CAMBRIDGE ENGLISH CLASSICS

Poems
by
George Crabbe

In Three Volumes

GEORGE CRABBE

Born, 1754

Died, 1832

GEORGE CRABBE

POEMS

EDITED BY

ADOLPHUS WILLIAM WARD,

Litt.D., Hon. LL.D., F.B.A.
Master of Peterhouse

Volume I

Cambridge:
at the University Press
1905

CAMBRIDGE
UNIVERSITY PRESS

University Printing House, Cambridge CB2 8BS, United Kingdom

Cambridge University Press is part of the University of Cambridge.

It furthers the University's mission by disseminating knowledge in the pursuit of education, learning and research at the highest international levels of excellence.

www.cambridge.org
Information on this title: www.cambridge.org/9781107432673

© Cambridge University Press 1905

First published 1905
First paperback edition 2014

A catalogue record for this publication is available from the British Library

ISBN 978-1-107-43267-3 Paperback

PREFATORY NOTE.

IN the present edition of Crabbe's Poems the general arrangement adopted is that of the chronological order of publication. The poem entitled *Midnight* has been inserted at a conjectural date as belonging to the period of the Juvenile Poems (1772–1780); but all other poems contained in this edition which have hitherto remained unpublished will be printed after the published poems, in the sequence of their production so far as this is ascertainable. With the poems hitherto unpublished I have also been fortunate enough to obtain permission to include in a later volume, among other posthumously printed pieces, the *Two Poetical Epistles* by Crabbe, first published, from a manuscript in the collection of Mr Buxton Forman, in Vol. II of *Literary Anecdotes of the Nineteenth Century* edited by W. Robertson Nicoll and Thomas J. Wise (London, 1896). From the second of these *Epistles* were taken, but not in their original order, the ten lines reproduced in the present volume from George Crabbe the younger's 1834 edition of his father's Poems.

The earliest of the Juvenile Poems here printed are taken from *The Lady's Magazine, or Entertaining Companion for the Fair Sex, appropriated solely to their Use and Amusement,* for the year 1772, printed at London for Robinson and Roberts, 25 Paternoster Row. The

PREFATORY NOTE

first volume of this Magazine seems to have been that for the year 1770, and to have comprised the numbers from August to December inclusive ; but the earlier portion of this volume had been previously published in the same year 1770 under the same title by J. Wheble at 20 Paternoster Row, ' by whom letters to the Editor are requested and received.' This then must be the ' Wheble's Magazine for 1772,' of which George Crabbe the younger in the Life prefixed to the 1834 edition of his father's Poems (p. 22) states that he had after long search discovered a copy. The Magazine seems itself to have been a revival of an earlier *Lady's Magazine*, of which portions of the volumes for 1760 and 1761 are extant, and which, according to the title-page of the volume for 1761, was printed for J. Wilkie at the Bible in St Paul's Churchyard.

But the younger Crabbe's account of his father's verses in ' Wheble's Magazine for 1772 ' does not tally with the actual contents of the volume for 1772 of *The Lady's Magazine* which has been used for the present edition. It is possible, of course, though there is no evidence to support the supposition, that *The Lady's Magazine* published by Wheble was continued at all events till 1772, parallel to *The Lady's Magazine* published by Robinson and Roberts, with which in 1770 it had been in some measure blended. It is equally possible that the younger Crabbe made some mistake or mistakes. In any case, his statement is, that Wheble's Magazine for 1772 ' contains besides the prize poem on Hope,' from which he proceeds to quote the concluding six lines, ' four other pieces, signed " G. C., Woodbridge, Suffolk," " To Mira," " The Atheist reclaimed," " The Bee," and " An Allegorical Fable."' The volume published by Robinson and Roberts contains no pieces corresponding to these, except that in

vi

PREFATORY NOTE

its October number there is printed an *Essay on Hope*, in which the lines cited by the younger Crabbe and reprinted, on his authority, in the present edition, do not appear, but of which the concluding lines seem to imply that it was a copy of verses written in competition for a prize. It cannot however be by Crabbe. For it is signed 'C. C., Rotherhithe, 1772'; and the July number of the same volume contains a piece of verse of some length entitled *The Rotherhithe Beauties* and signed 'C. C., Rotherhithe, July 15,' which is certainly not by Crabbe; and later in the volume follows another piece entitled *Night*, signed 'C. C., Rotherhithe, November 19, 1772,' which likewise cannot be attributed to Crabbe.

On the other hand the 1772 volume of *The Lady's Magazine* contains certain pieces of verse which may without hesitation be assigned to him, and which are accordingly reprinted in the present edition. These are, in the September number, *Solitude* and *A Song*, which bear as a signature the quasi-anagram 'G. EBBARE'; in the October number, the lines *To Emma*, with the quasi-anagram 'G. EBBAAC' and the date 'Suffolk'; and, in the November number, *Despair*, *Cupid*, and a *Song*, signed with the earlier form 'G. EBBARE.' This *Song* is followed by some lines in blank verse *On the Wonders of Creation*, and, further on, by some stanzas *To Friendship*, likewise signed 'C. C.'; but manifestly neither blank verse nor stanzas are by Crabbe.

Finally, it should be noted that in the October number in the same volume the following occurs among the notices *To our Correspondents*: 'The birth of a Maccaroni, by Ebbare, in the style of the Scriptures, seems to be taking too great a liberty with things sacred; and it is our maxim, as far as possible, to abstain from every appearance of evil.' The *Lady's*

PREFATORY NOTE

Magazine continued to be published by Robinson and Roberts for many subsequent years ; and it is a curious coincidence that No. 5 of Vol. xlvii (for May, 1816) contains some stanzas entitled *Myra's Wedding-Day.*

The remaining *Juvenilia* printed in the present edition are partly reproduced from the *Fragments of Verse, from Mr Crabbe's early Note-Books* in Vol. ii of the 1834 edition, partly from the *Life* in Vol. i of the same. The lines On the Death of William Springall Levett are quoted in the latter from Green's *History of Framlingham,* which has been compared.

Of the poems which follow in the present volume, *Inebriety* is here printed from a copy of the quarto of 1775, which lacks a title-page and which bears on p. 1 the following deprecation in Crabbe's handwriting : ' NB.—pray let not this be seen at [cipher] there is very little of it that I'm not heartily asham'd of.' The imprint of the title-page here given is taken from the *Life* (1834, p. 28).

Midnight, a Poem, is now first printed from the original manuscript which formed part of Dawson Turner's collection, in which it was numbered 121 at the sale of Dawson Turner's manuscripts in June, 1859. Its handwriting, as Professor Dowden points out, is identical with that of a *facsimile* in a passage from the *Two Epistles* mentioned above, given in the *Literary Ancedotes of the Nineteenth Century.*

The Candidate is printed from the edition of 1834 (Vol. ii, Appendix). This poem is not included in the edition of 1823, and after a long quest it has proved impossible to obtain a copy of the original edition of 1780 (published in quarto by H. Payne, opposite Marlborough House, Pall Mall). This edition is not in the British Museum. It was only possible to compare the forty-six lines of the poem quoted in *The Monthly*

PREFATORY NOTE

Review for September, 1780; but no variants have been found in these.

The subsequent poems contained in the present volume are all printed from the edition of 1823, the last edition published in England in the poet's lifetime. The *Variants* enumerated at the close of this volume are in each case the readings of the first editions of the several poems, viz., *The Library*, 1781, *The Village*, 1783, *The Newspaper*, 1785, *The Parish Register &c*, 1807, and *The Borough*, 1810. The address *To the Reader* prefixed to *The Newspaper*, which does not appear in the edition of 1823, has been restored from that of 1785, as it appears in the younger Crabbe's edition of 1834.

The list of *Errata* includes all the misprints, slips of the pen, and unintentional mistakes of spelling or quotation, which have been found in the texts which have been reprinted in this volume. The reading substituted here is in each case enclosed in square brackets. The list is a long one, for Crabbe was a careless writer ; and in the matter of quotations (as the concluding sentence of the *Preface* to *The Borough* indicates) was not given to over-conscientiousness. It has seemed permissible, where this could be done, to supplement the poet's statements as to the sources of his quotations ; but there are instances in which these statements themselves remain more or less doubtful. Crabbe's interpunctuation is so arbitrary, and, though no doubt largely determined by what might be described as the movement of the writer's mind, so frequently at variance even with the practice (it can hardly be called system) which he more usually follows, that it has been thought right to use as much freedom on this head as seemed consistent with a due respect for the author's intention. No alteration has been made in the matter of interpunctuation which was not

PREFATORY NOTE

warranted either by the poet's ordinary practice, or by the primary necessity of making his meaning clear.

As complete as possible a bibliography of Crabbe's Poems will, it is hoped, be published in the concluding volume of this edition.

There remains the pleasant duty of thanking those whose kindness has been of assistance in the preparation of this volume. The relatives of my dear friend the late Canon AINGER have allowed me to retain for this purpose the first editions of *Inebriety* (with Crabbe's autograph), *The Village* and *The Newspaper* which he had lent me not long before his death. The Vice-Master of Trinity, Mr W. ALDIS WRIGHT, besides enabling me to borrow from Trinity Library the first edition of *The Library*, kindly lent his own copy of the *Poems* published in 1807. I am indebted to Professor EDWARD DOWDEN, LL.D., of Trinity College, Dublin, for various services generously rendered by him to this edition of Crabbe, which will benefit from them in its concluding as it has in its opening volume. He has readily allowed me to print the whole of the interesting blank verse poem of *Midnight*, which, in his own words, 'unless it be a transcript by Crabbe from some other eighteenth-century poet, of which there is no evidence, may be assumed to be of his authorship.'

To the same kind friend, and to the special courtesy of Mr J. W. LYSTER, Librarian of the National Library of Ireland, Kildare Street, Dublin, I owe the opportunity of tracing *fide oculata*, so far as it seems possible to make sure of it, the elusive volume of *The Lady's Magazine* containing the earliest of Crabbe's printed verse.

Mr A. R. WALLER, of Peterhouse, Assistant Secretary to the Syndics of the University Press, has in many ways facilitated the preparation of this volume.

PREFATORY NOTE

And without the unstinting and unflagging cooperation of another member of my College, Mr A. T. BARTHOLOMEW, of the University Library, who has compiled the list of variants, besides giving me much other assistance, I could not, amidst other engagements, have carried so far the execution of a delightful task.

A. W. WARD.

PETERHOUSE LODGE, CAMBRIDGE.
July 24th, 1905.

CORRIGENDA.

p. 5, *for* Ovid *read* Ovid [?].

p. 48, l. 41, *for* Meonides *read* [Maeonides].

p. 55, l. 297, *for* [threat'ned] *read* [threaten'd].

p. 232, l. 319, *for* Rubens *read* [Rubens].

p. 252, l. 5, *for* dolor *read* [labor].

p. 256, l. 4, *for* deplorant *read* [deplangunt].

p. 329, l. 11, *for* and worship me *read* [and worship me].

ib. l. 12, *for* Part I *read* Part II.

p. 364, l. 12, *for* [erat] *read* erant.

CONTENTS.

CONTENTS

JUVENILIA.

(1772—1780.)

SOLITUDE.

[September, 1772.]

FREE from envy, strife and sorrow,
  Jealous doubts, and heart-felt fears;
Free from thoughts of what to-morrow
  May o'er-charge the soul with cares—

Live I in a peaceful valley,
  By a neighbouring lonely wood;
Giving way to melancholy,
  (Joy, when better understood).

Near me ancient ruins falling
  From a worn-out castle's brow;   10
Once the greatest [chiefs] installing,
  Where are all their honours now?

Here in midnight's gloomy terror
  I enjoy the silent night;
Darkness shews the soul her error,
  Darkness leads to inward light.

Here I walk in meditation,
  Pond'ring all sublunar things,
From the silent soft persuasion,
  Which from virtue's basis springs.   20

What, says truth, are pomp and riches?
  Guilded baits to folly lent;
Honour, which the soul bewitches,
  When obtain'd, we may repent.

GEORGE CRABBE

By me plays the stream meand'ring
   Slowly, as its waters glide ;
And, in gentle murmurs wand'ring,
   Lulls to downy rest my pride.

Silent as the gloomy graves are
   Now the mansions once so loud ;
Still and quiet as the brave, or
   All the horrors of a croud.

This was once the seat of plunder,
   Blood of heroes stain'd the floor ;
Heroes, nature's pride and wonder,
   Heroes heard of now no more.

Owls and ravens haunt the buildings,
   Sending gloomy dread to all ;
Yellow moss the summit yielding,
   Pellitory decks the wall.

Time with rapid speed still wanders,
   Journies on an even pace ;
Fame of greatest actions squanders,
   But perpetuates disgrace.

Sigh not then for pomp or glory ;
   What avails a heroe's name ?
Future times may tell your story,
   To your then disgrace and shame.

Chuse some humble cot as this is,
   In sweet philosophic ease ;
With dame Nature's frugal blisses
   Live in joy, and die in peace.

G. EBBARE.

30

40

50

2

JUVENILIA

A SONG.

[September, 1772.]

I.

AS Chloe fair, a new-made bride,
    Sat knotting in an arbour,
To Colin now the damsel ty'd,
No strange affection harbour.

II.

"How poor," says [she, "'s a] single life,
    "A maid's affected carriage;
"Spent in sighs and inward strife,
    "Things unknown in marriage.

III.

"Virgins vainly say they're free,
    "None so much confin'd are;
"Lovers kind and good may be,
    "Husbands may be kinder.

IV.

"Then shun not wedlock's happy chain,
    "Nor wantonly still fly man;
"A single life is care and pain,
    "Blessings wait on Hymen."

G. EBBARE.

GEORGE CRABBE

CONCLUDING LINES OF PRIZE POEM ON HOPE.

[Before October, 1772.]

*　　　*　　　*　　　*　　　*　　　*

BUT, above all, the POET owns thy powers—
　　Hope leads him on, and every fear devours;
He writes, and, unsuccessful, writes again,
Nor thinks the last laborious work in vain;
New schemes he forms, and various plots he tries
To win the laurel, and possess the PRIZE.

TO EMMA.

VIEW, my fair, the fading flower,
　　Clad like thee in [beauty's] arms,
Idle pageant of an hour;
Soon shall time its tints devour,
　　And what are then its charms?

Early pluck'd, it might produce
　　A remedy to mortal pain,
Afford a balmy cordial juice,
That might celestial ease diffuse,
　　Nor blossom quite in vain.　　　　　　　　10

So 'tis with thee, my Emma fair,
　　If nature's law's unpaid,
If thou refuse our vows to hear
And steel thy heart to ev'ry pray'r,
　　A cruel frozen maid.

But yield, my fair one, yield to love,
　　And joys unnumber'd find,
In Cupid's mystic circle move,
Eternal raptures thou shalt prove,
　　Which leave no pang behind.　　　　　　　20

　　　　　　　　　　　　　　G. EBBAAC.
Suffolk, Oct. 15, 1772.
　'*Multa cadunt inter calicem supremaque labra.*'

4

JUVENILIA

DESPAIR.

[November, 1772.]

Heu mihi!
Quod nullis amor medicabilis herbis. OVID.

TYRSIS *and* DAMON.

D. BEGIN, my Tyrsis ; songs shall sooth our cares,
Allay our sorrows, and dispel our fears ;
Shall glad thy heart, and bring its native peace,
And bid thy grief its weighty influence cease.
No more those tears of woe, dear shepherd, shed,
Nor ever mourn the lov'd Cordelia dead.

T. In vain, my Damon, urge thy fond request
To still the troubles of an anxious breast :
Cordelia's gone ! and now what pain is life
Without my fair, my friend, my lovely wife ?   10
Hope ! chearful hope ! to distant climes is fled,
And Nature mourns the fair Cordelia dead.

D. But can thy tears re-animate the earth,
Or give to sordid dust a second birth ?
Mistaken mortal ! learn to bear the ill,
Nor let that canker, grief, thy pleasures kill.
No more in Sorrow's sable garb array'd,
Still [mourn] thy lov'd, thy lost Cordelia dead.

T. Can I forget the fairest of her kind,
Beauteous in person, fairer still in mind ?   20
Can I forget she sooth'd my heart to rest,
And still'd the troubl'd motion in my breast ?
Can I, by soothing song or friendship led,
Forget to mourn my lov'd Cordelia dead ?

5

GEORGE CRABBE

D. Another fair may court thee to her arms,
Display her graces, and reveal her charms;
May catch thy wand'ring eye, dispel thy woe,
And give to sorrow final overthrow.
No longer, then, thy heart-felt anguish shed,
Nor mourn, in solitude, Cordelia dead.   30

T. Sooner shall lions fierce forget to roam,
And peaceful walk with gentle lambs at home;
Sooner shall Discord love her ancient hate,
And Peace and Love with Rage incorporate;
Sooner shall turtles with the sparrow wed,
Than I forget my lov'd Cordelia dead.

D. Must then Dorintha ever sigh in vain,
And Cælia breathe to echoing groves her pain?
Must Chloe hope in vain to steel that heart
In which each nymph would gladly share a part?   40
Must these, dejected shepherd, be betray'd,
And victims fall, because Cordelia's dead?

T. By those who love, my friend, it stands confest,
No second flame can fill a lover's breast:
For me no more the idle scenes of life
Shall vex with envy, hatred, noise, or strife;
But here, in melancholy form array'd,
I'll ever mourn my lov'd Cordelia dead.

G. EBBARE.

JUVENILIA

CUPID.

[November, 1772.]

Whoe'er thou art, thy master know;
He has been, is, or shall be so.

WHAT is he, who clad in arms,
    Hither seems in haste to move,
Bringing with him soft alarms,
    Fears the heart of man to prove;
Yet attended too by charms—
    Is he Cupid, God of Love?

Yes, it is, behold him nigh,
    Odd compound of ease and smart;
Near him [stands] a nymph, whose sigh
    Grief and joy, and love impart;   10
Pleasure dances in her eye,
    Yet she seems to grieve at heart.

Lo! a quiver by his side,
    Arm'd with darts, a fatal store!
See him, with a haughty pride,
    Ages, sexes, all devour;
Yet, as pleasure is describ'd,
    Glad we meet the tyrant's power.

Doubts and cares before him go,
    Canker'd jealousy behind;   20
Round about him spells he'll throw,
    Scatt'ring with each gust of wind
On the motley crew below,
    Who, like him, are render'd blind.

This is love! a tyrant kind,
    Giving extacy and pain;
Fond deluder of the mind,
    Ever feigning not to feign;
Whom no savage laws can bind,
    None escape his pleasing chain.   30

G. EBBARE.

GEORGE CRABBE

SONG.

[November, 1772.]

CEASE to bid me not to sing.
　　Spite of Fate I'll tune my lyre :
Hither, god of music, bring
　　Food to feed the gentle fire ;
And on Pægasean wing
　　Mount my soul enraptur'd higher.

Some there are who'd curb the mind,
　　And would blast the springing bays ;
All essays are vain, they'll find,
　　Nought shall drown the muse's lays,　　10
Nought shall curb a free-born mind,
　　Nought shall damp Apollo's praise.

G. EBBARE.

[ON THE DEATH OF WILLIAM
SPRINGALL LEVETT.]

[1774.]

WHAT though no trophies peer above his dust,
　　Nor sculptured conquests deck his sober bust ;
What though no earthly thunders sound his name,
Death gives him conquest, and our sorrows fame :
One sigh reflection heaves, but shuns excess—
More should we mourn him, did we love him less.

8

JUVENILIA

PARODY ON [BYROM'S] "MY TIME, OH YE MUSES."

[Woodbridge, about 1774.]

M Y days, oh ye lovers, were happily sped
    Ere you or your whimsies got into my head ;
I could laugh, I could sing, I could trifle and jest,
And my heart play'd a regular tune in my breast.
But now, lack-a-day ! what a change for the worse,
'Tis as heavy as lead, yet as wild as a horse.

My fingers, ere love had tormented my mind,
Could guide my pen gently to what I design'd.
I could make an enigma, a rebus, or riddle,
Or tell a short tale of a dog and a fiddle.   10
But, since this vile Cupid has got in my brain,
I beg of the gods to assist in my strain.
And whatever my subject, the fancy still roves,
And sings of hearts, raptures, flames, sorrows, and loves.

*   *   *   *   *   *

GEORGE CRABBE

THE WISH.

[Woodbridge, about 1774.]

M Y Mira, shepherds, is as fair
　　As sylvan nymphs who haunt the vale,
As sylphs who dwell in purest air,
　　As fays who skim the dusky dale,
As Venus was when Venus fled
From watery Triton's oozy bed.

My Mira, shepherds, has a voice
　　As soft as Syrinx in her grove,
As sweet as echo makes her choice,
　　As mild as whispering virgin-love ;　　　10
As gentle as the winding stream
Or fancy's song when poets dream.

＊　　＊　　＊　　＊　　＊　　＊

INEBRIETY.

[Inebriety, a Poem, in three Parts. Ipswich, printed and sold by C. Punchard, Bookseller, in the Butter-Market, 1775. Price one shilling and sixpence.]

The PREFACE.

PResumption or Meanness are but too often the only articles to be discovered in a Preface. Whilst one author haughtily affects to despise the publick attention, another timidly courts it. I would no more beg for than disdain applause, and therefore should advance nothing in Favor of the following little *Poem*, did it not appear a Cruelty and disregard to send a first Production naked into the WORLD.

The WORLD!——how pompous, and yet how trifling the sound. Every MAN, Gentle Reader, has a WORLD of his own, & whether it consists of half a score, or half a thousand Friends, 'tis his, and he loves to boast of it. Into my WORLD, therefore, I commit this, my Muse's earliest labor, nothing doubting the Clemency of the Climate, nor fearing the Partiality of the censorious.

Something by way of *Apology* for this trifle, is perhaps necessary; especially for those parts, wherein I have taken such great Liberties with Mr. POPE; that Gentleman, secure in immortal Fame, would forgive me; forgive me too, my friendly Critic; I promise thee, thou wilt find the Extracts from the Swan of Thames the best Parts of the Performance;

GEORGE CRABBE

Few, I dare venture to affirm, will pay me so great a Compliment, as to think I have injured Mr POPE; Fewer, I hope, will think I endeavoured to do it, and Fewest of all will think any thing about it.

The LADIES will doubtless favor my Attempt; for them indeed it was principally composed; I have endeavored to demonstrate that it is their own Faults, if they are not deemed as good MEN, as half the masculine World; that a personal Difference of Sex need not make a real Difference; and that a tender Languishment, a refin'd Delicacy, and a particular attention to shine in Dress, will render the *Beau-Animal* infinitely more feminine, than the generality of LADIES, whatever arcane Tokens of *Manhood* the said *Animal* may be indued with; and yet, ye FAIR! these creatures pass even in your catalogue for MEN; which I'm afraid is a Demonstration that the real MAN is very scarce.

Some grave *Head* or *other* may possibly tell me, that Vice is to be lash'd, not indulg'd; that true *Poetry* forbids, not encourages, Folly; and such other wise and weighty Sentences, picked from POPE and HORACE, as he shall think most appertaining to his own dignity. But this, my good Reader, is a trifle; *People* now a Days are not to be preach'd into Reflection, or they pay *Parsons*, not *Poets* for it, if they were; they listen indeed to a Discourse from the Pulpit, for MEN are too wise to give away their Money without any consideration; and though they don't mind what is said there, 'tis doubtless a great Satisfaction to think they might if they choose it; but a MAN reads a *Poem* for quite a different purpose: to be lul'd into ease from reflection, to be lul'd into an inclination for pleasure, and (where I confess it comes nearer the Sermon) to be lul'd—asleep.

But lest the *Apology* should have the latter effect in itself, and so take away the merit of the Performance by forestalling that agreeable Event: I without further ceremony bid thee Adieu!

INEBRIETY.

PART the FIRST.

THE mighty Spirit and its power which stains[1]
The bloodless cheek, and vivifies the brains,
I sing. Say ye, its fiery Vot'ries true,
The jovial Curate, and the shrill-tongu'd Shrew;
Ye, in the floods of limpid poison nurst,
Where Bowl the second charms like Bowl the first;
Say, how and why the sparkling ill is shed,
The Heart which hardens, and which rules the Head.
When Winter stern his gloomy front uprears,
A sable void the barren earth appears;   10
The meads no more their former verdure boast,
Fast bound their streams, and all their Beauty lost;
The herds, the flocks, their icy garments mourn,
And wildly murmur for the Spring's return;
The fallen branches from the sapless tree
With glittering fragments strow the glassy way;
From snow-top'd Hills the whirlwinds keenly blow,
Howl through the Woods, and pierce the vales below;
Through the sharp air a flaky torrent flies,
Mocks the slow sight, and hides the gloomy skies;   20
The fleecy clouds their chilly bosoms bare,
And shed their substance on the floating air;

[1] "The mighty Mother, and her Son, who brings
"The Smithfield Muses to the ear of Kings,
"I sing. Say ye, her instruments, the great,
"Call'd to this Work by Dulness, Jove, and Fate;
"You by whose care, in vain decry'd, and curst,
"Still Dunce the second reigns like Dunce the first;
"Say, how the Goddess bade Britania sleep,
"And pour'd her spirit o'er the land and deep."
                                    Pope's Dunciad.—

13

GEORGE CRABBE

The floating air their downy substance glides
Through springing Waters, and prevents their tides;
Seizes the rolling Waves, and, as a God,
Charms their swift race, and stops the refl'ent flood;
The opening valves, which fill the venal road,
Then scarcely urge along the sanguine flood;
The labouring Pulse a slower motion rules,
The Tendons stiffen, and the Spirit cools;   30
Each asks the aid of [Nature's] sister Art,
To chear the senses, and to warm the Heart.
The gentle fair on nervous tea relies,
Whilst gay good-nature sparkles in her eyes;
An inoffensive Scandal fluttering round,
Too rough to tickle, and too light to wound;
Champain the Courtier drinks, the spleen to chase,
The Colonel burgundy, and port his Grace;
Turtle and 'rrack the city rulers charm,
Ale and content the labouring peasants warm;   40
O'er the dull embers happy Colin sits,
Colin, the prince of joke and rural wits;
Whilst the wind whistles through the hollow panes,
He drinks, nor of the rude assault complains;
And tells the Tale, from sire to son retold,
Of spirits vanishing near hidden gold;
Of moon-clad Imps, that tremble by the dew,
Who skim the air, or glide o'er waters blue.
The throng invisible, that doubtless float
By mould'ring Tombs, and o'er the stagnant moat;   50
Fays dimly glancing on the russet plain,
And all the dreadful nothing of the Green.
And why not these? Less fictious is the tale,
Inspir'd by Hel'con's streams, than muddy ale?
Peace be to such, the happiest and the best,
Who with the forms of fancy urge their jest;
Who wage no war with an Avenger's Rod,
Nor in the pride of reason curse their God.

When in the vaulted arch Lucina gleams,
And gaily dances o'er the azure streams;   60
When in the wide cerulean space on high

INEBRIETY

The vivid stars shoot lustre through the sky;
On silent Ether when a trembling sound
Reverberates, and wildly floats around,
Breaking through trackless space upon the ear—
Conclude the Bachanalian Rustic near;
O'er Hills and vales the jovial Savage reels,
Fire in his head and Frenzy at his heels;
From paths direct the bending Hero swerves,
And shapes his way in ill-proportion'd curves;   70
Now safe arriv'd, his sleeping Rib he calls,
And madly thunders on the muddy walls;
The well-known sounds an equal fury move,
For rage meets rage, as love enkindles love;
The buxom Quean from bed of flocks descends   ⎞
With vengeful ire, a civil war portends,   ⎬
An oaken plant the Hero's breast defends.   ⎠
In vain the 'waken'd infant's accents shrill
The humble regions of the cottage fill;
In vain the Cricket chirps the mansion through,   80
'Tis war, and Blood and Battle must ensue.
As when, on humble stage, him Satan hight
Defies the brazen Hero to the fight;
From twanging strokes what dire misfortunes rise,
What fate to maple arms, and glassen eyes;
Here lies a leg of elm, and there a stroke
From ashen neck has whirl'd a Head of oak.
So drops from either power, with vengeance big,
A remnant night-cap, and an old cut wig;
Titles unmusical, retorted round,   90
On either ear with leaden vengeance sound;
'Till equal Valour equal Wounds create,
And drowsy peace concludes the fell debate;
Sleep in her woolen mantle wraps the pair,
And sheds her poppies on the ambient air;
Intoxication flies, as fury fled,
On rocky pinions quits the aching head;
Returning Reason cools the fiery blood,
And drives from memory's seat the rosy God.
Yet still he holds o'er some his madd'ning rule,   100
Still sways his Sceptre, and still knows his Fool;

15

GEORGE CRABBE

Witness the livid lip and fiery front,
With many a smarting trophy plac'd upon't;
The hollow Eye, which plays in misty springs,
And the hoarse Voice, which rough and broken rings.
These are his triumphs, and o'er these he reigns,
The blinking Deity of reeling brains.

See Inebriety! her wand she waves,
And lo! her pale, and lo! her purple slaves;
Sots in embroidery, and sots in crape,   110
Of every order, station, rank, and shape;
The King, who nods upon his rattle-throne;
The staggering Peer, to midnight revel prone;
The slow-tongu'd Bishop, and the Deacon sly,
The humble Pensioner, and Gownsman dry;
The proud, the mean, the selfish, and the great,
Swell the dull throng, and stagger into state.

Lo! proud Flaminius at the splendid board,
The easy chaplain of an atheist Lord,
Quaffs the bright juice, with all the gust of sense,   120
And clouds his brain in torpid elegance;
In china vases see the sparkling ill,
From gay Decanters view the rosy rill;
The neat-carv'd pipes in silver settle laid,
The screw by mathematic cunning made;
The whole a pompous and enticing scene,
And grandly glaring for the surplic'd Swain;
Oh! happy Priest whose God like Egypt's lies,
At once the Deity and sacrifice!
But is Flaminius, then, the man alone,   130
To whom the Joys of swimming brains are known?
Lo! the poor Toper whose untutor'd sense[1]
Sees bliss in ale, and can with wine dispense;
Whose head proud fancy never taught to steer
Beyond the muddy extacies of Beer;

---

[1] "Lo, the poor Indian! whose untutor'd mind
"Sees God in Clouds, and hears him in the wind;
"Whose Soul proud science never taught to stray
"Far as the solar walk, or milky way,

INEBRIETY

But simple nature can her longing quench
Behind the settle's curve, or humbler bench;
Some kitchen-fire diffusing warmth around,
The semi-globe by Hieroglyphics crown'd;
Where canvas purse displays the brass enroll'd,   140
Nor Waiters rave, nor Landlords thirst for gold;
Ale and content his fancy's bounds confine,
He asks no limpid Punch, no rosy Wine;
But sees, admitted to an equal share,
Each faithful swain the heady potion bear.
Go, wiser thou! and in thy scale of taste
Weigh gout and gravel against ale and rest.
Call vulgar palates, what thou judgest so;
Say, beer is heavy, windy, cold and slow;
Laugh at poor sots with insolent pretence,   150
Yet cry when tortur'd, where is Providence?
If thou alone art, head and heel, not clear,
Alone made steady here, untumour'd there;
Snatch from the Board the bottle and the bowl,
Curse the keen pain, and be a mad proud Fool.

> " Yet simple nature to his hope has given
> " Behind the cloud-top't hill an humbler Heaven;
> " Some safer world, in depth of woods embrac'd,
> " Some happier island, in a watry waste:
> " Where slaves once more their native land behold,
> " Nor friends torment, nor Christians thirst for Gold;
> " To live, contents his natural desire,
> " He asks no Seraph's wing, no Angel's fire,
> " But thinks admitted to that equal Sky,
> " His faithful Dog, shall bear him company:
> " Go, wiser thou! and in thy scale of sense
> " Weigh thy opinion against Providence;
> " Call imperfection what thou fancy'st such,
> " Say here he gives too little, here too much,
> " Destroy all creatures for thy sport and gust,
> " Yet cry, if man's unhappy, God's unjust;
> " If man alone engross not Heaven's high care,
> " Alone made perfect here, immortal there:
> " Snatch from his hand the balance and the rod,
> " Rejudge his Justice, and be God of God."
>
> Pope's Essay on Man.—

END OF PART THE FIRST.

GEORGE CRABBE

INEBRIETY.

PART the SECOND.

IN various forms the mad'ning Spirit moves,
This drinks and fights, another drinks and loves.
A bastard Zeal of different kinds it shows,
And now with rage, and now Religion glows;
The frantic Soul bright reason's path defies,
Now creeps on Earth, now triumphs in the Skies;
Swims in the seas of error and explores,
Through midnight mists, the fluctuating Shores;
From wave to wave in rocky Channel glides,
And sinks in woe, or on presumption slides;   10
In Pride exalted, or by Shame deprest,
An Angel-Devil, or a human-Beast.
Without a pilot who attempts to steer,
Has small discretion or has little care;
That pilot Reason, in the erring Soul,
Is lost, is blinded in the steaming Bowl,
Charm'd by its power, we cast our guide away,
And at the mercy of conjecture lay;
Discretion dies with reason, Revel wakes!
And o'er the head his fiery banners shakes.   20
With him come frenzy, folly and excess,
Blink-ey'd conceit and shallow emptiness;
At Folly's beck a train of Vices glide,
Murder in madness cloak'd, in choler, Pride;
Above, Impiety, with curses bound,
Lours at the skies, and whirls Damnation round.

Some rage, in all the strength of folly mad,
Some love stupidity, in silence clad,

18

Are never quarrelsome, are never gay,
But sleep and groan and drink the Night away;   30
Old Torpio nods, and, as the laugh goes round,
Grunts through the nasal Duct, and joins the sound;
Then sleeps again, and, as the liquors pass,
Wakes at the friendly Jog, and takes his Glass;
Alike to him who stands, or reels, or moves;
The elbow chair, good wine and Sleep he loves;
Nor cares of state disturb his easy head,
By grosser fumes and calmer follies fed;
Nor thoughts, of when, or where, or how to come,
The Canvass general, or the general Doom;   40
Extremes ne'er reach'd one passion of his Soul;
A villain tame, and an unmettled fool,
To half his Vices he has but pretence,
For they usurp the place of common sense;
To half his little Merits has no claim
But very Indolence has rais'd his name,
Happy in this, that under Satan's sway
His passions humble, but will not obey.

The Vicar at the table's front presides,
Whose presence a monastic life derides;   50
The reverend Wig, in sideway order plac'd,
The reverend Band, by rubric stains disgrac'd,
The leering Eye, in wayward circles roll'd,
Mark him the Pastor of a jovial Fold,
Whose various texts excite a loud applause,
Favouring the Bottle, and the good old Cause.
See! the dull smile which fearfully appears,
When gross Indecency her front uprears;
The joy conceal'd the fiercer burns within,
As masks afford the keenest gust to Sin;   60
Imagination helps the reverend Sire,
And spreads the sails of sub-divine desire.
But when the gay immoral joke goes round,
When Shame and all her blushing train are drown'd,
Rather than hear his God blasphem'd he takes
The last lov'd Glass, and then the board forsakes:
Not that Religion prompts the sober thought,

But slavish Custom has the practice taught.
Besides, this zealous son of warm devotion
Has a true levite Bias for promotion ;   70
Vicars must with discretion go astray,
Whilst Bishops may be d——n'd the nearest way ;
So puny robbers individuals kill,
When hector-Heroes murder as they will.

Good honest Curio elbows the [divine,]
And strives, a social sinner, how to shine ;
The dull quaint tale is his, the lengthen'd tale,
That Wilton Farmers give you with their ale :
How midnight Ghosts o'er vaults terrific pass,
Dance o'er the Grave, and slide along the grass ;   80
How Maids forsaken haunt the lonely wood,
And tye the Noose, or try the willow flood ;
How rural Heroes overcame the giants,
And through the ramshorn trumpet blew defiance ;
Or how pale Cicely, within the wood,
Call'd Satan forth and bargain'd with her blood.
These, honest Curio, are thine, and these
Are the dull Treasures of a brain at peace.
No wit intoxicates thy gentle skull,
Of heavy, native, [unwrought] folly full ;   90
Bowl upon Bowl in vain exert their force ;
The breathing Spirit takes a downward course,
Or, vainly soaring upwards to the head,
Meets an impenetrable tence of lead.

Hast thou, Oh Reader ! search'd o'er gentle Gay,
Where various animals their powers display ?
In one strange Group, a chattering race was hurl'd,
Led by the Monkey who had seen the world.
He, it is said, from woodland shepherds stole,
And went to Court, to greet each fellow fool.   100
Like him, Fabricio steals from guardian's side,
Swims not in [pleasure's] stream, but sips the tide ;
He hates the Bottle, yet but thinks it right ⎫
To boast next day the honours of the night ; ⎬
None like your Coward can describe a fight. ⎭

INEBRIETY

See him, as down the sparkling potion goes,
Labor to grin away the horrid dose;
In joy-feign'd gaze his misty eye-balls float,
Th' uncivil Spirit gurgling at his throat;
So looks dim Titan through a wintry scene,   110
And faintly chears the woe-foreboding swain;
But now, Alas! the hour, th'increasing flood,
Rolls round and round, and cannot be withstood;
Thrice he essays to stop the ruby flow,
To stem its Force, and keep it still below;
In vain his Art, it comes! at [distance] gaze,
Ye stancher Sots, and be not near the place.
As when a flood from Ossa's pendant brow
Rolls rapid to its fellow streams below,
It moves tempest'ous down the Mountain's sides,   120 ⎫
O'er lesser hills and vales like light'ning glides,   ⎬
And o'er their beauties fall'n triumphant rides,   ⎭
Each verdant spot and sunny bank defaces,
And forms a minor Ocean at its basis;
So from his rueful lips Fabricio pours,
With melancholy Force, the tinctur'd showers;
O'er the embroider'd vest they take their way,
And in the grave its tinsel honours lay.
No Nymph was there, to hold the helpless face,
Or save from ruin's spoil the luckless lace;   130
No guardian Fair, to turn the head aside
And to securer paths the torrent glide;
From silk to silk it drove its wayward Course,
And on the diamond buckle spent its Force.
Ah! gentle Fop! what luckless fate was thine
To sin through fashion, and in woe to shine.
But all our Numbers why should rascals claim[1]?
Rise, honest Muse, and sing a nobler name.
Pleas'd in his Eye good humour always smiles,
And Mirth unbought with strife the hour beguiles,   140

[1] " But all our praises why should Lords engross?
" Rise honest Muse and sing the Man of Ross.
" Pleas'd Vaga echo's, through her winding bounds,
" And rapid Severn hoarse applause resounds;

GEORGE CRABBE

Who smooth'd the frown on yonder surly brow?
From the dry Joke who bade gay Laughter flow?
Not of affected, empty rapture full,
Nor in proud Strain magnificently dull,
But gay and easy, giving without Art
Joy to each sense, and Solace to the heart.
Thrice happy Damon, able to pursue
What all so wish, but want the power to do.
No cares thy Head, no crimes thy Heart torment,
At home thou'rt happy, and abroad content;   150
Pleas'd with thyself, and therefore form'd to please,
With Moderation free, and gay with Ease,
Wise in a medium, just to an extreme,
"The soul of Humour, and the life of Whim,"
Plac'd from thy Sphere, amid the sons of shame,
Proud of thy Jest, but prouder of thy Name.

Pernicious streams from healthy fountains rise,
And Wit abus'd degenerates into vice;
Timon, long practic'd in the School of art,
Has lost each finer feeling of the Heart,   160
Triumphs o'er shame, and with delusive whiles,
Laughs at the Idiot he himself beguiles.
So matrons, past the awe of Censure's tongue,
Deride the blushes of the fair and young.
Few with more Fire on every subject spoke,
But chief he lov'd the gay immoral joke;
The Words most sacred, stole from holy writ,
He gave a newer form, and call'd them Wit;
Could twist a Sentence into various meaning,
And save himself in dubious explaining;   170
Could use a manner long taught art affords,
And hint Impiety in holy words.

" Who hung with woods, yon mountain's sultry brow?
" From the dry Rock, who bade the waters flow?
" Not to the skies in useless columns tost,
" Nor in proud falls, magnificently lost.
" But clear and artless, pouring through the plain
" Health to the Sick, and solace to the Swain."
POPE.—

22

INEBRIETY

Vice never had a more sincere ally,
So bold no Sinner, yet no Saint so sly;
Sophist and Cynic, mystically cool,
And still a very Sceptic at the soul;
Learn'd but not wise, and without Virtue brave,
A gay, deluding, philosophic Knave.
When Bacchus' joys his airy fancy fire,
They stir a new, but still a false desire;   180
The place of malice ridicule then holds,
And woe to teachers, ministers and scolds;
And, to the comfort of each untaught Fool,
Horace in English vindicates the Bowl.
"The man" (says Timon) "who is drunk is blest[1],
"No fears [disturb], no cares distroy his rest;
"In thoughtless joy he reels away his life,
"Nor dreads that worst of ills, a noisy wife.
"Of late I sat within the jangling bar,
"And heard my Rib's hoarse thunder from afar;   190
"Careless I spoke, and, when she found me drunk,
"She breath'd one Curse, and then away she slunk,
"Oh! place me, Jove, where none but women come,
"And thunders worse than thine afflict the room;
"Where one eternal Nothing flutters round,
"And senseless [titt'rings] sense of mirth confound;
"Or lead me bound to Garret, babel-high,
"Where frantic Poet rolls his crazy eye;
"Tiring the Ear, with oft-repeated chimes,
"And smiling at the never ending rhimes;   200
"E'en here or there, I'll be as blest as Jove,
"Give me tobacco, and the wine I love."
Applause from Hands the dying accents break
Of stagg'ring sots, who vainly try to speak;
From Milo, him who hangs upon each word,
And in loud praises splits the tortur'd board,
Collects each sentence, ere it's better known,
And makes the mutilated joke his own,

---

[1] "Integer vitæ, scelerisque [purus]
"Non eget &c. &c."
                                    HORACE.

23

At weekly club to flourish, where he rules,
The glorious President of grosser fools.   210

  But cease, my Muse ; of those or these enough,
The fools who listen, and the knaves who scoff ;
The jest profane, that mocks th' offended God,
Defies his power, and [sets] at nought his rod ;
The empty Laugh, discretion's vainest foe,
From fool to fool re-echo'd to and fro ;
The sly Indecency, that slowly springs
From barren wit, and halts on trembling wings :
Enough of these, and all the charms of Wine ;
Be sober joys and social evenings mine,   220
Where peace and Reason unsoil'd mirth improve,
The powers of friendship and the joys of love ;
Where thought meets thought ere Words its form array,
And all is sacred, elegant, and gay ;
Such pleasure leaves no Sorrow on the mind,
Too great to [pall], to sicken too [refin'd],
Too soft for Noise, and too sublime for art,
The social solace of the feeling Heart,
For sloth too rapid, and for wit too high,
'Tis Virtue's Pleasure, and can never die.   230

END OF PART THE SECOND.

INEBRIETY.

PART the THIRD.

NOW soar, my Muse! and leave the meaner crew[1],
  To aim at bliss, and vainly bliss pursue;
Let us (since Man no privilege can claim,
Than a contended, half superior name)
Expatiate o'er the raptures of the Fair,
Vot'ries to stolen joys, but yet sincere;
In secret Haunts, where never day-light gleams
By bottles, tempting with forbidden streams,
Together let us search; above, below,
Try what the Closets, what the Cellars show;   10
The latent vault with piercing view explore
Of her who hides the all reviving store.
Eye Beauty's walks, when round the welkin rolls,
And catch the stumbling Charmer as she falls;
Laugh where we must, but pity where we can,
And vindicate the sweet soft souls to Man.

[1] "Awake, my St. John, leave all meaner things
"To low ambition, and the pride of Kings;
"Let us (since Life can little more supply
"Than just to look about us, and to die)
"Expatiate free o'er all this scene of Man,
"A mighty maze, but not without a plan;
"A Wild, where weeds and flowers promiscuous shoot
"Or Garden, tempting with forbidden fruit.
"Together let us beat this ample field,
"Try what the open, what the covert yield;
"The latent tracts, the giddy heights explore,
"Of all who blindly creep, or sightless soar;
"Eye Nature's walks, shoot Folly as it flies,
"And catch the Manners, living as they rise;
"Laugh where we must, be candid where we can,
"But vindicate the ways of God to Man."
                    Pope's Essay on Man.—

GEORGE CRABBE

Pardon, ye Fair, the Poet and his Muse,
And what ye can't approve, at least excuse;
Far be from him the iron lash of Wit,
The jokes of Humour, and the sneers that hit;   20
He speaks of Freedom, and he speaks to you,
His Verse is simple, but his Subject new;
And novelty, ye Fair, beyond a doubt,
Is philosophic truth, the World throughout.

Hard is the lot of Woman, so have sung
The pensive old, and the presuming young;
Born without privilege, in bondage bred,
Slave from the Cradle to the marriage Bed;
Slave from the hour hymeneal to the grave,
In age, in youth, in infancy a Slave.   30
Happy the Bard, who, bold in pride of song
Shall free the chain, by Custom bound so long,
And show the Fair, to mean tradition prone,
Though Virtue may have sex, yet Vice has none.
If Man is licenc'd to confuse his mind,
Say, why should female Frailty be confin'd?
Is't right that she who dearly bought the fruit,   ⎫
Of all our wayward appetites the root,   ⎬
Who first made Man a fool and then a brute;   ⎭
Who fair in spells of tender kind can slay,   40
Like Israel's Judge, her thousands in a day;
Nay farther, has a far superior Pow'r,
And almost thousands in a day can cure;
She, the bright cause of fury in Man's breast;
And brighter cause who bids that fury rest;
Who raises peace or war at her command,
And bids a sword destroy a tipsy Land;
Say, is it right that she who kills and saves,
Makes wise Men mad, and takes the veil from Knaves,
Should want the pow'r, the magic, which alone,   50
Can Conquests boast more fatal than her own?
For Man alone did earth produce her fruit,
The sole, as well as the superior, brute;
Does he alone the glorious licence claim,
To put the human off, and loose his Name?

INEBRIETY

Woman in Knowledge was the earlier curst,
And tasted of forbidden Fruit the first;
Prior to Man, the law she disobey'd,
And shall she want the Freedom she convey'd?
By her first Theft each fiery ill we feel, 60
And yet compel the gen'rous Fair to steal;
First made by her for soaring actions fit,
Woman! the spring of super-human wit,
Shall we from her each dear bought bliss withhold,
As Spaniards use the Indians for their Gold?
Ungrateful Man! in pride so high to aim,
As to be sole inheritor of shame!

And you, ye Fair! why slumber on disdain,
Forbear to vindicate, yet can't refrain?
Why should Papilla seek the vaulted hoard, 70
And but in secret ape her honest Lord?
Why should'st thou, Celia, to thy stores repair,
And sip the generous Spirit in such fear?
Reform the Error, and revoke your plan,
And as ye dare to imitate, be——Man.

First know yourselves, and frame your passions all¹,
In proper order, how to rise and fall;
Woman's a Being, dubiously great,
Never contented with a passive state;
With too much Knowledge to give Man the sway, 80
With too much Pride his humours to obey,
She hangs in doubt, [too] humble or [too] brave;
In doubt to be a Mistress or a Slave;
In doubt herself or Husband to controul;
Born to be made a tyrant or a fool;

> ¹ "Know then thyself, presume not God to scan,
> "The proper study of Mankind is Man.
> "Plac'd on this isthmus of a middle state,
> "A Being darkly wise, and rudely great;
> "With too much knowledge for the Sceptic side,
> "With too much weakness for the Stoic's pride,
> "He hangs between: in doubt to act, or rest;
> "In doubt to deem himself a God, or Beast;
> "In doubt his Mind or Body to prefer;
> "Born but to die, and reas'ning but to err;

GEORGE CRABBE

In one extreme, her Power is always such
Either to show too little, or too much;
Bred up in Passions, by their sway abus'd,
The weaker for the stronger still refus'd;
Created oft' to rise, and oft' to fall,   90
Changing in all things, yet alike in all;
Soft Judge of right or wrong, or blest or curst;
The happiest, saddest, holiest, or the worst.

And why? because your failings ye suppress,
And what ye dare to act, dare not confess.
Would you, ye Fair, as Man your vices boast,
And she be most admir'd, who sins the most;
Would ye in open revel gaily spring,
And o'er the wanton Banquet vaunting sing;
The doubtful Precedence we then should own,   100
And you be first in [Error's] mazes known.

But why to Vices of the boist'rous kind
Tye the soft Soul, and urge the gentle Mind?
Forbid it, Nature! to the Fair I speak,
By her made strong, by Custom render'd weak;
Whose passions, trembling for unbounded sway,
Will thank the Bard, who points the nearest way;
All Vice through Folly's regions first should pass,
And Folly holds her sceptre o'er the glass.
Drink then, ye Fair! and nature's laws fulfill;   110
Be ev'ry thing at once, and all ye will;
Put off the mask that hides the Sex's claim
And makes Distinction but an empty name.

> " Alike in Ignorance, his reason such,
> " Whether he thinks too little or too much;
> " Chaos of Thought and Passion; all confus'd;
> " Still by himself abus'd, or disabus'd:
> " Created half to rise, and half to fall,
> " Great Lord of all things, yet a prey to all;
> " Sole judge of Truth, in endless Error hurl'd;
> " The glory, jest, and riddle of the World!"
>   Pope's Essay on Man.—

INEBRIETY

Go, wond'rous Creature! where the potion glides[1]
From Bowls unmeasur'd in illumin'd tides;
Instruct each other, in your due degrees;
Correct old Rules, and be e'en what you please;
Go, drink! for who shall jointed power contest?
Drink to the passable, the good, the best.
And, quitting Custom and her idle plan,   120
Call drowning reason imitating Man;
Like lovers' brains in giddy circles run,
And, all exhausting, imitate the Sun;
Go, and be Man in noise and glorious strife,
Then drop into his Arms and be a——Wife.

Ye Gods! what scenes upon my Fancy press,
The Consequence of unconfin'd excess;
When Vice in common has one general name,
And male and female Errors be the same;
For, as the strength of Spirit none contest,   130
That daring Ill shall introduce the rest;
Then, what a field of glory will arise,
What dazzling scenes, ye Fair, before your eyes:
As female duels, Jockies——what besides?
Gamblers in petticoats, and booted brides;
The tender Billet to the gentle swain,
That boldly dares avouch the am'rous pain;
Soft Beaux intreated, gentle Coxcombs prest,
And Fops asham'd half blush to be addrest.
Thus to sweet Strephon will his Chloris say,   140

[1] "Go, wondrous creature! mount where Science guides;
"Go, measure earth, weigh air, and state the tides;
"Instruct the planets in what orbs to run,
"Correct old Time, and regulate the Sun;
"Go, soar, with Plato, to th' empyreal sphere,
"To the first Good, first Perfect, and first Fair;
"Or tread the mazy round his foll'wers trod,
"And quitting sense call imitating God;
"As eastern Priests in giddy circles run,
"And turn their heads to imitate the Sun;
"Go, teach Eternal Wisdom how to rule;
"Then drop into thyself, and be a Fool."
                          Pope's Essay on Man.—

GEORGE CRABBE

One cup of Nectar having pav'd the way :
"Oh! why so dead to my emploring eyes,
"Deaf to my prayer, and speechless to my sighs?
"Sure never Nymph of old, my darling Boy,
"When Men intreated, and when we were coy,
"Was prest so warmly by a bleeding swain,
"Or shot from killing eyes such cold disdain."
And thus will run wild Flavia's Billetdoux,
The writing bold, and e'en the spelling true :
"No more, my Belmour, shun these longing arms,   150
"Thou quintessence of all thy Sex's charms ;
"At ten—behind the elm, where echoes sigh,
"Shall, taught [by] me, teach thee my swain to die ;
"The conscious Moon shall fill her lucid horn,
"And join thy Blush to mock the crimson morn ;
"The limpid Stream shall softly move along,
"And hear its own sweet warble from thy tongue ;
"There come, dear boy, or vainly flow the streams,
"There come, or vainly sheds the moon her beams ;
"Vainly on her my Moments I shall waste,   160
"She who like thee is cold, and who like thee is chaste."
But then what tender Stripling shall escape?
What blushing Boy avoid a Lady-Rape?
Where shall each lisping creature hide his head,
To amazonian desires betray'd?
Where from the wily Heroine remove,
Clad in the fortitude of Wine and Love?
Oh! hapless Lad, what refuge canst thou find
Too soft, too mild, too tender to be kind?
Yet this is no objection understood,   170
"For partial Evil's universal Good."

Nor think of Nature's state I make a jest[1] :
The state of Nature is a state undrest ;
The love of Pleasure at our birth began,
Pleasure the aim of all things, and of Man.

[1] "Nor think, in Nature's State they blindly trod ;
"The state of Nature was the reign of God :
"Self-love and social at her birth began,
"Union the bond of all things, and of Man.

INEBRIETY

Law then was not, the swelling flame to kill,
Man walk'd with beast, and—so he always will;
And Woman too, the same their board and bed,
And would be now, but Folks are better bred;
In some convenient grot, or tufted wood,   180
All human beings Nature's circuit trod;
The shrine was her's, with no gay vesture laid;
Unbrib'd, unmarried stood the willing maid;
Her attribute was universal Love,
And man's prerogative to range and rove.
But how unlike the Pairs of times to come,
Wedded, yet separate, abroad at home,
Who foes to Nature, and to evil prone,
Despising all, but hating most their own.
A wayward craving this Neglect succeeds,   190
As every Monster monst'rous children breeds;
Strange motly passions from this vice began,
And Man unnatural turn'd to worship Man.

For this the Muse now calls the Fair to rise,
To shew our failings, and to make us wise;
Be now to Bacchus, now to Venus prone,
And share each folly Man has thought his own;

> "Pride then was not; nor Arts, that Pride to aid;
> "Man walk'd with beast, joint tenant of the shade;
> "The same his table, and the same his bed;
> "No murder cloath'd him, and no murder fed.
> "In the same temple, the resounding wood,
> "All vocal beings hymn'd their equal God;
> "The shrine with gore unstain'd, with gold undrest;
> "Unbrib'd, unbloody, stood the blameless priest;
> "Heav'n's attribute was universal care,
> "And Man's prerogative to rule, but spare.
> "Ah! how unlike the man of times to come!
> "Of half that live the butcher and the tomb;
> "Who, foe to Nature, hears the gen'ral groan,
> "Murders their species, and betrays his own.
> "But just Disease to luxury succeeds,
> "And ev'ry death its own avenger breeds;
> "The Fury-passions from that blood began,
> "And turn'd on Man a fiercer savage, Man."
>
> Pope's Essay on Man.—

31

GEORGE CRABBE

Shame him from Vice, by shewing him your shame,
And part with yours, to reinstate his Fame;
Be generously vile, and this your view: 200
That Man may hate his errors seen in you.

Say, when the Coxcomb flatters and adores,
When (taking snuff) your pity he implores;
With many a gentle Dem'me swears to die,
And humbly begs Destruction from your eye;
When your own arts he takes, and speaks in smiles,
With Softness woos, and with a Voice beguiles;
Does it not move your pity and disdain,
Such flow'ry passion, and such mincing pain;
Your various Follies you with anger scan,   210
So shewn by one whom Nature meant for Man.
E'en so do we our faults in you despise,
And Vice has double malice in those Eyes.
When Chloe toasts her Beau, or raves too loud;
When Flavia leaves her home, and joins a croud;
When Silvia fearless rolls the roguish eye,
And Damon's want of confidence supply;
When betts, and duns, and every rougher name,
Sound in the ear of either Sex the same;
How should we tell, when thus you love and hate, 220
Who acts the Man, and who's effeminate?

Drink, then! disclaim your Sex, be Man in all,
Shew us at once, distinction ought to fall;
And from the humble things ye were of old,
Be reeling Cæsars in a cyprian mould.

Better for us, 'tis granted, it might be[1],
Were you all Softness, and all Honour we;
That never rougher Passion mov'd your mind;
That we were all or excellent or blind;

---

[1] " Better for us, I grant, it might appear,
" Were there all Harmony, all Virtue here;
" That never air or ocean felt the wind,
" That never passion discompos'd the mind;

32

But, as we now subsist by passions strife,   230
Which are (POPE writes) the elements of life,
The general order, since the whole began,
Should be dissolv'd, and Manners make the Man.

Nor fear, if once ye break through general Laws,
To draw in thousands, and gain our applause ;
Nor fear but Fame your merits shall make known,
And female Bravos trample Hectors down ;
From Man himself you'll learn the art he boasts,
Rule in his room, and govern in his posts.

Thus does the Muse in vein didactic speak——[1]   240
" Go, from proud Man thy full instructions take ;
" Learn from the Law, what gain its mazes yield ;
" Learn of the Brave the police of the field ;
" Thy arts of shuffling from the Courtier get ;
" Learn of his Grace to stare away a debt ;
" Learn from the Sot his poison to caress,
" Shake the mad room, and revel in excess ;
" From Man all forms of grand deception find,
" And so be tempted to delude Mankind.
" Here frantic schemes of wild Ambition see ;   250
" There all the plots, my Fair ! he lays for thee.
" Learn each small People's genius, humours, aims,

> " But all subsists by elemental strife,
> " And passions are the elements of life ;
> " The general Order, since the whole began
> " Is kept in Nature, and is kept in Man."

[1] " Thus then to Man the voice of Nature spake——
" ' Go, from the creatures thy instructions take :
" ' Learn from the birds what food the thickets yield ;
" ' Learn from the beasts the physic of the field ;
" ' Thy arts of building from the bee receive ;
" ' Learn of the mole to plough, the worm to weave ;
" ' Learn of the little nautilus to sail,
" ' Spread the thin oar, and catch the driving gale.
" ' Here too all forms of social union find,
" ' And hence let Reason, late, instruct Mankind ;
" ' Here subterranean works and cities see,
" ' There towns aerial on the waving tree.
" ' Learn each small people's genius, policies,

GEORGE CRABBE

" The Jocky's dealing, and Newmarket games;
" How there in common wealth in currents go,
" And poverty and riches ebb and flow;
" And these for ever, though a Saint deny'd,
" To splendour or contempt their Masters guide;
" Mark the nice rules of modern honour well,
" Rules which the laws of Nature far excell.
" In vain thy fancy finer whims shall draw;   260
" Good-breeding is as difficult as Law,
" And, form'd so complex, makes itself a science,
" To bid the Scholar and the Clown defiance.
" Go then, and thus thy present Lords survey,
" And let the Creatures feel they must obey;
" Learn all their Arts, be these thy choicest hoard,
" Be fear'd for these, and be for these ador'd."

And where are these? within the Bowl they lie;
Thence spring ambitious thoughts, there doubtings die;
From thence we trace the horrors of a War,   270
Chaotic counsel, ministerial jar;
This makes a gambling Lord, a Patriot vain,
The Soldier's fury, and the Lover's pain;
Fills Bedlam's wards with souls of ærial mould;
This makes the Madman, this supplies the Scold;
Here rules the one grand Passion in extreme,
A love of lucre, or a love of fame;

    " ' The ant's republic, and the realm of bees;
    " ' How those in common all their wealth bestow,
    " ' And anarchy without confusion know;
    " ' And these for ever, though a monarch reign,
    " ' Their sep'rate cells and properties maintain.
    " ' Mark what unvary'd laws preserv'd each state,
    " ' Laws wise as nature, and as fix'd as Fate.
    " ' In vain thy Reason finer webs shall draw,
    " ' Intangle Justice in her net of law,
    " ' And right, too rigid, harden into wrong,
    " ' Still for the strong too weak, the weak too strong.
    " ' Yet go! and thus o'er all the creatures sway;
    " ' Thus let the wiser make the rest obey;
    " ' And, for those arts mere Instinct could afford,
    " ' Be crown'd as Monarchs, or as Gods ador'd.' "

    Pope's Essay on Man.—

The Scholar's boast, the Politician's plan;
Here shines the Bubble, and here falls the Man.

Oh! happy fall of insolence and pride,   280
Which makes the humblest with the great allied;
Which levels like the Grave all earthly things,
For drunken Coblers are as proud as Kings;
Which plucks the sons of grandeur from their sphere,
For who is lower than a stagg'ring Peer?
Yet here, ye Fair, tho' ev'ry Soul's the same,
And Prince and Pedlar differ but in name,
Folly with Fashion is discreetly grac'd,
And, if all sin, not all can sin in taste;
For who, ye Gods! would ever go astray,   290
If 'twas not something in a modish way?

Oh! Fashion, caprice, pride—whate'er we call—
Thou something, nothing, dear attractive all;
Thou serious trifle of the gentle Soul,
Worship'd, yet changing, varying to controul;
Sweet Child of wanton fancy, artful whim,
Bred in an instant, born in an Extreme;
Folly's best friend, and luxury's ally,
Who, dying always, prov'st thou canst not die;
Attend us here; let us grow mad in Form,   300
Rage with an Air, and elegantly storm;
Invoke destruction with a Grace divine,
And call for Satan as a child of thine;
Genteely stagger from the common road;
And ape the brute, but ape him in the mode;
With a Court-grace make every action known,
For who'd be d——n'd for sins they blush to own?

Far as the power of human vice extends[1],
Her scale of sensual vanity ascends;
Mark how it rises to the gilded Throne,   310
From the poor wretch who dully topes alone.

[1] " Far as Creation's ample range extends,
" The scale of sensual, mental pow'rs ascends;
" Mark how it mounts to Man's imperial race,
" From the green myriads in the peopled grass

GEORGE CRABBE

What modes of folly, each in one extreme,
The sots dim sense, th' Epicurean's dream;
Of scent, what diff'rence 'twixt the pungent rum
And noxious vapours of fermenting stum;
Of hearing, to Champain's decanted swell
From the dull gurgle of expiring ale?
The touch, how distant in the mean and great,
Who feel all roughness, or who feed from plate;
In the nice Lord, behold what arts produce;   320
From vases carv'd is quaff'd the balmy juice;
How palates vary in the poor Divine,
Compar'd, half-reasoning Nobleman! with thine.

Thus every sense is fill'd in due degree,
And proper barriers bound his Grace and me;
Here every Passion is at length display'd,
Nations are ruin'd, Ministers betray'd;
And what, ye Fair, concerns your pleasures most,
Intrigues are plan'd, and Reputations lost:
By you persuaded, Man was overcome,   330
And conquer'd once, received a general doom;
Require the deed, partake a general Curse;
We fell with you, and you should fall with us.

> "What modes of sight, betwixt each wide extreme,
> "The mole's dim curtain, and the lynx's beam:
> "Of smell the head-long lioness between,
> "And hound sagacious on the tainted green.
> "Of hearing, from the life that fills the flood,
> "To that which warbles thro' the vernal wood,
> "The spider's touch, how exquisitely fine!
> "Feels at each thread, and lives along the line;
> "In the nice bee what art, so subtly true,
> "From pois'nous herbs extracts the healing dew;
> "How Instinct varies in the grov'ling swine,
> "Compar'd, half-reasoning elephant, with thine."
>   Pope's Essay on Man.—

FINIS.

36

JUVENILIA

[THE LEARNING OF LOVE.]

[About 1776.]

AH! blest be the days when with Mira I took
  The learning of Love . . . . .
When we pluck'd the wild blossoms that blush'd in the grass,
And I taught my dear maid of their species and class ;
For Conway, the friend of mankind, had decreed
That Hudson should show us the wealth of the mead.

YE GENTLE GALES.

Woodbridge, 1776.

YE gentle Gales, that softly move,
  Go whisper to the Fair I love ;
Tell her I languish and adore,
And pity in return implore.

But if she's cold to my request,
Ye louder Winds, proclaim the rest—
My sighs, my tears, my griefs proclaim,
And speak in strongest notes my flame.

Still, if she rests in mute disdain,
And thinks I feel a common pain—   10
Wing'd with my woes, ye Tempests, fly,
And tell the haughty Fair I die.

GEORGE CRABBE

MIRA.

Aldborough, 1777.

A WANTON chaos in my breast raged high,
A wanton transport darted in mine eye;
False pleasure urged, and ev'ry eager care,
That swell the soul to guilt and to despair.
My Mira came! be ever blest the hour,
That drew my thoughts half way from folly's power;
She first my soul with loftier notions fired;
I saw their truth, and as I saw admired;
With greater force returning reason moved,
And as returning reason urged, I loved;   10
Till pain, reflection, hope, and love allied
My bliss precarious to a surer guide—
To Him who gives pain, reason, hope, and love,
Each for that end that angels must approve.
One beam of light He gave my mind to see,
And gave that light, my heavenly fair, by thee;
That beam shall raise my thoughts, and mend my strain,
Nor shall my vows, nor prayers, nor verse be vain.

JUVENILIA

HYMN.

Beccles, 1778.

OH, Thou! who taught my infant eye
    To pierce the air, and view the sky,
To see my God in earth and seas,
To hear him in the vernal breeze,
To know him midnight thoughts among,
O guide my soul, and aid my song!
Spirit of Light! do thou impart
Majestic truths, and teach my heart;
Teach me to know how weak I am,
How vain my powers, how poor my frame;   10
Teach me celestial paths untrod—
The ways of glory and of God.

No more let me, in vain surprise,
To heathen art give up my eyes—
To piles laborious science rear'd
For heroes brave, or tyrants fear'd;
But quit Philosophy, and see
The Fountain of her works in Thee.

Fond man! yon glassy mirror eye—
Go, pierce the flood, and there descry   20
The miracles that float between
The rainy leaves of wat'ry green;
Old Ocean's hoary treasures scan;
See nations swimming round a span.

Then wilt thou say—and rear no more
Thy monuments in mystic lore—
My God! I quit my vain design,
And drop my work to gaze on Thine:
Henceforth I'll frame myself to be,
Oh, Lord! a monument of Thee.   30

39

GEORGE CRABBE

THE WISH.

Aldborough, 1778.

GIVE me, ye Powers that rule in gentle hearts,
The full design, complete in all its parts,
Th' enthusiastic glow, that swells the soul—
When swell'd too much the judgment to control—
The happy ear that feels the flowing force
Of the smooth line's uninterrupted course ;
Give me, oh give, if not in vain the prayer,
That sacred wealth, poetic worth, to share—
Be it my boast to please and to improve,
To warm the soul to virtue and to love ;   10
To paint the passions, and to teach mankind
Our greatest pleasures are the most refined ;
The cheerful tale with fancy to rehearse,
And gild the moral with the charm of verse.

THE COMPARISON.

Parham, 1778.

FRIENDSHIP is like the gold refined,
And all may weigh its worth ;
Love like the ore, brought undesign'd
In virgin beauty forth.

Friendship may pass from age to age,
And yet remain the same ;
Love must in many a toil engage,
And melt in lambent flame.

JUVENILIA

GOLDSMITH TO THE AUTHOR.
Aldborough, 1778.

Felix quem faciunt aliena pericula cautum.

YOU'RE in love with the Muses? Well, grant it be true,
When, good Sir, were the Muses enamour'd of you?
Read first—if my lectures your fancy delight—
Your taste is diseased, can your cure be to *write*?

You suppose you're a genius, that ought to engage
The attention of wits and the smiles of the age:
Would the wits of the age their opinion make known,
Why—every man thinks just the same of his own.

You imagine that Pope—but yourself you beguile—
Would have wrote the same things, had he chose the same
    style.   10
Delude not yourself with so fruitless a hope—
Had he chose the same style, he had never been Pope.

You think of *my* muse with a friendly regard,
And rejoice in her author's esteem and reward:
But let not his glory your spirits elate,
When pleased with his honours, remember his fate.

FRAGMENT.
Aldborough, 1778.

Lord, what is man, that thou art mindful of him?

PROUD, little Man, opinion's slave,
Error's fond child, too duteous to be free,
Say, from the cradle to the grave,
    Is not the earth thou tread'st too grand for thee?
This globe that turns thee, on her agile wheel
Moves by deep springs, which thou canst never feel;
Her day and night, her centre and her sun,
Untraced by thee, their annual courses run.
A busy fly, thou sharest the march divine,
And flattering fancy calls the motion thine;   10
Untaught how soon some hanging grave may burst,
And join thy flimsy substance to the dust.

GEORGE CRABBE

THE RESURRECTION.

Aldborough, 1778.

THE wintry winds have ceased to blow,
    And trembling leaves appear;
And fairest flowers succeed the snow,
    And hail the infant year.

So, when the world and all its woes
    Are vanish'd far away,
Fair scenes and wonderful repose
    Shall bless the new-born day—

When, from the confines of the grave,
    The body too shall rise,   10
No more precarious passion's slave,
    Nor error's sacrifice.

'Tis but a sleep—and Sion's king
    Will call the many dead;
'Tis but a sleep—and then we sing
    O'er dreams of sorrow fled.

Yes!—wintry winds have ceased to blow,
    And trembling leaves appear,
And Nature has her types to show
    Throughout the varying year.   20

42

JUVENILIA

MY BIRTH-DAY.

Aldborough, December 24, 1778.

THROUGH a dull tract of woe, of dread,
  The toiling year has pass'd and fled:
And, lo! in sad and pensive strain,
I sing my birth-day date again.

Trembling and poor, I saw the light,
New waking from unconscious night;
Trembling and poor I still remain,
To meet unconscious night again.

Time in my pathway strews few flowers,
To cheer or cheat the weary hours;   10
And those few strangers, dear indeed,
Are choked, are check'd, by many a weed.

TO ELIZA.

Beccles, 1779.

THE Hebrew king, with spleen possest,
  By David's harp was soothed to rest;
Yet, when the magic song was o'er,
The soft delusion charm'd no more;
The former fury fired the brain,
And every care return'd again.

  But had he known Eliza's skill
To bless the sense and bind the will,
To bid the gloom of care retire,
And fan the flame of fond desire,   10
Remembrance then had kept the strain,
And not a care return'd again.

GEORGE CRABBE

LIFE.

Aldborough, 1779.

THINK ye, the joys that fill our early day,
Are the poor prelude to some full repast?
Think you, they *promise*?—ah! believe they *pay*;
The purest ever, they are oft the last.
The jovial swain that yokes the morning team,
And all the verdure of the field enjoys,
See him, how languid, when the noontide beam
Plays on his brow, and all his force destroys.
So 'tis with us, when, love and pleasure fled,
We at the summit of our hill arrive: 10
Lo! the gay lights of Youth are past—are dead,
But what still deepening clouds of Care survive!

THE SACRAMENT.

Aldborough, 1779.

O SACRED gift of God to man,
A faith that looks above,
And sees the deep amazing plan
Of sanctifying love.

Thou dear and yet tremendous God,
Whose glory pride reviles;
How did'st thou change thy awful rod
To pard'ning grace and smiles!

Shut up with sin, with shame below,
I trust, this bondage past,   10
A great, a glorious change to know,
And to be bless'd at last.

I *do* believe, that, God of light!
Thou didst to earth descend,
With Satan and with Sin to fight—
Our great, our only friend.

I *know* thou did'st ordain for me,
Thy creature, bread and wine;
The depth of grace I cannot see,
But worship the design.   20

JUVENILIA

NIGHT.

Aldborough, 1779.

THE sober stillness of the night
 That fills the silent air,
And all that breathes along the shore,
 Invite to solemn prayer.

Vouchsafe to me that spirit, Lord!
 Which points the sacred way,
And let thy creatures here below
 Instruct me how to pray.

FRAGMENT, WRITTEN AT MIDNIGHT.

Aldborough, 1779.

OH, great Apollo! by whose equal aid
 The verse is written and the med'cine made,
Shall thus a boaster, with his fourfold powers,
In triumph scorn this sacred art of ours?
Insulting quack! on thy sad business go,
And land the stranger on this world of woe.
 Still I pass on, and now before me find
The restless ocean, emblem of my mind;
There wave on wave, here thought on thought succeeds,
Their produce idle works and idle weeds.   10
Dark is the prospect o'er the rolling sea,
But not more dark than my sad views to me;
Yet from the rising moon the light beams dance
In troubled splendour o'er the wide expanse;
So on my soul, whom cares and troubles fright,
The Muse pours comfort in a flood of light.—
Shine out, fair flood! until the day-star flings
His brighter rays on all sublunar things.

"Why in such haste? by all the powers of wit,
"I have against thee neither bond nor writ.   20
"If thou'rt a poet, now indulge the flight
"Of thy fine fancy in this dubious light;
"Cold, gloom, and silence shall assist thy rhyme,
"And all things meet to form the true sublime."—
    "Shall I, preserver deem'd around the place,
"With abject rhymes a doctor's name disgrace?
"Nor doctor solely, in the healing art
"I'm all in all, and all in every part;
"Wise Scotland's boast let that diploma be
"Which gave me right to claim the golden fee.   30
"Praise, then, I claim, to skilful surgeon due,
"For mine th' advice and operation too;
"And, fearing all the vile compounding tribe,
"I make myself the med'cines I prescribe.
"Mine, too, the chemic art; and not a drop
"Goes to my patients from a vulgar shop.
"But chief my fame and fortune I command
"From the rare skill of this obstetric hand:
"This our chaste dames and prudent wives allow,
"With her who calls me from thy wonder now."   40

MIDNIGHT.

A POEM.

[About 1779.]

L IFE is a Dream ;—it steals upon the Man,
    He knows not how, but thinks himself awake ;
'Tis like a Bubble dancing on the Deep,
That turns its glossy surface to the Sun,
Catches a Rainbow-Vest, and sparkles, proud
Of momentary Being—then it breaks—
To some tremendous Billow drops a prey,
And joins th' eternal Source, from whence it sprang.

But ah ! how dismal are the Dreams of Care,
How much of Care do e'en the happiest dream,   10
And some—hard Fortune theirs—of Care alone.

Forgive me then, ye Wise, who seem awake,
A Midnight Song, and let your Censure sleep ;
While Sorrow's Theme, and Contemplation sad,
And Soul-dilating Fancy's pensive Flight
Through Star-crown'd Gloom, I sing ; inspir'd by her,
Whom Virtue loves, whom Wisdom ; from whose Touch
Grief borrows Charm, and Expectation sits
On the cold Bosom of the Tomb serene.
Pale Melancholy she ; nor softer shines   20
The sabled Fair, her Votress, o'er the Grave
Of the departed Lover ; nor more mild
Sits yonder Moon's chaste ray upon the Rock,
That, rising from the Bosom of the Wave,
Flings Awe on Night. Thou Grave-enamour'd Fair,
Attune my Song, and, languid as thou art,
The Song shall please ; and I will paint the Dream
That Midnight gave thee, when with wintry Wing

47

She swept thy Grot, and shook her grisled Dew
Upon the frozen Garment of the pool ;   30
And I will drown mine Eye in Tears like thine,
And give my hollow Cheek a dewy pale,
And dress me in the Livery of the Dead ;
And o'er their dreary Mansions walk with thee ;
Bidding a brief Farewell to little Cares,
And Visionary Honour's frantic Sons,
Who feed on Adulation—let them feed,
Till the full Soul disdains the nauseous Trash,
And sickens with Repletion.—

                          I will ask,
No Voice of Fame to spread abroad my Song,   40
Nor Court Applause—Meonides had Fame,
And with her poverty and pain and Care,
Attendants on the Bard-deluding Nymph,
Who mock the Babbling of her loudest Note ;
From Heaven he stole Description, Nature's Key,
And loosen'd into Light her Mysteries ;
Ambition started when he sang of War,
In Language all her own ; and o'er his Lyre
Hung Devastation, glowing at the Sound,
And frantic for the Field; and there Distress,   50
As if enamour'd of the Mighty Man,
With cruel Constancy repaid his Muse ;
And chiding Fame, by whispering to the Soul
Domestic Ills, she [triumph'd] over praise,
And, through th' untasted Plaudit of a World,
Led the blind Bard in Sadness to the Tomb.—

I ask no Mantuan Muse with silver Wing
To bear me in some rapid even flight
Thro' distant Ages, tho' so sweet her Bard
That yet the Traveller o'er each Hill he sang,   60
Transported, [wanders], feeling power divine
New-rising on his Soul to chain its Cares.
Imagination turns the Tide of Time,
Unwinds each year, and, thro' reviving Light,
And thro' the vandal Gloom of Centuries drear,

MIDNIGHT

And falling Rome works back, till Nature smiles
And [Tityrus] sings anew ; then laughs each Scene,
And cloudless skies appear, and Beachen Boughs
That Shade the [Nereids] listning from their Streams.—

Nor Milton's muse I boast, to whom the Morn   70
And all her rosy Train, and blazing Noon,
Dipping his fiery Tresses in the Stream
Of Pison, bank'd with Gold, and tepid Eve,
Who in her soft recesses cradles Thought,
And Worlds unsung pay Homage, and the Suns,
From which the Light yet wings its rapid Way,
Nor on the gloomy Bosom of the Earth,
Sleeps from the Labour of its long Career.

Nor feels my Bosom that ambiguous Flame,
That now from Skies, and now from central Gloom,   80
Shot devious o'er the fervent Page of Young—
Young, Thought's Œconomist, who wove reproof
Her [gloomiest] Vest, and yet a Vest that shone ;
Whose Invitation was assault: he found
The World asleep and rent its drowsy Ear.

Nor shares my Soul the soft enchanting Stream,
The lambent Blaze, that [Thomson] knew to blend
With his Creation ; when he led the Eye
Through the [year's Verdant] Gate, the budding Spring ;
And from the Willow o'er the tuneless Stream,   90
And from the [Aspen] Rind, ere yet her Leaf
Unfolding flicker'd, and from limpid rills
Unmantled, cull'd Simplicity and Grace.
Ah ! who with mingled Modesty and Love
So paints the bathing Maid ; who so describes
The new-mown Meadow, and the new shorn Lamb?
Hard is the Task to strip the Muse's Wing
Of Learning's plume, yet leave enough to charm ;
But this was thine ! Grace beautify'd thy page,
And led thy weary plowman from the field,   100
And spread thy simple Foliage on the Sod,
And hung thy ponderous Treasures on the Bough,

And rov'd with thy Lavinia where the Winds,
Rustling along the golden [Valley], bear
The Grain just dropping from its withering Glume.
And Winter too was thine! permit me there
To bear a part, for mine are wintry Thoughts.—

Nor dare I hope his Dignity and Fire,
Who led the soul thro' Nature, and display'd
Imagination's pleasures to its Eye;   110
His the blest Task, a [gloomier] task is mine;
His were the Smiles of Fortune, mine her Frowns;
And when her Frowns and Smiles shall charm alike,
At that dread Hour when the officious Friend,
Stammering his Idiot-Comfort, soothes amiss,
May Joys he painted dart upon the Soul,
And, more than Fancy pointing to the Skies,
Whisper a noble [Challenge] to the Tomb.—
Tho' far behind my Song, my Hope the same,
And not behind my Song; with Vulgar souls,   120
Both sentenc'd to Contempt—unletter'd pride—
Grins the pale Bard Disgrace alike to him
Who soars above or labours in the Clouds,
Who travells the sublime, or dives profound
In the Wild Chaos of a School-boy's Dream:
He, tyed to some poor Spot, where e'en the rill
That owns him Lord untasted steals away,
Hallows a Clod, and spurns Immensity.

Ye gentle, nameless Bards, who float a-down
The soft smoothe Stream of silver poesy   130
And dream your pretty Dreams, permit my Song
Cold inspiration from a Winter's Night.
This is no Stanza'd Birth-Day of his Grace,
Your patron; no sad Satire of the Lord,
Your Foe; no Dunciad arm'd with power,
To dive into the Depths of your profound,
And with a vile assemblage gather'd there
Whip the pale Moonshine from your with'ring Bays.—

Is there, who sick of Pleasure's daily Draught,
In repetition mawkish, or who tir'd   140

MIDNIGHT

Thinks Life an Idiot's Tale ? or whom the Hand
Of [Disappointment] snatches from the Vice
That waits on power? or who has lost a friend,
And mingles with the dew that wets his Tomb
A frequent Tear? or who by Nature's mild
And melancholy Bias from the Womb
Was fashioned for the View of serious Things,
And with the sober chiding of his eye,
Freezes the [Current] within Laughter's Cheek,
And awes the Voice of loud Garrulity ?   150
Let him approach, and I will tell my Soul,
EUGENIO rises from the Grave, and give
The Living Youth the Manners of my Friend.
From the Enshrouded Tenant of the Sod
I'll call the speaking Eye, the open Heart,
The Tongue belov'd of Knowledge, and the Form
That, could Deceit put on, Grey-headed Guile,
That judges from his own embosom'd Guilt,
Would yet be won, and lend a ductile Ear.

Together, while the [Echo's] feeble Sound,   160
Halting in frozen regions of the Air,
Mocks our slow Step, we from the Mountain's Brow,
Will look around and court the Stars of Heav'n
For as much Light as guides the Miser's hand,
To grasp Delusion in her Guise of Gold.—

The Morn is banish'd now, nor down the Hill
Slopes the faint Shadow; now in other Realms
She drinks the Dew that on the Vi'lets Lip
Slept thro' the Night; and, with her golden Dart
Bays the pale Moon, retiring from the View.   170
In other Climates, from the rays of Noon
Embower'd, Content lies sleeping; and the palm
Drinking the fiery Stream, plays o'er the Brow
Of shadied Wearyness ; and distant now
Draws meek-ey'd Eve, with even hand and slow,
The fringèd Curtain of the setting Sun,
Ting'd with the golden Splendour he bequeaths,
The brief, but beauteous Legacy of Light.

GEORGE CRABBE

'Tis Midnight round us, canopied by Dim
And twinkling Orbs that, gleaming ghastly, gild   180
The restless Bosom of the briny Deep.
The fiery Meteor in the foggy Air
Rides emulous of Fame and apes the Star,
Till, in the Compass of a Maiden's Wish,
It mocks the Eye, and sheds an [igneous] Stream,
Within the bosom of Oblivion.

The Sea-Bird sleeps upon yon hoary Cliff,
Unconscious of the Surge that grates below
The frozen Shore; and Icy Friendship binds,
As Danger Wretches Destitute of Soul,   190
The wave-worn pebbles, which the ebbing Tide,
Left with the Salt-Flood shining; dark is now
The awfull Deep, and o'er the Seaman's Grave
Rolls pouring, and forbids the lucid Stream,
That silvers oft the way, a shining Vest,
Sprung from the scaly people's putrid Dead,
Hanging unhers'd upon the Coral Bough;
Or, as the Sage explains, from Stores of Light
Imprizon'd in the Bowels of the Deep,
And now escaping, when the parent Sun   200
Flings [out] his fiery Noon with Beam direct,
Upon the Glossy Surface of the wave.

Cold Vapour, falling on the putrid Fen,
Condenses grey, and wraps with glassy net
The wintry Fern, and throws along the Heath
A Hoary Garment, nor less fair than Spring
Drops on the Sod, of Texture near as frail.
The icy Atoms thro' the burden'd Air
Shed Languor, and enwrap with double Fleece
The Slumbering Fold; they cloathe the knotted oak,   210
Stretching its naked arms, as if to chide,
With [age's] stern and touching Eloquence
The ruthless Skies for Summer's slow return.
The winds that in converging Furrows plough
The freezing pool, and shake the [rattling] Wood,
Are arm'd with pain, and vitrified their Wings.

52

MIDNIGHT

In Winter's Livery sleeps this earthly Scene—
And, save where Ocean rolls his restless Flood,
The horizontal Eye grasps all things grey.—

Eugenio, see—for thou shalt bear His Name   220
Who sleeps beneath yon Sod, and was my Friend—
The Grave o'er which I weep; and give not thou
A Glance contemptuous to the grassy Tomb;
For oft the vaulted Chambers of the Dead,
Where Vanity amid the Mouldring Scrolls
Of Genealogy and mingled Bones
Moves in a formal join'd Solemnity,
House wretched Remnants of degenerate Man;
And oft the Green Turf's temporary swell,
Sepulchring all that Virtue leaves the Earth,   230
Stirs busy Memory to con o'er Deeds
Of high Renown in Heaven, the Deeds of Love;
Which in th' eternal Records of the Just,
Are written with an Angels pen, and sung
With [Symphony] of Harp, and there is Joy
And Gratulation with the Sons of God.—

Alas! how chang'd the Verdure of this [Scene],
How lost the Flowers, how winter-struck the Blade!
No more the wild Thyme wings the passing Gale
With Fragrance, nor invites the roving Bee   240
To taste its Sweets—and why this direful waste
Of Verdure? why this Vegetable Death?
Did all with Man commit mysterious Sin?
All in rebellion rise?—and tepid Meads,
And Lawns irriguous, and the blooming field,
And Hills, and Vallies, and intangling Woods,
Spurn GOD's Command and drink forbidden Dew?—

There was a Time, and Poets paint it fair,
(A wild, uncertain, musing, madning Race)
A Golden Age, when wealth was only Love: 250
Not even Fancy dreamt a Dream of Care,
The Sward was not—and Desolation slept
Till by a Crime awaken'd; not e'en Song

53

GEORGE CRABBE

Wore Semblatude of War;—Eternal Spring
From the unfurrow'd Field the heavy Ear
Drew smiling, and the undistinguish'd year
Brought willing plenty forth, nor scorn'd she then
A Common Call, enamour'd of her plough.
The Clinging Vine prest down the branching Elm
E'en to the Earth, and in her verdant Lap 260
The tributary Grape, yet growing, laid.
The simple Shepherd pip'd a silvan Lay;
Or, while the Fair who charm'd him prest beside,
The listning Vale sung hymeneal Strains,
And woo'd with melting Themes a ten years' Bride.

Eugenio, thus they taught; and after this
A silver age arose, and hers the Scenes
Not Gold could purchase now: when Vice, afraid,
Hid his pale Visage in the womb of Night,
And blush'd, if but a Moon-beam met his Eye. 270
The Seasons alter'd, but the Change was slow,
And Man forgot they chang'd; then Care began
To plow his Furrows on the Brow of Age,
And Falshood from the female Eye to steal
The silent Tear; then prudence took her Seat
Within the Soul, and reign'd in Virtue's room.
Then Vanity, a Child, first learn'd to bend
The ready Ear to tales of her own praise;
Nor knew she yet the Gross of Flattery,
But was, as Modesty is now, afraid 280
The Verse she lov'd should tickle her too much.
Then young Ambition wore his Russet Gown
Only in better Form, and Infant pomp
But saw his Garden smile in richer Bloom,
And propt his Cottage with a taller pier.—

Since these, dread Sorrow, consequent of Sin
And foul Deformity, the Breast of Man
And the Sad Surface of the Earth enrobes.—

From the Dark Bosom of the Giant Guilt
Leak'd all Things terrible, and Murder first, 290

54

MIDNIGHT

Who proul'd about the Earth and groan'd for Blood;
And treatchery, breaking up the League of Friends
And rending Nature's Bond, a solemn writ,
With Heaven's own Seal imprest : and Avarice pale,
A Woolfish-Visag'd Fiend [and] fang'd with Care.
Hence War, in all her guilty Majesty
In slow pomp riding o'er a [threat'ned] Land,
With all the murderous Whispers of the Camp
And shout of Ambush, castigates the Night.—

And hence the Spirits from th' Abyss of Hell,   300
That prey upon Mankind.—Eugenio, give
Thy Soul's pure Eye, that sees immortal things,
To the grim Spectres hovering in the Air,
And we will mark the dreary Train that vex
The mortal Man, and ride with ghostly pomp,
Frowning upon the Midnight's murky Wing.—

And who is he, from yonder antient roof,
With Horror in his Eye, who steals around
Each hollow Isle ; and with a fierce Embrace
Clasps the encrumbling ruin ? 'Tis the Foe   310
Of Men and Virtue, Eldest-born of Night,
And Superstition call'd, a Giant fond
Of Dead-Men's Bones, and vagrant [Rottenness],
Denied a Tomb ; around him turns the wheel,
And faggots blaze ; and prizons, with a Groan
Resounding loud, affright the Coward Soul
From Reason's Law, and Nature's. Hark! he Mourns
The fretted Abby where he reign'd Secure,
With Indolence and Folly, social pair,
Nurses to shrine-enamour'd Zeal, who built   320
The Cavern deep and dark, in which he chain'd
The drowsy Nine ; who yet at Morn or Eve
Hail'd the arising or descending Sun
With gothic Note, harmoniously sad.
But now no more the Votive Maiden clasps
The clay cold Saint, and mingles with her Vow
The Heaven-reproaching Sigh ; in these blest realms
No more the power-compelling Bigot plucks

GEORGE CRABBE

The robe from Kings, and consecrates the Tomb
That hides a Brother-Saint with Zeal-enforc'd 330
And ceremonious Solemnity.—

O'er the Opaque of Nature and of Night
Fair Truth rose smiling, with the Heaven-born Art
That shews the Man his Fellow's Thought imprest
Within the Volumes' varied Character,
Where to the wondering Eye the Soul reveals
Her Store immortal. Hence a Bacon shone
And Newton thro' the World, and Light on Light
Pour'd on the human Breast, as when of old,
From the Eternal Fountains of the God, 340
Etherial Streams assail'd the groaning Mass;
Then Chaos and the Sun's large Eye survey'd
The first [distinguish'd] Forms of mortal Things,
Till then in Congregate Confusion hurl'd
Without a Station, and without a Name.
Then Wit began, the younger-born of Light,
To sport in hallow'd Cloysters, where the arm
Of Superstition, red with slaughter'd Foes,
Held high the Torch of Discord. Stroke on Stroke
The smiling Boy repeated with his Sword, 350
Sharp as the [Whirlwind's] Eye: yet fear'd the fight,
And oft drew back, his silver wing born down
By the foul Breath of Malice; till at length
The Monster, rousing in Collected Might,
Shook with his Roar the Earth, and at the Sound
Red Tyranny, and Torture, with his Limbs
Disjoint, and Ignorance that blows the blast
For every Fire, prepar'd each bloody Form
Of Death, and woo'd Destruction for her Wheel.—

Then on the Father dead the dying Son 360
Implor'd Heavn's Vengence. Execration shrill
Shot from the lurid Flame, and to the Skies
Sail'd with the Speed of Light. The Virgin's Eye
Met the grey Ruffian's, speaking Nature's Fear
Of Death and Pain: the Bigot's stern Reply,
Forbidding Hope, on the affrightned Soul

56

Flung Terror; till, in pity to the World,
Came Wisdom, whispering to the Ear of power,
And peace arose; and then the Brother wept
A Brother's Death, for distant seem'd his own.   370

And now the Spirit of uneasy Man,
That weds Extreme, and, ever on the Wing
For Wonder, baffles peace, high o'er the Cells
Of monkish Zeal, built with the base remains
The tow'ring Palace of Impiety.
There Jest profane, and Quibbling Mockery
Of all divine grew fast, as from the Earth
Enrich'd Ill-Weeds first spring; and here the Fools,
Of Laughter vain, [despis'd] the Voice of Truth,
And labour'd in the ludicrous obscene.   380

To these succeed, and ah! with sad Success,
A Sceptic herd more cool, and fair of form,
And smoothe of Tongue and apt to gloss a Lye
With Semblance strong of Nature and the Truth;
They shine as Serpents, and as Serpents bite,
With poison'd Tooth.   Alas! the State of Man,
Or doom'd the Victim of ungovern'd Zeal,
Or led the Captive of unquiet Doubt!—

And now, Eugenio, turn thine Eye, and view
Yon Sire bare-headed to the ruthless Wind,   390
And heedless of its Force.   Upon the Brow
Of yon huge shapeless Ruin, see, he kneels,
And urges the departed Saints who sleep,
To lend a Prayer; Repentance sent him forth,
Her Son, but late th' adopted of her dark
And gloomy Train.   Ah! heavy weighs the Crime
Of Murder on his Soul, and haunts his Bed!
And, shrieking by, unseals the Eye of Sleep,
Or scatters on the dark and restless Mind
A thousand sooty Images of Death,   400
All horrible, and making Guilt's repose
Like to the fearfull rest the Vessell feels
In the dread Chasm of the tempestuous Sea,

GEORGE CRABBE

Arch'd by the Wave that pauses o'er the Gulph,
While Sea-men urge their momentary prayer,
And with Heart-shrinking Horror view their Grave.

But hark, he speaks—attend the Wretches Tale—
Spreading his Soul upon the Wings of Night,
And seeking peace by giving Themes of pain
To the rude Air:

                " Come, all ye little Ills,   410
"Contempt, and poverty, and pale Disease
"With Dewy Front, and Envy-struck applause
"That sickens on the World, and all of Care
"That shed your daily Drops of bitter Dew
"Upon the Brow of mortal Man, here strike,
"That I may feel your force, and call it Joy,
"So made when weigh'd against the Load that Guilt,
"With leaden Hand, deposits on my Heart,
"And when a momentary Comfort strives,
"Lifted by hope, to spread her downy Wing,   420
"Dispair, with Icy palm, arrests the Thought,
"And nips the still-born Joy.—

                " To me no more
"The Good I coveted brings Joy, brings peace,
"Or stifles Truth's reproof that will be heard;
"And did I think a base and sordid Heap
"Had in it the Ability to pluck
"The Sting from Guilt, and smother how it came
"In the vile Knowledge that it came to me?
"It was a Madman's Dream—O ye good Gods!
"If Envy knew her Mark, she would beset   430
"The poor Man's Table and the Shepherd's Hut,
"Unroof'd to the cold Winter's wildest Blast,
"Or the Embay'd Explorers of the Deep,
"At their still howling North; and leave the Throne,
"The Sceptre and the chested Gold to plant
"The Thorn of Care upon the Brow of State,
"On which Distraction drives his plow-share deep,
"And helps the Scythe of Time to wrinkle there.—

58

MIDNIGHT

" When shall I rest—O! let me, Night, [besiege]
" Thy drowsy Ear with wailing, but be thou　　　440
" [Tenacious] of my Guilt; and with her Band
" Let everlasting Silence Tye thy Tongue;
" The pent-up Woe now struggles to o'er-leap
" Murder's Discretion, and with fearfull Speech
" To free the Heart by telling Deeds of Death:
" [Death, Thought's] repose, whom the abhor'd of Man,
" The base assassin, gives, and after longs
" With Lover's Ardour to embrace, be mine,
" And I will yield all Hope of After-Life,
" All Saints have promis'd, and all poets sung—　　450
" Elysium water'd with immortal Streams,
" And gifted with Eternity of peace,
" Balm-breathing Fields, and Bowers of soft repose,
" Walks amaranthine, and the pillowy Moss,
" On Banks where Harpers, to celestial Strings
" Attuning Nature, warble Notes of Love,
" The Anodyne to all-rebellious Thought.—

" These, for Oblivion, I forego, with these
" Foregoing pain eternal. Why then strive
" From off Life's galling Load to elbow Care,　　460
" When Life and Care may be remov'd together?—
" If I were not a very Coward Wretch,
" A very Shadow of the Man, a thing
" Made to feel Burdens of my Fear, and drag
" A hated Being on—'twere but to leap
" From this rough [Eminence], and all is done—
" All that is done on this Side of the Bier.
" But there, surrounded with impervious Fog,
" Sits Doubt and Questions of the Scenes to come;
" Oh! Death, what moves beyond thee? Fears and Hopes, 470
" Dread and Confusion, Envy and Disease,
" Sleeping and waking Lusts, War-moving Pride,
" Windy Ambition, and slow Avarice,
" Slay in thy path; within thy Sepulchre
" Mould Dead Men's Bones, feed worms, rust Epitaphs,
" Sleep brainless Skulls in blest Vacuity!
" But what comes then? O for a Seraph's Eye

59

"That, piercing thro' the Mask of Mortal Things,
"Might scale the cloudless Battlements of Light,
"And in its Immaterial Robe detect   480
"The Spirit, stript of the encumbring Clay."—

Alas, Eugenio! Life, Deception's Child,
Gives us her fairer Side, and gives no more;
The rest we seek in our reflecting View
Of Self, and Guilt's o'erheard Soliloquy.
How smiles the World in pain, and smiles believ'd!
Yon Wretch who, muffled in the Garb of Night,
Gave her the Tortures of a weary Soul,
Meets—may he not?—the jovial Eye of Day,
With a depictur'd Laughter in his Cheek,   490
Or the smoothe Visage of habitual Ease?

How have I mourn'd my Lot, as if the Fates
Cull'd me, the vilest from their pitchy Stores
That ere in Mortal Bosom planted Woe,
And pain'd the Care-fraught Soul! I'll grieve no more,
But take it patient with a sober hope,
That soon Distress may vary his assault,
Or soon the Welcome Tomb exclude Distress.—

But see another Son of Night and Care,
A Shepherd watching o'er his frozen Fold,   500
Himself benumb'd and murmuring at his Fate.
Sigh not, fond Man; thy bosom only feels
The gentler Blows of Nature, and receives
The Common Visit of Calamity.

JUVENILIA

[A FAREWELL.]

[1779?]

THE hour arrived! I sigh'd and said,
How soon the happiest hours are fled!
On wings of down they lately flew,
But then their moments pass'd with you;
And still with you could I but be,
On downy wings they'd always flee.

Say, did you not, the way you went,
Feel the soft balm of gay content?
Say, did you not all pleasures find,
Of which you left so few behind?   10
I think you did: for well I know
My parting prayer would make it so.

"May she," I said, "life's choicest goods partake;
"Those, late in life, for nobler still forsake—
"The bliss of one, th' esteem'd of many live,
"With all that Friendship would, and all that Love can give!"

GEORGE CRABBE

TIME.

London, February, 1780.

" THE clock struck one! we take no thought of Time,"
　　Wrapt up in Night, and meditating rhyme.
All big with vision, we despise the powers
That vulgar beings link to days and hours—
Those vile, mechanic things that rule our hearts,
And cut our lives in momentary parts.
　　That speech of Time was Wisdom's gift, said Young.
Ah, Doctor! better, Time would hold his tongue:
What serves the clock? " To warn the careless crew,
" How much in little space they have to do;　　　　10
" To bid the busy world resign their breath,
" And beat each moment a soft call for death—
" To give it, then, a tongue, was wise in man."
Support the assertion, Doctor, if you can.
It tells the ruffian when his comrades wait;
It calls the duns to crowd my hapless gate;
It tells my heart the paralysing tale
Of hours to come, when Misery must prevail.

JUVENILIA

THE CHOICE.

London, February, 1780.

WHAT vulgar title thus salutes the eye,
    The schoolboy's first attempt at poesy?
The long-worn theme of every humbler Muse,
For wits to scorn and nurses to peruse;
The dull description of a scribbler's brain,
And sigh'd-for wealth, for which he sighs in vain;
A glowing chart of fairy-land estate,
Romantic scenes, and visions out of date,
Clear skies, clear streams, soft banks, and sober bowers,
Deer, whimpering brooks, and wind-perfuming flowers?   10

Not thus! too long have I in fancy wove
My slender webs of wealth, and peace, and love;
Have dream'd of plenty, in the midst of want,
And sought, by Hope, what Hope can never grant;
Been fool'd by wishes, and still wish'd again,
And loved the flattery, while I knew it vain!
"Gain by the Muse!"—alas! thou might'st as soon
Pluck gain (as Percy honour) from the moon;
As soon grow rich by ministerial nods,
As soon divine by dreaming of the gods,   20
As soon succeed by telling ladies truth,
Or preaching moral documents to youth;
To as much purpose, mortal! thy desires,
As Tully's flourishes to country squires;
As simple truth within St. James's state,
Or the soft lute in shrill-tongued Billingsgate.
"Gain by the Muse!" alas, preposterous hope!
Who ever gain'd by poetry—but Pope?
And what art thou? No St. John takes thy part;

GEORGE CRABBE

No potent Dean commends thy head or heart!   30
What gain'st thou but the praises of the poor?
They bribe no milkman to thy lofty door,
They wipe no scrawl from thy increasing score.
What did the Muse, or Fame, for Dryden, say?
What for poor Butler? what for honest Gay?
For Thomson, what? or what to Savage give?
Or how did Johnson—how did Otway live?
Like thee, dependent on to-morrow's good,
Their thin revénue never understood;
Like thee, elate at what thou canst not know;   40
Like thee, repining at each puny blow;
Like thee they lived, each dream of Hope to mock,
Upon their wits—but with a larger stock.
  No, if for food thy unambitious pray'r,
With supple acts to supple minds repair;
Learn of the base in soft grimace to deal,
And deck thee with the livery genteel;
Or trim the wherry, or the flail invite,
Draw teeth, or any viler thing but write.
Writers, whom once th' astonish'd vulgar saw   50
Give nations language, and great cities law;
Whom gods, they said—and surely gods—inspired,
Whom emp'rors honour'd, and the world admired,
Now common grown, they awe mankind no more,
But vassals are, who judges were before.
Blockheads on wits their little talents waste,
As files gnaw metal that they cannot taste;
Though still some good the trial may produce,
To shape the useful to a nobler use.
Some few of these a statue and a stone   60
Has Fame decreed—but deals out bread to none.
Unhappy art! decreed thine owner's curse,
Vile diagnostic of consumptive purse;
Members by bribes, and ministers by lies,
Gamesters by luck, by courage soldiers rise:
Beaux by the outside of their heads may win,
And wily sergeants by the craft within:
Who but the race, by Fancy's demon led,
Starve by the means they use to gain their bread?

JUVENILIA

Oft have I read, and, reading, mourn'd the fate   70
Of garret-bard, and his unpitied mate ;
Of children stinted in their daily meal,—
The joke of wealthier wits who could not feel.
Portentous spoke that pity in my breast,
And pleaded self—who ever pleads the best.
No ! thank my stars, my misery's all my own—
To friends, to family, to foes unknown ;
Who hates my verse, and damns the mean design,
Shall wound no peace—shall grieve no heart but mine.
One trial past, let sober Reason speak: 80
Here shall we rest, or shall we further seek ?
Rest here, if our relenting stars ordain
A placid harbour from the stormy main;
Or, that denied, the fond remembrance weep,
And sink, forgotten, in the mighty deep.

[A HUMBLE INVOCATION.]

[1780.]

WHEN summer's tribe, her rosy tribe, are fled,
And drooping beauty mourns her blossoms shed,
Some humbler sweet may cheer the pensive swain,
And simpler beauties deck the withering plain.
And thus, when Verse her wintry prospect weeps,
When Pope is gone, and mighty Milton sleeps,
When Gray in lofty lines has ceased to soar,
And gentle Goldsmith charms the town no more,
An humbler Bard the widow'd Muse invites,
Who led by hope and inclination writes ;   10
With half their art, he tries the soul to move,
And swell the softer strain with themes of love.

GEORGE CRABBE

[FROM AN EPISTLE TO MIRA.]

[April, 1780.]

*   *   *   *   *   *

OF substance I've thought, and the varied disputes
    On the nature of man and the notions of brutes;
Of systems confuted, and systems explain'd;
Of science disputed, and tenets maintain'd.
These, and such speculations on these kind of things,
Have robb'd my poor Muse of her plume and her wings;
Consumed the phlogiston you used to admire,
The spirit extracted, extinguish'd the fire;
Let out all the ether, so pure and refined,
And left but a mere *caput mortuum* behind.   10

*   *   *   *   *   *

[CONCLUDING LINES OF AN EPISTLE TO PRINCE WILLIAM HENRY, AFTER-WARDS KING WILLIAM IV.]

[April, 1780.]

*   *   *   *   *   *

WHO thus aspiring sings, would'st thou explore?
    A Bard replies, who ne'er assumed before—
One taught in hard affliction's school to bear
Life's ills, where every lesson costs a tear;
Who sees from thence the proper point of view,
What the wise heed not, and the weak pursue.

*   *   *   *   *   *

"And now farewell," the drooping Muse exclaims;
She lothly leaves thee to the shock of war,

And, fondly dwelling on her princely tar,
Wishes the noblest good her Harry's share,   10
Without her misery and without her care.
For, ah! unknown to thee, a rueful train,
Her hapless children sigh, and sigh in vain;
A numerous band, denied the boon to die,
Half-starved, half-fed by fits of charity.
Unknown to thee! and yet, perhaps, thy ear
Has chanced each sad, amusing tale to hear,
How some, like Budgell, madly sank for ease;
How some, like Savage, sicken'd by degrees;
How a pale crew, like helpless Otway, shed   20
The proud, big tear on song-extorted bread;
Or knew, like Goldsmith, some would stoop to choose
Contempt, and for the mortar quit the Muse.

One of this train—and of these wretches one—
Slave to the Muses, and to Misery son—
Now prays the Father of all Fates to shed
On Henry, laurels, on his poet, bread!
Unhappy art! decreed thine owner's curse;
Vile diagnostic of consumptive purse;
Still shall thy fatal force my soul perplex,   30
And every friend, and every brother vex—
Each fond companion?—No, I thank my God.
There rests my torment—there is hung the rod.
To friend, to fame, to family unknown,
Sour disappointments frown on me alone.
Who hates my song, and damns the poor design,
Shall wound no peace—shall grieve no heart but mine!

Pardon, sweet Prince! the thoughts that will intrude,
For want is absent, and dejection rude.
Methinks I hear, amid the shouts of Fame,   40
Each jolly victor hail my Henry's name;
And Heaven forbid that, in that jovial day,
One British bard should grieve when all are gay.
No! let him find his country has redress,
And bid adieu to every fond distress;
Or, touch'd too near, from joyful scenes retire,
Scorn to complain, and with one sigh expire!

GEORGE CRABBE

[DRIFTING.]

[May, 1780.]

LIKE some poor bark on the rough ocean tost,
  My rudder broken, and my compass lost,
My sails the coarsest, and too thin to last,
Pelted by rains, and bare to many a blast,
My anchor, Hope, scarce fix'd enough to stay
Where the strong current Grief sweeps all away,
I sail along, unknowing how to steer,
Where quicksands lie and frowning rocks appear.
Life's ocean teems with foes to my frail bark,
The rapid sword-fish, and the rav'ning shark,   10
Where torpid things crawl forth in splendid shell,
And knaves and fools and sycophants live well.
What have I left in such tempestuous sea?
No Tritons shield, no Naiads shelter me!
A gloomy Muse, in Mira's absence, hears
My plaintive prayer, and sheds consoling tears—
Some fairer prospect, though at distance, brings,
Soothes me with song, and flatters as she sings.

*   *   *   *   *   *

JUVENILIA

TO THE RIGHT HONOURABLE THE EARL OF SHELBURNE.

[June, 1780.]

AH! SHELBURNE, blest with all that's good or great
 T'adorn a rich, or save a sinking, state—
If public Ills engross not all thy care,
Let private Woe assail a patriot's ear ;
Pity confined, but not less warm, impart,
And unresisted win thy noble heart ;
Nor deem I rob thy soul of Britain's share,
Because I hope to have some interest there.
Still wilt thou shine on all a fostering sun,
Though with more fav'ring beams enlight'ning one ; 10
As Heaven will oft make some more amply blest,
Yet still in general bounty feeds the rest.
Oh, hear the Virtue thou reverest plead ;
She'll swell thy breast, and there applaud the deed.
She bids thy thoughts one hour from greatness stray,
And leads thee on to fame a shorter way ;
Where, if no withering laurel's thy reward,
There's shouting Conscience, and a grateful Bard ;
A bard untrained in all but misery's school,
Who never bribed a knave or praised a fool. 20
'Tis Glory prompts, and, as thou read'st, attend ;
She dictates pity, and becomes my friend ;
She bids each cold and dull reflection flee,
And yields her Shelburne to distress and me !

GEORGE CRABBE

AN EPISTLE TO A FRIEND.

[June, 1780.]

WHY, true, thou say'st the fools, at Court denied,
Growl vengeance—and then take the other side;
The unfed flatterer borrows satire's power,
As sweets unshelter'd run to vapid sour.
But thou, the counsel to my closest thought,
Beheld'st it ne'er in fulsome stanzas wrought.
The Muse I court ne'er fawn'd on venal souls,
Whom suppliants angle, and poor praise controls;
She, yet unskill'd in all but fancy's dream,
Sang to the woods, and Mira was her theme.   10
But, when she sees a titled nothing stand
The ready cipher of a trembling land—
Not of that simple kind that, placed alone,
Are useless, harmless things, and threaten none;
But those which, join'd to figures, well express
A strengthen'd tribe that amplify distress,
Grow in proportion to their number great,
And help each other in the ranks of state—
When this and more the pensive Muses see,
They leave the vales and willing nymphs to thee;   20
To Court on wings of agile anger speed,
And paint to freedom's sons each guileful deed.
Hence rascals teach the virtues they detest,
And fright base action from sin's wavering breast;
For, though the Knave may scorn the Muse's arts,
Her sting may haply pierce more timid hearts.
Some, though they wish it, are not steel'd enough,
Nor is each would-be villain conscience-proof.

And what, my friend, is left my song besides?
No school-day wealth that roll'd in silver tides, 30
No dreams of hope that won my early will,
Nor love, that pain'd in temporary thrill;

No gold to deck my pleasure-scorn'd abode,
No friend to whisper peace, to give me food.
Poor to the World, I'd yet not live in vain,
But show its lords their hearts, and my disdain.

Yet shall not Satire all my song engage
In indiscriminate and idle rage;
True praise, where Virtue prompts, shall gild each line,
And long—if Vanity deceives not—shine.   40
For, though in harsher strains, the strains of woe,
And unadorn'd my heart-felt murmurs flow,
Yet time shall be when this thine humbled friend
Shall to more lofty heights his notes extend.
A Man—for other title were too poor—
Such as 'twere almost virtue to adore,
He shall the ill that loads my heart exhale,
As the sun vapours from the dew-press'd vale;
Himself uninjuring, shall new warmth infuse,
And call to blossom every want-nipp'd Muse.   50
Then shall my grateful strains his ear rejoice,
His name harmonious thrill'd on Mira's voice;
Round the reviving bays new sweets shall spring,
And SHELBURNE's fame through laughing valleys ring.

THE CANDIDATE;

A POETICAL EPISTLE TO THE AUTHORS OF THE
MONTHLY REVIEW.

Multa quidem nobis facimus mala sæpe poetæ,
(Ut vineta egomet cædam mea) cum tibi librum
Sollicito damus, aut fesso, &c.

Hor. Lib. ii. Ep. i.

[London, 1780.]

AN INTRODUCTORY ADDRESS OF THE AUTHOR TO HIS POEMS.

YE idler things, that soothed my hours of care,
    Where would ye wander, triflers, tell me where?
As maids neglected, do ye fondly dote
On the fair type, or the embroider'd coat;
Detest my modest shelf, and long to fly,
Where princely Popes and mighty Miltons lie?
Taught but to sing, and that in simple style,
Of Lycia's lip, and Musidora's smile,
Go, then! and taste a yet unfelt distress,
The fear that guards the captivating press;   10
Whose maddening region should ye once explore,
No refuge yields my tongueless mansion more.
But thus ye'll grieve, Ambition's plumage stript,
"Ah, would to Heaven, we'd died in manuscript!"
Your unsoil'd page each yawning wit shall flee
—For few will read, and none admire like me.—

73

Its place, where spiders silent bards enrobe,
Squeezed betwixt Cibber's Odes and Blackmore's Job ;
Where froth and mud, that varnish and deform,
Feed the lean critic and the fattening worm ;   20
Then sent disgraced—the unpaid printer's bane—
To mad Moorfields, or sober Chancery Lane,
On dirty stalls I see your hopes expire,
Vex'd by the grin of your unheeded sire,
Who half reluctant has his care resign'd,
Like a teased parent, and is rashly kind.

Yet rush not all, but let some scout go forth,
View the strange land, and tell us of its worth ;
And, should he there barbarian usage meet,
The patriot scrap shall warn us to retreat.   30

And thou, the first of thy eccentric race,
A forward imp, go, search the dangerous place,
Where Fame's eternal blossoms tempt each bard,
Though dragon-wits there keep eternal guard.
Hope not unhurt the golden spoil to seize,
The Muses yield, as the Hesperides ;
Who bribes the guardian, all his labour's done,
For every maid is willing to be won.

Before the lords of verse a suppliant stand,
And beg our passage through the fairy land: 40
Beg more—to search for sweets each blooming field,
And crop the blossoms woods and valleys yield ;
To snatch the tints that beam on Fancy's bow,
And feel the fires on Genius' wings that glow ;
Praise without meanness, without flattery stoop,
Soothe without fear, and without trembling hope.

THE CANDIDATE

TO THE READER.

THE following Poem being itself of an introductory nature, its author supposes it can require but little preface.

It is published with a view of obtaining the opinion of the candid and judicious reader on the merits of the writer as a poet; very few, he apprehends, being in such cases sufficiently impartial to decide for themselves.

It is addressed to the Authors of the Monthly Review, as to critics of acknowledged merit; an acquaintance with whose labours has afforded the writer of this Epistle a reason for directing it to them in particular, and, he presumes, will yield to others a just and sufficient plea for the preference.

Familiar with disappointment, he shall not be much surprised to find he has mistaken his talent. However, if not egregiously the dupe of his vanity, he promises to his readers some entertainment, and is assured that, however little in the ensuing Poem is worthy of applause, there is yet less that merits contempt.

GEORGE CRABBE

TO THE AUTHORS OF THE MONTHLY REVIEW.

THE pious pilot, whom the Gods provide,
   Through the rough seas the shatter'd bark to guide,
Trusts not alone his knowledge of the deep,
Its rocks that threaten, and its sands that sleep;
But, whilst with nicest skill he steers his way,
The guardian Tritons hear their favourite pray.
Hence borne his vows to Neptune's coral dome,
The God relents, and shuts each gulfy tomb.

Thus as on fatal floods to fame I steer,
I dread the storm, that ever rattles here;   10
Nor think enough, that long my yielding soul
Has felt the Muse's soft, but strong, control;
Nor think enough that manly strength and ease,
Such as have pleased a friend, will strangers please;
But, suppliant, to the critic's throne I bow,
Here burn my incense, and here pay my vow;
That censure hush'd, may every blast give o'er,
And the lash'd coxcomb hiss contempt no more.
And ye, whom authors dread or dare in vain,
Affecting modest hopes or poor disdain,   20
Receive a bard, who, neither mad nor mean,
Despises each extreme, and sails between;
Who fears; but has, amid his fears confess'd,
The conscious virtue of a Muse oppress'd;
A Muse in changing times and stations nursed,
By nature honour'd and by fortune cursed.

No servile strain of abject hope she brings,
Nor soars presumptuous, with unwearied wings;
But, pruned for flight—the future all her care—
Would know her strength, and, if not strong, forbear.   30

76

THE CANDIDATE

The supple slave to regal pomp bows down,
Prostrate to power, and cringing to a crown;
The bolder villain spurns a decent awe,
Tramples on rule, and breaks through every law;
But he whose soul on honest truth relies,
Nor meanly flatters power, nor madly flies.
Thus timid authors bear an abject mind,
And plead for mercy they but seldom find.
Some, as the desperate to the halter run,
Boldly deride the fate they cannot shun;   40
But such there are, whose minds, not taught to stoop,
Yet hope for fame, and dare avow their hope;
Who neither brave the judges of their cause,
Nor beg in soothing strains a brief applause.
And such I'd be;—and, ere my fate is past,
Ere clear'd with honour, or with culprits cast,
Humbly at Learning's bar I'll state my case,
And welcome then distinction or disgrace!

When in the man the flights of fancy reign,
Rule in the heart, or revel in the brain,   50
As busy Thought her wild creation apes,
And hangs delighted o'er her varying shapes,
It asks a judgment, weighty and discreet,
To know where wisdom prompts, and where conceit;
Alike their draughts to every scribbler's mind
(Blind to their faults as to their danger blind)—
We write enraptured, and we write in haste,
Dream idle dreams, and call them things of taste;
Improvement trace in every paltry line,
And see, transported, every dull design;   60
Are seldom cautious, all advice detest,
And ever think our own opinions best;
Nor shows my Muse a muse-like spirit here,
Who bids me pause, before I persevere.

But she—who shrinks, while meditating flight
In the wide way, whose bounds delude her sight,
Yet tired in her own mazes still to roam,
And cull poor banquets for the soul at home—

Would, ere she ventures, ponder on the way,
Lest dangers yet unthought-of flight betray;   70
Lest her Icarian wing, by wits unplumed,
Be robb'd of all the honours she assumed;
And Dulness swell—a black and dismal sea,
Gaping her grave, while censures madden me.

   Such was his fate, who flew too near the sun,
Shot far beyond his strength, and was undone;
Such is his fate, who creeping at the shore
The billow sweeps him, and he's found no more.
Oh! for some God, to bear my fortunes fair
Midway betwixt presumption and despair!   80

   "Has then some friendly critic's former blow
"Taught thee a prudence authors seldom know?"

   Not so! their anger and their love untried,
A wo-taught prudence deigns to tend my side:
Life's hopes ill-sped, the Muse's hopes grow poor,
And though they flatter, yet they charm no more;
Experience points where lurking dangers lay,
And as I run, throws caution in my way.

   There was a night, when wintry winds did rage,
Hard by a ruin'd pile I met a sage;   90
Resembling him the time-struck place appear'd,
Hollow its voice, and moss its spreading beard;
Whose fate-lopp'd brow, the bat's and beetle's dome,
Shook, as the hunted owl flew hooting home.
His breast was bronzed by many an eastern blast,
And fourscore winters seem'd he to have past;
His thread-bare coat the supple osier bound,
And with slow feet he press'd the sodden ground;
Where, as he heard the wild-wing'd Eurus blow,
He shook, from locks as white, December's snow;   100
Inured to storm, his soul ne'er bid it cease,
But lock'd within him meditated peace.

   "Father," I said—for silver hairs inspire,
And oft I call the bending peasant Sire—

THE CANDIDATE

"Tell me, as here beneath this ivy bower,
"That works fantastic round its trembling tower,
"We hear Heaven's guilt-alarming thunders roar,
"Tell me the pains and pleasures of the poor;
"For Hope, just spent, requires a sad adieu,
"And Fear acquaints me I shall live with you.   110

        "There was a time when, by Delusion led,
"A scene of sacred bliss around me spread;
"On Hope's, as Pisgah's lofty top, I stood,
"And saw my Canaan there, my promised good.
"A thousand scenes of joy the clime bestow'd,
"And wine and oil through vision's valleys flow'd;
"As Moses his, I call'd my prospect bless'd,
"And gazed upon the good I ne'er possess'd :
"On this side Jordan doom'd by fate to stand,
"Whilst happier Joshuas win the promised land."   120
"Son," said the Sage—"be this thy care suppress'd;
"The state the Gods shall choose thee is the best:
"Rich if thou art, they ask thy praises more,
"And would thy patience, when they make thee poor.
"But other thoughts within thy bosom reign,
"And other subjects vex thy busy brain;
"Poetic wreaths thy vainer dreams excite,
"And thy sad stars have destined thee to write.
"Then, since that task the ruthless fates decree,
"Take a few precepts from the Gods and me!   130

        "Be not too eager in the arduous chace :
"Who pants for triumph seldom wins the race;
"Venture not all, but wisely hoard thy worth,
"And let thy labours one by one go forth;
"Some happier scrap capricious wits may find
"On a fair day, and be profusely kind;
"Which, buried in the rubbish of a throng,
"Had pleased as little as a new-year's song,
"Or lover's verse, that cloy'd with nauseous sweet,
"Or birth-day ode, that ran on ill-pair'd feet.   140
"Merit not always—Fortune feeds the bard,
"And, as the whim inclines, bestows reward;

GEORGE CRABBE

" None without wit, nor with it numbers gain;
" To please is hard, but none shall please in vain.
" As a coy mistress is the humour'd town,
" Loth every lover with success to crown;
" He who would win must every effort try,
" Sail in the mode, and to the fashion fly;
" Must gay or grave to every humour dress,
" And watch the lucky Moment of Success;   150
" That caught, no more his eager hopes are crost;
" But vain are Wit and Love, when that is lost."

   Thus said the God; for now a God he grew,
His white locks changing to a golden hue,
And from his shoulders hung a mantle azure-blue. [}]
His softening eyes the winning charm disclosed
Of dove-like Delia, when her doubts reposed;
Mira's alone a softer lustre bear,
When wo beguiles them of an angel's tear;
Beauteous and young the smiling phantom stood,   160
Then sought on airy wing his blest abode.

   Ah! truth distasteful in poetic theme,
Why is the Muse compell'd to own her dream?
Whilst forward wits had sworn to every line,
I only wish to make its moral mine.

   Say then, O ye who tell how authors speed,
May Hope indulge her flight, and I succeed?
Say, shall my name, to future song prefix'd,
Be with the meanest of the tuneful mix'd?
Shall my soft strains the modest maid engage,   170
My graver numbers move the silver'd sage,
My tender themes delight the lover's heart,
And comfort to the poor my solemn songs impart?

   For O! thou, Hope's—thou, Thought's eternal King,
Who gav'st them power to charm, and me to sing,
Chief to thy praise my willing numbers soar,
And in my happier transports I adore;

THE CANDIDATE

Mercy thy softest attribute proclaim,
Thyself in abstract, thy more lovely name;
That flings o'er all my grief a cheering ray,   180
As the full moon-beam gilds the watery way.
And then too, Love, my soul's resistless lord,
Shall many a gentle, generous strain afford,
To all the soil of sooty passions blind,
Pure as embracing angels, and as kind;
Our Mira's name in future times shall shine,
And—though the harshest—Shepherds envy mine.

Then let me (pleasing task!) however hard,
Join, as of old, the prophet and the bard;
If not, ah! shield me from the dire disgrace   190
That haunts the wild and visionary race;
Let me not draw my lengthen'd lines along,
And tire in untamed infamy of song;
Lest, in some dismal Dunciad's future page,
I stand the CIBBER of this tuneless age;
Lest, if another POPE th' indulgent skies
Should give, inspired by all their deities,
My luckless name, in his immortal strain,
Should, blasted, brand me as a second Cain;
Doom'd in that song to live against my will,   200
Whom all must scorn, and yet whom none could kill.

The youth, resisted by the maiden's art,
Persists, and time subdues her kindling heart;
To strong entreaty yields the widow's vow,
As mighty walls to bold besiegers bow;
Repeated prayers draw bounty from the sky,
And heaven is won by importunity.
Ours, a projecting tribe, pursue in vain,
In tedious trials, an uncertain gain;
Madly plunge on through every hope's defeat,   210
And with our ruin only, find the cheat.

"And why then seek that luckless doom to share?"
Who, I?—To shun it is my only care.

GEORGE CRABBE

I grant it true, that others better tell
Of mighty Wolfe, who conquer'd as he fell[1];
Of heroes born their threaten'd realms to save,
Whom Fame anoints, and Envy tends whose grave;
Of crimson'd fields, where Fate, in dire array,
Gives to the breathless the short-breathing clay;
Ours, a young train, by humbler fountains dream,   220
Nor taste presumptuous the Pierian stream;
When Rodney's triumph comes on eagle-wing,
We hail the victor, whom we fear to sing;
Nor tell we how each hostile chief goes on,
The luckless Lee, or wary Washington;
How Spanish bombast blusters—they were beat,
And French politeness dulcifies—defeat.
My modest Muse forbears to speak of kings,
Lest fainting stanzas blast the name she sings;
For who, the tenant of the beechen shade,   230
Dares the big thought in regal breasts pervade?
Or search his soul, whom each too-favouring God
Gives to delight in plunder, pomp, and blood?
No; let me, free from Cupid's frolic round,
Rejoice, or more rejoice by Cupid bound;
Of laughing girls in smiling ·couplets tell,
And paint the dark-brow'd grove, where wood-nymphs dwell,
Who bid invading youths their vengeance feel,
And pierce the votive hearts they mean to heal.
Such were the themes I knew in school-day ease,   240
When first the moral magic learn'd to please;
Ere Judgment told how transports warm'd the breast,
Transported Fancy there her stores imprest;
The soul in varied raptures learn'd to fly,
Felt all their force, and never question'd why.
No idle doubts could then her peace molest;
She found delight, and left to heaven the rest.
Soft joys in Evening's placid shades were born,

[1] IMIT.—Scriberis Vario fortis, et hostium
Victor, Mæonii carminis alite,
Quam rem cumque ferox navibus aut equis
Miles, te duce, gesserit, &c. &c.
Hor. Lib. i. Od. [6].

THE CANDIDATE

And where sweet fragrance wing'd the balmy morn.
When the wild thought roved vision's circuit o'er,   250
And caught the raptures, caught, alas! no more:
No care did then a dull attention ask,
For study pleased, and that was every task;
No guilty dreams stalk'd that heaven-favour'd round,
Heaven-guarded too; no Envy entrance found;
Nor numerous wants, that vex advancing age,
Nor Flattery's silver'd tale, nor Sorrow's sage;
Frugal Affliction kept each growing dart,
T' o'erwhelm in future days the bleeding heart.
No sceptic art veil'd Pride in Truth's disguise,   260
But prayer, unsoil'd of doubt, besieged the skies;
Ambition, avarice, care, to man retired,
Nor came desires more quick, than joys desired.

A summer morn there was, and passing fair;
Still was the breeze, and health perfumed the air;
The glowing east in crimson'd splendour shone,
What time the eye just marks the pallid moon;
Vi'let-wing'd Zephyr fann'd each opening flower,
And brush'd from fragrant cups the limpid shower;
A distant huntsman fill'd his cheerful horn,   270
The vivid dew hung trembling on the thorn,
And mists, like creeping rocks, arose to meet the morn. [∫]
Huge giant shadows spread along the plain,
Or shot from towering rocks o'er half the main.
There to the slumbering bark the gentle tide
Stole soft, and faintly beat against its side;
Such is that sound, which fond designs convey,
When, true to love, the damsel speeds away;
The sails, unshaken, hung aloft unfurl'd,
And, simpering nigh, the languid current curl'd;   280
A crumbling ruin, once a city's pride,
The well-pleased eye through withering oaks descried,
Where Sadness, gazing on time's ravage, hung,
And Silence to Destruction's trophy clung—
Save that, as morning songsters swell'd their lays,
Awaken'd Echo humm'd repeated praise.

GEORGE CRABBE

The lark on quavering pinion woo'd the day,
Less towering linnets fill'd the vocal spray,
And song-invited pilgrims rose to pray. [ ]]
Here at a pine-prest hill's embroider'd base 290
I stood, and hail'd the Genius of the place.
Then was it doom'd by fate, my idle heart,
Soften'd by Nature, gave access to Art;
The Muse approach'd, her syren-song I heard,
Her magic felt, and all her charms revered:
E'er since she rules in absolute control,
And Mira only dearer to my soul.
Ah! tell me not these empty joys to fly;
If they deceive, I would deluded die;
To the fond themes my heart so early wed, 300
So soon in life to blooming visions led,
So prone to run the vague uncertain course—
'Tis more than death to think of a divorce.

What wills the poet of the favouring gods,
Led to their shrine, and blest in their abodes[1]?
What, when he fills the glass, and to each youth
Names his loved maid, and glories in his truth?
Not India's spoils, the splendid nabob's pride,
Not the full trade of Hermes' own Cheapside,
Nor gold itself, nor all the Ganges laves, 310
Or shrouds, well shrouded in his sacred waves;
Nor gorgeous vessels deck'd in trim array,
Which the more noble Thames bears far away.
Let those whose nod makes sooty subjects flee,
Hack with blunt steel the savory callipee;
Let those whose ill-used wealth their country fly,
Virtue-scorn'd wines from hostile France to buy:
Favour'd by fate, let such in joy appear,
Their smuggled cargoes landed thrice a year; 320
Disdaining these, for simpler food I'll look,
And crop my beverage at the mantled brook.

[1] IMIT.—Quid dedicatum poscit Apollinem
 Vates? quid orat, de paterâ novum
 Fundens liquorem? &c. &c.
 HOR. Lib. i. *Carm.* xxxi.

THE CANDIDATE

O Virtue! brighter than the noon-tide ray,
My humble prayers with sacred joys repay!
Health to my limbs may the kind Gods impart,
And thy fair form delight my yielding heart!
Grant me to shun each vile inglorious road,
To see thy way, and trace each moral good;
If more—let Wisdom's sons my page peruse,
And decent credit deck my modest Muse.

Nor deem it pride that prophesies, my song   330
Shall please the sons of taste, and please them long.
Say, ye, to whom my Muse submissive brings
Her first-fruit offering, and on trembling wings,
May she not hope in future days to soar,
Where fancy's sons have led the way before?
Where genius strives in each ambrosial bower
To snatch with agile hand the opening flower?
To cull what sweets adorn the mountain's brow,
What humbler blossoms crown the vales below?
To blend with these the stores by art refined,   340
And give the moral Flora to the mind?

Far other scenes my timid hour admits,
Relentless critics, and avenging wits;
E'en coxcombs take a licence from their pen,
And to each " let-him-perish " cry Amen!
And thus, with wits or fools my heart shall cry,
For if they please not, let the trifles die—
Die, and be lost in dark oblivion's shore,
And never rise to vex their author more.

I would not dream o'er some soft liquid line,   350
Amid a thousand blunders form'd to shine;
Yet rather this, than that dull scribbler be,
From every fault, and every beauty free,
Curst with tame thoughts and mediocrity.   [ʃ]
Some have I found so thick beset with spots,
'Twas hard to trace their beauties through their blots;
And these, as tapers round a sick-man's room,
Or passing chimes, but warn'd me of the tomb!

85

GEORGE CRABBE

O! if you blast, at once consume my bays,
And damn me not with mutilated praise.   360
With candour judge; and, a young bard in view,
Allow for that, and judge with kindness too.
Faults he must own, though hard for him to find,
Not to some happier merits quite so blind;
These if mistaken Fancy only sees,
Or Hope, that takes Deformity for these;
If Dunce, the crowd-befitting title, falls
His lot, and Dulness her new subject calls:
To the poor bard alone your censures give—
Let his fame die, but let his honour live;   370
Laugh if you must—be candid as you can,
And when you lash the Poet, spare the Man.

POEMS.

Ipse per Ausonias Æneïa carmina gentes
Qui sonat, ingenti qui nomine pulsat Olympum,
Mæoniumque senem Romano provocat ore:
Forsitan illius nemoris latuisset in umbrâ
Quod canit, et sterili tantum cantâsset avenâ
Ignotus populi, si Mæcenate careret.

Paneg. ad Pisones.

GEORGE CRABBE

TO THE

RIGHT HONOURABLE HENRY RICHARD FOX,

LORD HOLLAND,

OF HOLLAND, IN LINCOLNSHIRE; LORD HOLLAND
OF FOXLEY; AND FELLOW OF THE SOCIETY
OF ANTIQUARIES.

My Lord,

THAT the longest poem in this collection was honoured by the notice of your Lordship's right honourable and ever-valued relation, Mr. Fox; that it should be the last which engaged his attention; and that some parts of it were marked with his approbation : are circumstances productive of better hopes of ultimate success than I had dared to entertain before I was gratified with a knowledge of them; and the hope thus raised leads me to ask permission that I may dedicate this book to your Lordship, to whom that truly great and greatly lamented personage was so nearly allied in family, so closely bound in affection, and in whose mind presides the same critical taste which he exerted to the delight of all who heard him. He doubtless united with his unequalled abilities a fund of good-nature; and this possibly led him to speak favourably of, and give satisfaction to writers, with whose productions he might not be entirely satisfied; nor must I allow myself to suppose his desire of obliging was withholden, when he honoured any effort of mine with his approbation. But, my Lord, as there was discrimination in the opinion he gave; as he did not veil indifference for insipid mediocrity of composition under any

88

DEDICATION

general expression of cool approval : I allow myself to draw a favourable conclusion from the verdict of one who had the superiority of intellect few would dispute, which he made manifest by a force of eloquence peculiar to himself ; whose excellent judgment no one of his friends found cause to distrust, and whose acknowledged candour no enemy had the temerity to deny.

With such encouragement, I present my book to your Lordship : the Account of the *Life and Writings of Lopez de Vega* has taught me what I am to expect ; I there perceive how your Lordship can write, and am there taught how you can judge of writers : my faults, however numerous, I know will none of them escape through inattention, nor will any merit be lost for want of discernment ; my verses are before him who has written elegantly, who has judged with accuracy, and who has given unequivocal proof of abilities in a work of difficulty— a translation of poetry, which few persons in this kingdom are able to read, and in the estimation of talents not hitherto justly appreciated. In this view, I cannot but feel some apprehension ; but I know also, that your Lordship is apprised of the great difficulty of writing well ; that you will make much allowance for failures, if not too frequently repeated ; and, as you can accurately discern, so you will readily approve, all the better and more happy efforts of one who places the highest value upon your Lordship's approbation, and who has the honour to be,

My Lord,

Your Lordship's most faithful

and obliged humble servant,

GEO. CRABBE.

GEORGE CRABBE

PREFACE.

ABOUT twenty-five years since was published a poem called "The Library," which, in no long time, was followed by two others, "The Village," and "The Newspaper." These, with a few alterations and additions, are here reprinted; and are accompanied by a poem of greater length, and several shorter attempts, now, for the first time, before the public; whose reception of them creates in their author something more than common solicitude, because he conceives that, with the judgment to be formed of these latter productions, upon whatever may be found intrinsically meritorious or defective, there will be united an inquiry into the relative degree of praise or blame which they may be thought to deserve, when compared with the more early attempts of the same writer.

And certainly, were it the principal employment of a man's life to compose verses, it might seem reasonable to expect that he would continue to improve as long as he continued to live; though, even then, there is some doubt whether such improvement would follow, and perhaps proof might be adduced to show it would not. But when, to this "*idle trade*," is added some "*calling*," with superior claims upon his time and attention, his progress in the art of versification will probably be in proportion neither to the years he has lived, nor even to the attempts he has made.

While composing the first-published of these poems, the author was honoured with the notice and assisted by the advice of the Right Honourable Edmund Burke; part of it was written in his presence, and the whole submitted to his judgment; receiving, in its progress, the benefit of his correction. I hope, therefore, to obtain pardon of the reader, if I eagerly

PREFACE

seize the occasion, and, after so long a silence, endeavour to express a grateful sense of the benefits I have received from this gentleman, who was solicitous for my more essential interests, as well as benevolently anxious for my credit as a writer.

I will not enter upon the subject of his extraordinary abilities; it would be vanity, it would be weakness, in me to believe that I could make them better known or more admired than they now are. But of his private worth, of his wishes to do good, of his affability and condescension; his readiness to lend assistance when he knew it was wanted, and his delight to give praise where he thought it was deserved : of these I may write with some propriety. All know that his powers were vast, his acquirements various; and I take leave to add, that he applied them with unremitted attention to those objects which he believed tended to the honour and welfare of his country. But it may not be so generally understood that he was ever assiduous in the more private duties of a benevolent nature; that he delighted to give encouragement to any promise of ability, and assistance to any appearance of desert. To what purposes he employed his pen, and with what eloquence he spake in the senate, will be told by many, who yet may be ignorant of the solid instruction, as well as the fascinating pleasantry, found in his common conversation, amongst his friends, and his affectionate manners, amiable disposition, and zeal for their happiness, which he manifested in the hours of retirement with his family.

To this gentleman I was indebted for my knowledge of Sir Joshua Reynolds, who was as well known to his friends for his perpetual fund of good-humour and his unceasing wishes to oblige, as he was to the public for the extraordinary productions of his pencil and his pen. By him I was favoured with an introduction to Doctor Johnson, who honoured me with his notice, and assisted me, as Mr. Boswell has told, with remarks and emendations for a poem I was about to publish. The doctor had been often wearied by applications, and did not readily comply with requests for his opinion : not from any unwillingness to oblige, but from a painful contention in his mind between a desire of giving pleasure and a determination to speak truth. No man can, I think, publish a work without some expectation of satisfying those who are to judge of its merit; but I can, with the utmost regard to veracity, speak my fears, as predominating over every pre-indulged thought of a more favourable nature, when I was told that a judge so discerning had consented to read and give his opinion of "The Village," the poem I had prepared for publication. The time of suspense was not long protracted; I was soon favoured with a few words from Sir Joshua, who observed, "If I knew how "cautious Doctor Johnson was in giving commendation, I should "be well satisfied with the portion dealt to me in his letter." Of that letter the following is a copy:

"SIR,

"I have sent you back Mr. Crabbe's poem; which "I read with great delight. It is original, vigorous, and elegant. "The alterations which I have made, I do not require him to "adopt; for my lines are, perhaps, not often better [than] his "own: but he may take mine and his own together, and "perhaps, between them, produce something better than "either.—He is not to think his copy wantonly defaced; a "wet sponge will wash all the red lines away, and leave the "pages clean.—His Dedication will be least liked: it were "better to contract it into a short sprightly address.—I do not "doubt of Mr. Crabbe's success.

"I am, Sir, your most humble servant,

"SAM. JOHNSON."

"*March* 4, 1783."

That I was fully satisfied, my readers will do me the justice to believe; and I hope they will pardon me, if there should appear to them any impropriety in publishing the favourable opinion expressed in a private letter: they will judge, and truly, that by so doing, I wish to bespeak their good opinion, but have no design of extorting their applause. I would not hazard an appearance so ostentatious to gratify my vanity, but I venture to do it in compliance with my fears.

PREFACE

After these was published "The Newspaper": it had not the advantage of such previous criticism from any friends, nor perhaps so much of my own attention as I ought to have given to it; but the impression was disposed of, and I will not pay so little respect to the judgment of my readers as now to suppress what they then approved.

Since the publication of this poem more than twenty years have elapsed, and I am not without apprehension, lest so long a silence should be construed into a blamable neglect of my own interest, which those excellent friends were desirous of promoting; or, what is yet worse, into a want of gratitude for their assistance; since it becomes me to suppose, they considered these first attempts as promises of better things, and their favours as stimulants to future exertion. And here, be the construction put upon my apparent negligence what it *may*, let me not suppress my testimony to the liberality of those who are looked up to as patrons and encouragers of literary merit, or indeed of merit of any kind: their patronage has never been refused, I conceive, when it has been reasonably expected or modestly required; and it would be difficult, probably, to instance, in these times and in this country, any one who merited or was supposed to merit assistance, but who nevertheless languished in obscurity or necessity for want of it; unless in those cases where it was prevented by the resolution of impatient pride, or wearied by the solicitations of determined profligacy. And, while the subject is before me, I am unwilling to pass silently over the debt of gratitude which I owe to the memory of two deceased noblemen, His Grace the late Duke of Rutland, and the Right Honourable the Lord Thurlow: sensible of the honour done me by their notice, and the benefits received from them, I trust this acknowledgment will be imputed to its only motive, a grateful sense of their favours.

Upon this subject I could dwell with much pleasure; but, to give a reason for that appearance of neglect, as it is more difficult, so, happily, it is less required. In truth, I have, for many years, intended a republication of these poems, as soon as I should be able to join with them such other of later date as might not deprive me of the little credit the former had obtained.

93

GEORGE CRABBE

Long indeed has this purpose been procrastinated; and, if the duties of a profession, not before pressing upon me—if the claims of a situation, at that time untried—if diffidence of my own judgment, and the loss of my earliest friends, will not sufficiently account for my delay, I must rely upon the good-nature of my reader, that he will let them avail as far as he can, and find an additional apology in my fears of his censure.

These fears being so prevalent with me, I determined not to publish any thing more, unless I could first obtain the sanction of such an opinion as I might with some confidence rely upon. I looked for a friend who, having the discerning taste of Mr. Burke, and the critical sagacity of Doctor Johnson, would bestow upon my MS. the attention requisite to form his opinion, and would then favour me with the result of his observations; and it was my singular good fortune to gain such assistance; the opinion of a critic so qualified, and a friend so disposed to favour me. I had been honoured by an introduction to the Right Honourable Charles James Fox some years before, at the seat of Mr. Burke; and, being again with him, I received a promise that he would peruse any work I might send to him previous to its publication, and would give me his opinion. At that time, I did not think myself sufficiently prepared; and when, afterwards, I had collected some poems for his inspection, I found my right honourable friend engaged by the affairs of a great empire, and struggling with the inveteracy of a fatal disease; at such time, upon such mind, ever disposed to oblige as that mind was, I could not obtrude the petty business of criticising verses; but he remembered the promise he had kindly given, and repeated an offer, which, though I had not presumed to expect, I was happy to receive. A copy of the poems, now first published, was immediately sent to him, and (as I have the information from Lord Holland, and his Lordship's permission to inform my readers) the poem which I have named " The Parish Register " was heard by Mr. Fox, and it excited interest enough, by some of its parts, to gain for me the benefit of his judgment upon the whole. Whatever he approved, the reader will readily believe, I have carefully retained; the parts he disliked are totally expunged, and others are substituted, which I hope resemble those, more conformable to the taste of so

PREFACE

admirable a judge. Nor can I deny myself the melancholy satisfaction of adding, that this poem (and more especially the story of Phœbe Dawson, with some parts of the second book), were the last compositions of their kind that engaged and amused the capacious, the candid, the benevolent mind of this great man.

The above information I owe to the favour of the Right Honourable Lord Holland ; nor this only, but to his Lordship I am indebted for some excellent remarks upon the other parts of my MS. It was not indeed my good fortune then to know that my verses were in the hands of a nobleman who had given proof of his accurate judgment as a critic, and his elegance as a writer, by favouring the public with an easy and spirited translation of some interesting scenes of a dramatic poet, not often read in this kingdom. The Life of Lopez de Vega was then unknown to me ; I had, in common with many English readers, heard of him, but could not judge whether his far-extended reputation was caused by the sublime efforts of a mighty genius, or the unequalled facility of a rapid composer, aided by peculiar and fortunate circumstances. That any part of my MS. was honoured by the remarks of Lord Holland yields me a high degree of satisfaction, and his Lordship will perceive the use I have made of them ; but I must feel some regret when I know to what small portion they were limited ; and discerning, as I do, the taste and judgment bestowed upon the verses of Lopez de Vega, I must perceive how much my own needed the assistance afforded to one who cannot be sensible of the benefit he has received.

But how much soever I may lament the advantages lost, let me remember with gratitude the helps I have obtained. With a single exception, every poem in the ensuing collection has been submitted to the critical sagacity of a gentleman, upon whose skill and candour their author could rely. To publish by advice of friends has been severely ridiculed, and that too by a poet, who probably, without such advice, never made public any verses of his own : in fact, it may not be easily determined who acts with less discretion, the writer who is encouraged to publish his works, merely by the advice of friends whom he consulted, or he who, against advice, publishes from the sole encouragement of his own opinion. These are deceptions to be carefully avoided ; and I was happy to escape the latter, by the friendly attentions of the Reverend Richard Turner, minister of Great Yarmouth. To this gentleman I am indebted more than I am able to describe, or than he is willing to allow, for the time he has bestowed upon the attempts I have made. He is, indeed, the kind of critic for whom every poet should devoutly wish, and the friend whom every man would be happy to acquire ; he has taste to discern all that is meritorious, and sagacity to detect whatsoever should be discarded ; he gives just the opinion an author's wisdom should covet, however his vanity might prompt him to reject it; what altogether to expunge and what to improve he has repeatedly taught me, and, could I have obeyed him in the latter direction, as I invariably have in the former, the public would have found this collection more worthy its attention, and I should have sought the opinion of the critic more void of apprehension.

But whatever I may hope or fear, whatever assistance I have had or have needed, it becomes me to leave my verses to the judgment of the reader, without my endeavour to point out their merit, or an apology for their defects. Yet as, among the poetical attempts of one who has been for many years a priest, it may seem a want of respect for the legitimate objects of his study, that nothing occurs, unless it be incidentally, of the great subjects of religion : so it may appear a kind of ingratitude of a beneficed clergyman, that he has not employed his talent (be it estimated as it may) to some patriotic purpose—as in celebrating the unsubdued spirit of his countrymen in their glorious resistance of those enemies, who would have no peace throughout the world, except that which is dictated to the drooping spirit of suffering humanity by the triumphant insolence of military success.

Credit will be given to me, I hope, when I affirm that subjects so interesting have the due weight with me, which the sacred nature of the one, and the national importance of the other, must impress upon every mind not seduced into carelessness for religion by the lethargic influence of a perverted

PREFACE

philosophy, nor into indifference for the cause of our country by hyperbolical or hypocritical professions of universal philanthropy; but, after many efforts to satisfy myself by various trials on these subjects, I declined all further attempt, from a conviction that I should not be able to give satisfaction to my readers. Poetry of religious nature must indeed ever be clogged with almost insuperable difficulty; but there are doubtless to be found poets who are well qualified to celebrate the unanimous and heroic spirit of our countrymen, and to describe in appropriate colours some of those extraordinary scenes, which have been and are shifting in the face of Europe, with such dreadful celerity; and to such I relinquish the duty.

It remains for me to give the reader a brief view of those articles in the following collection, which for the first time solicit his attention.

In the " Parish Register," he will find an endeavour once more to describe village-manners, not by adopting the notion of pastoral simplicity or assuming ideas of rustic barbarity, but by more natural views of the peasantry, considered as a mixed body of persons, sober or profligate, and hence, in a great measure, contented or miserable. To this more general description are added the various characters which occur in the three parts of a Register : Baptism, Marriages, and Burials.

If the " Birth of Flattery " offer no moral, as an appendage to the fable, it is hoped that nothing of an immoral, nothing of improper, tendency will be imputed to a piece of poetical playfulness. In fact, genuine praise, like all other species of truth, is known by its bearing full investigation : it is what the giver is happy that he can justly bestow, and the receiver conscious that he may boldly accept; but adulation must ever be afraid of inquiry, and must, in proportion to their degrees of moral sensibility,

> Be shame "to him that gives and him that takes."

The verses in page[s 234-7] want a title; nor does the motto, although it gave occasion to them, altogether express the sense of the writer, who meant to observe that some of our best acquisitions, and some of our nobler conquests, are rendered

Crabbe   G   97

GEORGE CRABBE

ineffectual, by the passing away of opportunity, and the changes made by time : an argument that such acquirements and moral habits are reserved for a state of being in which they have the uses here denied them.

In the story of "Sir Eustace Grey," an attempt is made to describe the wanderings of a mind first irritated by the consequences of error and misfortune, and afterwards soothed by a species of enthusiastic conversion, still keeping him insane : a task very difficult, and, if the presumption of the attempt may find pardon, it will not be refused to the failure of the poet. It is said of our Shakspeare, respecting madness,

"In that circle none dare walk but he."

Yet be it granted to one who dares not to pass the boundary fixed for common minds, at least to step near to the tremendous verge, and form some idea of the terrors that are stalking in the interdicted space.

When first I had written "Aaron, or The Gipsy," I had no unfavourable opinion of it ; and, had I been collecting my verses at that time for publication, I should certainly have included this tale. Nine years have since elapsed, and I continue to judge the same of it, thus literally obeying one of the directions given by the prudence of criticism to the eagerness of the poet ; but how far I may have conformed to rules of more importance must be left to the less partial judgment of the readers.

The concluding poem, entitled "Woman!" was written at the time when the quotation from Mr. Ledyard was first made public ; the expression has since become hackneyed ; but the sentiment is congenial with our feelings, and though somewhat amplified in these verses, it is hoped they are not so far extended as to become tedious.

After this brief account of his subjects, the author leaves them to their fate, not presuming to make any remarks upon the kinds of versification he has chosen, or the merit of the execution. He has indeed brought forward the favourable

PREFACE

opinion of his friends, and for that he earnestly hopes his motives will be rightly understood ; it was a step of which he felt the advantage while he foresaw the danger ; he was aware of the benefit, if his readers would consider him as one who puts on a defensive armour against hasty and determined severity ; but he feels also the hazard, lest they should suppose he looks upon himself to be guarded by his friends, and so secure in the defence, that he may defy the fair judgment of legal criticism. It will probably be said, " he has brought with him his testimonials to the bar of the public," and he must admit the truth of the remark ; but he begs leave to observe in reply, that of those who bear testimonials of any kind the greater numbers feel apprehension, and not security : they are indeed so far from the enjoyment of victory, of the exultation of triumph, that, with all they can do for themselves, with all their friends have done for them, they are, like him, in dread of examination, and in fear of disappointment.

Muston, Leicestershire,
September, 1807.

THE LIBRARY.

Books afford Consolation to the troubled Mind, by substituting a lighter Kind of Distress for its own—They are productive of other Advantages—An Author's Hope of being known in distant Times—Arrangement of the Library—Size and Form of the Volumes—The ancient Folio, clasped and chained—Fashion prevalent even in this Place—The Mode of publishing in Numbers, Pamphlets, &c.—Subjects of the different Classes—Divinity—Controversy—The Friends of Religion often more dangerous than her Foes—Sceptical Authors—Reason too much rejected by the former Converts; exclusively relied upon by the latter—Philosophy ascending through the Scale of Being to moral Subjects—Books of Medicine: their Variety, Variance, and Proneness to System: the Evil of this, and the Difficulty it causes—Farewell to this Study—Law: the increasing Number of its Volumes—Supposed happy State of Man without Laws—Progress of Society—Historians: their Subjects—Dramatic Authors, Tragic and Comic—Ancient Romances—The Captive Heroine—Happiness in the Perusal of such Books: why—Criticism—Apprehensions of the Author, removed by the Appearance of the Genius of the Place; whose Reasoning and Admonition conclude the Subject.

THE LIBRARY.

WHEN the sad soul, by care and grief oppress'd,
    Looks round the world, but looks in vain for rest;
When every object that appears in view,
Partakes her gloom and seems dejected too:
Where shall affliction from itself retire?
Where fade away and placidly expire?
Alas! we fly to silent scenes in vain;
Care blasts the honours of the flow'ry plain:
Care veils in clouds the sun's meridian beam,
Sighs through the grove and murmurs in the stream.   10
For, when the soul is labouring in despair,
In vain the body breathes a purer air:
No storm-toss'd sailor sighs for slumbering seas—
He dreads the tempest, but invokes the breeze;
On the smooth mirror of the deep resides
Reflected wo, and o'er unruffled tides
The ghost of every former danger glides.   []]
Thus, in the calms of life, we only see
A steadier image of our misery;
But lively gales and gently-clouded skies   20
Disperse the sad reflections as they rise;
And busy thoughts and little cares avail
To ease the mind, when rest and reason fail.
When the dull thought, by no designs employ'd,
Dwells on the past, or suffer'd or enjoy'd,
We bleed anew in every former grief,
And joys departed furnish no relief.
    Not Hope herself, with all her flattering art,
Can cure this stubborn sickness of the heart:
The soul disdains each comfort she prepares,   30

GEORGE CRABBE

And anxious searches for congenial cares—
Those lenient cares, which, with our own combined,)
By mix'd sensations ease th' afflicted mind,   }
And steal our grief away and leave their own behind : [ )]
A lighter grief! which feeling hearts endure
Without regret, nor e'en demand a cure.
  But what strange art, what magic can dispose
The troubled mind to change its native woes?
Or lead us willing from ourselves, to see
Others more wretched, more undone than we?   40
This, books can do—nor this alone : they give
New views to life, and teach us how to live;
They soothe the grieved, the stubborn they chastise;
Fools they admonish, and confirm the wise.
Their aid they yield to all : they never shun
The man of sorrow, nor the wretch undone;
Unlike the hard, the selfish, and the proud,
They fly not sullen from the suppliant crowd;
Nor tell to various people various things,
But show to subjects, what they show to kings.   50
  Come, Child of Care! to make thy soul serene,
Approach the treasures of this tranquil scene;
Survey the dome, and, as the doors unfold,
The soul's best cure in all her cares behold!
Where mental wealth the poor in thought may find,
And mental physic the diseased in mind.
See here the balms that passion's wounds assuage;
See coolers here, that damp the fire of rage;
Here alt'ratives by slow degrees control
The chronic habits of the sickly soul;   60
And round the heart, and o'er the aching head,
Mild opiates here their sober influence shed.
Now bid thy soul man's busy scenes exclude,
And view composed this silent multitude :—
Silent they are, but, though deprived of sound,
Here all the living languages abound,
Here all that live no more; preserved they lie,
In tombs that open to the curious eye.
  Bless'd be the gracious Power, who taught mankind
To stamp a lasting image of the mind!—   70

THE LIBRARY

Beasts may convey, and tuneful birds may sing,
Their mutual feelings in the opening spring;
But man alone has skill and power to send
The heart's warm dictates to the distant friend;
'Tis his alone to please, instruct, advise
Ages remote, and nations yet to rise.
In sweet repose, when labour's children sleep,
When joy forgets to smile and care to weep,
When passion slumbers in the lover's breast,
And fear and guilt partake the balm of rest—   80
Why then denies the studious man to share
Man's common good, who feels his common care?
Because the hope is his, that bids him fly
Night's soft repose, and sleep's mild power defy;
That after-ages may repeat his praise,
And fame's fair meed be his for length of days.
Delightful prospect! when we leave behind
A worthy offspring of the fruitful mind,
Which, born and nursed through many an anxious day,
Shall all our labour, all our care repay.   90
Yet all are not these births of noble kind,
Not all the children of a vigorous mind;
But, where the wisest should alone preside,
The weak would rule us, and the blind would guide;
Nay, man's best efforts taste of man, and show
The poor and troubled source from which they flow:
Where most he triumphs, we his wants perceive,
And for his weakness in his wisdom grieve.
But, though imperfect all, yet wisdom loves
This seat serene, and virtue's self approves;   100
Here come the grieved, a change of thought to find,
The curious here, to feed a craving mind;
Here the devout their peaceful temple choose;
And here the poet meets his favouring muse.
With awe around these silent walks I tread:
These are the lasting mansions of the dead.—
"The dead," methinks, a thousand tongues reply;
"These are the tombs of such as cannot die!
"Crown'd with eternal fame, they sit sublime,
"And laugh at all the little strife of time."   110

GEORGE CRABBE

Hail, then, immortals! ye who shine above,
Each in his sphere the literary Jove;
And ye, the common people of these skies,
A humbler crowd of nameless deities:
Whether 'tis yours to lead the willing mind
Through history's mazes, and the turnings find;
Or whether, led by science, ye retire,
Lost and bewilder'd in the vast desire;
Whether the Muse invites you to her bowers,
And crowns your placid brows with living flowers;   120
Or godlike wisdom teaches you to show
The noblest road to happiness below;
Or men and manners prompt the easy page
To mark the flying follies of the age:
Whatever good ye boast, that good impart;
Inform the head and rectify the heart!

Lo! all in silence, all in order stand;
And mighty folios first, a lordly band,
Then quartos, their well-order'd ranks maintain,
And light octavos fill a spacious plain;   130
See yonder, ranged in more frequented rows,
A humbler band of duodecimos;
While undistinguish'd trifles swell the scene,
The last new play and fritter'd magazine.
Thus 'tis in life, where first the proud, the great,
In leagued assembly keep their cumbrous state;
Heavy and huge, they fill the world with dread,
Are much admired, and are but little read:
The commons next, a middle rank, are found;
Professions fruitful pour their offspring round;   140
Reasoners and wits are next their place allow'd,
And last, of vulgar tribes a countless crowd.
    First, let us view the form, the size, the dress;
For these the manners, nay the mind express;
That weight of wood, with leathern coat o'erlaid;
Those ample clasps, of solid metal made;
The close-press'd leaves, unclosed for many an age;
The dull red edging of the well-fill'd page;
On the broad back the stubborn ridges roll'd,

THE LIBRARY

Where yet the title stands in tarnish'd gold;   150
These all a sage and labour'd work proclaim,
A painful candidate for lasting fame:
No idle wit, no trifling verse can lurk
In the deep bosom of that weighty work;
No playful thoughts degrade the solemn style,
Nor one light sentence claims a transient smile.
   Hence, in these times, untouch'd the pages lie,
And slumber out their immortality:
They *had* their day, when, after all his toil,
His morning study, and his midnight oil,   160
At length an author's ONE great work appear'd,
By patient hope, and length of days, endear'd:
Expecting nations hail'd it from the press;
Poetic friends prefix'd each kind address;
Princes and kings received the pond'rous gift,
And ladies read the work they could not lift.
Fashion, though Folly's child, and guide of fools,
Rules e'en the wisest, and in learning rules;
From crowds and courts to Wisdom's seat she goes,
And reigns triumphant o'er her mother's foes.   170
For lo! these fav'rites of the ancient mode
Lie all neglected like the Birth-day Ode;
Ah! needless now this weight of massy chain[1];
Safe in themselves, the once-loved works remain;
No readers now invade their still retreat,
None try to steal them from their parent-seat;
Like ancient beauties, they may now discard
Chains, bolts, and locks, and lie without a guard.
   Our patient fathers trifling themes laid by,
And roll'd o'er labour'd works th' attentive eye;   180
Page after page, the much-enduring men
Explored the deeps and shallows of the pen;
Till, every former note and comment known,
They mark'd the spacious margin with their own:
Minute corrections proved their studious care;
The little index, pointing, told us where;

---

[1] In the more ancient libraries, works of value and importance were
fastened to their places by a length of chain; and might so be perused, but
not taken away.

And many an emendation show'd the age
Look'd far beyond the rubric title-page.
  Our nicer palates lighter labours seek,
Cloy'd with a folio-*Number* once a week ;   190
Bibles, with cuts and comments, thus go down :
E'en light Voltaire is *number'd* through the town :
Thus physic flies abroad, and thus the law,
From men of study, and from men of straw ;
Abstracts, abridgments, please the fickle times,
Pamphlets and plays, and politics and rhymes :
But though to write be now a task of ease,
The task is hard by manly arts to please,
When all our weakness is exposed to view,
And half our judges are our rivals too.   200

  Amid these works, on which the eager eye
Delights to fix, or glides reluctant by,
When all combined, their decent pomp display,
Where shall we first our early offering pay?

  To thee, DIVINITY! to thee, the light
And guide of mortals through their mental night ;
By whom we learn our hopes and fears to guide ;
To bear with pain, and to contend with pride ;
When grieved, to pray ; when injured, to forgive ;
And with the world in charity to live.   210
Not truths like these inspired that numerous race,
Whose pious labours fill this ample space ;
But questions nice, where doubt on doubt arose,
Awaked to war the long-contending foes.
For dubious meanings, learn'd polemics strove,
And wars on faith prevented works of love ;
The brands of discord far around were hurl'd,
And holy wrath inflamed a sinful world—
Dull though impatient, peevish though devout,
With wit disgusting and despised without ;   220
Saints in design, in execution men,
Peace in their looks, and vengeance in their pen.

  Methinks, I see, and sicken at the sight,
Spirits of spleen from yonder pile alight :

Spirits who prompted every damning page,
With pontiff pride and still-increasing rage.
Lo! how they stretch their gloomy wings around,
And lash with furious strokes the trembling ground!
They pray, they fight, they murder, and they weep—
Wolves in their vengeance, in their manners sheep; 230
Too well they act the prophet's fatal part,
Denouncing evil with a zealous heart;
And each, like Jonas, is displeased, if God
Repent his anger, or withhold his rod.
    But here the dormant fury rests unsought,
And Zeal sleeps soundly by the foes she fought;
Here all the rage of controversy ends,
And rival zealots rest like bosom-friends:
An Athanasian here, in deep repose,
Sleeps with the fiercest of his Arian foes; 240
Socinians here with Calvinists abide,
And thin partitions angry chiefs divide;
Here wily Jesuits simple Quakers meet,
And Bellarmine has rest at Luther's feet.
Great authors, for the church's glory fired,
Are, for the church's peace, to rest retired;
And close beside, a mystic, maudlin race,
Lie, "Crums of Comfort for the Babes of Grace."
    Against her foes Religion well defends
Her sacred truths, but often fears her friends; 250
If learn'd, their pride, if weak, their zeal she dreads,
And their hearts' weakness, who have soundest heads.
But most she fears the controversial pen,
The holy strife of disputatious men;
Who the bless'd Gospel's peaceful page explore,
Only to fight against its precepts more.
    Near to these seats, behold yon slender frames,
All closely fill'd and mark'd with modern names;
Where no fair science ever shows her face,
Few sparks of genius, and no spark of grace. 260
There sceptics rest, a still-increasing throng,
And stretch their widening wings ten thousand strong:
Some in close fight their dubious claims maintain;
Some skirmish lightly, fly and fight again;

Coldly profane, and impiously gay;
Their end the same, though various in their way.
When first Religion came to bless the land,
Her friends were then a firm believing band;
To doubt was, then, to plunge in guilt extreme,
And all was gospel that a monk could dream;   270
Insulted Reason fled the grov'ling soul,
For Fear to guide, and visions to control.
But now, when Reason has assumed her throne,
She, in her turn, demands to reign alone;
Rejecting all that lies beyond her view,
And, being judge, will be a witness too.
Insulted Faith then leaves the doubtful mind,
To seek for truth, without a power to find;
Ah! when will both in friendly beams unite,
And pour on erring man resistless light?   280

    Next to the seats, well stored with works divine,
An ample space, PHILOSOPHY! is thine;
Our reason's guide, by whose assisting light
We trace the moral bounds of wrong and right;
Our guide through nature, from the sterile clay,
To the bright orbs of yon celestial way!
'Tis thine, the great, the golden chain to trace,
Which runs through all, connecting race with race;
Save where those puzzling, stubborn links remain,
Which thy inferior light pursues in vain:—   290
    How vice and virtue in the soul contend;
How widely differ, yet how nearly blend!
What various passions war on either part,
And now confirm, now melt the yielding heart;
How Fancy loves around the world to stray,
While Judgment slowly picks his sober way!
The stores of memory, and the flights sublime
Of genius, bound by neither space nor time—
All these divine Philosophy explores,
Till, lost in awe, she wonders and adores.   300
From these, descending to the earth, she turns,
And matter, in its various form, discerns;
She parts the beamy light with skill profound,

Metes the thin air, and weighs the flying sound;
'Tis hers the lightning from the clouds to call,
And teach the fiery mischief where to fall.
Yet more her volumes teach—on these we look
As abstracts drawn from Nature's larger book:
Here, first described, the torpid earth appears,
And next, the vegetable robe it wears: 310
Where flow'ry tribes, in valleys, fields and groves,
Nurse the still flame, and feed the silent loves—
Loves, where no grief, nor joy, nor bliss, nor pain,
Warm the glad heart or vex the labouring brain;
But as the green blood moves along the blade,
The bed of Flora on the branch is made;
Where, without passion, love instinctive lives,
And gives new life, unconscious that it gives.
Advancing still in Nature's maze, we trace,
In dens and burning plains, her savage race;   320
With those tame tribes who on their lord attend,
And find, in man, a master and a friend;
Man crowns the scene, a world of wonders new,
A moral world, that well demands our view.
This world is here; for, of more lofty kind,
These neighbouring volumes reason on the mind;
They paint the state of man, ere yet endued
With knowledge—man, poor, ignorant, and rude;
Then, as his state improves, their pages swell,
And all its cares, and all its comforts, tell: 330
Here we behold how inexperience buys,
At little price, the wisdom of the wise;
Without the troubles of an active state,
Without the cares and dangers of the great,
Without the miseries of the poor, we know
What wisdom, wealth, and poverty bestow;
We see how reason calms the raging mind,
And how contending passions urge mankind.
Some, won by virtue, glow with sacred fire;
Some, lured by vice, indulge the low desire;   340
Whilst others, won by either, now pursue
The guilty chase, now keep the good in view;
For ever wretched, with themselves at strife,

GEORGE CRABBE

They lead a puzzled, vex'd, uncertain life;
For transient vice bequeaths a lingering pain,
Which transient virtue seeks to cure in vain.

Whilst thus engaged, high views enlarge the soul,
New interests draw, new principles control:
Nor thus the soul alone resigns her grief,
But here the tortured body finds relief;   350
For see where yonder sage Arachnè shapes
Her subtile gin, that not a fly escapes!
There PHYSIC fills the space, and far around,
Pile above pile, her learned works abound:
Glorious their aim—to ease the labouring heart;
To war with death, and stop his flying dart;
To trace the source whence the fierce contest grew,
And life's short lease on easier terms renew;
To calm the frenzy of the burning brain;
To heal the tortures of imploring pain;   360
Or, when more powerful ills all efforts brave,
To ease the victim no device can save,
And smooth the stormy passage to the grave.   [ʃ]
    But man, who knows no good unmix'd and pure,
Oft finds a poison where he sought a cure;
For grave deceivers lodge their labours here,
And cloud the science they pretend to clear.
Scourges for sin, the solemn tribe are sent;
Like fire and storms, they call us to repent;
But storms subside, and fires forget to rage,   370
These are eternal scourges of the age.
'Tis not enough that each terrific hand
Spreads desolation round a guilty land;
But, train'd to ill, and harden'd by its crimes,
Their pen relentless kills through future times.
    Say ye, who search these records of the dead,
Who read huge works, to boast what ye have read:
Can all the real knowledge ye possess,
Or those (if such there are) who more than guess,
Atone for each impostor's wild mistakes,   380
And mend the blunders pride or folly makes?
    What thought so wild, what airy dream so light,

That will not prompt a theorist to write?
What art so prevalent, what proof so strong,
That will convince him his attempt is wrong?
One in the solids finds each lurking ill,
Nor grants the passive fluids power to kill;
A learned friend some subtler reason brings
Absolves the channels, but condemns their springs;
The subtile nerves, that shun the doctor's eye,   390
Escape no more his subtler theory;
The vital heat, that warms the labouring heart,
Lends a fair system to these sons of art;
The vital air, a pure and subtile stream,
Serves a foundation for an airy scheme,   [ ]
Assists the doctor, and supports his dream.
Some have their favourite ills, and each disease
Is but a younger branch that kills from these.
One to the gout contracts all human pain;
He views it raging in the frantic brain;   400
Finds it in fevers all his efforts mar,
And sees it lurking in the cold catarrh.
Bilious by some, by others nervous seen,
Rage the fantastic demons of the spleen;
And every symptom of the strange disease
With every system of the sage agrees.
　　Ye frigid tribe, on whom I wasted long
The tedious hours, and ne'er indulged in song;
Ye first seducers of my easy heart,
Who promised knowledge ye could not impart;   410
Ye dull deluders, truth's destructive foes;
Ye sons of fiction, clad in stupid prose;
Ye treacherous leaders, who, yourselves in doubt,
Light up false fires, and send us far about—
Still may yon spider round your pages spin,
Subtile and slow, her emblematic gin!
Buried in dust and lost in silence, dwell;
Most potent, grave, and reverend friends—farewell!

　　Near these, and where the setting sun displays
Through the dim window his departing rays,   420
And gilds yon columns, there, on either side,

The huge abridgments of the LAW abide.
Fruitful as vice the dread correctors stand,
And spread their guardian terrors round the land ;
Yet, as the best that human care can do,
Is mix'd with error, oft with evil too,
Skill'd in deceit, and practised to evade,
Knaves stand secure, for whom these laws were made ;
And justice vainly each expedient tries,
While art eludes it, or while power defies.   430
" Ah! happy age," the youthful poet sings,
" When the free nations knew not laws nor kings ;
" When all were bless'd to share a common store,
" And none were proud of wealth, for none were poor;
" No wars nor tumults vex'd each still domain,
" No thirst of empire, no desire of gain ;
" No proud great man, nor one who would be great,
" Drove modest merit from its proper state ;
" Nor into distant climes would avarice roam,
" To fetch delights for luxury at home :   440
" Bound by no ties which kept the soul in awe,
" They dwelt at liberty, and love was law!"
    " Mistaken youth! each nation first was rude,
" Each man a cheerless son of solitude,
" To whom no joys of social life were known ;
" None felt a care that was not all his own ;
" Or in some languid clime his abject soul
" Bow'd to a little tyrant's stern control ;
" A slave, with slaves his monarch's throne he raised,
" And in rude song his ruder idol praised ;   450
" The meaner cares of life were all he knew ;
" Bounded his pleasures, and his wishes few.
" But when by slow degrees the Arts arose,
" And Science waken'd from her long repose ;
" When Commerce, rising from the bed of ease,
" Ran round the land, and pointed to the seas ;
" When Emulation, born with jealous eye,
" And Avarice, lent their spurs to industry ;
" Then one by one the numerous laws were made,
" Those to control, and these to succour trade ;   460
" To curb the insolence of rude command,

THE LIBRARY

"To snatch the victim from the usurer's hand;
"To awe the bold, to yield the wrong'd redress,
"And feed the poor with Luxury's excess."
Like some vast flood, unbounded, fierce, and strong,
His nature leads ungovern'd man along;
Like mighty bulwarks made to stem that tide,
The laws are form'd and placed on ev'ry side:
Whene'er it breaks the bounds by these decreed,
New statutes rise, and stronger laws succeed;   470
More and more gentle grows the dying stream,
More and more strong the rising bulwarks seem;
Till, like a miner working sure and slow,
Luxury creeps on, and ruins all below;
The basis sinks, the ample piles decay;
The stately fabric shakes and falls away;
Primeval want and ignorance come on,
But freedom, that exalts the savage state, is gone.

Next, HISTORY ranks;—there full in front she lies,
And every nation her dread tale supplies.   480
Yet History has her doubts, and every age
With sceptic queries marks the passing page;
Records of old nor later date are clear—
Too distant those, and these are placed too near;
There time conceals the objects from our view,
Here our own passions and a writer's too.
Yet, in these volumes, see how states arose,
Guarded by virtue from surrounding foes;
Their virtue lost, and of their triumphs vain,
Lo! how they sunk to slavery again!   490
Satiate with power, of fame and wealth possess'd,
A nation grows too glorious to be bless'd;
Conspicuous made, she stands the mark of all,
And foes join foes to triumph in her fall.
Thus speaks the page that paints ambition's race,
The monarch's pride, his glory, his disgrace;
The headlong course, that madd'ning heroes run,
How soon triumphant, and how soon undone;
How slaves, turn'd tyrants, offer crowns to sale,
And each fall'n nation's melancholy tale.   500

Crabbe   H   113

GEORGE CRABBE

Lo ! where of late the Book of Martyrs stood,
Old pious tracts, and Bibles bound in wood :
There, such the taste of our degenerate age,
Stand the profane delusions of the STAGE.
Yet virtue owns the TRAGIC MUSE a friend—
Fable her means, morality her end ;
For this she rules all passions in their turns,
And now the bosom bleeds, and now it burns ;
Pity with weeping eye surveys her bowl ;
Her anger swells, her terror chills the soul ;   510
She makes the vile to virtue yield applause,
And own her sceptre while they break her laws ;
For vice in others is abhorr'd of all,
And villains triumph when the worthless fall.

Not thus her sister COMEDY prevails,
Who shoots at folly, for her arrow fails :
Folly, by dulness arm'd, eludes the wound,
And harmless sees the feather'd shafts rebound ;
Unhurt she stands, applauds the archer's skill,
Laughs at her malice, and is folly still.   520
Yet well the Muse portrays in fancied scenes
What pride will stoop to, what profession means ;
How formal fools the farce of state applaud ;
How caution watches at the lips of fraud ;
The wordy variance of domestic life ;
The tyrant husband, the retorting wife ;
The snares for innocence, the lie of trade,
And the smooth tongue's habitual masquerade.
With her the virtues too obtain a place,
Each gentle passion, each becoming grace ;   530
The social joy in life's securer road,
Its easy pleasure, its substantial good ;
The happy thought that conscious virtue gives,
And all that ought to live, and all that lives.

But who are these ? Methinks, a noble mien
And awful grandeur in their form are seen—
Now in disgrace. What, though by time is spread
Polluting dust o'er every reverend head ;

THE LIBRARY

What, though beneath yon gilded tribe they lie,
And dull observers pass insulting by :⠀⠀⠀⠀⠀540
Forbid it shame, forbid it decent awe,
What seems so grave, should no attention draw !
Come, let us then with [reverent] step advance,
And greet—the ancient worthies of ROMANCE.
⠀⠀Hence, ye profane ! I feel a former dread ;
A thousand visions float around my head.
Hark ! hollow blasts through empty courts resound,
And shadowy forms with staring eyes stalk round ;
See ! moats and bridges, walls and castles rise,
Ghosts, fairies, demons, dance before our eyes ;⠀⠀550
Lo ! magic verse inscribed on golden gate,
And bloody hand that beckons on to fate :—
" And who art thou, thou little page, unfold !
" Say, doth thy lord my Claribel withhold ?
" Go tell him straight, Sir Knight, thou must resign
" The captive queen—for Claribel is mine."
Away he flies ; and now for bloody deeds,
Black suits of armour, masks, and foaming steeds ;
The giant falls ; his recreant throat I seize,
And from his corslet take the massy keys ;⠀⠀560
Dukes, lords, and knights in long procession move,
Released from bondage with my virgin love ;
She comes ! she comes ! in all the charms of youth,
Unequall'd love and unsuspected truth !
⠀⠀Ah ! happy he who thus, in magic themes,
O'er worlds bewitch'd in early rapture dreams,
Where wild Enchantment waves her potent wand,
And Fancy's beauties fill her fairy land ;
Where doubtful objects strange desires excite,
And Fear and Ignorance afford delight.⠀⠀570
⠀⠀But lost, for ever lost, to me these joys,
Which Reason scatters, and which Time destroys—
Too dearly bought : maturer judgment calls
My busied mind from tales and madrigals ;
My doughty giants all are slain or fled,
And all my knights, blue, green, and yellow, dead !
No more the midnight fairy tribe I view,
All in the merry moonshine tippling dew ;

⠀⠀⠀⠀⠀⠀⠀⠀H 2⠀⠀⠀⠀⠀⠀⠀⠀⠀115

GEORGE CRABBE

E'en the last lingering fiction of the brain,
The church-yard ghost, is now at rest again; 580
And all these wayward wanderings of my youth
Fly Reason's power and shun the light of truth.
  With fiction, then, does real joy reside,
And is our reason the delusive guide?
Is it, then, right to dream the syrens sing,
Or mount enraptured on the dragon's wing?
No, 'tis the infant mind, to care unknown,
That makes th' imagined paradise its own;
Soon as reflections in the bosom rise,
Light slumbers vanish from the clouded eyes; 590
The tear and smile, that once together rose,
Are then divorced; the head and heart are foes:
Enchantment bows to Wisdom's serious plan,
And Pain and Prudence make and mar the man.

  While thus, of power and fancied empire vain,
With various thoughts my mind I entertain;
While books, my slaves, with tyrant hand I seize,
Pleased with the pride that will not let them please;
Sudden I find terrific thoughts arise,
And sympathetic sorrow fills my eyes; 600
For, lo! while yet my heart admits the wound,
I see the CRITIC army ranged around.
  Foes to our race! if ever ye have known
A father's fears for offspring of your own.—
If ever, smiling o'er a lucky line,
Ye thought the sudden sentiment divine,
Then paused and doubted, and then, tired of doubt,
With rage as sudden dash'd the stanza out—
If, after fearing much and pausing long,
Ye ventured on the world your labour'd song, 610
And from the crusty critics of those days
Implored the feeble tribute of their praise:
Remember now the fears that moved you then,
And, spite of truth, let mercy guide your pen!
  What vent'rous race are ours! what mighty foes
Lie waiting all around them to oppose!
What treacherous friends betray them to the fight!

THE LIBRARY

What dangers threaten them—yet still they write:
A hapless tribe! to every evil born,
Whom villains hate, and fools affect to scorn;   620
Strangers they come amid a world of wo,
And taste the largest portion ere they go.

Pensive I spoke, and cast mine eyes around;
The roof, methought, return'd a solemn sound;
Each column seem'd to shake, and clouds, like smoke,
From dusty piles and ancient volumes broke;
Gathering above, like mists condensed they seem,
Exhaled in summer from the rushy stream;
Like flowing robes they now appear, and twine
Round the large members of a form divine;   630
His silver beard, that swept his aged breast,
His piercing eye, that inward light express'd,
Were seen—but clouds and darkness veil'd the rest.   [J]
Fear chill'd my heart: to one of mortal race,
How awful seem'd the Genius of the place!
So, in Cimmerian shores, Ulysses saw
His parent-shade, and shrunk in pious awe;
Like him I stood, and wrapt in thought profound,
When from the pitying power broke forth a solemn sound:—
  "Care lives with all; no rules, no precepts save   640
"The wise from wo, no fortitude the brave;
"Grief is to man as certain as the grave: [J]
"Tempests and storms in life's whole progress rise,
"And hope shines dimly through o'erclouded skies;
"Some drops of comfort on the favour'd fall,
"But showers of sorrow are the lot of *all*:
"Partial to talents, then, shall Heav'n withdraw
"Th' afflicting rod, or break the general law?
"Shall he who soars, inspired by loftier views,
"Life's little cares and little pains refuse?   650
"Shall he not rather feel a double share
"Of mortal wo, when doubly arm'd to bear?
  "Hard is his fate who builds his peace of mind
"On the precarious mercy of mankind;
"Who hopes for wild and visionary things,
"And mounts o'er unknown seas with vent'rous wings:

GEORGE CRABBE

"But as, of various evils that befal
"The human race, some portion goes to all:
"To him perhaps the milder lot's assign'd,
"Who feels his consolation in his mind;   660
"And, lock'd within his bosom, bears about
"A mental charm for every care without.
"E'en in the pangs of each domestic grief,
"Or health or vigorous hope affords relief;
"And every wound the tortured bosom feels,
"Or virtue bears, or some preserver heals;
"Some generous friend, of ample power possess'd;
"Some feeling heart that bleeds for the distress'd;
"Some breast that glows with virtues all divine;
"Some noble RUTLAND, Misery's friend and thine.   670
"Nor say, the Muse's song, the Poet's pen,
"Merit the scorn they meet from little men.
"With cautious freedom if the numbers flow,
"Not wildly high, nor pitifully low;
"If vice alone their honest aims oppose,
"Why so ashamed their friends, so loud their foes?
"Happy for men in every age and clime,
"If all the sons of vision dealt in rhyme!
"Go on then, Son of Vision! still pursue
"Thy airy dreams; the world is dreaming too.   680
"Ambition's lofty views, the pomp of state,
"The pride of wealth, the splendour of the great,
"Stripp'd of their mask, their cares and troubles known,
"Are visions far less happy than thy own:
"Go on! and, while the sons of care complain,
"Be wisely gay and innocently vain;
"While serious souls are by their fears undone,
"Blow sportive bladders in the beamy sun,
"And call them worlds! and bid the greatest show
"More radiant colours in their worlds below;   690
"Then, as they break, the slaves of care reprove,
"And tell them, Such are all the toys they love."

118

THE VILLAGE.

IN TWO BOOKS.

BOOK I.

The Subject proposed—Remarks upon Pastoral Poetry—A Tract of
Country near the Coast described—An impoverished Borough—
Smugglers and their Assistants—Rude Manners of the Inhabitants—
Ruinous Effects of a high Tide—The Village Life more generally
considered: Evils of it—The youthful Labourer—The old Man: his
Soliloquy—The Parish Workhouse: its Inhabitants—The sick Poor:
their Apothecary—The dying Pauper—The Village Priest.

GEORGE CRABBE

THE VILLAGE.

BOOK I.

THE Village Life, and every care that reigns
  O'er youthful peasants and declining swains;
What labour yields, and what, that labour past,
Age, in its hour of languor, finds at last;
What form the real picture of the poor,
Demand a song—the Muse can give no more.
  Fled are those times when, in harmonious strains,
The rustic poet praised his native plains.
No shepherds now, in smooth alternate verse,
Their country's beauty or their nymphs' rehearse;   10
Yet still for these we frame the tender strain,
Still in our lays fond Corydons complain,
And shepherds' boys their amorous pains reveal,
The only pains, alas! they never feel.
  On Mincio's banks, in Cæsar's bounteous reign,
If Tityrus found the Golden Age again,
Must sleepy bards the flattering dream prolong,
Mechanic echoes of the Mantuan song?
From Truth and Nature shall we widely stray,
Where Virgil, not where Fancy, leads the way?   20
  Yes, thus the Muses sing of happy swains,
Because the Muses never knew their pains.
They boast their peasants' pipes; but peasants now
Resign their pipes and plod behind the plough;
And few, amid the rural-tribe, have time
To number syllables, and play with rhyme;
Save honest Duck, what son of verse could share
The poet's rapture, and the peasant's care?
Or the great labours of the field degrade,
With the new peril of a poorer trade?   30

THE VILLAGE

From this chief cause these idle praises spring,
That themes so easy few forbear to sing;
For no deep thought the trifling subjects ask :
To sing of shepherds is an easy task.
The happy youth assumes the common strain,
A nymph his mistress, and himself a swain ;
With no sad scenes he clouds his tuneful prayer,
But all, to look like her, is painted fair.
I grant indeed that fields and flocks have charms
For him that grazes or for him that farms ;   40
But, when amid such pleasing scenes I trace
The poor laborious natives of the place,
And see the mid-day sun, with fervid ray,
On their bare heads and dewy temples play ;
While some, with feebler heads and fainter hearts,
Deplore their fortune, yet sustain their parts :
Then shall I dare these real ills to hide
In tinsel trappings of poetic pride?
No ; cast by Fortune on a frowning coast,
Which neither groves nor happy valleys boast ;   50
Where other cares than those the Muse relates,
And other shepherds dwell with other mates ;
By such examples taught, I paint the Cot,
As Truth will paint it, and as Bards will not :
Nor you, ye poor, of letter'd scorn complain,
To you the smoothest song is smooth in vain ;
O'ercome by labour, and bow'd down by time,
Feel you the barren flattery of a rhyme?
Can poets soothe you, when you pine for bread,
By winding myrtles round your ruin'd shed?   60
Can their light tales your weighty griefs o'erpower,
Or glad with airy mirth the toilsome hour?
Lo! where the heath, with withering brake grown o'er,
Lends the light turf that warms the neighbouring poor ;
From thence a length of burning sand appears,
Where the thin harvest waves its wither'd ears ;
Rank weeds, that every art and care defy,
Reign o'er the land, and rob the blighted rye :
There thistles stretch their prickly arms afar,
And to the ragged infant threaten war ;   70

GEORGE CRABBE

There poppies, nodding, mock the hope of toil;
There the blue bugloss paints the sterile soil;
Hardy and high, above the slender sheaf,
The slimy mallow waves her silky leaf;
O'er the young shoot the charlock throws a shade,
And clasping tares cling round the sickly blade;
With mingled tints the rocky coasts abound,
And a sad splendour vainly shines around.
So looks the nymph whom wretched arts adorn,
Betray'd by man, then left for man to scorn; 80
Whose cheek in vain assumes the mimic rose,
While her sad eyes the troubled breast disclose;
Whose outward splendour is but folly's dress,
Exposing most, when most it gilds distress.
 Here joyless roam a wild amphibious race,
With sullen wo display'd in every face;
Who far from civil arts and social fly,
And scowl at strangers with suspicious eye.
 Here too the lawless merchant of the main
Draws from his plough th' intoxicated swain; 90
Want only claim'd the labour of the day,
But vice now steals his nightly rest away.
 Where are the swains, who, daily labour done,
With rural games play'd down the setting sun;
Who struck with matchless force the bounding ball,
Or made the pond'rous quoit obliquely fall;
While some huge Ajax, terrible and strong,
Engaged some artful stripling of the throng,
And fell beneath him, foil'd, while far around
Hoarse triumph rose, and rocks return'd the sound? 100
Where now are these?—Beneath yon cliff they stand,
To show the freighted pinnace where to land;
To load the ready steed with guilty haste;
To fly in terror o'er the pathless waste;
Or, when detected in their straggling course,
To foil their foes by cunning or by force;
Or, yielding part (which equal knaves demand),
To gain a lawless passport through the land.
 Here, wand'ring long amid these frowning fields,
I sought the simple life that Nature yields; 110

THE VILLAGE

Rapine and Wrong and Fear usurp'd her place,
And a bold, artful, surly, savage race;
Who, only skill'd to take the finny tribe,
The yearly dinner, or septennial bribe,
Wait on the shore, and, as the waves run high,
On the tost vessel bend their eager eye,
Which to their coast directs its vent'rous way;
[Their], or the ocean's, miserable prey.
  As on their neighbouring beach yon swallows stand,
And wait for favouring winds to leave the land,   120
While still for flight the ready wing is spread:
So waited I the favouring hour, and fled—
Fled from these shores where guilt and famine reign,
And cried, Ah! hapless they who still remain;
Who still remain to hear the ocean roar,
Whose greedy waves devour the lessening shore;
Till some fierce tide, with more imperious sway,
Sweeps the low hut and all it holds away;
When the sad tenant weeps from door to door,
And begs a poor protection from the poor!   130
  But these are scenes where Nature's niggard hand
Gave a spare portion to the famish'd land;
Hers is the fault, if here mankind complain
Of fruitless toil and labour spent in vain.
But yet in other scenes, more fair in view,
Where Plenty smiles —alas! she smiles for few—
And those who taste not, yet behold her store,   ⎱
Are as the slaves that dig the golden ore,   ⎰
The wealth around them makes them doubly poor   [ʃ]
  Or will you deem them amply paid in health,   140
Labour's fair child, that languishes with wealth?
Go, then! and see them rising with the sun,
Through a long course of daily toil to run;
See them beneath the dog-star's raging heat,
When the knees tremble and the temples beat;
Behold them, leaning on their scythes, look o'er
The labour past, and toils to come explore;
See them alternate suns and showers engage,
And hoard up aches and anguish for their age;
Through fens and marshy moors their steps pursue, 150

123

GEORGE CRABBE

When their warm pores imbibe the evening dew;
Then own that labour may as fatal be
To these thy slaves, as thine excess to thee.
  Amid this tribe too oft a manly pride
Strives in strong toil the fainting heart to hide;
There may you see the youth of slender frame
Contend with weakness, weariness, and shame;
Yet, urged along, and proudly loth to yield,
He strives to join his fellows of the field;
Till long-contending nature droops at last,   160
Declining health rejects his poor repast,
His cheerless spouse the coming danger sees,
And mutual murmurs urge the slow disease.
  Yet grant them health, 'tis not for us to tell,
Though the head droops not, that the heart is well;
Or will you praise that homely, healthy fare,
Plenteous and plain, that happy peasants share?
Oh! trifle not with wants you cannot feel,
Nor mock the misery of a stinted meal—
Homely, not wholesome; plain, not plenteous; such   170
As you who praise would never deign to touch.
  Ye gentle souls, who dream of rural ease,
Whom the smooth stream and smoother sonnet please;
Go! if the peaceful cot your praises share,
Go, look within, and ask if peace be there:
If peace be his—that drooping weary sire,
Or theirs, that offspring round their feeble fire;
Or hers, that matron pale, whose trembling hand
Turns on the wretched hearth th' expiring brand!
  Nor yet can Time itself obtain for these   180
Life's latest comforts, due respect and ease:
For yonder see that hoary swain, whose age
Can with no cares except his own engage;
Who, propp'd on that rude staff, looks up to see
The bare arms broken from the withering tree,
On which, a boy, he climb'd the loftiest bough,
Then his first joy, but his sad emblem now.
  He once was chief in all the rustic trade;
His steady hand the straightest furrow made;
Full many a prize he won, and still is proud   190

THE VILLAGE

To find the triumphs of his youth allow'd.
A transient pleasure sparkles in his eyes;
He hears and smiles, then thinks again and sighs:
For now he journeys to his grave in pain;
The rich disdain him, nay, the poor disdain;
Alternate masters now their slave command,
Urge the weak efforts of his feeble hand;
And, when his age attempts its task in vain,
With ruthless taunts, of lazy poor complain[1].

 Oft may you see him, when he tends the sheep, 200
His winter-charge, beneath the hillock weep;
Oft hear him murmur to the winds that blow
O'er his white locks and bury them in snow,
When, roused by rage and muttering in the morn,
He mends the broken hedge with icy thorn:—
 "Why do I live, when I desire to be
"At once from life and life's long labour free?
"Like leaves in spring, the young are blown away,
"Without the sorrows of a slow decay;
"I, like yon wither'd leaf, remain behind, 210
"Nipp'd by the frost, and shivering in the wind;
"There it abides till younger buds come on,
"As I, now all my fellow-swains are gone;
"Then, from the rising generation thrust,
"It falls, like me, unnoticed to the dust.
 "These fruitful fields, these numerous flocks I see,
"Are others' gain, but killing cares to me:
"To me the children of my youth are lords,
"Cool in their looks, but hasty in their words:
"Wants of their own demand their care; and who 220
"Feels his own want and succours others too?
"A lonely, wretched man, in pain I go,
"None need my help, and none relieve my wo;
"Then let my bones beneath the turf be laid,
"And men forget the wretch they would not aid!"
 Thus groan the old, till, by disease oppress'd,
They taste a final wo, and then they rest.
 Theirs is yon house that holds the parish poor,
Whose walls of mud scarce bear the broken door;
There, where the putrid vapours, flagging, play, 230

125

And the dull wheel hums doleful through the day—
There children dwell, who know no parents' care;
Parents, who know no children's love, dwell there!
Heart-broken matrons on their joyless bed,
Forsaken wives, and mothers never wed;
Dejeĉted widows with unheeded tears,
And crippled age with more than childhood fears;
The lame, the blind, and, far the happiest they!
The moping idiot and the madman gay.
Here too the sick their final doom receive,   240
Here brought, amid the scenes of grief, to grieve,
Where the loud groans from some sad chamber flow,
Mix'd with the clamours of the crowd below;
Here, sorrowing, they each kindred sorrow scan,
And the cold charities of man to man:
Whose laws indeed for ruin'd age provide,
And strong compulsion plucks the scrap from pride;
But still that scrap is bought with many a sigh,
And pride embitters what it can't deny.
Say ye, oppress'd by some fantastic woes,   250
Some jarring nerve that baffles your repose;
Who press the downy couch, while slaves advance
With timid eye to read the distant glance;
Who with sad prayers the weary doĉtor tease,
To name the nameless ever-new disease;
Who with mock patience dire complaints endure,
Which real pain, and that alone, can cure—
How would ye bear in real pain to lie,
Despised, negleĉted, left alone to die?
How would ye bear to draw your latest breath,   260
Where all that's wretched paves the way for death?
Such is that room which one rude beam divides,
And naked rafters form the sloping sides;
Where the vile bands that bind the thatch are seen,
And lath and mud are all that lie between,
Save one dull pane, that, coarsely patch'd, gives way
To the rude tempest, yet excludes the day.
Here, on a matted flock, with dust o'erspread,
The drooping wretch reclines his languid head;
For him no hand the cordial cup applies,   270

THE VILLAGE

Or wipes the tear that stagnates in his eyes;
No friends with soft discourse his pain beguile,
Or promise hope till sickness wears a smile.
    But soon a loud and hasty summons calls,
Shakes the thin roof, and echoes round the walls.
Anon, a figure enters, quaintly neat,
All pride and business, bustle and conceit;
With looks unalter'd by these scenes of wo,
With speed that, entering, speaks his haste to go,
He bids the gazing throng around him fly,   280
And carries fate and physic in his eye:
A potent quack, long versed in human ills,
Who first insults the victim whom he kills;
Whose murd'rous hand a drowsy Bench protect,
And whose most tender mercy is neglect.
    Paid by the parish for attendance here,
He wears contempt upon his sapient sneer;
In haste he seeks the bed where Misery lies,
Impatience mark'd in his averted eyes;
And, some habitual queries hurried o'er,   290
Without reply, he rushes on the door.
His drooping patient, long inured to pain,
And long unheeded, knows remonstrance vain;
He ceases now the feeble help to crave
Of man; and silent sinks into the grave.
    But ere his death some pious doubts arise,
Some simple fears, which "bold bad" men despise:
Fain would he ask the parish-priest to prove
His title certain to the joys above;
For this he sends the murmuring nurse, who calls   300
The holy stranger to these dismal walls;
And doth not he, the pious man, appear,
He, "passing rich with forty pounds a year"?
Ah! no; a shepherd of a different stock,
And far unlike him, feeds this little flock:
A jovial youth, who thinks his Sunday's task
As much as God or man can fairly ask;
The rest he gives to loves and labours light,
To fields the morning, and to feasts the night;
None better skill'd the noisy pack to guide,   310

GEORGE CRABBE

To urge their chase, to cheer them or to chide;
A sportsman keen, he shoots through half the day,
And, skill'd at whist, devotes the night to play.
Then, while such honours bloom around his head,
Shall he sit sadly by the sick man's bed,
To raise the hope he feels not, or with zeal
To combat fears that e'en the pious feel?
Now once again the gloomy scene explore,
Less gloomy now; the bitter hour is o'er,
The man of many sorrows sighs no more.—   320[ ]]
Up yonder hill, behold how sadly slow
The bier moves winding from the vale below;
There lie the happy dead, from trouble free,
And the glad parish pays the frugal fee.
No more, O Death! thy victim starts to hear
Churchwarden stern, or kingly overseer;
No more the farmer claims his humble bow,
Thou art his lord, the best of tyrants thou!
Now to the church behold the mourners come,
Sedately torpid and devoutly dumb;   330
The village children now their games suspend,
To see the bier that bears their ancient friend:
For he was one in all their idle sport,
And like a monarch ruled their little court;
The pliant bow he form'd, the flying ball,
The bat, the wicket, were his labours all;
Him now they follow to his grave, and stand
Silent and sad, and gazing, hand in hand;
While bending low, their eager eyes explore
The mingled relics of the parish poor.   340
The bell tolls late, the moping owl flies round,
Fear marks the flight and magnifies the sound;
The busy priest, detain'd by weightier care,
Defers his duty till the day of prayer;
And, waiting long, the crowd retire distress'd,
To think a poor man's bones should lie unbless'd[2].

128

THE VILLAGE.

BOOK II.

There are found, amid the Evils of a laborious Life, some Views of
Tranquillity and Happiness—The Repose and Pleasure of a Summer
Sabbath: interrupted by Intoxication and Dispute—Village Detrac-
tion—Complaints of the 'Squire—The Evening Riots—Justice—
Reasons for this unpleasant View of Rustic Life: the Effect it should
have upon the Lower Classes; and the Higher—These last have their
peculiar Distresses: Exemplified in the Life and heroic Death of Lord
Robert Manners—Concluding Address to His Grace the Duke of
Rutland.

THE VILLAGE.

BOOK II.

NO longer truth, though shown in verse, disdain,
But own the Village Life a life of pain.
I too must yield, that oft amid these woes
Are gleams of transient mirth and hours of sweet repose,
Such as you find on yonder sportive Green,
The 'squire's tall gate and churchway-walk between;
Where loitering stray a little tribe of friends,
On a fair Sunday when the sermon ends.
Then rural beaux their best attire put on,
To win their nymphs, as other nymphs are won; 10
While those long wed go plain, and, by degrees,
Like other husbands, quit their care to please.
Some of the sermon talk, a sober crowd,
And loudly praise, if it were preach'd aloud;
Some on the labours of the week look round,
Feel their own worth, and think their toil renown'd;
While some, whose hopes to no renown extend,
Are only pleased to find their labours end.
  Thus, as their hours glide on, with pleasure fraught,
Their careful masters brood the painful thought; 20
Much in their mind they murmur and lament,
That one fair day should be so idly spent;
And think that Heaven deals hard, to tithe their store
And tax their time for preachers and the poor.
  Yet still, ye humbler friends, enjoy your hour,
This is your portion, yet unclaim'd of power;
This is Heaven's gift to weary men oppress'd,
And seems the type of their expected rest.
But yours, alas! are joys that soon decay;
Frail joys, begun and ended with the day; 30

THE VILLAGE

Or yet, while day permits those joys to reign,
The village vices drive them from the plain.
    See the stout churl, in drunken fury great,
Strike the bare bosom of his teeming mate!
His naked vices, rude and unrefined,
Exert their open empire o'er the mind;
But can we less the senseless rage despise,
Because the savage acts without disguise?
    Yet here disguise, the city's vice, is seen,
And Slander steals along and taints the Green: 40
At her approach domestic peace is gone,
Domestic broils at her approach come on;
She to the wife the husband's crime conveys,
She tells the husband when his consort strays,
Her busy tongue through all the little state
Diffuses doubt, suspicion, and debate;
Peace, tim'rous goddess! quits her old domain,
In sentiment and song content to reign.
    Nor are the nymphs that breathe the rural air
So fair as Cynthia's, nor so chaste as fair: 50
These to the town afford each fresher face,
And the clown's trull receives the peer's embrace;
From whom, should chance again convey her down,
The peer's disease in turn attacks the clown.
    Here too the 'squire, or 'squire-like farmer, talk,
How round their regions nightly pilferers walk;
How from their ponds the fish are borne, and all
The rip'ning treasures from their lofty wall;
How meaner rivals in their sports delight,
Just rich enough to claim a doubtful right;   60
Who take a licence round their fields to stray,
A mongrel race! the poachers of the day.
    And hark! the riots of the Green begin,
That sprang at first from yonder noisy inn;
What time the weekly pay was vanish'd all,
And the slow hostess scored the threat'ning wall;
What time they ask'd, their friendly feast to close,
A final cup, and that will make them foes;
When blows ensue that break the arm of toil,
And rustic battle ends the boobies' broil.   70

Save when to yonder Hall they bend their way,
Where the grave justice ends the grievous fray;
He who recites, to keep the poor in awe,
The law's vast volume—for he knows the law:—
To him with anger or with shame repair
The injured peasant and deluded fair.
   Lo! at his throne the silent nymph appears,
Frail by her shape, but modest in her tears;
And while she stands abash'd, with conscious eye,
Some favourite female of her judge glides by,   80
Who views with scornful glance the strumpet's fate,
And thanks the stars that made her keeper great;
Near her the swain, about to bear for life
One certain evil, doubts 'twixt war and wife;
But, while the falt'ring damsel takes her oath,
Consents to wed, and so secures them both.
   Yet, why, you ask, these humble crimes relate,
Why make the poor as guilty as the great?
To show the great, those mightier sons of pride,
How near in vice the lowest are allied;   90
Such are their natures and their passions such,
But these disguise too little, those too much:
So shall the man of power and pleasure see
In his own slave as vile a wretch as he;
In his luxurious lord the servant find
His own low pleasures and degenerate mind:
And each in all the kindred vices trace
Of a poor, blind, bewilder'd, erring race;
Who, a short time in varied fortune past,
Die, and are equal in the dust at last.   100
   And you, ye poor, who still lament your fate,
Forbear to envy those you call the great;
And know, amid those blessings they possess,
They are, like you, the victims of distress;
While sloth with many a pang torments her slave,
Fear waits on guilt, and danger shakes the brave.
   Oh! if in life one noble chief appears,
Great in his name, while blooming in his years;
Born to enjoy whate'er delights mankind,
And yet to all you feel or fear resign'd;   110

THE VILLAGE

Who gave up joys and hopes, to you unknown,
For pains and dangers greater than your own :
If such there be, then let your murmurs cease,
Think, think of him, and take your lot in peace.
　　And such there was :—Oh ! grief, that checks our pride !
Weeping we say, there was—for Manners died :
Beloved of Heaven, these humble lines forgive,
That sing of Thee [(3)], and thus aspire to live.
　　As the tall oak, whose vigorous branches form
An ample shade and brave the wildest storm,　　　　120
High o'er the subject wood is seen to grow,
The guard and glory of the trees below ;
Till on its head the fiery bolt descends,
And o'er the plain the shatter'd trunk extends ;
Yet then it lies, all wond'rous as before,
And still the glory, though the guard no more :
　　So THOU, when every virtue, every grace,
Rose in thy soul, or shone within thy face ;
When, though the son of Granby, thou wert known
Less by thy father's glory than thy own ;　　　　130
When Honour loved and gave thee every charm,
Fire to thy eye and vigour to thy arm ;
Then from our lofty hopes and longing eyes,
Fate and thy virtues call'd thee to the skies ;
Yet still we wonder at thy tow'ring fame,
And, losing thee, still dwell upon thy name.
　　Oh ! ever honour'd, ever valued ! say,
What verse can praise thee, or what work repay ?
Yet verse (in all we can) thy worth repays,
Nor trusts the tardy zeal of future days ;—　　　　140
Honours for thee thy country shall prepare,
Thee in their hearts, the good, the brave shall bear ;
To deeds like thine shall noblest chiefs aspire,
The Muse shall mourn thee, and the world admire.
　　In future times, when, smit with Glory's charms,
The untried youth first quits a father's arms ;—
"Oh ! be like him," the weeping sire shall say ;
"Like Manners walk, who walk'd in Honour's way ;
"In danger foremost, yet in death sedate,
"Oh ! be like him in all things, but his fate ! "　　　　150

GEORGE CRABBE

If for that fate such public tears be shed,
That Victory seems to die now THOU art dead;
How shall a friend his nearer hope resign,
That friend a brother, and whose soul was thine?
By what bold lines shall we his grief express,
Or by what soothing numbers make it less?
'Tis not, I know, the chiming of a song,
Nor all the powers that to the Muse belong,
Words aptly cull'd and meanings well express'd,
Can calm the sorrows of a wounded breast;   160
But Virtue, soother of the fiercest pains,
Shall heal that bosom, Rutland, where she reigns.
Yet hard the task to heal the bleeding heart,
To bid the still-recurring thoughts depart,
Tame the fierce grief and stem the rising sigh,
And curb rebellious passion with reply;
Calmly to dwell on all that pleased before,
And yet to know that all shall please no more—
Oh! glorious labour of the soul, to save
Her captive powers, and bravely mourn the brave.   170
To such these thoughts will lasting comfort give—
Life is not measured by the time we live:
'Tis not an even course of threescore years,
A life of narrow views and paltry fears,
Gray hairs and wrinkles and the cares they bring,
That take from death the terrors or the sting;
But 'tis the gen'rous spirit, mounting high
Above the world, that native of the sky;
The noble spirit, that, in dangers brave,
Calmly looks on, or looks beyond the grave:—   180
Such Manners was, so he resign'd his breath,
If in a glorious, then a timely death.
Cease then that grief, and let those tears subside;
If Passion rule us, be that passion pride;
If Reason, Reason bids us strive to raise
Our fallen hearts, and be like him we praise;
Or, if Affection still the soul subdue,
Bring all his virtues, all his worth in view,
And let Affection find its comfort too:
For how can Grief so deeply wound the heart,   190

134

THE VILLAGE

When Admiration claims so large a part?
  Grief is a foe; expel him, then, thy soul;
Let nobler thoughts the nearer views control!
Oh! make the age to come thy better care;
See other Rutlands, other Granbys there!
And, as thy thoughts through streaming ages glide,
See other heroes die as Manners died:
And, from their fate, thy race shall nobler grow,
As trees shoot upwards that are pruned below;
Or as old Thames, borne down with decent pride,   200
Sees his young streams run warbling at his side;
Though some, by art cut off, no longer run,
And some are lost beneath the summer's sun—
Yet the pure stream moves on, and, as it moves,
Its power increases and its use improves;
While plenty round its spacious waves bestow,
Still it flows on, and shall for ever flow.

GEORGE CRABBE

NOTES TO THE VILLAGE.

Note 1, page 125, lines 198 and 199.

And, when his age attempts its task in vain,
With ruthless taunts, of lazy poor complain.

A pauper who, being nearly past his labour, is employed by different masters for a length of time, proportioned to their occupations.

Note 2, page 128, lines 345 and 346.

And, waiting long, the crowd retire distress'd
To think a poor man's bones should lie unbless'd.

Some apology is due for the insertion of a circumstance by no means common: that it has been a subject for complaint in any place is a sufficient reason for its being reckoned among the evils which may happen to the poor, and which must happen to them exclusively; nevertheless, it is just to remark, that such neglect is very rare in any part of the kingdom, and in many parts is totally unknown.

Note 3, page 133, lines 117 and 118.

Beloved of Heaven, these humble lines forgive,
That sing of Thee, and thus aspire to live.

Lord Robert Manners, the youngest son of the Marquis of Granby and the Lady Frances Seymour, daughter of Charles Duke of Somerset, was born the 5th of February, 1758; and was placed with his brother, the late Duke of Rutland, at Eton school, where he acquired, and ever after retained, a considerable knowledge of the classical authors.

Lord Robert, after going through the duties of his profession on board different ships, was made captain of the Resolution, and commanded her in nine different actions, besides the last memorable one on the 2nd of April, 1782, when, in breaking the French line of battle, he received the wounds which terminated his life, in the twenty-fourth year of his age.—*See the Annual Register, printed for Mr. Dodsley.*

THE NEWSPAPER.

E quibus, hi vacuas implent sermonibus aures,
Hi narrata ferunt alio : Mensuraque ficti
Crescit, et auditis aliquid novus adjicit auctor:
Illic Credulitas, illic temerarius Error,
Vanaque Lætitia est, consternatique Timores,
Seditioque recens, dubioque auctore Susurri.

Ovid. Metamorph. lib. xii.

GEORGE CRABBE

TO THE RIGHT HONOURABLE

EDWARD LORD THURLOW,

LORD HIGH CHANCELLOR OF GREAT BRITAIN; ONE OF HIS MAJESTY'S MOST HONOURABLE PRIVY COUNCIL, ETC. ETC.

My Lord,

My obligations to your Lordship, great as they are, have not induced me to prefix your name to the following Poem ; nor is it your Lordship's station, exalted as that is, which prevailed upon me to solicit the honour of your protection for it. But, when I considered your Lordship's great abilities and good taste, so well known and so universally acknowledged, I became anxious for the privilege with which you have indulged me ; well knowing that the Public would not be easily persuaded to disregard a performance, marked, in any degree, with your Lordship's approbation.

It is, my Lord, the province of superior rank, in general, to bestow this kind of patronage ; but superior talents only can render it valuable. Of the value of your Lordship's I am fully sensible ; and, while I make my acknowledgments for that, and for many other favours, I cannot suppress the pride I have in thus publishing my gratitude, and declaring how much I have the honour to be,

My Lord,

Your Lordship's most obedient,

most obliged,

and devoted servant,

GEORGE CRABBE.

Belvoir Castle,
February 20th, 1785.

THE NEWSPAPER

TO THE READER.

THE Poem which I now offer to the Public, is, I believe, the only one written on the subject; at least, it is the only one which I have any knowledge of; and, fearing there may not be found in it many things to engage the Reader's attention, I am willing to take the strongest hold I can upon him, by offering something which has the claim of novelty.

When the subject first occurred to me, I meant, in a few lines only, to give some description of that variety of dissociating articles which are huddled together in our Daily Papers. As the thought dwelt upon me, I conceived this might be done methodically, and with some connection of parts, by taking a larger scope; which notwithstanding I have done, I must still apologize for a want of union and coherence in my Poem. Subjects like this will not easily admit of them : we cannot slide from theme to theme in an easy and graceful succession; but, on quitting one thought, there will be an unavoidable hiatus, and in general an awkward transition into that which follows.

That, in writing upon the subject of our Newspapers, I have avoided every thing which might appear like the opinion of a party, is to be accounted for from the knowledge I have gained from them; since, the more of these Instructors a man reads, the less he will infallibly understand; nor would it have been very consistent in me, at the same time to censure their temerity and ignorance, and to adopt their rage.

GEORGE CRABBE

I should have been glad to have made some discrimination in my remarks on these productions. There is, indeed, some difference ; and I have observed, that one editor will sometimes convey his abuse with more decency, and colour his falsehood with more appearance of probability, than another : but till I see that paper, wherein no great character is wantonly abused, nor groundless insinuation wilfully disseminated, I shall not make any distinction in my remarks upon them.

It must, however, be confessed, that these things have their use, and are, besides, vehicles of much amusement ; but this does not outweigh the evil they do to society, and the irreparable injury they bring upon the characters of individuals. In the following Work I have given those good properties their due weight : they have changed indignation into mirth, and turned, what would otherwise have been abhorrence, into derision.

THE NEWSPAPER.

This not a Time favourable to poetical Composition; and why—
Newspapers Enemies to Literature, and their general Influence—
Their Numbers—The Sunday Monitor—Their general Character—
Their Effect upon Individuals—upon Society—in the Country—The
Village Freeholder—What Kind of Composition a Newspaper is;
and the Amusement it affords—Of what Parts it is chiefly composed
—Articles of Intelligence: Advertisements: The Stage: Quacks:
Puffing—The Correspondents to a Newspaper; political and poetical
—Advice to the latter—Conclusion.

GEORGE CRABBE

THE NEWSPAPER.

A TIME like this, a busy, bustling time,
　　Suits ill with writers, very ill with rhyme:
Unheard we sing, when party-rage runs strong,
And mightier madness checks the flowing song:
Or, should we force the peaceful Muse to wield
Her feeble arms amid the furious field,
Where party-pens a wordy war maintain,
Poor is her anger, and her friendship vain;
And oft the foes who feel her sting, combine,
Till serious vengeance pays an idle line;　　　　10
For party-poets are like wasps, who dart
Death to themselves, and to their foes but smart.
　　Hard then our fate: if general themes we choose,
Neglect awaits the song, and chills the Muse;
Or, should we sing the subject of the day,
To-morrow's wonder puffs our praise away.
More bless'd the bards of that poetic time,
When all found readers who could find a rhyme;
Green grew the bays on every teeming head,
And Cibber was enthroned, and Settle read.　　　20
Sing, drooping Muse, the cause of thy decline;
Why reign no more the once-triumphant Nine?
Alas! new charms the wavering many gain,
And rival sheets the reader's eye detain;
A daily swarm, that banish every Muse,
Come flying forth, and mortals call them News:
For these unread the noblest volumes lie;
For these in sheets unsoil'd the Muses die;
Unbought, unbless'd, the virgin copies wait
In vain for fame, and sink, unseen, to fate.　　　30
　　Since, then, the town forsakes us for our foes,

THE NEWSPAPER

The smoothest numbers for the harshest prose;
Let us, with generous scorn, the taste deride,
And sing our rivals with a rival's pride.
　　Ye gentle poets, who so oft complain
That foul neglect is all your labours gain;
That pity only checks your growing spite
To erring man, and prompts you still to write;
That your choice works on humble stalls are laid,
Or vainly grace the windows of the trade;　　　　40
Be ye my friends, if friendship e'er can warm
Those rival bosoms whom the Muses charm:
Think of the common cause wherein we go,
Like gallant Greeks against the Trojan foe;
Nor let one peevish chief his leader blame,
Till, crown'd with conquest, we regain our fame;
And let us join our forces to subdue
This bold assuming but successful crew.

　　I sing of NEWS, and all those vapid sheets
The rattling hawker vends through gaping streets;　　50
Whate'er their name, whate'er the time they fly,
Damp from the press, to charm the reader's eye:
For, soon as morning dawns with roseate hue,
The Herald of the morn arises too;
Post after Post succeeds, and, all day long,
Gazettes and Ledgers swarm, a noisy throng.
When evening comes, she comes with all her train
Of Ledgers, Chronicles, and Posts again—
Like bats, appearing, when the sun goes down,
From holes obscure and corners of the town.　　　　60
Of all these triflers, all like these, I write;
Oh! like my subject could my song delight,
The crowd at Lloyd's one poet's name should raise,
And all the Alley echo to his praise.
　　In shoals the hours their constant numbers bring,
Like insects waking to th' advancing spring;
Which take their rise from grubs obscene that lie
In shallow pools, or thence ascend the sky:
Such are these base ephemeras, so born
To die before the next revolving morn.　　　　70

GEORGE CRABBE

Yet thus they differ: insect-tribes are lost
In the first visit of a winter's frost;
While these remain, a base but constant breed,
Whose swarming sons their short-lived sires succeed;
No changing season makes their number less,
Nor Sunday shines a sabbath on the press!
Then, lo! the sainted Monitor is born,
Whose pious face some sacred texts adorn:
As artful sinners cloak the secret sin,
To veil with seeming grace the guile within;   80
So Moral Essays on his front appear,
But all is carnal business in the rear;
The fresh-coin'd lie, the secret whisper'd last,
And all the gleanings of the six days past.

With these retired, through half the Sabbath-day,
The London-lounger yawns his hours away:
Not so, my little flock! your preacher fly,
Nor waste the time no worldly wealth can buy;
But let the decent maid and sober clown
Pray for these idlers of the sinful town: 90
This day, at least, on nobler themes bestow,
Nor give to Woodfall, or the world below.

But, Sunday pass'd, what numbers flourish then,
What wond'rous labours of the press and pen!
Diurnal most, some thrice each week affords,
Some only once—O avarice of words!
When thousand starving minds such manna seek[1],
To drop the precious food but once a week.
Endless it were to sing the powers of all,
Their names, their numbers; how they rise and fall: 100
Like baneful herbs the gazer's eye they seize,
Rush to the head, and poison where they please:
Like idle flies, a busy, buzzing train,
They drop their maggots in the trifler's brain;
That genial soil receives the fruitful store,
And there they grow, and breed a thousand more.

Now be their arts display'd, how first they choose
A cause and party, as the bard his muse;

144

Inspired by these, with clamorous zeal they cry,
And through the town their dreams and omens fly:
So the Sibylline leaves were blown about[2],
Disjointed scraps of fate involved in doubt;
So idle dreams, the journals of the night,
Are right and wrong by turns, and mingle wrong with right.
Some champions for the rights that prop the crown,
Some sturdy patriots, sworn to pull them down;
Some neutral powers, with secret forces fraught,
Wishing for war, but willing to be bought:
While some to every side and party go,
Shift every friend, and join with every foe;
Like sturdy rogues in privateers, they strike
This side and that, the foes of both alike;
A traitor-crew, who thrive in troubled times,
Fear'd for their force, and courted for their crimes.
Chief to the prosperous side the numbers sail,
Fickle and false, they veer with every gale;
As birds that migrate from a freezing shore,
In search of warmer climes, come skimming o'er,
Some bold adventurers first prepare to try
The doubtful sunshine of the distant sky;
But soon the growing Summer's certain sun
Wins more and more, till all at last are won:
So, on the early prospect of disgrace,
Fly in vast troops this apprehensive race;
Instinctive tribes! their failing food they dread,
And buy, with timely change, their future bread.

Such are our guides; how many a peaceful head,
Born to be still, have they to wrangling led!
How many an honest zealot stol'n from trade,
And factious tools of pious pastors made!
With clews like these they tread the maze of state,
These oracles explore, to learn our fate;
Pleased with the guides who can so well deceive,
Who cannot lie so fast as they believe.

Oft lend I, loth, to some sage friend an ear,
(For we who will not speak are doom'd to hear);

GEORGE CRABBE

While he, bewilder'd, tells his anxious thought,
Infectious fear from tainted scribblers caught,
Or idiot hope ; for each his mind assails,
As Lloyd's court-light or Stockdale's gloom prevails.　　150
Yet stand I patient while but one declaims,
Or gives dull comments on the speech he maims :
But oh ! ye Muses, keep your votary's feet
From tavern-haunts where politicians meet ;
Where rector, doctor, and attorney pause,
First on each parish, then each public cause :
[Indicted] roads and rates that still increase ;
The murmuring poor, who will not fast in peace ;
Election-zeal and friendship, since declined ;
A tax commuted, or a tithe in kind ;　　160
The Dutch and Germans kindling into strife ;
Dull port and poachers vile, the serious ills of life.
　　Here comes the neighbouring justice, pleased to guide
His little club, and in the chair preside.
In private business his commands prevail,
On public themes his reasoning turns the scale ;
Assenting silence soothes his happy ear,
And, in or out, his party triumphs here.

　　Nor here th' infectious rage for party stops,
But flits along from palaces to shops ;　　170
Our weekly journals o'er the land abound,
And spread their plague and influenzas round ;
The village, too, the peaceful, pleasant plain,
Breeds the Whig-farmer and the Tory-swain ;
Brookes' and St. Alban's boasts not, but, instead,
Stares the Red Ram, and swings the Rodney's Head :—
Hither, with all a patriot's care, comes he
Who owns the little hut that makes him free ;
Whose yearly forty shillings buy the smile
Of mightier men, and never waste the while ;　　180
Who feels his freehold's worth, and looks elate,
A little prop and pillar of the state.
　　Here he delights the weekly news to con,
And mingle comments as he blunders on ;
To swallow all their varying authors teach,

146

THE NEWSPAPER

To spell a title, and confound a speech :
Till with a muddled mind he quits the news,
And claims his nation's licence to abuse ;
Then joins the cry, " That all the courtly race
" Are venal candidates for power and place " ;   190
Yet feels some joy, amid the general vice,
That his own vote will bring its wonted price.
  These are the ills the teeming press supplies,
The pois'nous springs from learning's fountain rise ;
Not there the wise alone their entrance find,
Imparting useful light to mortals blind ;
But, blind themselves, these erring guides hold out
Alluring lights, to lead us far about ;
Screen'd by such means, here Scandal whets her quill,
Here Slander shoots unseen, whene'er she will ;   200
Here Fraud and Falsehood labour to deceive,
And Folly aids them both, impatient to believe.

  Such, sons of Britain ! are the guides ye trust ;
So wise their counsel, their reports so just :—
Yet, though we cannot call their morals pure,
Their judgment nice, or their decisions sure ;
Merit they have, to mightier works unknown,
A style, a manner, and a fate their own.
  We, who for longer fame with labour strive,
Are pain'd to keep our sickly works alive ;   210
Studious we toil, with patient care refine,
Nor let our love protect one languid line.
Severe ourselves, at last our works appear,
When, ah ! we find our readers more severe ;
For after all our care and pains, how few
Acquire applause, or keep it if they do !—
  Not so these sheets, ordain'd to happier fate,
Praised through their day, and but that day their date ;
Their careless authors only strive to join
As many words as make an even line [3] ;   220
As many lines as fill a row complete ;
As many rows as furnish up a sheet :
From side to side, with ready types they run,
The measure's ended, and the work is done ;

GEORGE CRABBE

Oh, born with ease, how envied and how blest!
Your fate to-day and your to-morrow's rest.
To you all readers turn, and they can look
Pleased on a paper, who abhor a book;
Those, who ne'er deign'd their Bible to peruse,
Would think it hard to be denied their news;   230
Sinners and saints, the wisest with the weak,
Here mingle tastes, and one amusement seek;
This, like the public inn, provides a treat,
Where each promiscuous guest sits down to eat;
And such this mental food, as we may call
Something to all men, and to some men all.

    Next, in what rare production shall we trace
Such various subjects in so small a space?
As the first ship upon the waters bore
Incongruous kinds who never met before;   240
Or as some curious virtuoso joins,
In one small room, moths, minerals, and coins,
Birds, beasts, and fishes; nor refuses place
To serpents, toads, and all the reptile race:
So here, compress'd within a single sheet,
Great things and small, the mean and mighty meet:
'Tis this which makes all Europe's business known,
Yet here a private man may place his own;
And, where he reads of Lords and Commons, he
May tell their honours that he sells rappee.   250
    Add next th' amusement which the motley page
Affords to either sex and every age:
Lo! where it comes before the cheerful fire—
Damps from the press in smoky curls aspire
(As from the earth the sun exhales the dew),
Ere we can read the wonders that ensue:
Then, eager, every eye surveys the part,
That brings its favourite subject to the heart;
Grave politicians look for facts alone,
And gravely add conjectures of their own: 260
The sprightly nymph, who never broke her rest
For tottering crowns, or mighty lands oppress'd,
Finds broils and battles, but neglects them all

148

THE NEWSPAPER

For songs and suits, a birth-day, or a ball ;
The keen warm man o'erlooks each idle tale
For " Money's wanted," and " Estates on Sale " ;
While some with equal minds to all attend,
Pleased with each part, and grieved to find an end.

So charm the News ; but we, who, far from town,
Wait till the postman brings the packet down,   270
Once in the week a vacant day behold,
And stay for tidings, till they're three days old :
That day arrives ; no welcome post appears,
But the dull morn a sullen aspect wears ;
We meet, but ah ! without our wonted smile,
To talk of headaches, and complain of bile ;
Sullen, we ponder o'er a dull repast,
Nor feast the body while the mind must fast.
A master-passion is the love of news,
Not music so commands, nor so the Muse :   280
Give poets claret, they grow idle soon ;
Feed the musician, and he's out of tune ;
But the sick mind, of this disease possess'd,
Flies from all cure, and sickens when at rest.

Now sing, my Muse, what various parts compose
These rival sheets of politics and prose.
First, from each brother's hoard a part they draw,
A mutual theft that never fear'd a law ;
Whate'er they gain, to each man's portion fall,
And read it once, you read it through them all :   290
For this their runners ramble day and night,
To drag each lurking deed to open light ;
For daily bread the dirty trade they ply,
Coin their fresh tales, and live upon the lie.
Like bees for honey, forth for news they spring—
Industrious creatures ! ever on the wing ;
Home to their several cells they bear the store,
Cull'd of all kinds, then roam abroad for more.

No anxious virgin flies to " fair Tweed-side " ;
No injured husband mourns his faithless bride ;   300

GEORGE CRABBE

No duel dooms the fiery youth to bleed,
But through the town transpires each vent'rous deed.

Should some fair frail-one drive her prancing pair,
Where rival peers contend to please the fair;
When, with new force, she aids her conquering eyes,
And beauty decks with all that beauty buys—
Quickly we learn whose heart her influence feels,
Whose acres melt before her glowing wheels.
To these a thousand idle themes succeed,
Deeds of all kinds, and comments to each deed.   310
Here stocks, the state-barometers, we view,
That rise or fall, by causes known to few;
Promotion's ladder who goes up or down;
Who wed, or who seduced, amuse the town;
What new-born heir has made his father blest;
What heir exults, his father now at rest;
That ample list the Tyburn-herald gives,
And each known knave, who still for Tyburn lives.

So grows the work, and now the printer tries
His powers no more, but leans on his allies.   320

When, lo! the advertising tribe succeed,
Pay to be read, yet find but few will read;
And chief th' illustrious race, whose drops and pills
Have patent powers to vanquish human ills:
These, with their cures, a constant aid remain,
To bless the pale composer's fertile brain;
Fertile it is, but still the noblest soil
Requires some pause, some intervals from toil;
And they at least a certain ease obtain
From Katterfelto's skill, and Graham's glowing strain.   330

I too must aid, and pay to see my name
Hung in these dirty avenues to fame;
Nor pay in vain, if aught the Muse has seen
And sung, could make those avenues more clean;
Could stop one slander ere it found its way,
And gave to public scorn its helpless prey.
By the same aid, the Stage invites her friends,

THE NEWSPAPER

And kindly tells the banquet she intends;
Thither from real life the many run,
With Siddons weep, or laugh with Abingdon; 340
Pleased, in fictitious joy or grief, to see
The mimic passion with their own agree;
To steal a few enchanted hours away
From care, and drop the curtain on the day.
 But who can steal from self that wretched wight,
Whose darling work is tried, some fatal night?
Most wretched man! when, bane to every bliss,
He hears the serpent-critic's rising hiss;
Then groans succeed; not traitors on the wheel
Can feel like him, or have such pangs to feel. 350
Nor end they here: next day he reads his fall
In every paper; critics are they all;
He sees his branded name, with wild affright,
And hears again the cat-calls of the night.

 Such help the STAGE affords; a larger space
Is fill'd by PUFFS and all the puffing race.
Physic had once alone the lofty style,
The well-known boast, that ceased to raise a smile;
Now all the province of that tribe invade,
And we abound in quacks of every trade. 360

 The simple barber, once an honest name—
Cervantes founded, Fielding raised his fame—
Barber no more, a gay perfumer comes,
On whose soft cheek his own cosmetic blooms;
Here he appears, each simple mind to move,
And advertises beauty, grace, and love.
—"Come, faded belles, who would your youth renew,
"And learn the wonders of Olympian dew;
"Restore the roses that begin to faint,
"Nor think celestial washes vulgar paint; 370
"Your former features, airs, and arts assume,
"Circassian virtues, with Circassian bloom.
"—Come, batter'd beaux, whose locks are turn'd to grey,
"And crop Discretion's lying badge away;
"Read where they vend these smart engaging things,

GEORGE CRABBE

"These flaxen frontlets with elastic springs;
"No female eye the fair deception sees,
"Not Nature's self so natural as these."
Such are their arts, but not confined to them,
The Muse impartial must her sons condemn: 380
For they, degenerate! join the venal throng,
And puff a lazy Pegasus along:
More guilty these, by Nature less design'd
For little arts that suit the vulgar-kind;
That barbers' boys, who would to trade advance,
Wish us to call them, smart Friseurs from France;
That he who builds a chop-house, on his door
Paints "The true old original Blue Boar!"
These are the arts by which a thousand live,
Where Truth may smile, and Justice may forgive;   390
But when, amid this rabble-rout, we find
A puffing poet to his honour blind;
Who [slily] drops quotations all about,
Packet or Post, and points their merit out;
Who advertises what reviewers say,
With sham editions every second day;
Who dares not trust his praises out of sight,
But hurries into fame with all his might;
Although the verse some transient praise obtains,
Contempt is all the anxious poet gains.   400
Now, puffs exhausted, advertisements past,
Their correspondents stand exposed at last;
These are a numerous tribe, to fame unknown,
Who for the public good forego their own;
Who, volunteers, in paper-war engage,
With double portion of their party's rage:
Such are the Bruti, Decii, who appear
Wooing the printer for admission here;
Whose generous souls can condescend to pray
For leave to throw their precious time away.   410
Oh! cruel Woodfall! when a patriot draws
His grey-goose quill in his dear country's cause,
To vex and maul a ministerial race,
Can thy stern soul refuse the champion place?
Alas! thou know'st not with what anxious heart

152

THE NEWSPAPER

He longs his best-loved labours to impart ;
How he has sent them to thy brethren round,
And still the same unkind reception found :
At length indignant will he damn the state,
Turn to his trade, and leave us to our fate.   420

These Roman souls, like Rome's great sons, are known
To live in cells on labours of their own.
Thus Milo, could we see the noble chief,
Feeds, for his country's good, on legs of beef ;
Camillus copies deeds for sordid pay,
Yet fights the public battles twice a day ;
E'en now the godlike Brutus views his score
Scroll'd on the bar-board, swinging with the door ;
Where, tippling punch, grave Cato's self you'll see,
And *Amor Patriæ* vending smuggled tea.   430

Last in these ranks and least, their art's disgrace,
Neglected stand the Muse's meanest race :
Scribblers who court contempt, whose verse the eye
Disdainful views, and glances swiftly by :
This Poet's Corner is the place they choose,
A fatal nursery for an infant Muse ;
Unlike that corner where true poets lie,
These cannot live, and they shall never die ;
Hapless the lad whose mind such dreams invade,
And win to verse the talents due to trade.   440

Curb, then, O youth ! these raptures as they rise ;
Keep down the evil spirit and be wise ;
Follow your calling, think the Muses foes,
Nor lean upon the pestle and compose.

I know your day-dreams, and I know the snare
Hid in your flow'ry path, and cry "Beware."
Thoughtless of ill, and to the future blind,
A sudden couplet rushes on your mind ;
Here you may nameless print your idle rhymes,
And read your first-born work a thousand times ;   450
Th' infection spreads, your couplet grows apace—

Stanzas to Delia's dog or Celia's face;
You take a name : Philander's odes are seen,
Printed, and praised, in every magazine;
Diarian sages greet their brother sage,
And your dark pages please th' enlighten'd age.—
Alas! what years you thus consume in vain,
Ruled by this wretched bias of the brain!

   Go! to your desks and counters all return;
Your sonnets scatter, your acrostics burn;   460
Trade, and be rich; or, should your careful sires
Bequeath you wealth, indulge the nobler fires;
Should love of fame your youthful heart betray,
Pursue fair fame, but in a glorious way,
Nor in the idle scenes of Fancy's painting stray.   [ʃ]

   Of all the good that mortal men pursue,
The Muse has least to give, and gives to few;
Like some coquettish fair, she leads us on,
With smiles and hopes, till youth and peace are gone;
Then, wed for life, the restless wrangling pair   470
Forget how constant one, and one how fair:
Meanwhile, Ambition, like a blooming bride,
Brings power and wealth to grace her lover's side;
And, though she smiles not with such flattering charms,
The brave will sooner win her to their arms.
   Then wed to her, if Virtue tie the bands,
Go spread your country's fame in hostile lands;
Her court, her senate, or her arms adorn,
And let her foes lament that you were born:
Or weigh her laws, their ancient rights defend,   480
Though hosts oppose, be theirs and Reason's friend;
Arm'd with strong powers, in their defence engage,
And rise the Thurlow of the future age!

THE NEWSPAPER

NOTES TO THE NEWSPAPER.

Note 1, page 144, line 97.

When thousand starving minds such manna seek.

The Manna of the Day. *Green's Spleen.*

Note 2, page 145, line 111.

So the Sibylline leaves were blown about.

. . . . in foliis descripsit carmina Virgo ;—
. . . . et [teneras] turbavit janua frondes.
$\qquad\qquad$ *Virg. Æneid.* lib. iii. [vv. 445, 447.]

Note 3, page 147, lines 220—2.

As many words as make an even line;
As many lines as fill a row complete;
As many rows as furnish up a sheet.

How many hours bring about the day;
How many days will furnish up the year;
How many years a mortal man may live. &c.
$\qquad$ *Shakspeare's Henry VI.* [Part III. Act II. Sc. 5.]

THE PARISH REGISTER.

IN THREE PARTS.

INTRODUCTION.

The Village Register considered, as containing principally the Annals of the Poor—State of the Peasantry as meliorated by Frugality and Industry—The Cottage of an industrious Peasant; its Ornaments—Prints and Books—The Garden; its Satisfactions—The State of the Poor, when improvident and vicious—The Row or Street, and its Inhabitants—The Dwelling of one of these—A Public House—Garden and its Appendages—Gamesters; rustic Sharpers, &c.—Conclusion of the Introductory Part.

PART I.

BAPTISMS.

The Child of the Miller's Daughter, and Relation of her Misfortune—A frugal Couple: their Kind of Frugality—Plea of the Mother of a natural Child: her Churching—Large Family of Gerard Ablett: his Apprehensions: Comparison between his State and that of the wealthy Farmer his Master: his Consolation—An old Man's Anxiety for an Heir: the Jealousy of another on having many—Characters of the Grocer Dawkins and his Friend: their different Kinds of Disappointment—Three Infants named—An Orphan Girl and Village Schoolmistress—Gardener's Child: Pedantry and Conceit of the Father: his Botanical Discourse: Method of fixing the Embryo-fruit of Cucumbers—Absurd Effects of Rustic Vanity: observed in the Names of their Children—Relation of the Vestry Debate on a Foundling: Sir Richard Monday—Children of various Inhabitants—The poor Farmer—Children of a Profligate: his Character and Fate —Conclusion.

GEORGE CRABBE

THE PARISH REGISTER.

PART I.

BAPTISMS.

Tum porro puer (ut sævis projeƈtus ab undis
Navita) nudus humi jacet, infans, indigus omni
Vitali auxilio——
Vagituque locum lugubri complet, ut æquum est,
Cui tantum in vitâ [restet] transire malorum.
Lucret. de Nat. Rerum, lib. v. [vv. 223—5, 227—8.]

THE year revolves, and I again explore
    The simple annals of my parish poor :
What infant-members in my flock appear ;
What pairs I bless'd in the departed year ;
And who, of old or young, or nymphs or swains,
Are lost to life, its pleasures and its pains.
    No Muse I ask, before my view to bring
The humble actions of the swains I sing—
How pass'd the youthful, how the old their days ;
Who sank in sloth, and who aspired to praise ;   10
Their tempers, manners, morals, customs, arts ;
What parts they had, and how they 'mploy'd their parts ;
By what elated, soothed, seduced, depress'd,
Full well I know—these records give the rest.
    Is there a place, save one the poet sees,
A land of love, of liberty and ease ;
Where labour wearies not, nor cares suppress
Th' eternal flow of rustic happiness ;
Where no proud mansion frowns in awful state,
Or keeps the sunshine from the cottage-gate ;   20

158

THE PARISH REGISTER

Where young and old, intent on pleasure, throng,
And half man's life is holiday and song?
Vain search for scenes like these! no view appears,
By sighs unruffled or unstain'd by tears;
Since vice the world subdued and waters drown'd,
Auburn and Eden can no more be found.
　　Hence good and evil mix'd, but man has skill
And power to part them, when he feels the will!
Toil, care, and patience bless th' abstemious few,
Fear, shame, and want the thoughtless herd pursue.　　30
　　Behold the cot! where thrives th' industrious swain,
Source of his pride, his pleasure, and his gain;
Screen'd from the winter's wind, the sun's last ray
Smiles on the window and prolongs the day;
Projecting thatch the woodbine's branches stop,
And turn their blossoms to the casement's top:
All need requires is in that cot contain'd,
And much that taste, untaught and unrestrain'd,
Surveys delighted; there she loves to trace,
In one gay picture, all the royal race;　　40
Around the walls are heroes, lovers, kings;
The print that shows them and the verse that sings.
　　Here the last Lewis on his throne is seen,
And there he stands imprison'd, and his queen;
To these the mother takes her child, and shows
What grateful duty to his God he owes;
Who gives to him a happy home, where he
Lives and enjoys his freedom with the free;
When kings and queens, dethroned, insulted, tried,
Are all these blessings of the poor denied.　　50
　　There is King Charles, and all his Golden Rules,
Who proved Misfortune's was the best of schools:
And there his son, who, tried by years of pain,
Proved that misfortunes may be sent in vain.
　　The magic-mill that grinds the gran'nams young,
Close at the side of kind Godiva hung;
She, of her favourite place the pride and joy,
Of charms at once most lavish and most coy,
By wanton act the purest fame could raise,
And give the boldest deed the chastest praise.　　60

GEORGE CRABBE

There stands the stoutest Ox in England fed ;
There fights the boldest Jew, Whitechapel-bred ;
And here Saint Monday's worthy votaries live
In all the joys that ale and skittles give.
Now, lo ! in Egypt's coast that hostile fleet,
By nations dreaded and by Nelson beat ;
And here shall soon another triumph come,
A deed of glory in a day of gloom—
Distressing glory ! grievous boon of fate !
The proudest conquest, at the dearest rate.   70
On shelf of deal, beside the cuckoo-clock,
Of cottage-reading rests the chosen stock ;
Learning we lack, not books, but have a kind
For all our wants, a meat for every mind :
The tale for wonder and the joke for whim,
The half-sung sermon and the half-groan'd hymn.
No need of classing ; each within its place,
The feeling finger in the dark can trace ;
"First from the corner, farthest from the wall " :
Such all the rules, and they suffice for all.   80
There pious works for Sunday's use are found,
Companions for that Bible newly bound :
That Bible, bought by sixpence weekly saved,
Has choicest prints by famous hands engraved ;
Has choicest notes by many a famous head,
Such as to doubt have rustic readers led ;
Have made them stop to reason, *why?* and *how?*
And, where they once agreed, to cavil now.
Oh ! rather give me commentators plain,
Who with no deep researches vex the brain ;   90
Who from the dark and doubtful love to run,
And hold their glimmering tapers to the sun ;
Who simple truth with nine-fold reasons back,
And guard the point no enemies attack.
Bunyan's famed Pilgrim rests that shelf upon ;
A genius rare but rude was honest John :
Not one who, early by the Muse beguiled,
Drank from her well the waters undefiled ;
Not one who slowly gain'd the hill sublime,
Then often sipp'd and little at a time ;   100

160

THE PARISH REGISTER

But one who dabbled in the sacred springs,
And drank them muddy, mix'd with baser things.
Here, to interpret dreams we read the rules—
Science our own, and never taught in schools;
In moles and specks we Fortune's gifts discern,
And Fate's fix'd will from Nature's wanderings learn.
Of Hermit Quarle we read, in island rare,
Far from mankind and seeming far from care;
Safe from all want, and sound in every limb;
Yes! there was he, and there was care with him.   110
Unbound and heap'd, these valued works beside,
Lay humbler works the pedler's pack supplied;
Yet these, long since, have all acquired a name:
The Wandering Jew has found his way to fame;
And fame, denied to many a labour'd song,
Crowns Thumb the great, and Hickerthrift the strong.
There too is he, by wizard-power upheld,
Jack, by whose arm the giant-brood were quell'd:
His shoes of swiftness on his feet he placed;
His coat of darkness on his loins he braced;   120
His sword of sharpness in his hand he took,
And off the heads of doughty giants stroke:
Their glaring eyes beheld no mortal near;
No sound of feet alarm'd the drowsy ear;
No English blood their pagan sense could smell,
But heads dropp'd headlong, wondering why they fell.
These are the peasant's joy, when, placed at ease,
Half his delighted offspring mount his knees.
To every cot the lord's indulgent mind
Has a small space for garden-ground assign'd;   130
Here—till return of morn dismiss'd the farm—
The careful peasant plies the sinewy arm,
Warm'd as he works, and casts his look around
On every foot of that improving ground:
It is his own he sees; his master's eye
Peers not about, some secret fault to spy;
Nor voice severe is there, nor censure known;—
Hope, profit, pleasure,—they are all his own.
Here grow the humble [chives], and, hard by them,
The leek with crown globose and reedy stem;   140

Crabbe   L   161

High climb his pulse in many an even row,
Deep strike the ponderous roots in soil below;
And herbs of potent smell and pungent taste
Give a warm relish to the night's repast;
Apples and cherries grafted by his hand,
And cluster'd nuts for neighbouring market stand.
　　Nor thus concludes his labour : near the cot,
The reed-fence rises round some fav'rite spot;
Where rich carnations, pinks with purple eyes,
Proud hyacinths, the least some florist's prize,　　150
Tulips tall-stemm'd and pounced auriculas rise.
　　Here on a Sunday-eve, when service ends,
Meet and rejoice a family of friends;
All speak aloud, are happy and are free,
And glad they seem, and gaily they agree.
　　What, though fastidious ears may shun the speech,
Where all are talkers and where none can teach;
Where still the welcome and the words are old,
And the same stories are for ever told—
Yet theirs is joy that, bursting from the heart,　　160
Prompts the glad tongue these nothings to impart;
That forms these tones of gladness we despise,
That lifts their steps, that sparkles in their eyes;
That talks or laughs or runs or shouts or plays,
And speaks in all their looks and all their ways.
　　Fair scenes of peace! ye might detain us long;
But vice and misery now demand the song,
And turn our view from dwellings simply neat,
To this infected row we term our street.
　　Here, in cabal, a disputatious crew　　170
Each evening meet: the sot, the cheat, the shrew;
Riots are nightly heard—the curse, the cries
Of beaten wife, perverse in her replies;
While shrieking children hold each threat'ning hand,
And sometimes life, and sometimes food, demand:
Boys, in their first-stol'n rags, to swear begin,
And girls, who heed not dress, are skill'd in gin:
Snarers and smugglers here their gains divide;
Ensnaring females here their victims hide;
And here is one, the sibyl of the row,　　180

THE PARISH REGISTER

Who knows all secrets, or affects to know.
Seeking their fate, to her the simple run,
To her the guilty, theirs awhile to shun;
Mistress of worthless arts, depraved in will,
Her care unbless'd and unrepaid her skill,
Slave to the tribe, to whose command she stoops,
And poorer than the poorest maid she dupes.
  Between the road-way and the walls, offence
Invades all eyes and strikes on every sense:
There lie, obscene, at every open door,   190
Heaps from the hearth and sweepings from the floor;
And day by day the mingled masses grow,
As sinks are disembogued and kennels flow.
  There hungry dogs from hungry children steal;
There pigs and chickens quarrel for a meal;
There dropsied infants wail without redress,
And all is want and wo and wretchedness:
Yet, should these boys, with bodies bronzed and bare,
High-swoln and hard, outlive that lack of care,
Forced on some farm, the unexerted strength,   200
Though loth to action, is compell'd at length,
When warm'd by health, as serpents in the spring
Aside their slough of indolence they fling.
  Yet, ere they go, a greater evil comes—
See! crowded beds in those contiguous rooms;
Beds but ill parted by a paltry screen
Of paper'd lath or curtain dropp'd between;
Daughters and sons to yon compartments creep,
And parents here beside their children sleep.
Ye who have power, these thoughtless people part,   210
Nor let the ear be first to taint the heart!
  Come! search within, nor sight nor smell regard;
The true physician walks the foulest ward.
See! on the floor what frouzy patches rest!
What nauseous fragments on yon fractured chest!
What downy dust beneath yon window-seat!
And round these posts that serve this bed for feet;
This bed, where all those tatter'd garments lie,
Worn by each sex, and now perforce thrown by!
  See! as we gaze, an infant lifts its head,   220

Left by neglect and burrow'd in that bed;
The mother-gossip has the love suppress'd
An infant's cry once waken'd in her breast;
And daily prattles, as her round she takes,
(With strong resentment) of the want she makes.
   Whence all these woes?—From want of virtuous will,
Of honest shame, of time-improving skill;
From want of care t'employ the vacant hour,
And want of ev'ry kind but want of power.
   Here are no wheels for either wool or flax,   230
But packs of cards—made up of sundry packs;
Here is no clock, nor will they turn the glass,
And see how swift th'important moments pass;
Here are no books, but ballads on the wall
Are some abusive, and indecent all;
Pistols are here, unpair'd; with nets and hooks,
Of every kind, for rivers, ponds, and brooks;
An ample flask, that nightly rovers fill
With recent poison from the Dutchman's still;
A box of tools, with wires of various size,   240
Frocks, wigs, and hats, for night or day disguise,
And bludgeons stout to gain or guard a prize.   [ ]]
   To every house belongs a space of ground,
Of equal size, once fenced with paling round;
That paling now by slothful waste destroy'd,
Dead gorse and stumps of elder fill the void,
Save in the centre-spot, whose walls of clay
Hide sots and striplings at their drink or play.
Within, a board, beneath a tiled retreat,
Allures the bubble and maintains the cheat;   250
Where heavy ale in spots like varnish shows;
Where chalky tallies yet remain in rows;
Black pipes and broken jugs the seats defile,
The walls and windows, rhymes and reck'nings vile;
Prints of the meanest kind disgrace the door,
And cards, in curses torn, lie fragments on the floor.
   Here his poor bird th'inhuman cocker brings,
Arms his hard heel and clips his golden wings;
With spicy food th'impatient spirit feeds,
And shouts and curses as the battle bleeds.   260

THE PARISH REGISTER

Struck through the brain, deprived of both his eyes,
The vanquish'd bird must combat till he dies;
Must faintly peck at his victorious foe,
And reel and stagger at each feeble blow.
When fall'n, the savage grasps his dabbled plumes,
His blood-stain'd arms, for other deaths assumes;
And damns the craven-fowl, that lost his stake,
And only bled and perish'd for his sake.
   Such are our peasants, those to whom we yield
Praise with relief, the fathers of the field;   270
And these who take, from our reluctant hands,
What Burn advises or the Bench commands.
   Our farmers round, well pleased with constant gain,
Like other farmers, flourish and complain.—
These are our groups; our portraits next appear,
And close our exhibition for the year.

WITH evil omen we that year begin:
     A Child of Shame—stern Justice adds, of Sin—
Is first recorded; I would hide the deed,
But vain the wish; I sigh and I proceed: 280
And could I well th' instructive truth convey,
'Twould warn the giddy and awake the gay.
   Of all the nymphs who gave our village grace,
The Miller's daughter had the fairest face.
Proud was the Miller; money was his pride;
He rode to market, as our farmers ride;
And 'twas his boast, inspired by spirits, there,
His favourite Lucy should be rich as fair;
But she must meek and still obedient prove,
And not presume, without his leave, to love.   290
   A youthful Sailor heard him;—"Ha!" quoth he,
"This Miller's maiden is a prize for me;
"Her charms I love, his riches I desire,
"And all his threats but fan the kindling fire;
"My ebbing purse no more the foe shall fill,
"But Love's kind act and Lucy at the mill."

GEORGE CRABBE

Thus thought the youth, and soon the chase began,
Stretch'd all his sail, nor thought of pause or plan :
His trusty staff in his bold hand he took,
Like him and like his frigate, heart of oak ;   300
Fresh were his features, his attire was new ;
Clean was his linen, and his jacket blue :
Of finest jean, his trowsers, tight and trim,
Brush'd the large buckle at the silver rim.
    He soon arrived, he traced the village-green ;
There saw the maid, and was with pleasure seen ;
Then talk'd of love, till Lucy's yielding heart
Confess'd 'twas painful, though 'twas right, to part.
    "For ah ! my father has a haughty soul ;
"Whom best he loves, he loves but to control ;   310
"Me to some churl in bargain he'll consign,
"And make some tyrant of the parish mine :
"Cold is his heart, and he with looks severe
"Has often forced but never shed the tear ;
"Save, when my mother died, some drops express'd
"A kind of sorrow for a wife at rest.—
"To me a master's stern regard is shown,
"I'm like his steed, prized highly as his own ;
"Stroked but corrected, threaten'd when supplied,
"His slave and boast, his victim and his pride."   320
    "Cheer up, my lass ! I'll to thy father go—
"The Miller cannot be the Sailor's foe ;
"Both live by Heaven's free gale, that plays aloud
"In the stretch'd canvas and the piping shroud ;
"The rush of winds, the flapping sails above,
"And rattling planks within, are sounds *we* love ;
"Calms are our dread ; when tempests plough the deep,
"We take a reef, and to the rocking sleep."
    "Ha !" quoth the Miller, moved at speech so rash,
"Art thou like me ? then, where thy notes and cash ?   330
"Away to Wapping, and a wife command,
"With all thy wealth, a guinea, in thine hand ;
"There with thy messmates quaff the muddy cheer,
"And leave my Lucy for thy betters here."
    "Revenge ! revenge !" the angry lover cried,
Then sought the nymph, and "Be thou now my bride."

THE PARISH REGISTER

Bride had she been, but they no priest could move
To bind in law the couple bound by love.
What sought these lovers then by day, by night,
But stolen moments of disturb'd delight—   340
Soft trembling tumults, terrors dearly prized,
Transports that pain'd, and joys that agonized :
Till the fond damsel, pleased with lad so trim,
Awed by her parent, and enticed by him,
Her lovely form from savage power to save,
Gave—not her hand, but ALL she could, she gave.
 Then came the day of shame, the grievous night,
The varying look, the wandering appetite ;
The joy assumed, while sorrow dimm'd the eyes ;
The forced sad smiles that follow'd sudden sighs ;   350
And every art, long used, but used in vain,
To hide thy progress, Nature, and thy pain.
 Too eager caution shows some danger's near,
The bully's bluster proves the coward's fear ;
His sober step the drunkard vainly tries,
And nymphs expose the failings they disguise.
 First, whispering gossips were in parties seen ;
Then louder Scandal walk'd the village-green ;
Next babbling Folly told the growing ill,
And busy Malice dropp'd it at the mill.   360
 "Go ! to thy curse and mine," the Father said,
" Strife and confusion stalk around thy bed ;
" Want and a wailing brat thy portion be,
" Plague to thy fondness, as thy fault to me.—
" Where skulks the villain ? "—" On the ocean wide
" My William seeks a portion for his bride."—
 " Vain be his search ! but, till the traitor come,
" The higgler's cottage be thy future home ;
" There with his ancient shrew and care abide,
" And hide thy head—thy shame thou canst not hide."   370
 Day after day was pass'd in pains and grief ;
Week follow'd week—and still was no relief.
Her boy was born—no lads nor lasses came
To grace the rite or give the child a name ;
Nor grave conceited nurse, of office proud,
Bore the young Christian roaring through the crowd :

167

GEORGE CRABBE

In a small chamber was my office done,
Where blinks through paper'd panes the setting sun;
Where noisy sparrows, perch'd on penthouse near,
Chirp tuneless joy, and mock the frequent tear;   380
Bats on their webby wings in darkness move,
And feebly shriek their melancholy love.
  No Sailor came; the months in terror fled!
Then news arrived: he fought, and he was DEAD!
  At the lone cottage Lucy lives, and still
Walks for her weekly pittance to the mill;
A mean seraglio there her father keeps,
Whose mirth insults her, as she stands and weeps,
And sees the plenty, while compell'd to stay,
Her father's pride become his harlot's prey.   390
  Throughout the lanes she glides, at evening's close,
And softly lulls her infant to repose;
Then sits and gazes, but with viewless look,
As gilds the moon the rippling of the brook;
And sings her vespers, but in voice so low,
She hears their murmurs as the waters flow:
And she too murmurs, and begins to find
The solemn wanderings of a wounded mind.
Visions of terror, views of wo succeed,
The mind's impatience, to the body's need;   400
By turns to that, by turns to this, a prey,
She knows what reason yields, and dreads what madness may.

  Next, with their boy, a decent couple came,
And call'd him Robert, 'twas his father's name;
Three girls preceded, all by time endear'd,
And future births were neither hoped nor fear'd.
Bless'd in each other, but to no excess,
Health, quiet, comfort, form'd their happiness;
Love, all made up of torture and delight,
Was but mere madness in this couple's sight: 410
Susan could think, though not without a sigh,
If she were gone, who should her place supply;
And Robert, half in earnest, half in jest,
Talk of her spouse when he should be at rest:

THE PARISH REGISTER

Yet strange would either think it to be told,
Their love was cooling or their hearts were cold.
Few were their acres,—but, with these content,
They were, each pay-day, ready with their rent;
And few their wishes—what their farm denied,
The neighbouring town, at trifling cost, supplied.   420
If at the draper's window Susan cast
A longing look, as with her goods she pass'd,
And, with the produce of the wheel and churn,
Bought her a Sunday-robe on her return;
True to her maxim, she would take no rest,
Till care repaid that portion to the chest:
Or if, when loitering at the Whitsun-fair,
Her Robert spent some idle shillings there;
Up at the barn, before the break of day,
He made his labour for th'indulgence pay: 430
Thus both—that waste itself might work in vain—
Wrought double tides, and all was well again.
    Yet, though so prudent, there were times of joy,
(The day they wed, the christening of the boy,)
When to the wealthier farmers there was shown
Welcome unfeign'd, and plenty like their own;
For Susan served the great, and had some pride
Among our topmost people to preside.
Yet in that plenty, in that welcome free,
There was the guiding nice frugality,   440
That, in the festal as the frugal day,
Has, in a different mode, a sovereign sway;
As tides the same 'attractive influence know,
In the least ebb and in their proudest flow:
The wise frugality, that does not give
A life to saving, but that saves to live;
Sparing, not pinching, mindful though not mean,
O'er all presiding, yet in nothing seen.

    Recorded next, a babe of love I trace,
Of many loves the mother's fresh disgrace.—   450
    "Again, thou harlot! could not all thy pain,
"All my reproof, thy wanton thoughts restrain?"
    "Alas! your reverence, wanton thoughts, I grant,

GEORGE CRABBE

"Were once my motive, now the thoughts of want;
"Women, like me, as ducks in a decoy,
"Swim down a stream, and seem to swim in joy;
"Your sex pursue us, and our own disdain;
"Return is dreadful, and escape is vain.
"Would men forsake us, and would women strive
"To help the fall'n, their virtue might revive."   460
   For rite of churching soon she made her way,
In dread of scandal, should she miss the day.—
Two matrons came! with them she humbly knelt,
Their action copied and their comforts felt,
From that great pain and peril to be free,
Though still in peril of that pain to be;
Alas! what numbers, like this amorous dame,
Are quick to censure, but are dead to shame!

   Twin-infants then appear: a girl, a boy,
Th' o'erflowing cup of Gerard Ablett's joy.   470
One had I named in every year that pass'd
Since Gerard wed, and twins behold at last!
Well pleased, the bridegroom smiled to hear—"A vine
"Fruitful and spreading round the walls be thine,
"And branch-like be thine offspring!"—Gerard then
Look'd joyful love, and softly said, "Amen."
Now of that vine he'd have no more increase,
Those playful branches now disturb his peace:
Them he beholds around his table spread,
But finds, the more the branch, the less the bread;   480
And while they run his humble walls about,
They keep the sunshine of good-humour out.
   Cease, man, to grieve! thy master's lot survey,
Whom wife and children, thou and thine, obey;
A farmer proud beyond a farmer's pride,
Of all around the envy or the guide;
Who trots to market on a steed so fine,
That when I meet him, I'm ashamed of mine;
Whose board is high up-heap'd with generous fare,
Which five stout sons and three tall daughters share: 490
Cease, man, to grieve, and listen to his care.
   A few years fled, and all thy boys shall be

THE PARISH REGISTER

Lords of a cot, and labourers like thee:
Thy girls, unportion'd, neighb'ring youths shall lead
Brides from my church, and thenceforth thou art freed;
But then thy master shall of cares complain,
Care after care, a long connected train;
His sons for farms shall ask a large supply,
For farmers' sons each gentle miss shall sigh;
Thy mistress, reasoning well of life's decay,   500
Shall ask a chaise, and hardly brook delay;
The smart young cornet who, with so much grace,
Rode in the ranks and betted at the race,
While the vex'd parent rails at deeds so rash,
Shall d—n his luck, and stretch his hand for cash.
Sad troubles, Gerard! now pertain to thee,
When thy rich master seems from trouble free;
But 'tis one fate at different times assign'd,
And thou shalt lose the cares that he must find.

"Ah!" quoth our village Grocer, rich and old,   510
"Would I might one such cause for care behold!"
To whom his Friend, "Mine greater bliss would be,
"Would Heav'n take those my spouse assigns to me."

Aged were both, that Dawkins, Ditchem this,
Who much of marriage thought, and much amiss;
Both would delay, the one, till, riches gain'd,
The son he wish'd might be to honour train'd;
His Friend—lest fierce intruding heirs should come,
To waste his hoard and vex his quiet home.
Dawkins, a dealer once on burthen'd back   520
Bore his whole substance in a pedler's pack;
To dames discreet, the duties yet unpaid,
His stores of lace and hyson he convey'd.
When thus enrich'd, he chose at home to stop,
And fleece his neighbours in a new-built shop;
Then woo'd a spinster blithe, and hoped, when wed,
For love's fair favours and a fruitful bed.
Not so his Friend;—on widow fair and staid
He fix'd his eye; but he was much afraid,
Yet woo'd; while she his hair of silver hue   530

Demurely noticed, and her eye withdrew.
Doubtful he paused—"Ah! were I sure," he cried,
"No craving children would my gains divide:
"Fair as she is, I would my widow take,
"And live more largely for my partner's sake."
  With such their views, some thoughtful years they pass'd,
And hoping, dreading, they were bound at last.
And what their fate? Observe them as they go,
Comparing fear with fear and wo with wo.
"Humphrey!" said Dawkins, "envy in my breast   540
"Sickens to see thee in thy children bless'd;
"They are thy joys, while I go grieving home
"To a sad spouse, and our eternal gloom.
"We look despondency; no infant near,
"To bless the eye or win the parent's ear;
"Our sudden heats and quarrels to allay,
"And soothe the petty sufferings of the day.
"Alike our want, yet both the want reprove;
"Where are, I cry, these pledges of our love?
"When she, like Jacob's wife, makes fierce reply,   550
"Yet fond—'Oh! give me children, or I die';
"And I return—still childless doom'd to live,
"Like the vex'd patriarch—'Are they mine to give?'
"Ah! much I envy thee thy boys, who ride
"On poplar branch, and canter at thy side;
"And girls, whose cheeks thy chin's fierce fondness know,
"And with fresh beauty at the contact glow."
  "Oh! simple friend," said Ditchem, "would'st thou gain
"A father's pleasure by a husband's pain?
"Alas! what pleasure—when some vig'rous boy   560
"Should swell thy pride, some rosy girl thy joy—
"Is it to doubt who grafted this sweet flower,
"Or whence arose that spirit and that power?
  "Four years I've wed; not one has pass'd in vain:
"Behold the fifth! behold, a babe again!
"My wife's gay friends th' unwelcome imp admire,
"And fill the room with gratulation dire.
"While I in silence sate, revolving all
"That influence ancient men, or that befall,
"A gay pert guest—Heav'n knows his business—came;   570

172

THE PARISH REGISTER

"'A glorious boy,' he cried, 'and what the name?'
"Angry I growl'd, 'My spirit cease to tease,
"'Name it yourselves,—Cain, Judas, if you please;
"'His father's give him—should you that explore,
"'The devil's or yours,' I said, and sought the door.
"My tender partner not a word or sigh
"Gives to my wrath, nor to my speech reply;
"But takes her comforts, triumphs in my pain,
"And looks undaunted for a birth again."
Heirs thus denied afflict the pining heart,   580
And, thus afforded, jealous pangs impart;
Let, therefore, none avoid, and none demand
These arrows number'd for the giant's hand.

Then with their infants three, the parents came,
And each assign'd—'twas all they had—a name:
Names of no mark or price; of them not one
Shall court our view on the sepulchral stone,
Or stop the clerk, th' engraven scrolls to spell,
Or keep the sexton from the sermon bell.

An orphan-girl succeeds; ere she was born   590
Her father died, her mother on that morn;
The pious mistress of the school sustains
Her parents' part, nor their affection feigns,
But pitying feels; with due respect and joy,
I trace the matron at her loved employ.
What time the striplings, wearied e'en with play,   ⎫
Part at the closing of the summer's day,   ⎬ [ ]]
And each by different path returns the well-known way— ⎭
Then I behold her at her cottage-door,
Frugal of light, her Bible laid before,   600
When on her double duty she proceeds,
Of time as frugal, knitting as she reads.
Her idle neighbours, who approach to tell
Some trifling tale, her serious looks compel,
To hear reluctant—while the lads who pass,
In pure respect walk silent on the grass.
Then sinks the day; but not to rest she goes,
Till solemn prayers the daily duties close.

GEORGE CRABBE

But I digress, and lo! an infant train
Appear, and call me to my task again.   610
"Why Lonicera wilt thou name thy child?"
I ask'd the Gardener's wife, in accents mild.
"We have a right," replied the sturdy dame—
And Lonicera was the infant's name.
If next a son shall yield our Gardener joy,
Then Hyacinthus shall be that fair boy;
And if a girl, they will at length agree,
That Belladonna that fair maid shall be.
  High-sounding words our worthy Gardener gets,
And at his club to wondering swains repeats;   620
He then of Rhus and Rhododendron speaks,
And Allium calls his onions and his leeks;
Nor weeds are now, for whence arose the weed,
Scarce plants, fair herbs, and curious flowers proceed;
Where Cuckoo-pints and Dandelions sprung,
(Gross names had they our plainer sires among,)
There Arums, there Leontodons we view,
And Artemisia grows, where Wormwood grew.
  But though no weed exists his garden round,
From Rumex strong our Gardener frees his ground; 630
Takes soft Senicio from the yielding land,
And grasps the arm'd Urtica in his hand.
  Not Darwin's self had more delight to sing
Of floral courtship, in th' awaken'd Spring,
Than Peter Pratt, who, simpering, loves to tell
How rise the Stamens, as the Pistils swell;
How bend and curl the moist-top to the spouse,
And give and take the vegetable vows;
How those esteem'd of old but tips and chives,
Are tender husbands and obedient wives;   640
Who live and love within the sacred bower—
That bridal bed the vulgar term a flower.
  Hear Peter proudly, to some humble friend,
A wondrous secret in his science lend:—
"Would you advance the nuptial hour, and bring
"The fruit of Autumn with the flowers of Spring:
"View that light frame where Cucumis lies spread,
"And trace the husbands in their golden bed,

174

THE PARISH REGISTER

" Three powder'd Anthers ;—then no more delay,
" But to the Stigma's tip their dust convey ;   650
" Then by thyself, from prying glance secure,
" Twirl the full tip and make your purpose sure ;
" A long-abiding race the deed shall pay,
" Nor one unbless'd abortion pine away."
  T' admire their friend's discourse our swains agree,
And call it science and philosophy.
  'Tis good, 'tis pleasant, through th' advancing year,
To see unnumber'd growing forms appear.
What leafy-life from Earth's broad bosom rise !
What insect-myriads seek the summer skies !   660
What scaly tribes in every streamlet move !
What plumy people sing in every grove !
All with the year awaked to life, delight, and love.   [ ]
Then names are good ; for how, without their aid,
Is knowledge, gain'd by man, to man convey'd ?
But from that source shall all our pleasures flow ?
Shall all our knowledge be those names to know ?
Then he, with memory bless'd, shall bear away
The palm from Grew, and Middleton, and Ray.
No ! let us rather seek, in grove and field,   670
What food for wonder, what for use they yield ;
Some just remark from Nature's people bring,
And some new source of homage for her King.

  Pride lives with all ; strange names our rustics give
To helpless infants, that their own may live ;
Pleased to be known, they'll some attention claim,
And find some by-way to the house of fame.
  The straightest furrow lifts the ploughman's art ;
The hat he gain'd has warmth for head and heart ;
The bowl that beats the greater number down   680
Of tottering nine-pins, gives to fame the clown ;
Or, foil'd in these, he opes his ample jaws,
And lets a frog leap down, to gain applause ;
Or grins for hours, or tipples for a week ;
Or challenges a well-pinch'd pig to squeak.
Some idle deed, some child's preposterous name,
Shall make him known, and give his folly fame.

175

GEORGE CRABBE

To name an infant meet our village-sires,
Assembled all, as such event requires;
Frequent and full, the rural sages sate,　　　　690
And speakers many urged the long debate.
Some harden'd knaves, who roved the country round,
Had left a babe within the parish-bound.—
First, of the fact they question'd—"Was it true?"
The child was brought—"What then remain'd to do?
"Was't dead or living?" This was fairly proved:
'Twas pinch'd, it roar'd, and every doubt removed.
Then by what name th' unwelcome guest to call
Was long a question, and it posed them all;
For he who lent it to a babe unknown,　　　　700
Censorious men might take it for his own:
They look'd about, they gravely spoke to all,
And not one Richard answer'd to the call.
Next they inquired the day, when, passing by,
Th' unlucky peasant heard the stranger's cry:
This known, how food and raiment they might give,
Was next debated—for the rogue would live;
At last, with all their words and work content,
Back to their homes the prudent vestry went,
And Richard Monday to the workhouse sent.　　710 [ ]]
There was he pinch'd and pitied, thump'd and fed,
And duly took his beatings and his bread;
Patient in all control, in all abuse,
He found contempt and kicking have their use—
Sad, silent, supple; bending to the blow,
A slave of slaves, the lowest of the low;
His pliant soul gave way to all things base;
He knew no shame, he dreaded no disgrace.
It seem'd, so well his passions he suppress'd,
No feeling stirr'd his ever-torpid breast;　　　720
Him might the meanest pauper bruise and cheat,
He was a footstool for the beggar's feet;
His were the legs that ran at all commands;
They used on all occasions Richard's hands.
His very soul was not his own; he stole
As others order'd, and without a dole;
In all disputes, on either part he lied,

176

And freely pledged his oath on either side ;
In all rebellions Richard join'd the rest,
In all detections Richard first confess'd.   730
Yet, though disgraced, he watch'd his time so well,
He rose in favour, when in fame he fell ;
Base was his usage, vile his whole employ,
And all despised and fed the pliant boy.
At length, " 'tis time he should abroad be sent,"
Was whisper'd near him—and abroad he went.
One morn they call'd him, Richard answer'd not ;
They deem'd him hanging, and in time forgot ;
Yet miss'd him long, as each, throughout the clan,
Found he "had better spared a better man."   740
  Now Richard's talents for the world were fit,
He'd no small cunning, and had some small wit ;
Had that calm look which seem'd to all assent,
And that complacent speech which nothing meant ;
He'd but one care, and that he strove to hide,
How best for Richard Monday to provide.
Steel, through opposing plates, the magnet draws,
And steely atoms culls from dust and straws ;
And thus our hero, to his interest true,
Gold through all bars and from each trifle drew ;   750
But, still more surely round the world to go,
This fortune's child had neither friend nor foe.
  Long lost to us, at last our man we trace—
Sir Richard Monday died at Monday-place.
His lady's worth, his daughter's, we peruse,
And find his grandsons all as rich as Jews ;
He gave reforming charities a sum,
And bought the blessings of the blind and dumb ;
Bequeathed to missions money from the stocks,
And Bibles issued from his private box ;   760
But, to his native place severely just,
He left a pittance bound in rigid trust—
Two paltry pounds, on every quarter's-day,
(At church produced) for forty loaves should pay :
A stinted gift, that to the parish shows
He kept in mind their bounty and their blows !

To farmers three, the year has given a son :
Finch on the Moor, and French, and Middleton.
Twice in this year a female Giles I see :
A Spalding once, and once a Barnaby—   770
A humble man is he, and, when they meet,
Our farmers find him on a distant seat ;
There for their wit he serves a constant theme—
They praise his dairy, they extol his team,
They ask the price of each unrivall'd steed,
And whence his sheep, that admirable breed ?
His thriving arts they beg he would explain,
And where he puts the money he must gain.
They have their daughters, but they fear their friend
Would think his sons too much would condescend ;   780
They have their sons who would their fortunes try,
But fear his daughters will their suit deny.
So runs the joke, while James, with sigh profound,
And face of care, looks moveless on the ground ;
His cares, his sighs, provoke the insult more,
And point the jest—for Barnaby is poor.

Last in my list, five untaught lads appear ;
Their father dead, compassion sent them here—
For still that rustic infidel denied
To have their names with solemn rite applied.   790
His, a lone house, by Deadman's Dyke-way stood ;
And his, a nightly haunt, in Lonely-wood.
Each village inn has heard the ruffian boast,
That he believed in neither God nor ghost ;
That, when the sod upon the sinner press'd,
He, like the saint, had everlasting rest ;
That never priest believed his doctrines true,
But would, for profit, own himself a Jew,
Or worship wood and stone, as honest heathen do ;
That fools alone on future worlds rely,   800
And all who die for faith, deserve to die.
These maxims, part th' attorney's clerk profess'd ;
His own transcendent genius found the rest.
Our pious matrons heard, and, much amazed,
Gazed on the man, and trembled as they gazed ;

THE PARISH REGISTER

And now his face explored, and now his feet,
Man's dreaded foe, in this bad man, to meet.
But him our drunkards as their champion raised,
Their bishop call'd, and as their hero praised;
Though most, when sober, and the rest, when sick,   810
Had little question whence his bishopric.
　But he, triumphant spirit! all things dared,
He poach'd the wood, and on the warren snared;
'Twas his, at cards, each novice to trepan,
And call the wants of rogues the rights of man;
Wild as the winds, he let his offspring rove,
And deem'd the marriage-bond the bane of love.
　What age and sickness, for a man so bold,
Had done, we know not—none beheld him old.
By night, as business urged, he sought the wood—   820
The ditch was deep—the rain had caused a flood—
The foot-bridge fail'd—he plunged beneath the deep,
And slept, if truth were his, th' eternal sleep.

　These have we named; on life's rough sea they sail,
With many a prosperous, many an adverse gale!
Where passion soon, like powerful winds, will rage,
And prudence, wearied, with their strength engage.
Then each, in aid, shall some companion ask,
For help or comfort in the tedious task;
And what that help—what joys from union flow,   830
What good or ill, we next prepare to show;
And row, meantime, our weary bark ashore,
As Spenser his—but not with Spenser's oar[1].

[1] Allusions of this kind are to be found in the Fairy Queen.　See the
end of the First Book, and other places.

THE PARISH REGISTER.

PART II.

MARRIAGES.

Previous Consideration necessary: yet not too long Delay—Imprudent
Marriage of old Kirk and his Servant—Comparison between an
ancient and youthful Partner to a young Man—Prudence of Donald
the Gardener—Parish Wedding: the compelled Bridegroom; Day of
Marriage, how spent—Relation of the Accomplishments of Phœbe
Dawson, a rustic Beauty; her Lover: his Courtship; their Marriage
— Misery of Precipitation—The wealthy Couple: Reluctance in the
Husband; why?—Unusually fair Signatures in the Register: the
common Kind—Seduction of Lucy Collins by Footman Daniel: her
rustic Lover; her Return to him—An ancient Couple: Comparisons
on the Occasion—More pleasant View of Village Matrimony: Farmers
celebrating the Day of Marriage; their Wives—Reuben and Rachel,
a happy Pair: an Example of prudent Delay—Reflections on their
State who were not so prudent, and its Improvement towards the
Termination of Life; an old Man so circumstanced—Attempt to
seduce a Village Beauty: Persuasion and Reply; the Event.

THE PARISH REGISTER.

PART II.

MARRIAGES.

Nubere si quà voles, quamvis properabitis ambo,
Differ; habent parvæ commoda magna moræ.
Ovid. Fast. lib. iii. [vv. 393—4.]

" DISPOSED to wed, e'en while you hasten, stay ;
There's great advantage in a small delay : "—
Thus Ovid sang, and much the wise approve
This prudent maxim of the priest of Love.
If poor, delay for future want prepares,
And eases humble life of half its cares ;
If rich, delay shall brace the thoughtful mind,
T' endure the ills that e'en the happiest find :
Delay shall knowledge yield on either part,
And show the value of the vanquish'd heart ;   10
The humours, passions, merits, failings prove,
And gently raise the veil that's worn by Love ;
Love, that impatient guide—too proud to think
Of vulgar wants, of clothing, meat and drink—
Urges our amorous swains their joys to seize,
And then, at rags and hunger frighten'd, flees.—
Yet not too long in cold debate remain :
Till age, refrain not—but if old, refrain.

By no such rule would Gaffer Kirk be tried ;
First in the year he led a blooming bride,   20
And stood a wither'd elder at her side.
Oh ! Nathan ! Nathan ! at thy years, trepann'd
To take a wanton harlot by the hand !

GEORGE CRABBE

Thou, who wert used so tartly to express
Thy sense of matrimonial happiness,
Till every youth, whose bans at church were read,
Strove not to meet, or meeting, hung his head;
And every lass forbore at thee to look,
A sly old fish, too cunning for the hook;—
And now at sixty, that pert dame to see   30
Of all thy savings mistress, and of thee;
Now will the lads, rememb'ring insults past,
Cry, "What, the wise-one in the trap at last!"
   Fie! Nathan! fie! to let an artful jade
The close recesses of thine heart invade;
What grievous pangs, what suffering, she'll impart,
And fill with anguish that rebellious heart;
For thou wilt strive incessantly, in vain,
By threatening speech, thy freedom to regain:
But she for conquest married, nor will prove   40
A dupe to thee, thine anger, or thy love.
Clamorous her tongue will be;—of either sex,
She'll gather friends around thee, and perplex
Thy doubtful soul; thy money she will waste
In the vain ramblings of a vulgar taste;
And will be happy to exert her power,
In every eye, in thine, at every hour.
   Then wilt thou bluster—"No! I will not rest,
"And see consumed each shilling of my chest":
Thou wilt be valiant—"When thy cousins call,   50
"I will abuse and shut my door on all";
Thou wilt be cruel—"What the law allows,
"That be thy portion, my ungrateful spouse!
"Nor other shillings shalt thou then receive,
"And when I die——What! may I this believe?   ⎫
"Are these true tender tears? and does my Kitty grieve? [ʃ]⎬
"Ah! crafty vixen, thine old man has fears;   ⎭
"But weep no more! I'm melted by thy tears;
"Spare but my money; thou shalt rule ME still,
"And see thy cousins—there! I burn the will."—   60
   Thus, with example sad, our year began,
A wanton vixen and a weary man;
But had this tale in other guise been told,

THE PARISH REGISTER

Young let the lover be, the lady old,
And that disparity of years shall prove
No bane of peace, although some bar to love :
'Tis not the worst, our nuptial ties among,
That joins the ancient bride and bridegroom young ;—
Young wives, like changing winds, their power display,
By shifting points and varying day by day ;   70
Now zephyrs mild, now whirlwinds in their force,
They sometimes speed, but often thwart our course ;
And much experienced should that pilot be,
Who sails with them on life's tempestuous sea.
But like a trade-wind is the ancient dame,
Mild to your wish, and every day the same ;
Steady as time, no sudden squalls you fear,
But set full sail and with assurance steer ;
Till every danger in your way be pass'd,
And then she gently, mildly breathes her last ;   80
Rich you arrive, in port awhile remain,
And for a second venture sail again.

For this, blithe Donald southward made his way,
And left the lasses on the banks of Tay ;
Him to a neighbouring garden fortune sent,
Whom we beheld, aspiringly content :
Patient and mild, he sought the dame to please,
Who ruled the kitchen and who bore the keys.
Fair Lucy first, the laundry's grace and pride,
With smiles and gracious looks, her fortune tried ;   90
But all in vain she praised his "pawky eyne,"
Where never fondness was for Lucy seen :
Him the mild Susan, boast of dairies, loved,
And found him civil, cautious, and unmoved :
From many a fragrant simple, Catharine's skill
Drew oil and essence from the boiling still ;
But not her warmth, nor all her winning ways,
From his cool phlegm could Donald's spirit raise :
Of beauty heedless, with the merry mute,
To Mistress Dobson he preferr'd his suit ;   100
There proved his service, there address'd his vows,
And saw her mistress—friend—protectress—spouse ;

A butler now, he thanks his powerful bride,
And, like her keys, keeps constant at her side.

Next at our altar stood a luckless pair,
Brought by strong passions and a warrant there;
By long rent cloak, hung loosely, strove the bride,
From ev'ry eye what all perceived to hide;
While the boy-bridegroom, shuffling in his pace,
Now hid awhile and then exposed his face;   110
As shame alternately with anger strove
The brain confused with muddy ale to move.
In haste and stammering he perform'd his part,
And look'd the rage that rankled in his heart;
(So will each lover inly curse his fate,
Too soon made happy and made wise too late;)
I saw his features take a savage gloom,
And deeply threaten for the days to come.
Low spake the lass, and lisp'd and minced the while,
Look'd on the lad, and faintly tried to smile;   120
With soften'd speech and humbled tone she strove
To stir the embers of departed love:
While he, a tyrant, frowning walk'd before,
Felt the poor purse and sought the public door,
She, sadly following, in submission went,
And saw the final shilling foully spent;
Then to her father's hut the pair withdrew,
And bade to love and comfort long adieu!
   Ah! fly temptation, youth, refrain! refrain!
I preach for ever; but I preach in vain!   130

   Two summers since, I saw, at Lammas Fair,
The sweetest flower that ever blossom'd there,
When Phœbe Dawson gaily cross'd the Green,
In haste to see and happy to be seen:
Her air, her manners, all who saw admired,
Courteous though coy, and gentle though retired;
The joy of youth and health her eyes display'd,
And ease of heart her every look convey'd;
A native skill her simple robes express'd,
As with untutor'd elegance she dress'd;   140

The lads around admired so fair a sight,
And Phœbe felt, and felt she gave, delight.
Admirers soon of every age she gain'd,
Her beauty won them and her worth retain'd;
Envy itself could no contempt display,
They wish'd her well, whom yet they wish'd away.
Correct in thought, she judged a servant's place
Preserved a rustic beauty from disgrace;
But yet on Sunday-eve, in freedom's hour,
With secret joy she felt that beauty's power,   150
When some proud bliss upon the heart would steal,
That, poor or rich, a beauty still must feel.—
    At length, the youth, ordain'd to move her breast,
Before the swains with bolder spirit press'd;
With looks less timid made his passion known,
And pleased by manners most unlike her own;
Loud though in love, and confident though young;
Fierce in his air, and voluble of tongue;
By trade a tailor, though, in scorn of trade,
He served the 'Squire, and brush'd the coat he made: 160
Yet now, would Phœbe her consent afford,
Her slave alone, again he'd mount the board;
With her should years of growing love be spent,
And growing wealth—she sigh'd and look'd consent.
    Now, through the lane, up hill, and 'cross the green,
(Seen by but few, and blushing to be seen—
Dejected, thoughtful, anxious, and afraid,)
Led by the lover, walk'd the silent maid.
Slow through the meadows roved they many a mile,
Toy'd by each bank and trifled at each stile;   170
Where, as he painted every blissful view,
And highly colour'd what he strongly drew,
The pensive damsel, prone to tender fears,
Dimm'd the false prospect with prophetic tears.—
Thus pass'd th' allotted hours, till, lingering late,
The lover loiter'd at the master's gate;
There he pronounced adieu! and yet would stay,
Till chidden—soothed—entreated—forced away,
He would of coldness, though indulged, complain,
And oft retire and oft return again;   180

GEORGE CRABBE

When, if his teasing vex'd her gentle mind,
The grief assumed, compell'd her to be kind!
For he would proof of plighted kindness crave,
That she resented first and then forgave,
And to his grief and penance yielded more
Than his presumption had required before.—
    Ah! fly temptation, youth; refrain! refrain,
Each yielding maid and each presuming swain!

    Lo! now with red rent cloak and bonnet black,
And torn green gown loose hanging at her back,   190
One who an infant in her arms sustains,
And seems in patience striving with her pains;
Pinch'd are her looks, as one who pines for bread,
Whose cares are growing and whose hopes are fled;
Pale her parch'd lips, her heavy eyes sunk low,
And tears unnoticed from their channels flow;
Serene her manner, till some sudden pain
Frets the meek soul, and then she's calm again.—
Her broken pitcher to the pool she takes,
And every step with cautious terror makes;   200
For not alone that infant in her arms,
But nearer cause, her anxious soul alarms.
With water burthen'd, then she picks her way,
Slowly and cautious, in the clinging clay;
Till, in mid-green, she trusts a place unsound,
And deeply plunges in th' adhesive ground;
Thence, but with pain, her slender foot she takes,
While hope the mind, as strength the frame, forsakes:
For, when so full the cup of sorrow grows,
Add but a drop, it instantly o'erflows.   210
And now her path, but not her peace, she gains,
Safe from her task, but shivering with her pains;
Her home she reaches, open leaves the door,
And, placing first her infant on the floor,
She bares her bosom to the wind, and sits,
And sobbing struggles with the rising fits.
In vain, they come; she feels th' inflating grief,
That shuts the swelling bosom from relief;
That speaks in feeble cries a soul distress'd,

THE PARISH REGISTER

Or the sad laugh that cannot be repress'd.   220
The neighbour-matron leaves her wheel and flies
With all the aid her poverty supplies ;
Unfee'd, the calls of Nature she obeys,
Not led by profit, nor allured by praise ;
And, waiting long, till these contentions cease,
She speaks of comfort, and departs in peace.
    Friend of distress ! the mourner feels thy aid,
She cannot pay thee, but thou wilt be paid.

    But who this child of weakness, want, and care ?
'Tis Phœbe Dawson, pride of Lammas Fair ;   230
Who took her lover for his sparkling eyes,
Expressions warm, and love-inspiring lies.
Compassion first assail'd her gentle heart,
For all his suffering, all his bosom's smart :
And then his prayers ! they would a savage move,
And win the coldest of the sex to love.
But ah ! too soon his looks success declared,
Too late her loss the marriage-rite repaired ;
The faithless flatterer then his vows forgot,
A captious tyrant or a noisy sot :   240
If present, railing, till he saw her pain'd ;
If absent, spending what their labours gain'd ;
Till that fair form in want and sickness pined,
And hope and comfort fled that gentle mind.
    Then fly temptation, youth ; resist, refrain !
Nor let me preach for ever and in vain !

    Next came a well-dress'd pair, who left their coach,
And made, in long procession, slow approach ;
For this gay bride had many a female friend,
And youths were there, this favour'd youth t' attend.   250
Silent, nor wanting due respect, the crowd
Stood humbly round, and gratulation bow'd ;
But not that silent crowd, in wonder fix'd,
Not numerous friends, who praise and envy mix'd,
Nor nymphs attending near to swell the pride
Of one more fair, the ever-smiling bride ;

GEORGE CRABBE

Nor that gay bride, adorn'd with every grace,
Nor love nor joy triumphant in her face,
Could from the youth's sad signs of sorrow chase.   [ ]]
Why didst thou grieve? wealth, pleasure, freedom thine;   260
Vex'd it thy soul, that freedom to resign?
Spake Scandal truth? "Thou didst not then intend
"So soon to bring thy wooing to an end"?
Or, was it, as our prating rustics say,
To end as soon, but in a different way?
'Tis told, thy Phillis is a skilful dame,
Who play'd uninjured with the dangerous flame:
That, while, like Lovelace, thou thy coat display'd,
And hid the snare for her affection laid,
Thee, with her net, she found the means to catch,   270
And, at the amorous see-saw, won the match[1].
Yet others tell, the Captain fix'd thy doubt,
He'd call thee brother, or he'd call thee out.—
But rest the motive—all retreat too late,
Joy like thy bride's should on thy brow have sate;
The deed had then appear'd thine own intent,
A glorious day, by gracious fortune sent,
In each revolving year to be in triumph spent.   [ ]]
Then in few weeks that cloudy brow had been
Without a wonder or a whisper seen;   280
And none had been so weak as to inquire,
"Why pouts my Lady?" or "why frowns the Squire?"

How fair these names, how much unlike they look
To all the blurr'd subscriptions in my book:
The bridegroom's letters stand in row above,
Tapering yet stout, like pine-trees in his grove;
While free and fine the bride's appear below,
As light and slender as her jasmines grow.
Mark now in what confusion, stoop or stand,
The crooked scrawls of many a clownish hand;   290
Now out, now in, they droop, they fall, they rise,
Like raw recruits drawn forth for exercise;
Ere yet reform'd and modell'd by the drill,
The free-born legs stand striding as they will.

[1] Clarissa, vol. vii. Lovelace's Letter.

THE PARISH REGISTER

Much have I tried to guide the fist along,
But still the blunderers placed their blottings wrong:
Behold these marks uncouth! how strange that men,
Who guide the plough, should fail to guide the pen.
For half a mile the furrows even lie;
For half an inch the letters stand awry;— 300
Our peasants, strong and sturdy in the field,
Cannot these arms of idle students wield;
Like them, in feudal days, their valiant lords
Resign'd the pen and grasp'd their conqu'ring swords;
They to robed clerks and poor dependent men
Left the light duties of the peaceful pen;
Nor to their ladies wrote, but sought to prove,
By deeds of death, their hearts were fill'd with love.
  But yet, small arts have charms for female eyes;
Our rustic nymphs the beau and scholar prize; 310
Unletter'd swains and ploughmen coarse they slight,
For those who dress, and amorous scrolls indite.

  For Lucy Collins happier days had been,
Had Footman Daniel scorn'd his native green;
Or when he came an idle coxcomb down,
Had he his love reserved for lass in town;
To Stephen Hill she then had pledged her truth,—
A sturdy, sober, kind, unpolish'd youth;
But from the day, that fatal day she spied
The pride of Daniel, Daniel was her pride. 320
In all concerns was Stephen just and true;
But coarse his doublet was and patch'd in view,
And felt his stockings were, and blacker than his shoe; [ ]
While Daniel's linen all was fine and fair—
His master wore it, and he deign'd to wear;
(To wear his livery, some respect might prove;
To wear his linen, must be sign of love :)
Blue was his coat, unsoil'd by spot or stain;
His hose were silk, his shoes of Spanish-grain;
A silver knot his breadth of shoulder bore; 330
A diamond buckle blazed his breast before—
Diamond he swore it was! and show'd it as he swore; [ ]
Rings on his fingers shone; his milk-white hand

Could pick-tooth case and box for snuff command :
And thus, with clouded cane, a fop complete,
He stalk'd, the jest and glory of the street.
Join'd with these powers, he could so sweetly sing,
Talk with such toss, and saunter with such swing ;
Laugh with such glee, and trifle with such art,
That Lucy's promise fail'd to shield her heart.   340
   Stephen, meantime, to ease his amorous cares,
Fix'd his full mind upon his farm's affairs ;
Two pigs, a cow, and wethers half a score,
Increased his stock, and still he look'd for more.
He, for his acres few, so duly paid,
That yet more acres to his lot were laid ;
Till our chaste nymphs no longer felt disdain,
And prudent matrons praised the frugal swain ;
Who, thriving well, through many a fruitful year,
Now clothed himself anew, and acted overseer.   350
   Just then poor Lucy, from her friend in town,
Fled in pure fear, and came a beggar down ;
Trembling, at Stephen's door she knock'd for bread—
Was chidden first, next pitied, and then fed ;
Then sat at Stephen's board, then shared in Stephen's bed : [}]
All hope of marriage lost in her disgrace,
He mourns a flame revived, and she a love of lace.

   Now to be wed a well-match'd couple came ;
Twice had old Lodge been tied, and twice the dame ;
Tottering they came and toying, (odious scene !)   360
And fond and simple, as they'd always been.
Children from wedlock we by laws restrain ;
Why not prevent them, when they're such again ?
Why not forbid the doting souls, to prove
Th' indecent fondling of preposterous love ?
In spite of prudence, uncontroll'd by shame,
The amorous senior woos the toothless dame,
Relating idly, at the closing eve,
The youthful follies he disdains to leave ;
Till youthful follies wake a transient fire,   370
When arm in arm they totter and retire.
   So a fond pair of solemn birds, all day,

Blink in their seat and doze the hours away ;
Then, by the moon awaken'd, forth they move,
And fright the songsters with their cheerless love.
   So two sear trees, dry, stunted, and unsound,
Each other catch, when dropping to the ground ;
Entwine their wither'd arms 'gainst wind and weather,
And shake their leafless heads, and drop together.
   So two cold limbs, touch'd by Galvani's wire,   380
Move with new life, and feel awaken'd fire ;
Quivering awhile, their flaccid forms remain,
Then turn to cold torpidity again.

   " But ever frowns your Hymen ? man and maid,
" Are all repenting, suffering, or betray'd ? "
Forbid it, Love ! we have our couples here
Who hail the day in each revolving year :
These are with us, as in the world around ;
They are not frequent, but they may be found.
   Our farmers, too ; what, though they fail to prove,   390
In Hymen's bonds, the tenderest slaves of love,
(Nor, like those pairs whom sentiment unites,
Feel they the fervour of the mind's delights :)
Yet, coarsely kind and comfortably gay,
They heap the board and hail the happy day :
And, though the bride, now freed from school, admits
Of pride implanted there some transient fits ;
Yet soon she casts her girlish flights aside,
And in substantial blessings rests her pride.
   No more she moves in measured steps, no more   400
Runs, with bewilder'd ear, her music o'er ;
No more recites her French the hinds among,
But chides her maidens in her mother-tongue ;
Her tambour-frame she leaves and diet spare,
Plain work and plenty with her house to share ;
Till, all her varnish lost, in few short years,
In all her worth, the farmer's wife appears.
   Yet not the ancient kind ; nor she who gave
Her soul to gain—a mistress and a slave :
Who not to sleep allow'd the needful time ;   410
To whom repose was loss, and sport a crime ;

GEORGE CRABBE

Who, in her meanest room (and all were mean),
A noisy drudge, from morn till night was seen;—
But she, the daughter, boasts a decent room,
Adorn'd with carpet, form'd in Wilton's loom;
Fair prints along the paper'd wall are spread;
There, Werter sees the sportive children fed,
And Charlotte, here, bewails her lover dead.   [ ]]
   'Tis here, assembled, while in space apart
Their husbands, drinking, warm the opening heart,   420
Our neighbouring dames, on festal days, unite
With tongues more fluent and with hearts as light;
Theirs is that art, which English wives alone
Profess—a boast and privilege their own;
An art it is, where each at once attends
To all, and claims attention from her friends,
When they engage the tongue, the eye, the ear,
Reply when list'ning, and when speaking hear:
The ready converse knows no dull delays,
"But double are the pains, and double be the praise[1]."   430

   Yet not to those alone who bear command
Heaven gives a heart to hail the marriage band;
Among their servants, we the pairs can show,
Who much to love and more to prudence owe.
Reuben and Rachel, though as fond as doves,
Were yet discreet and cautious in their loves;
Nor would attend to Cupid's wild commands,
Till cool reflection bade them join their hands.
When both were poor, they thought it argued ill
Of hasty love to make them poorer still;   440
Year after year, with savings long laid by,
They bought the future dwelling's full supply;
Her frugal fancy cull'd the smaller ware,
The weightier purchase ask'd her Reuben's care;
Together then their last year's gain they threw,
And lo! an auction'd bed, with curtains neat and new.
Thus both, as prudence counsell'd, wisely stay'd,
And cheerful then the calls of Love obey'd:
What if, when Rachel gave her hand, 'twas one

     [1] Spenser[, The Faerie Queene, Bk. II. c. ii. st. xxv.]

192

Embrown'd by Winter's ice and Summer's sun?   450
What if, in Reuben's hair, the female eye
Usurping grey among the black could spy?
What if, in both, life's bloomy flush was lost,
And their full autumn felt the mellowing frost?
Yet time, who blow'd the rose of youth away,
Had left the vigorous stem without decay;
Like those tall elms, in Farmer Frankford's ground,
They'll grow no more—but all their growth is sound;
By time confirm'd and rooted in the land,
The storms they've stood, still promise they shall stand.   460

These are the happier pairs: their life has rest,
Their hopes are strong, their humble portion bless'd;
While those, more rash, to hasty marriage led,
Lament th' impatience which now stints their bread.
When such their union, years their cares increase;
Their love grows colder, and their pleasures cease;
In health just fed, in sickness just relieved;
By hardships harass'd and by children grieved;
In petty quarrels and in peevish strife
The once fond couple waste the spring of life;   470
But, when to age mature those children grown,
Find hopes and homes and hardships of their own,
The harass'd couple feel their lingering woes
Receding slowly, till they find repose.
Complaints and murmurs then are laid aside,
(By reason these subdued, and those by pride;)
And, taught by care, the patient man and wife
Agree to share the bitter-sweet of life;
(Life that has sorrow much and sorrow's cure,
Where they who most enjoy shall much endure;)   480
Their rest, their labours, duties, sufferings, prayers,
Compose the soul, and fit it for its cares;
Their graves before them, and their griefs behind,
Have each a med'cine for the rustic mind;
Nor has he care to whom his wealth shall go,
Or who shall labour with his spade and hoe;
But, as he lends the strength that yet remains,
And some dead neighbour on his bier sustains,

Crabbe   N   193

(One with whom oft he whirl'd the bounding flail,
Toss'd the broad coit, or took th' inspiring ale,)   490
"For me," (he meditates,) "shall soon be done
"This friendly duty, when my race be run;
"'Twas first in trouble as in error pass'd,
"Dark clouds and stormy cares whole years o'ercast,
"But calm my setting day, and sunshine smiles at last: [ʃ]
"My vices punish'd and my follies spent,
"Not loth to die, but yet to live content,
"I rest";—then, casting on the grave his eye,
His friend compels a tear, and his own griefs a sigh.

    Last on my list appears a match of love,   500
And one of virtue—happy may it prove!—
Sir Edward Archer is an amorous knight,
And maidens chaste and lovely shun his sight;
His bailiff's daughter suited much his taste,
For Fanny Price was lovely and was chaste;
To her the Knight with gentle looks drew near,
And timid voice assumed, to banish fear.—
    "Hope of my life, dear sovereign of my breast,
"Which, since I knew thee, knows not joy nor rest;
"Know, thou art all that my delighted eyes,   510
"My fondest thoughts, my proudest wishes prize;
"And is that bosom—(what on earth so fair!)
"To cradle some coarse peasant's sprawling heir?
"To be that pillow which some surly swain
"May treat with scorn and agonize with pain?
"Art thou, sweet maid, a ploughman's wants to share,
"To dread his insult, to support his care;
"To hear his follies, his contempt to prove,
"And (oh! the torment!) to endure his love;
"Till want and deep regret those charms destroy,   520
"That time would spare, if time were pass'd in joy?
"With him, in varied pains, from morn till night,
"Your hours shall pass, yourself a ruffian's right;
"Your softest bed shall be the knotted wool;
"Your purest drink the waters of the pool;
"Your sweetest food will but your life sustain,
"And your best pleasure be a rest from pain;

"While, through each year, as health and strength abate,
"You'll weep your woes and wonder at your fate;
"And cry, 'Behold, as life's last cares come on,   530
"'My burthens growing when my strength is gone!'
  "Now turn with me, and all the young desire,
"That taste can form, that fancy can require;
"All that excites enjoyment, or procures
"Wealth, health, respect, delight, and love, are yours:
"Sparkling, in cups of gold, your wines shall flow,
"Grace that fair hand, in that dear bosom glow;
"Fruits of each clime, and flowers, through all the year,
"Shall on your walls and in your walks appear;
"Where all, beholding, shall your praise repeat,   540
"No fruit so tempting and no flower so sweet.
"The softest carpets in your rooms shall lie,
"Pictures of happiest loves shall meet your eye,
"And tallest mirrors, reaching to the floor,
"Shall show you all the object I adore;
"Who, by the hands of wealth and fashion dress'd,
"By slaves attended and by friends caress'd,
"Shall move, a wonder, through the public ways,
"And hear the whispers of adoring praise.
"Your female friends, though gayest of the gay,   550
"Shall see you happy, and shall, sighing, say,
"While smother'd envy rises in the breast—
"'Oh! that we lived so beauteous and so bless'd!'
  "Come then, my mistress, and my wife; for she
"Who trusts my honour is the wife for me;
"Your slave, your husband, and your friend employ,
"In search of pleasures we may both enjoy."
  To this the damsel, meekly firm, replied:
"My mother loved, was married, toil'd, and died;
"With joys, she'd griefs, had troubles in her course,   560
"But not one grief was pointed by remorse;
"My mind is fix'd, to Heaven I resign,
"And be her love, her life, her comforts mine."
  Tyrants have wept; and those with hearts of steel,
Unused the anguish of the heart to heal,
Have yet the transient power of virtue known,
And felt th' imparted joy promote their own.

GEORGE CRABBE

Our Knight, relenting, now befriends a youth,
Who to the yielding maid had vow'd his truth;
And finds in that fair deed a sacred joy,   570
That will not perish, and that cannot cloy—
A living joy, that shall its spirit keep,
When every beauty fades, and all the passions sleep.

THE PARISH REGISTER.

PART III.

BURIALS.

True Christian Resignation not frequently to be seen—The Register a melancholy Record—A dying Man, who at length sends for a Priest: for what Purpose? answered—Old Collett of the Inn, an Instance of Dr. Young's slow-sudden Death: his Character and Conduct—The Manners and Management of the Widow Goe: her successful Attention to Business; her Decease unexpected—The Infant-Boy of Gerard Ablett dies: Reflections on his Death, and the Survivor his Sister-Twin—The Funeral of the deceased Lady of the Manor described: her neglected Mansion; Undertaker and Train; the Character which her Monument will hereafter display—Burial of an ancient Maiden: some former Drawback on her Virgin-fame; Description of her House and Household; Her Manners, Apprehensions, Death—Isaac Ashford, a virtuous Peasant, dies: his manly Character; Reluctance to enter the Poor-House; and why—Misfortune and Derangement of Intellect in Robin Dingley: whence they proceeded: he is not restrained by Misery from a wandering Life; his various Returns to his Parish; his final Return—Wife of Farmer Frankford dies in Prime of Life; Affliction in Consequence of such Death; melancholy View of her House, &c. on her Family's Return from her Funeral: Address to Sorrow—Leah Cousins, a Midwife: her Character; and successful Practice; at length opposed by Doctor Glibb; Opposition in the Parish: Argument of the Doctor; of Leah: her Failure and Decease—Burial of Roger Cuff, a Sailor: his Enmity to his Family; how it originated: his Experiment and its Consequence—The Register terminates—A Bell heard: Inquiry, for whom? The Sexton—Character of old Dibble, and the five Rectors whom he served—Reflections—Conclusion.

GEORGE CRABBE

THE PARISH REGISTER.

PART III.

BURIALS.

Qui vultus Acherontis atri,
Qui Stygia tristem, non tristis, videt,—
. . . .
Par ille Regi, par Superis erit.
Seneca in Agamem. [Act III. vv. 606—8.]

THERE was, 'tis said, and I believe, a time,
  When humble Christians died with views sublime ;
When all were ready for their faith to bleed,
But few to write or wrangle for their creed ;
When lively Faith upheld the sinking heart,
And friends, assured to meet, prepared to part ;
When Love felt hope, when Sorrow grew serene,
And all was comfort in the death-bed scene.
  Alas ! when now the gloomy king they wait,
'Tis weakness yielding to resistless fate ;   10
Like wretched men upon the ocean cast,
They labour hard and struggle to the last,
" Hope against hope," and wildly gaze around,
In search of help that never shall be found :
Nor, till the last strong billow stops the breath,
Will they believe them in the jaws of Death !

  When these my records I reflecting read,
And find what ills these numerous births succeed ;
What powerful griefs these nuptial ties attend,
With what regret these painful journeys end ;   20
When from the cradle to the grave I look,
Mine I conceive a melancholy book.

THE PARISH REGISTER

Where now is perfect resignation seen?
Alas! it is not on the village-green:—
I've seldom known, though I have often read,
Of happy peasants on their dying-bed;
Whose looks proclaim'd that sunshine of the breast,
That more than hope, that Heaven itself express'd.
 What I behold are feverish fits of strife,
'Twixt fears of dying and desire of life: 30
Those earthly hopes, that to the last endure;
Those fears, that hopes superior fail to cure;
At best a sad submission to the doom,
Which, turning from the danger, lets it come.

 Sick lies the man, bewilder'd, lost, afraid,
His spirits vanquish'd and his strength decay'd;
No hope the friend, the nurse, the doctor lend—
"Call then a priest, and fit him for his end."
A priest is call'd; 'tis now, alas! too late,
Death enters with him at the cottage-gate;   40
Or, time allow'd, he goes, assured to find
The self-commending, all-confiding mind;
And sighs to hear, what we may justly call
Death's common-place, the train of thought in all.
 "True, I'm a sinner," feebly he begins,
"But trust in Mercy to forgive my sins";
(Such cool confession no past crimes excite;
Such claim on Mercy seems the sinner's right!)
"I know, mankind are frail, that God is just,
"And pardons those who in his mercy trust;   50
"We're sorely tempted in a world like this;
"All men have done, and I like all, amiss;
"But now, if spared, it is my full intent
"On all the past to ponder and repent:
"Wrongs against me I pardon great and small,
"And if I die, I die in peace with all."
 His merits thus and not his sins confess'd,
He speaks his hopes, and leaves to Heaven the rest.
Alas! are these the prospects, dull and cold,
That dying Christians to their priests unfold?   60
Or mends. the prospect when th' enthusiast cries,

"I die assured!" and in a rapture dies?
Ah, where that humble, self-abasing mind,
With that confiding spirit, shall we find—
The mind that, feeling what repentance brings,
Dejection's terrors and Contrition's stings,
Feels then the hope, that mounts all care above,
And the pure joy that flows from pardoning love?
Such have I seen in death, and much deplore,
So many dying, that I see no more.   70
Lo! now my records, where I grieve to trace,
How Death has triumph'd in so short a space;
Who are the dead, how died they, I relate,
And snatch some portion of their acts from fate.

With Andrew Collett we the year begin,
The blind, fat landlord of the Old Crown Inn—
Big as his butt, and, for the self-same use,
To take in stores of strong fermenting juice.
On his huge chair beside the fire he sate,
In revel chief, and umpire in debate;   80
Each night his string of vulgar tales he told,
When ale was cheap and bachelors were bold:
His heroes all were famous in their days,
Cheats were his boast and drunkards had his praise;
"One, in three draughts, three mugs of ale took down,
"As mugs were then—the champion of the Crown;
"For thrice three days another lived on ale,
"And knew no change but that of mild and stale;
"Two thirsty soakers watch'd a vessel's side,
"When he the tap, with dexterous hand, applied;   90
"Nor from their seats departed, till they found
"That butt was out and heard the mournful sound."
He praised a poacher, precious child of fun!
Who shot the keeper with his own spring-gun;
Nor less the smuggler who the exciseman tied,
And left him hanging at the birch-wood side,
There to expire; but one who saw him hang
Cut the good cord—a traitor of the gang.
His own exploits with boastful glee he told,
What ponds he emptied and what pikes he sold;   100

THE PARISH REGISTER

And how, when bless'd with sight alert and gay,
The night's amusements kept him through the day.
  He sang the praises of those times, when all
"For cards and dice, as for their drink, might call;
"When justice wink'd on every jovial crew,
"And ten-pins tumbled in the parson's view."
  He told, when angry wives, provoked to rail,
Or drive a third-day drunkard from his ale,
What were his triumphs, and how great the skill
That won the vex'd virago to his will :   110
Who raving came—then talk'd in milder strain—
Then wept, then drank, and pledged her spouse again.
Such were his themes : how knaves o'er laws prevail,
Or, when made captives, how they fly from jail;
The young how brave, how subtle were the old;
And oaths attested all that Folly told.
  On death like his what name shall we bestow,
So very sudden! yet so very slow?
'Twas slow :—Disease, augmenting year by year,
Show'd the grim king by gradual steps brought near.   120
'Twas not less sudden : in the night he died,
He drank, he swore, he jested, and he lied;
Thus aiding folly with departing breath.—
"Beware, Lorenzo, the slow-sudden death[1]."

  Next died the Widow Goe, an active dame,
Famed ten miles round, and worthy all her fame;
She lost her husband when their loves were young,
But kept her farm, her credit, and her tongue :
Full thirty years she ruled, with matchless skill,
With guiding judgment and resistless will;   130
Advice she scorn'd, rebellions she suppress'd,
And sons and servants bow'd at her behest.
Like that great man's, who to his Saviour came,
Were the strong words of this commanding dame :—
"Come," if she said, they came; if "go," were gone;
And if "do this,"—that instant it was done.
Her maidens told she was all eye and ear,
In darkness saw and could at distance hear;—

[1 Young's *The Complaint, or Night Thoughts, Night* I.]

GEORGE CRABBE

No parish-business in the place could stir,
Without direction or assent from her;   140
In turn she took each office as it fell,
Knew all their duties, and discharged them well;
The lazy vagrants in her presence shook,
And pregnant damsels fear'd her stern rebuke;
She look'd on want with judgment clear and cool,
And felt with reason and bestow'd by rule;
She match'd both sons and daughters to her mind,
And lent them eyes—for Love, she heard, was blind;
Yet ceaseless still she throve, alert, alive,
The working bee, in full or empty hive;   150
Busy and careful, like that working bee,
No time for love nor tender cares had she;
But when our farmers made their amorous vows,
She talk'd of market-steeds and patent-ploughs.
Not unemploy'd her evenings pass'd away,
Amusement closed, as business waked the day;
When to her toilet's brief concern she ran,
And conversation with her friends began,
Who all were welcome, what they saw, to share;
And joyous neighbours praised her Christmas fare,   160
That none around might, in their scorn, complain
Of Gossip Goe as greedy in her gain.
   Thus long she reign'd, admired, if not approved;
Praised, if not honour'd; fear'd, if not beloved;—
When, as the busy days of Spring drew near,
That call'd for all the forecast of the year;
When lively hope the rising crops survey'd,
And April promised what September paid;
When stray'd her lambs where gorse and greenweed grow;
When rose her grass in richer vales below;   170
When pleased she look'd on all the smiling land,
And view'd the hinds who wrought at her command;
(Poultry in groups still follow'd where she went;)
Then dread o'ercame her—that her days were spent.
   "Bless me! I die, and not a warning giv'n,—
"With *much* to do on Earth, and ALL for Heav'n!—
"No reparation for my soul's affairs,
"No leave petition'd for the barn's repairs;

202

THE PARISH REGISTER

"Accounts perplex'd, my interest yet unpaid,
"My mind unsettled, and my will unmade ;—   180
"A lawyer, haste, and, in your way, a priest ;
"And let me die in one good work at least."
She spake, and, trembling, dropp'd upon her knees,
Heaven in her eye, and in her hand her keys ;
And still the more she found her life decay,
With greater force she grasp'd those signs of sway :
Then fell and died !—In haste her sons drew near,
And dropp'd, in haste, the tributary tear ;
Then from th' adhering clasp the keys unbound,
And consolation for their sorrows found.   190

Death has his infant-train ; his bony arm
Strikes from the baby-cheek the rosy charm ;
The brightest eye his glazing film makes dim,
And his cold touch sets fast the lithest limb :
He seized the sick'ning boy to Gerard lent[1],
When three days' life, in feeble cries, were spent ;
In pain brought forth, those painful hours to stay,
To breathe in pain and sigh its soul away !
   "But why thus lent, if thus recall'd again,
"To cause and feel, to live and die, in pain ?"   200
Or rather say, Why grievous these appear,
If all it pays for Heaven's eternal year ;
If these sad sobs and piteous sighs secure
Delights that live, when worlds no more endure ?
   The sister-spirit long may lodge below,
And pains from nature, pains from reason, know ;
Through all the common ills of life may run,
By hope perverted and by love undone ;
A wife's distress, a mother's pangs, may dread,
And widow-tears, in bitter anguish, shed ;   210
May at old age arrive through numerous harms,
With children's children in those feeble arms :
Nor, till by years of want and grief oppress'd,
Shall the sad spirit flee and be at rest !
   Yet happier therefore shall we deem the boy,
Secured from anxious care and dangerous joy ?

[1] See p. 170.

203

GEORGE CRABBE

Not so! for then would Love Divine in vain
Send all the burthens weary men sustain;
All that now curb the passions when they rage,
The checks of youth and the regrets of age;   220
All that now bid us hope, believe, endure,
Our sorrow's comfort and our vice's cure;
All that for Heaven's high joys the spirits train,
And charity, the crown of all, were vain.
    Say, will you call the breathless infant bless'd,
Because no cares the silent grave molest?
So would you deem the nursling from the wing
Untimely thrust and never train'd to sing;
But far more bless'd the bird whose grateful voice
Sings its own joy and makes the woods rejoice,   230
Though, while untaught, ere yet he charm'd the ear,
Hard were his trials and his pains severe!

    Next died the Lady who yon Hall possess'd;
And here they brought her noble bones to rest.
In Town she dwelt;—forsaken stood the Hall:
Worms ate the floors, the tap'stry fled the wall;
No fire the kitchen's cheerless grate display'd;
No cheerful light the long-closed sash convey'd;
The crawling worm, that turns a summer-fly,
Here spun his shroud and laid him up to die   240
The winter-death:—upon the bed of state,
The bat shrill-shrieking woo'd his flickering mate;
To empty rooms the curious came no more,
From empty cellars turn'd the angry poor,
And surly beggars cursed the ever-bolted door.
To one small room the steward found his way,
Where tenants follow'd to complain and pay;
Yet no complaint before the Lady came,
The feeling servant spared the feeble dame;
Who saw her farms with his observing eyes,   250
And answer'd all requests with his replies.
She came not down, her falling groves to view;
Why should she know, what one so faithful knew?
Why come, from many clamorous tongues to hear,
What one so just might whisper in her ear?

THE PARISH REGISTER

Her oaks or acres why with care explore;
Why learn the wants, the sufferings of the poor;
When one so knowing all their worth could trace,
And one so piteous govern'd in her place?
Lo! now, what dismal sons of Darkness come,   260
To bear this daughter of Indulgence home;
Tragedians all, and well arranged in black!
Who nature, feeling, force, expression lack;
Who cause no tear, but gloomily pass by,
And shake their sables in the wearied eye,
That turns disgusted from the pompous scene,
Proud without grandeur, with profusion, mean!
The tear for kindness past affection owes;
For worth deceased the sigh from reason flows;
E'en well-feign'd passion[s] for our sorrows call,   270
And real tears for mimic miseries fall—
But this poor farce has neither truth nor art,
To please the fancy or to touch the heart;
Unlike the darkness of the sky, that pours
On the dry ground its fertilizing showers;
Unlike to that which strikes the soul with dread,
When thunders roar and forky fires are shed;
Dark but not awful, dismal but yet mean,
With anxious bustle moves the cumbrous scene;
Presents no objects tender or profound,   280
But spreads its cold unmeaning gloom around.
   When woes are feign'd, how ill such forms appear;
And oh! how needless, when the wo's sincere.
   Slow to the vault they come, with heavy tread,
Bending beneath the Lady and her lead;
A case of elm surrounds that ponderous chest,
Close on that case the crimson velvet's press'd;
Ungenerous this, that to the worm denies,
With niggard-caution,. his appointed prize;
For now, ere yet he works his tedious way,   290
Through cloth and wood and metal to his prey,
That prey dissolving shall a mass remain,
That fancy loathes and worms themselves disdain.
   But see! the master-mourner makes his way,
To end his office for the coffin'd clay;

Pleased that our rustic men and maids behold
His plate like silver, and his studs like gold,
As they approach to spell the age, the name,
And all the titles of th' illustrious dame.—
This as (my duty done) some scholar read,   300
A village-father look'd disdain and said :
" Away, my friends ! why take such pains to know
" What some brave marble soon in church shall show ?
" Where not alone her gracious name shall stand,
" But how she lived—the blessing of the land ;
" How much we all deplored the noble dead,
" What groans we utter'd and what tears we shed ;
" Tears, true as those, which in the sleepy eyes
" Of weeping cherubs on the stone shall rise ;
" Tears, true as those, which, ere she found her grave, 310
" The noble Lady to our sorrows gave."

    Down by the church-way walk, and where the brook
Winds round the chancel like a shepherd's crook,
In that small house, with those green pales before,
Where jasmine trails on either side the door ;
Where those dark shrubs that now grow wild at will,
Were clipp'd in form and tantalized with skill ;
Where cockles blanch'd and pebbles neatly spread,
Form'd shining borders for the larkspurs' bed—
There lived a Lady, wise, austere, and nice,   320
Who show'd her virtue by her scorn of vice.
In the dear fashions of her youth she dress'd,
A pea-green Joseph was her favourite vest ;
Erect she stood, she walk'd with stately mien,
Tight was her length of stays, and she was tall and lean.
    There long she lived in maiden-state immured,
From looks of love and treacherous man secured ;
Though evil fame (but that was long before)
Had blown her dubious blast at Catherine's door.
A Captain thither, rich from India, came,   330
And though a cousin call'd, it touch'd her fame :
Her annual stipend rose from his behest,
And all the long-prized treasures she possess'd :—
If aught like joy awhile appear'd to stay

In that stern face, and chase those frowns away,
'Twas when her treasures she disposed for view,
And heard the praises to their splendour due;
Silks beyond price, so rich, they'd stand alone,
And diamonds blazing on the buckled zone;
Rows of rare pearls by curious workmen set,　340
And bracelets fair in box of glossy jet;
Bright polish'd amber precious from its size,
Or forms the fairest fancy could devise.
Her drawers of cedar, shut with secret springs,
Conceal'd the watch of gold and rubied rings;
Letters, long proofs of love, and verses fine
Round the pink'd rims of crisped Valentine.
Her china-closet, cause of daily care,
For woman's wonder held her pencill'd ware;
That pictured wealth of China and Japan,　350
Like its cold mistress, shunn'd the eye of man.
　Her neat small room, adorn'd with maiden-taste,
A clipp'd French puppy, first of favourites, graced;
A parrot next, but dead and stuff'd with art;
(For Poll, when living, lost the Lady's heart,
And then his life; for he was heard to speak
Such frightful words as tinged his Lady's cheek;)
Unhappy bird! who had no power to prove,
Save by such speech, his gratitude and love.
A grey old cat his whiskers lick'd beside;　360
A type of sadness in the house of pride.
The polish'd surface of an India chest,
A glassy globe, in frame of ivory, press'd;
Where swam two finny creatures: one of gold,
Of silver one, both beauteous to behold.
All these were form'd the guiding taste to suit;
The beasts well-manner'd and the fishes mute.
A widow'd Aunt was there, compell'd by need
The nymph to flatter and her tribe to feed;
Who, veiling well her scorn, endured the clog,　370
Mute as the fish and fawning as the dog.
　As years increased, these treasures, her delight,
Arose in value in their owner's sight:
A miser knows that, view it as he will,

GEORGE CRABBE

A guinea kept is but a guinea still ;
And so he puts it to its proper use,
That something more this guinea may produce :
But silks and rings, in the possessor's eyes,
The oft'ner seen, the more in value rise,
And thus are wisely hoarded to bestow   380
The kind of pleasure that with years will grow.
　But what avail'd their worth—if worth had they—
In the sad summer of her slow decay ?
　Then we beheld her turn an anxious look
From trunks and chests, and fix it on her book—
A rich-bound Book of Prayer the Captain gave,
(Some Princess had it, or was said to have ;)
And then once more, on all her stores, look round,
And draw a sigh so piteous and profound,
That told, " Alas ! how hard from these to part,   390
" And for new hopes and habits form the heart !
" What shall I do," (she cried,) " my peace of mind
" To gain in dying, and to die resign'd ? "
　" Hear," we return'd ;—" these baubles cast aside,
" Nor give thy God a rival in thy pride ;
" Thy closets shut, and ope thy kitchen's door ;
" *There* own thy failings, *here* invite the poor ;
" A friend of Mammon let thy bounty make ;
" For widows' prayers thy vanities forsake ;
" And let the hungry of thy pride partake :   400[ ]]
" Then shall thy inward eye with joy survey
" The angel Mercy tempering Death's delay ! "
　Alas ! 'twas hard ; the treasures still had charms,
Hope still its flattery, sickness its alarms ;
Still was the same unsettled, clouded view,
And the same plaintive cry, " What shall I do ? "
　Nor change appear'd : for when her race was run,
Doubtful we all exclaim'd, " What has been done ? "
Apart she lived, and still she lies alone ;
Yon earthy heap awaits the flattering stone,   410
On which invention shall be long employ'd,
To show the various worth of Catherine Lloyd.

　Next to these ladies, but in nought allied,

THE PARISH REGISTER

A noble Peasant, Isaac Ashford, died.
Noble he was, contemning all things mean,
His truth unquestion'd and his soul serene;
Of no man's presence Isaac felt afraid;
At no man's question Isaac look'd dismay'd:
Shame knew him not, he dreaded no disgrace;
Truth, simple truth, was written in his face;   420
Yet while the serious thought his soul approved,
Cheerful he seem'd, and gentleness he loved.
To bliss domestic he his heart resign'd,
And, with the firmest, had the fondest mind.
Were others joyful, he look'd smiling on,
And gave allowance where he needed none;
Good he refused with future ill to buy,
Nor knew a joy that caused reflection's sigh;
A friend to virtue, his unclouded breast
No envy stung, no jealousy distress'd;   430
(Bane of the poor! it wounds their weaker mind,
To miss one favour which their neighbours find.)
Yet far was he from stoic pride removed;
He felt humanely, and he warmly loved.
I mark'd his action, when his infant died,
And his old neighbour for offence was tried;
The still tears, stealing down that furrow'd cheek,
Spoke pity, plainer than the tongue can speak.
If pride were his, 'twas not their vulgar pride,
Who, in their base contempt, the great deride;   440
Nor pride in learning,—though my clerk agreed,
If fate should call him, Ashford might succeed;
Nor pride in rustic skill, although we knew
None his superior, and his equals few:—
But, if that spirit in his soul had place,
It was the jealous pride that shuns disgrace:
A pride in honest fame, by virtue gain'd,
In sturdy boys to virtuous labours train'd;
Pride in the power that guards his country's coast,
And all that Englishmen enjoy and boast;   450
Pride in a life that slander's tongue defied,—
In fact, a noble passion, misnamed pride.
   He had no party's rage, no sect'ry's whim;

Crabbe   o   209

Christian and countryman was all with him.
True to his church he came; no Sunday-shower
Kept him at home in that important hour;
Nor his firm feet could one persuading sect,
By the strong glare of their new light, direct;—
"On hope, in mine own sober light, I gaze,
"But should be blind and lose it, in your blaze."   460
    In times severe, when many a sturdy swain
Felt it his pride, his comfort, to complain,
Isaac their wants would soothe, his own would hide,
And feel in that his comfort and his pride.
    At length he found, when seventy years were run,
His strength departed, and his labour done;
When he, save honest fame, retain'd no more,
But lost his wife and saw his children poor:
'Twas then, a spark of—say not, discontent—
Struck on his mind, and thus he gave it vent: 470
    "Kind are your laws, ('tis not to be denied,)
"That in yon house for ruin'd age provide,
"And they are just;—when young, we give you all,
"And for assistance in our weakness call.—
"Why then this proud reluctance to be fed,
"To join your poor, and eat the parish-bread?
"But yet I linger, loth with him to feed,
"Who gains his plenty by the sons of need;
"He who, by contract, all your paupers took,
"And gauges stomachs with an anxious look.   480
"On some old master I could well depend;
"See him with joy and thank him as a friend;
"But ill on him, who doles the day's supply,
"And counts our chances, who at night may die:
"Yet help me, Heav'n! and let me not complain
"Of what I suffer, but my fate sustain."
    Such were his thoughts, and so resign'd he grew;
Daily he placed the workhouse in his view!
But came not there, for sudden was his fate:
He dropp'd, expiring, at his cottage-gate.   490
    I feel his absence in the hours of prayer,
And view his seat and sigh for Isaac there:
I see no more those white locks thinly spread

Round the bald polish of that honour'd head;
No more that awful glance on playful wight,
Compell'd to kneel and tremble at the sight,
To fold his fingers, all in dread the while,
Till Mister Ashford soften'd to a smile;
No more that meek and suppliant look in prayer,
Nor the pure faith (to give it force), are there;—   500
But he is bless'd, and I lament no more
A wise good man, contented to be poor.

Then died a Rambler: not the one who sails
And trucks, for female favours, beads and nails;
Not one, who posts from place to place—of men
And manners treating with a flying pen;
Not he, who climbs, for prospects, Snowd[o]n's height,
And chides the clouds that intercept the sight;
No curious shell, rare plant, or brilliant spar,
Enticed our traveller from his home so far;   510
But all the reason, by himself assign'd
For so much rambling, was, a restless mind;
As on, from place to place, without intent,
Without reflection, Robin Dingley went.
    Not thus by nature;—never man was found
Less prone to wander from his parish-bound:
Claudian's old Man, to whom all scenes were new,
Save those where he and where his apples grew,
Resembled Robin, who around would look,
And his horizon for the earth's mistook.   520
    To this poor swain a keen Attorney came:—
"I give thee joy, good fellow! on thy name;
"The rich old Dingley's dead;—no child has he,
"Nor wife, nor will; his ALL is left for thee:
"To be his fortune's heir thy claim is good;
"Thou hast the name, and we will prove the blood."
    The claim was made; 'twas tried—it would not stand;
They proved the blood, but were refused the land.
    Assured of wealth, this man of simple heart,
To every friend had predisposed a part: 530
His wife had hopes indulged of various kind;
The three Miss Dingleys had their school assign'd,

GEORGE CRABBE

Masters were sought for what they each required,
And books were bought and harpsichords were hired:
So high was hope;—the failure touch'd his brain,
And Robin never was himself again.
Yet he no wrath, no angry wish express'd,
But tried, in vain, to labour or to rest;
Then cast his bundle on his back, and went
He knew not whither, nor for what intent.   540
     Years fled;—of Robin all remembrance past,
When home he wander'd in his rags at last.
A sailor's jacket on his limbs was thrown,
A sailor's story he had made his own;
Had suffer'd battles, prisons, tempests, storms,
Encountering death in all his ugliest forms.
His cheeks were haggard, hollow was his eye,
Where madness lurk'd, conceal'd in misery;
Want, and th' ungentle world, had taught a part,
And prompted cunning to that simple heart: 550
He now bethought him, he would roam no more,
But live at home and labour as before.
     Here clothed and fed, no sooner he began
To round and redden, than away he ran;
His wife was dead, their children past his aid:
So, unmolested, from his home he stray'd.
Six years elapsed, when, worn with want and pain,
Came Robin, wrapt in all his rags, again.—
We chide, we pity;—placed among our poor,
He fed again, and was a man once more.   560
     As when a gaunt and hungry fox is found,
Entrapp'd alive in some rich hunter's ground;
Fed for the field, although each day's a feast,
Fatten you may, but never *tame* the beast;
A house protects him, savoury viands sustain;
But loose his neck and off he goes again:
So stole our vagrant from his warm retreat,
To rove a prowler and be deem'd a cheat.
     Hard was his fare; for, him at length we saw,
In cart convey'd and laid supine on straw.   570
His feeble voice now spoke a sinking heart;
His groans now told the motions of the cart;

212

And when it stopp'd, he tried in vain to stand;
Closed was his eye, and clench'd his clammy hand;
Life ebb'd apace, and our best aid no more
Could his weak sense or dying heart restore:
But now he fell, a victim to the snare,
That vile attorneys for the weak prepare—
They who, when profit or resentment call,
Heed not the groaning victim they enthrall.   580

Then died lamented, in the strength of life,
A valued Mother and a faithful Wife;
Call'd not away, when time had loosed each hold
On the fond heart, and each desire grew cold;
But when, to all that knit us to our kind,
She felt fast-bound, as charity can bind—
Not, when the ills of age, its pain, its care,
The drooping spirit for its fate prepare;
And each affection, failing, leaves the heart
Loosed from life's charm and willing to depart—   590
But all her ties the strong invader broke,
In all their strength, by one tremendous stroke!
Sudden and swift the eager pest came on,
And terror grew, till every hope was gone;
Still those around appear'd for hope to seek!
But view'd the sick, and were afraid to speak.—
Slowly they bore, with solemn step, the dead;
When grief grew loud and bitter tears were shed,
My part began; a crowd drew near the place,
Awe in each eye, alarm in every face: 600
So swift the ill, and of so fierce a kind,
That fear with pity mingled in each mind;
Friends with the husband came their griefs to blend;
For good-man Frankford was to all a friend.
The last-born boy they held above the bier;
He knew not grief, but cries express'd his fear;
Each different age and sex reveal'd its pain,
In now a louder, now a lower strain;
While the meek father, listening to their tones,
Swell'd the full cadence of the grief by groans.   610
The elder sister strove her pangs to hide,

And soothing words to younger minds applied :
" Be still, be patient," oft she strove to say ;
But fail'd as oft, and weeping turn'd away.
   Curious and sad, upon the fresh-dug hill,
The village-lads stood melancholy still ;
And idle children, wandering to-and-fro,
As Nature guided, took the tone of wo.
   Arrived at home, how then they gazed around,
In every place—where she no more was found ;   620
The seat at table she was wont to fill ;
The fire-side chair, still set, but vacant still ;
The garden-walks, a labour all her own ;
The latticed bower, with trailing shrubs o'ergrown ;
The Sunday-pew she fill'd with all her race—
Each place of hers, was now a sacred place,
That, while it call'd up sorrows in the eyes,
Pierced the full heart and forced them still to rise.
   Oh sacred sorrow ! by whom souls are tried,
Sent not to punish mortals, but to guide ;   630
If thou art mine, (and who shall proudly dare
To tell his Maker, he has had his share ?)
Still let me feel for what thy pangs are sent,
And be my guide and not my punishment !

   Of Leah Cousins next the name appears,
With honours crown'd and bless'd with length of years,
Save that she lived to feel, in life's decay,
The pleasure die, the honours drop away.
A matron she, whom every village-wife
View'd as the help and guardian of her life ;   640
Fathers and sons, indebted to her aid,
Respect to her and her profession paid ;
Who in the house of plenty largely fed,
Yet took her station at the pauper's bed ;
Nor from that duty could be bribed again,
While fear or danger urged her to remain.
In her experience all her friends relied ;
Heaven was her help and nature was her guide.
   Thus Leah lived, long trusted, much caress'd,
Till a Town-Dame a youthful Farmer bless'd ;   650

THE PARISH REGISTER

A gay vain bride, who would example give
To that poor village where she deign'd to live;
Some few months past, she sent, in hour of need,
For Doctor Glibb, who came with wond'rous speed:
Two days he waited, all his art applied,
To save the mother when her infant died :—
"'Twas well I came," at last he deign'd to say;
"'Twas wondrous well"—and proudly rode away.
    The news ran round :—" How vast the Doctor's pow'r!
"He saved the Lady in the trying hour;   660
"Saved her from death, when she was dead to hope,
"And her fond husband had resign'd her up:
"So all, like her, may evil fate defy,
"If Doctor Glibb, with saving hand, be nigh."
    Fame (now his friend), fear, novelty, and whim,
And fashion, sent the varying sex to him:
From this, contention in the village rose,
And *these* the Dame espoused, the Doctor *those* :
The wealthier part, to him and science went;
With luck and her the poor remain'd content.   670
    The matron sigh'd; for she was vex'd at heart,
With so much profit, so much fame, to part:
"So long successful in my art," she cried,
"And this proud man, so young and so untried!"
    "Nay," said the Doctor, "dare you trust your wives,
"The joy, the pride, the solace of your lives,
"To one who acts and knows no reason why,
"But trusts, poor hag! to luck for an ally?—
"Who, on experience, can her claims advance,
"And own the powers of accident and chance?   680
"A whining dame, who prays in danger's view,
"(A proof she knows not what beside to do;)
"What's her experience? In the time that's gone,
"Blundering she wrought, and still she blunders on :—
"And what is Nature? One who acts in aid
"Of gossips half asleep, and half afraid.
"With such allies I scorn my fame to blend,
"Skill is my luck and courage is my friend;
"No slave to Nature, 'tis my chief delight
"To win my way and act in her despite :—   690

215

GEORGE CRABBE

"Trust then my art, that, in itself complete,
"Needs no assistance and fears no defeat."
Warm'd by her well-spiced ale and aiding pipe,
The angry matron grew for contest ripe.
  "Can you," she said, "ungrateful and unjust,
"Before experience, ostentation trust!
"What is your hazard, foolish daughters, tell?
"If safe, you're certain; if secure, you're well:
"That I have luck must friend and foe confess,
"And what's good judgment but a lucky guess?   700
"*He* boasts but what he *can* do:—will you run
"From me, your friend! who, all *he* boasts, *have* done?
"By proud and learned words his powers are known;
"By healthy boys and handsome girls my own.
"Wives! fathers! children! by my help you live;
"Has this pale Doctor more than life to give?
"No stunted cripple hops the village round;
"Your hands are active and your heads are sound:
"My lads are all your fields and flocks require;
"My lasses all those sturdy lads admire.   710
"Can this proud leech, with all his boasted skill,
"Amend the soul or body, wit or will?
"Does he for courts the sons of farmers frame,
"Or make the daughter differ from the dame?
"Or, whom he brings into this world of wo,
"Prepares he them their part to undergo?
"If not, this stranger from your doors repel,
"And be content to *be*, and to be *well*."
  She spake; but, ah! with words too strong and plain;
Her warmth offended, and her truth was vain: 720
The *many* left her, and the friendly *few*,
If never colder, yet they older grew;
Till, unemploy'd, she felt her spirits droop,
And took, insidious aid! th' inspiring cup;
Grew poor and peevish as her powers decay'd,
And propp'd the tottering frame with stronger aid;—
Then died!—I saw our careful swains convey,
From this our changeful world, the matron's clay,
Who to this world, at least, with equal care,
Brought them its changes, good and ill to share.   730

216

THE PARISH REGISTER

Now to his grave was Roger Cuff convey'd,
And strong resentment's lingering spirit laid.
Shipwreck'd in youth, he home return'd, and found
His brethren three—and thrice they wish'd him drown'd.
"Is this a landman's love? Be certain then,
"We part for ever!"—and they cried, "Amen!"
His words were truth's.—Some forty summers fled;
His brethren died; his kin supposed him dead:
Three nephews these, one sprightly niece, and one,
Less near in blood—they call'd him *surly John*;   740
He work'd in woods apart from all his kind,
Fierce were his looks and moody was his mind.
　For home the Sailor now began to sigh:—
"The dogs are dead, and I'll return and die;
"When all I have, my gains, in years of care,
"The younger Cuffs with kinder souls shall share.—
"Yet hold! I'm rich;—with one consent they'll say,
"'You're welcome, Uncle, as the flowers in May.'
"No; I'll disguise me, be in tatters dress'd,
"And best befriend the lads who treat me best."   750
　Now all his kindred,—neither rich nor poor—
Kept the wolf want some distance from the door.
　In piteous plight he knock'd at George's gate,
And begg'd for aid, as he described his state;—
But stern was George:—"Let them who had thee strong,
"Help thee to drag thy weaken'd frame along;
"To us a stranger, while your limbs would move,
"From us depart and try a stranger's love:—
"Ha! dost thou murmur?"—for, in Roger's throat,
Was "Rascal!" rising with disdainful note.   760
　To pious James he then his prayer address'd;—
"Good lack," quoth James, "thy sorrows pierce my breast;
"And, had I wealth, as have my brethren twain,
"One board should feed us and one roof contain.
"But plead I will thy cause and I will pray;
"And so farewell! Heaven help thee on thy way!"
　"Scoundrel!" said Roger, (but apart;)—and told
His case to Peter;—Peter too was cold;—
"The rates are high; we have a-many poor;
"But I will think,"—he said, and shut the door.   770

GEORGE CRABBE

Then the gay Niece the seeming pauper press'd :—
"Turn, Nancy, turn, and view this form distress'd ;
"Akin to thine is this declining frame,
"And this poor beggar claims an Uncle's name."
"Avaunt ! begone !" the courteous maiden said,
"Thou vile impostor ! Uncle Roger's dead :
"I hate thee, beast ; thy look my spirit shocks !
"Oh ! that I saw thee starving in the stocks !"
"My gentle niece !" he said—and sought the wood.—
"I hunger, fellow ; prithee, give me food !"   780
"Give ! am I rich ? This hatchet take, and try
"Thy proper strength, nor give those limbs the lie ;
"Work, feed thyself, to thine own powers appeal,
"Nor whine out woes, thine own right-hand can heal :
"And while that hand is thine and thine a leg,
"Scorn of the proud or of the base to beg."
"Come, surly John, thy wealthy kinsman view,"
Old Roger said :—"thy words are brave and true ;
"Come, live with me : we'll vex those scoundrel-boys,
"And that prim shrew shall, envying, hear our joys.—   790
"Tobacco's glorious fume all day we'll share,
"With beef and brandy kill all kinds of care ;
"We'll beer and biscuit on our table heap,
"And rail at rascals, till we fall asleep."
Such was their life ; but when the woodman died,
His grieving kin for Roger's smiles applied—
In vain ; he shut, with stern rebuke, the door,
And dying, built a refuge for the poor :
With this restriction, That no Cuff should share
One meal, or shelter for one moment there.   800

My record ends :—But hark ! e'en now I hear
The bell of death, and know not whose to fear.
Our farmers all, and all our hinds were well ;
In no man's cottage danger seem'd to dwell ;—
Yet death of man proclaim these heavy chimes,
For thrice they sound, with pausing space, three times.
"Go ; of my sexton seek, Whose days are sped ?—
"What ! he, himself !—and is old Dibble dead ?"
His eightieth year he reach'd, still undecay'd,

218

And rectors five to one close vault convey'd :—   810
But he is gone; his care and skill I lose,
And gain a mournful subject for my Muse :
His masters lost, he'd oft in turn deplore,
And kindly add,—"Heaven grant, I lose no more!"
Yet, while he spake, a sly and pleasant glance
Appear'd at variance with his complaisance :
For, as he told their fate and varying worth,
He archly look'd,—"I yet may bear thee forth."
"When first "—(he so began)—"my trade I plied,
"Good master Addle was the parish-guide;   820
"His clerk and sexton, I beheld with fear
"His stride majestic, and his frown severe;
"A noble pillar of the church he stood,
"Adorn'd with college-gown and parish-hood.
"Then as he paced the hallow'd aisles about,
"He fill'd the sevenfold surplice fairly out!
"But in his pulpit, wearied down with prayer,
"He sat and seem'd as in his study's chair;
"For while the anthem swell'd, and when it ceased,
"Th' expecting people view'd their slumbering priest : 830
"Who, dozing, died.—Our Parson Peele was next;
"'I will not spare you,' was his favourite text;
"Nor did he spare, but raised them many a pound;
"Ev'n me he mulct for my poor rood of ground;
"Yet cared he nought, but with a gibing speech,
"'What should I do,' quoth he, 'but what *I* preach?'
"His piercing jokes (and he'd a plenteous store)
"Were daily offer'd both to rich and poor;
"His scorn, his love, in playful words he spoke;
"His pity, praise, and promise, were a joke :   840
"But though so young and bless'd with spirits high,
"He died as grave as any judge could die :
"The strong attack subdued his lively powers,—
"His was the grave, and Doctor Grandspear ours.
"Then were there golden times the village round;
"In his abundance all appear'd t' abound;
"Liberal and rich, a plenteous board he spread,
"E'en cool Dissenters at his table fed,
"Who wish'd, and hoped,—and thought a man so kind

GEORGE CRABBE

" A way to Heaven, though not their own, might find ;   850
" To them, to all, he was polite and free,
" Kind to the poor, and, ah ! most kind to me :
" ' Ralph,' would he say, ' Ralph Dibble, thou art old ;
" ' That doublet fit, 'twill keep thee from the cold.
" ' How does my sexton ?—What ! the times are hard ;
" ' Drive that stout pig, and pen him in thy yard.'
" But most, his rev'rence loved a mirthful jest :—
" ' Thy coat is thin ; why, man, thou'rt *barely* dress'd ;
" ' It's worn to th' thread ; but I have nappy beer ;
" ' Clap that within, and see how they will wear !'   860
"   " Gay days were these ; but they were quickly past :
" When first he came, we found he cou'dn't last :
" A whoreson cough (and at the fall of leaf)
" Upset him quite ;—but what's the gain of grief ?
"   " Then came the Author-Rector : his delight
" Was all in books ; to read them, or to write :
" Women and men he strove alike to shun,
" And hurried homeward when his tasks were done.
" Courteous enough, but careless what he said,
" For points of learning he reserved his head ;   870
" And, when addressing either poor or rich,
" He knew no better than his cassock which.
" He, like an osier, was of pliant kind,
" Erect by nature, but to bend inclined ;
" Not like a creeper falling to the ground,
" Or meanly catching on the neighbours round.—
" Careless was he of surplice, hood, and band—
" And kindly took them as they came to hand ;
" Nor, like the doctor, wore a world of hat,
" As if he sought for dignity in that.   880
" He talk'd, he gave, but not with cautious rules,
" Nor turn'd from gipsies, vagabonds, or fools ;
" It was his nature, but they thought it whim,
" And so our beaux and beauties turn'd from him.
" Of questions much he wrote, profound and dark—
" How spake the serpent, and where stopp'd the ark ;
" From what far land the Queen of Sheba came ;
" Who Salem's priest, and what his father's name ;
" He made the Song of Songs its mysteries yield,

220

THE PARISH REGISTER

"And Revelations, to the world, reveal'd. 890
"He sleeps i' the aisle—but not a stone records
"His name or fame, his actions or his words:
"And, truth, your reverence, when I look around,
"And mark the tombs in our sepulchral ground,
"(Though dare I not of one man's hope to doubt),
"I'd join the party who repose without.
  "Next came a youth from Cambridge, and, in truth,
"He was a sober and a comely youth;
"He blush'd in meekness as a modest man,
"And gain'd attention ere his task began; 900
"When preaching, seldom ventured on reproof,
"But touch'd his neighbours tenderly enough.
"Him, in his youth, a clamorous sect assail'd,
"Advised and censured, flatter'd,—and prevail'd.—
"Then did he much his sober hearers vex,
"Confound the simple, and the sad perplex;
"To a new style his reverence rashly took;
"Loud grew his voice, to threat'ning swell'd his look;
"Above, below, on either side, he gazed,
"Amazing all, and most himself amazed: 910
"No more he read his preachments pure and plain,
"But launch'd outright, and rose and sank again:
"At times he smiled in scorn, at times he wept,
"And such sad coil with words of vengeance kept,
"That our best sleepers started as they slept. [}]
  "'Conviction comes like lightning,' he would cry;
"'In vain you seek it, and in vain you fly;
"''Tis like the rushing of the mighty wind,
"'Unseen its progress, but its power you find;
"'It strikes the child ere yet its reason wakes; 920
"'His reason fled, the ancient sire it shakes.
"'The proud, learn'd man, and him who loves to know
"'How and from whence these gusts of grace will blow,
"'It shuns,—but sinners in their way impedes,
"'And sots and harlots visits in their deeds:
"'Of faith and penance it supplies the place;
"'Assures the' vilest that they live by grace,
"'And, without running, makes them win the race.' [}]
  "Such was the doctrine our young prophet taught;
"And here conviction, there confusion wrought; 930

221

GEORGE CRABBE

"When his thin cheek assumed a deadly hue,
"And all the rose to one small spot withdrew:
"They call'd it hectic; 'twas a fiery flush,
"More fix'd and deeper than the maiden blush;
"His paler lips the pearly teeth disclosed,
"And lab'ring lungs the length'ning speech opposed.
"No more his span-girth shanks and quiv'ring thighs
"Upheld a body of the smaller size;
"But down he sank upon his dying bed,
"And gloomy crotchets fill'd his wandering head.— 940
"'Spite of my faith, all-saving faith,' he cried,
"'I fear of worldly works the wicked pride;
"'Poor as I am, degraded, abject, blind,
"'The good I've wrought still rankles in my mind;
"'My alms-deeds all, and every deed I've done,
"'My moral-rags defile me, every one;
"'It should not be—what say'st thou? tell me, Ralph.'
"Quoth I, 'Your reverence, I believe, you're safe;
"'Your faith's your prop, nor have you pass'd such time
"'In life's good-works as swell them to a crime. 950
"'If I of pardon for my sins were sure,
"'About my goodness I would rest secure.'
"Such was his end; and mine approaches fast;
"I've seen my best of preachers—and my last."—
He bow'd, and archly smiled at what he said,
Civil but sly:—"And is old Dibble dead?"
Yes! he is gone: and WE are going all;
Like flowers we wither, and like leaves we fall;—
Here, with an infant, joyful sponsors come,
Then bear the new-made Christian to its home; 960
A few short years, and we behold him stand,
To ask a blessing, with his bride in hand:
A few, still seeming shorter, and we hear
His widow weeping at her husband's bier:—
Thus, as the months succeed, shall infants take
Their names; thus parents shall the child forsake;
Thus brides again and bridegrooms blithe shall kneel,
By love or law compell'd their vows to seal,
Ere I again, or one like me, explore
These simple annals of the VILLAGE POOR. 970

THE BIRTH OF FLATTERY.

The Subject—Poverty and Cunning described—When united, a jarring Couple—Mutual Reproof—The Wife consoled by a Dream—Birth of a Daughter—Description and Prediction of Envy—How to be rendered ineffectual, explained in a Vision—Simulation foretells the future Success and Triumphs of Flattery—Her Power over various Characters and different Minds; over certain Classes of Men; over Envy himself—Her successful Art of softening the Evils of Life; of changing Characters; of meliorating Prospects, and affixing Value to Possessions, Pictures, &c.—Conclusion.

GEORGE CRABBE

THE BIRTH OF FLATTERY.

Omnia habeo, nec quicquam habeo [. . . . . . .]
Quidquid dicunt, laudo; id rursum si negant, laudo id quoque.
Negat quis, nego; ait, aio. Postremò imperavi egomet mihi
Omnia assentari.

Terent. in Eunuch. [Aƈt II. Sc. 2.]

It has been held in ancient rules,
That flattery is the food of fools;
Yet now and then your men of wit
Will condescend to taste a bit.
Swift[, Cadenus and Vanessa.]

MUSE of my Spenser, who so well could sing
The passions all, their bearings and their ties;
Who could in view those shadowy beings bring,
And with bold hand remove each dark disguise,
Wherein love, hatred, scorn, or anger lies:
Guide him to Fairy-land, who now intends
That way his flight; assist him as he flies,
To mark those passions, Virtue's foes and friends,
By whom when led she droops, when leading she ascends.

Yes! they appear, I see the fairy-train!   10
And who that modest nymph of meek address?
Not Vanity, though loved by all the vain;
Not Hope, though promising to all success;
Nor Mirth, nor Joy, though foe to all distress;
Thee, sprightly syren, from this train I choose,
Thy birth relate, thy soothing arts confess;
'Tis not in thy mild nature to refuse,
When poets ask thine aid, so oft their meed and muse.

In Fairy-land, on wide and cheerless plain,
Dwelt, in the house of Care, a sturdy swain;   20

224

THE BIRTH OF FLATTERY

A hireling he, who, when he till'd the soil,
Look'd to the pittance that repaid his toil;
And to a master left the mingled joy
And anxious care that follow'd his employ.
Sullen and patient he at once appear'd,
As one who murmur'd, yet as one who fear'd;
Th' attire was coarse that clothed his sinewy frame,
Rude his address, and Poverty his name.

    In that same plain a nymph, of curious taste,
A cottage (plann'd with all her skill) had placed;   30
Strange the materials, and for what design'd
The various parts, no simple man might find;
What seem'd the door, each entering guest withstood,
What seem'd a window was but painted wood;
But by a secret spring the wall would move,
And daylight drop through glassy door above.
'Twas all her pride, new traps for praise to lay,
And all her wisdom was to hide her way;
In small attempts incessant were her pains,
And Cunning was her name among the swains.   40

    Now, whether fate decreed this pair should wed,
And blindly drove them to the marriage-bed;
Or whether love in some soft hour inclined
The damsel's heart, and won her to be kind,
Is yet unsung: they were an ill-match'd pair,
But both disposed to wed—and wed they were.

Yet, though united in their fortune, still
Their ways were diverse; varying was their will;
Nor long the maid had bless'd the simple man,
Before dissensions rose, and she began:—   50

    "Wretch that I am! since to thy fortune bound,
"What plan, what project, with success is crown'd?
"I, who a thousand secret arts possess;
"Who every rank approach with right address;
"Who've loosed a guinea from a miser's chest,
"And worm'd his secret from a traitor's breast;

Crabbe   P   225

"Thence gifts and gains collecting, great and small,
"Have brought to thee, and thou consum'st them all:
"For want like thine—a bog without a base—
"Ingulfs all gains I gather for the place;   60
"Feeding, unfill'd; destroying, undestroy'd;
"It craves for ever, and is ever void:—
"Wretch that I am! what misery have I found,
"Since my sure craft was to thy calling bound!"

"Oh! vaunt of worthless art," the swain replied,
Scowling contempt, "how pitiful this pride!
"What are these specious gifts, these paltry gains,
"But base rewards for ignominious pains?
"With all thy tricking, still for bread we strive;
"Thine is, proud wretch! the care that cannot thrive;   70
"By all thy boasted skill and baffled hooks
"Thou gain'st no more than students by their books;
"No more than I for my poor deeds am paid,
"Whom none can blame, will help, or dare upbraid.
"Call this our need, a bog that all devours—
"Then what thy petty arts but summer-flowers,
"Gaudy and mean, and serving to betray
"The place they make unprofitably gay?
"Who know it not, some useless beauties see—
"But ah! to prove it, was reserved for me."   80

Unhappy state! that, in decay of love,
Permits harsh truth his errors to disprove;
While he remains, to wrangle and to jar
Is friendly tournament, not fatal war;
Love in his play will borrow arms of hate,
Anger and rage, upbraiding and debate;
And by his power the desperate weapons thrown,
Become as safe and pleasant as his own;
But left by him, their natures they assume,
And fatal, in their poisoning force, become.   90

Time fled, and now the swain compell'd to see
New cause for fear—"Is this thy thrift?" quoth he.
To whom the wife with cheerful voice replied:—

THE BIRTH OF FLATTERY

"Thou moody man, lay all thy fears aside,
"I've seen a vision;—they, from whom I came,
"A daughter promise, promise wealth and fame;
"Born with my features, with my arts, yet she
"Shall patient, pliant, persevering be,
"And in thy better ways resemble thee.   [*J*]
"The fairies round shall at her birth attend;   100
"The friend of all in all shall find a friend;
"And, save that one sad star that hour must gleam
"On our fair child, how glorious were my dream!"

This heard the husband, and, in surly smile,
Aim'd at contempt, but yet he hoped the while :
For as, when sinking, wretched men are found
To catch at rushes rather than be drown'd;
So on a dream our peasant placed his hope,
And found that rush as valid as a rope.

Swift fled the days, for now in hope they fled,   110
When a fair daughter bless'd the nuptial bed;
Her infant-face the mother's pains beguiled,
She look'd so pleasing, and so softly smiled;
Those smiles, those looks, with sweet sensations moved
The gazer's soul, and, as he look'd, he loved.

And now the fairies came, with gifts, to grace
So mild a nature and so fair a face.
They gave, with beauty, that bewitching art,
That holds in easy chains the human heart;
They gave her skill to win the stubborn mind,   120
To make the suffering to their sorrows blind,
To bring on pensive looks the pleasing smile,
And Care's stern brow of every frown beguile.
These magic favours graced the infant-maid,
Whose more enlivening smile the charming gifts repaid.

Now Fortune changed, who, were she constant long,
Would leave us few adventures for our song.
A wicked elfin roved this land around,
Whose joys proceeded from the griefs he found;

P 2

Envy his name :—his fascinating eye   130
From the light bosom drew the sudden sigh ;
Unsocial he, but with malignant mind,
He dwelt with man, that he might curse mankind ;
Like the first foe, he sought th' abode of Joy,
Grieved to behold, but eager to destroy ;
Round blooming beauty, like the wasp, he flew,
Soil'd the fresh sweet, and changed the rosy hue ;
The wise, the good, with anxious heart, he saw,
And here a failing found, and there a flaw ;
Discord in families 'twas his to move,   140
Distrust in friendship, jealousy in love ;
He told the poor, what joys the great possess'd,
The great—what calm content the cottage bless'd ;
To part the learned and the rich he tried,
Till their slow friendship perish'd in their pride.
Such was the fiend, and so secure of prey,
That only Misery pass'd unstung away.

Soon as he heard the fairy-babe was born,
Scornful he smiled, but felt no more than scorn ;
For why, when Fortune placed her state so low,   150
In useless spite his lofty malice show ?
Why, in a mischief of the meaner kind,
Exhaust the vigour of a ranc'rous mind ?
But, soon as Fame the fairy-gifts proclaim'd,
Quick-rising wrath his ready soul inflamed,
To swear, by vows that e'en the wicked tie,
The nymph should weep her varied destiny ;
That every gift, that now appear'd to shine
In her fair face, and make her smiles divine,
Should all the poison of his magic prove,   160
And they should scorn her, whom she sought for love.

His spell prepared, in form an ancient dame,
A fiend in spirit, to the cot he came ;
There gain'd admittance, and the infant press'd
(Muttering his wicked magic) to his breast ;
And thus he said :—" Of all the powers, who wait
" On Jove's decrees, and do the work of fate,

THE BIRTH OF FLATTERY

"Was I alone, despised or worthless, found,
"Weak to protect, or impotent to wound?
"See then thy foe, regret the friendship lost,   170
"And learn my skill, but learn it at your cost.
  "Know then, O child! devote to fates severe,
"The good shall hate thy name, the wise shall fear;
"Wit shall deride, and no protecting friend
"Thy shame shall cover, or thy name defend.
"Thy gentle sex, who, more than ours, should spare
"A humble foe, will greater scorn declare;
"The base alone thy advocates shall be,
"Or boast alliance with a wretch like thee."

He spake and vanish'd, other prey to find,   180
And waste in slow disease the conquer'd mind.

Awed by the elfin's threats, and fill'd with dread,
The parents wept, and sought their infant's bed:
Despair alone the father's soul possess'd,
But hope rose gently in the mother's breast;
For well she knew that neither grief nor joy
Pain'd without hope, or pleased without alloy;
And while these hopes and fears her heart divide,
A cheerful vision bade the fears subside.

She saw descending to the world below   190
An ancient form, with solemn pace and slow.

  "Daughter, no more be sad," (the phantom cried,)
"Success is seldom to the wise denied;
"In idle wishes fools supinely stay—
"Be there a will, and wisdom finds a way:
"Why art thou grieved? Be rather glad, that he,
"Who hates the happy, aims his darts at thee,
"But aims in vain; thy favour'd daughter lies,
"Serenely blest, and shall to joy arise.
"For, grant that curses on her name shall wait,   200
"(So envy wills and such the voice of fate,)
"Yet, if that name be prudently suppress'd,

"She shall be courted, favour'd, and caress'd.
"For what are names? and where agree mankind
"In those to persons or to acts assign'd?
"Brave, learn'd, or wise, if some their favourites call,
"Have they the titles or the praise from all?
"Not so, but others will the brave disdain
"As rash, and deem the sons of wisdom vain ;
"The self-same mind shall scorn or kindness move,   210
"And the same deed attract contempt and love.

  "So all the powers who move the human soul,
"With all the passions who the will control,
"Have various names—[one] giv'n by Truth Divine,
"(As Simulation thus was fix'd for mine,)
"The rest by man, who now, as wisdom's, prize
"My secret counsels, now as art despise ;
"One hour, as just, those counsels they embrace,
"And spurn, the next, as pitiful and base.

  "Thee, too, my child, those fools as Cunning fly,   220
"Who on thy counsel and thy craft rely ;
"That worthy craft in others they condemn,
"But 'tis their prudence, while conducting them.

  "Be FLATTERY, then, thy happy infant's name,
"Let Honour scorn her and let Wit defame ;
"Let all be true that Envy dooms, yet all,
"Not on herself, but on her name, shall fall ;
"While she thy fortune and her own shall raise,
"And decent Truth be call'd, and loved as modest Praise.

  "O happy child! the glorious day shall shine,   230⎫
"When every ear shall to thy speech incline,   ⎬
"Thy words alluring and thy voice divine.   [ʃ]
"The sullen pedant and the sprightly wit,
"To hear thy soothing eloquence, shall sit ;
"And both, abjuring Flattery, will agree
"That truth inspires, and they must honour thee.

  "Envy himself shall to thy accents bend,   ⎫
"Force a faint smile and sullenly attend,   ⎬
"When thou shalt call him Virtue's jealous friend,   [ʃ]
"Whose bosom glows with generous rage to find   240
"How fools and knaves are flatter'd by mankind.

  "The sage retired, who spends alone his days,

THE BIRTH OF FLATTERY

"And flies th' obstreperous voice of public praise;
"The vain, the vulgar cry shall gladly meet,
"And bid thee welcome to his still retreat;
"Much will he wonder, how thou cam'st to find
"A man to glory dead, to peace consign'd.
"'O Fame!' he'll cry, (for he will call thee Fame,)
"'From thee I fly, from thee conceal my name.'
"But thou shalt say, 'Though Genius takes his flight,   250
"He leaves behind a glorious train of light,
"And hides in vain;—yet prudent he that flies
"The flatterer's art, and for himself is wise.'
 "Yes, happy child! I mark th' approaching day,
"When warring natures will confess thy sway;
"When thou shalt Saturn's golden reign restore,
"And vice and folly shall be known no more.
 "Pride shall not then in human-kind have place,
"Changed, by thy skill, to Dignity and Grace;
"While Shame, who now betrays the inward sense   260
"Of secret ill, shall be thy Diffidence;
"Avarice shall thenceforth prudent Forecast be,
"And bloody Vengeance, Magnanimity;
"The lavish tongue shall honest truths impart,   ⎫
"The lavish hand shall show the generous heart, ⎬
"And Indiscretion be contempt of art: [ʃ]
"Folly and Vice shall then, no longer known,
"Be, this as Virtue, that as Wisdom, shown.
 "Then shall the Robber, as the Hero, rise
"To seize the good that churlish law denies;   270
"Throughout the world shall rove the generous band,
"And deal the gifts of Heaven from hand to hand.
 "In thy blest days no tyrant shall be seen,
"Thy gracious king shall rule contented men;
"In thy blest days shall not a rebel be,
"But patriots all and well approved of thee.
 "Such powers are thine, that man, by thee, shall wrest
"The gainful secret from the cautious breast;
"Nor then, with all his care, the good retain,
"But yield to thee the secret and the gain.   280
"In vain shall much experience guard the heart
"Against the charm of thy prevailing art;

231

GEORGE CRABBE

"Admitted once, so soothing is thy strain,
"It comes the sweeter, when it comes again;
"And when confess'd as thine, what mind so strong
"Forbears the pleasure it indulged so long?
    "Soft'ner of every ill! of all our woes
"The balmy solace! friend of fiercest foes!
"Begin thy reign, and like the morning rise!
"Bring joy, bring beauty, to our eager eyes;   290
"Break on the drowsy world like opening day,
"While grace and gladness join thy flow'ry way;
"While every voice is praise, while every heart is gay. [ʃ]
    "From thee all prospects shall new beauties take,
"'Tis thine to seek them and 'tis thine to make;
"On the cold fen I see thee turn thine eyes,
"Its mists recede, its chilling vapour flies;
"Th' enraptured lord th' improving ground surveys,
"And for his Eden asks the traveller's praise,
"Which yet, unview'd of thee, a bog had been,   300
"Where spungy rushes hide the plashy green.
    "I see thee breathing on the barren moor,
"That seems to bloom although so bleak before;
"There, if beneath the gorse the primrose spring,
"Or the pied daisy smile below the ling,
"They shall new charms, at thy command, disclose,
"And none shall miss the myrtle or the rose.
"The wiry moss, that whitens all the hill,
"Shall live a beauty by thy matchless skill;
"Gale[1] from the bog shall yield Arabian balm,   310
"And the grey willow wave a golden palm.
    "I see thee smiling in the pictured room,
"Now breathing beauty, now reviving bloom;
"There, each immortal name 'tis thine to give
"To graceless forms, and bid the lumber live.
"Should'st thou coarse boors or gloomy martyrs see,
"These shall thy Guidos, those thy Teniers' be;
"There shalt thou Raphael's saints and angels trace,
"There make for Rubens and for Reynolds place,
"And all the pride of art [shalt] find in her disgrace.   320 [ʃ]

---

1 " Myrica gale," a shrub growing in boggy and fenny grounds.

THE BIRTH OF FLATTERY

"Delight of either sex! thy reign commence;
"With balmy sweetness soothe the weary sense,
"And to the sickening soul thy cheering aid dispense.   [ʃ]
"Queen of the mind! thy golden age begin;
"In mortal bosoms varnish shame and sin;
"Let all be fair without, let all be calm within."   [ʃ]

The Vision fled; the happy mother rose,
Kiss'd the fair infant, smiled at all her foes,
And FLATTERY made her name:—her reign began,
Her own dear sex she ruled, then vanquish'd man;   330
A smiling friend, to every class, she spoke,
Assumed their manners, and their habits took;
Her, for her humble mien, the modest loved;
Her cheerful looks the light and gay approved;
The just beheld her, firm; the valiant, brave;
Her mirth the free, her silence pleased the grave;
Zeal heard her voice, and, as he preach'd aloud,
Well-pleased he caught her whispers from the crowd—
(Those whispers, soothing-sweet to every ear,
Which some refuse to pay, but none to hear);   340
Shame fled her presence; at her gentle strain,
Care softly smiled, and guilt forgot its pain;
The wretched thought, the happy found her true;
The learn'd confess'd that she their merits knew;
The rich—could they a constant friend condemn?
The poor believed—for who should flatter them?

Thus on her name though all disgrace attend,
In every creature she beholds a friend.

GEORGE CRABBE

REFLECTIONS

UPON THE SUBJECT——

Quid juvat errores, mersâ jam puppe, fateri?
Quid lacrymæ delicta juvant commissa secutæ?
Claudian. in Eutrop. lib. ii. lin. 7

What avails it, when shipwreck'd, that error appears?
Are the crimes we commit wash'd away by our tears?

WHEN all the fiercer passions cease
   (The glory and disgrace of youth);
When the deluded soul, in peace,
   Can listen to the voice of truth;
When we are taught in whom to trust,
   And how to spare, to spend, to give,
(Our prudence kind, our pity just)—
   'Tis then we rightly learn to live.

Its weakness when the body feels,
   Nor danger in contempt defies;   10
To reason when desire appeals,
   When on experience hope relies;
When every passing hour we prize,
   Nor rashly on our follies spend;
But use it, as it quickly flies,
   With sober aim to serious end;
When prudence bounds our utmost views,
   And bids us wrath and wrong forgive;
When we can calmly gain or lose—
   'Tis then we rightly learn to live.   20

REFLECTIONS

Yet thus, when we our way discern,
 And can upon our care depend,
To travel safely when we learn,
 Behold! we're near our journey's end.
We've trod the maze of error round,
 Long wand'ring in the winding glade;
And now the torch of truth is found,
 It only shows us where we stray'd:
Light for ourselves, what is it worth,
 When we no more our way can choose? 30
For others when we hold it forth,
 They, in their pride, the boon refuse.

By long experience taught, we now
 Can rightly judge of friends and foes,
Can all the worth of these allow,
 And all their faults discern in those;
Relentless hatred, erring love,
 We can for sacred truth forego;
We can the warmest friend reprove,
 And bear to praise the fiercest foe: 40
To what effect? Our friends are gone,
 Beyond reproof, regard, or care;
And of our foes remains there one,
 The mild relenting thoughts to share?

Now 'tis our boast that we can quell
 The wildest passions in their rage;
Can their destructive force repel,
 And their impetuous wrath assuage:
Ah! Virtue, dost thou arm, when now
 This bold rebellious race are fled; 50
When all these tyrants rest, and thou
 Art warring with the mighty dead?
Revenge, ambition, scorn, and pride,
 And strong desire and fierce disdain,
The giant-brood, by thee defied,
 Lo! Time's resistless strokes have slain.

235

Yet Time, who could that race subdue,
    (O'erpow'ring strength, appeasing rage,)
Leaves yet a persevering crew,
    To try the failing powers of age.   60
Vex'd by the constant call of these,
    Virtue awhile for conquest tries,
But weary grown and fond of ease,
    She makes with them a compromise:
Av'rice himself she gives to rest,
    But rules him with her strict commands;
Bids Pity touch his torpid breast,
    And Justice hold his eager hands.

Yet is there nothing men can do,
    When chilling Age comes creeping on?   70
Cannot we yet some good pursue?
    Are talents buried? genius gone?
If passions slumber in the breast,
    If follies from the heart be fled:
Of laurels let us go in quest,
    And place them on the poet's head.

Yes, we'll redeem the wasted time,
    And to neglected studies flee;
We'll build again the lofty rhyme,
    Or live, Philosophy, with thee;   80
For reasoning clear, for flight sublime,
    Eternal fame reward shall be;
And to what glorious heights we'll climb,
    Th' admiring crowd shall envying see.

Begin the song! begin the theme!—
    Alas! and is Invention dead?
Dream we no more the golden dream?
    Is Mem'ry with her treasures fled?
Yes, 'tis too late—now Reason guides
    The mind, sole judge in all debate;   90
And thus th' important point decides,
    For laurels, 'tis, alas! too late.
        What is possess'd we may retain,
        But for new conquests strive in vain.

REFLECTIONS

Beware then, Age, that what was won,
[In] life's past labours, studies, views,
Be lost not, now the labour's done,
    When all thy part is—not to lose:
      When thou canst toil or gain no more,
      Destroy not what was gain'd before.   100

For, all that's gain'd of all that's good,
  When time shall his weak frame destroy,
(Their use then rightly understood,)
  Shall man, in happier state, enjoy.
Oh! argument for truth divine,
  For study's cares, for virtue's strife:
To know th' enjoyment will be thine,
  In that renew'd, that endless life!

GEORGE CRABBE

SIR EUSTACE GREY.

SCENE—A MAD-HOUSE.

PERSONS—VISITOR, PHYSICIAN, AND PATIENT.

Veris miscens falsa.—
   Seneca in Herc. furente [Aĉt IV. v. 1070].

VISITOR.

I 'LL know no more;—the heart is torn
    By views of wo we cannot heal;
Long shall I see these things forlorn,
    And oft again their griefs shall feel,
    As each upon the mind shall steal;
    That wan projeĉtor's mystic style,
    That lumpish idiot leering by,
That peevish idler's ceaseless wile,
And that poor maiden's half-form'd smile,
    While struggling for the full-drawn sigh!—   10

I'll know no more.

PHYSICIAN.

                    —Yes, turn again;
    Then speed to happier scenes thy way,
When thou hast view'd, what yet remain,
    The ruins of Sir Eustace Grey,
    The sport of madness, misery's prey.
But he will no historian need;
    His cares, his crimes, will he display,
And show (as one from frenzy freed)
The proud-lost mind, the rash-done deed.

SIR EUSTACE GREY

That cell to him is Greyling Hall:—   20
    Approach; he'll bid thee welcome there;
Will sometimes for his servant call,
    And sometimes point the vacant chair:
He can, with free and easy air,
    Appear attentive and polite;
Can veil his woes in manners fair,
    And pity with respect excite.

PATIENT.

Who comes?—Approach!—'tis kindly done:—
    My learn'd physician, and a friend,
Their pleasures quit, to visit one   30
    Who cannot to their ease attend,
Nor joys bestow, nor comforts lend,
    As when I lived so bless'd, so well,
And dreamt not I must soon contend
    With those malignant powers of hell.

PHYSICIAN.

Less warmth, Sir Eustace, or we go.—

PATIENT.

See! I am calm as infant-love,
A very child, but one of wo,
    Whom you should pity, not reprove:—
But men at ease, who never strove   40
    With passions wild, will calmly show
How soon we may their ills remove,
    And masters of their madness grow.

Some twenty years I think are gone;—
    (Time flies, I know not how, away;)—
The sun upon no happier shone,
    Nor prouder man, than Eustace Grey.
Ask where you would, and all would say,
    The man admired and praised of all,
By rich and poor, by grave and gay.   50
    Was the young lord of Greyling Hall.

GEORGE CRABBE

Yes! I had youth and rosy health;
   Was nobly form'd, as man might be;
For sickness then, of all my wealth,
   I never gave a single fee:
The ladies fair, the maidens free,
   Were all accustom'd then to say,
Who would a handsome figure see
   Should look upon Sir Eustace Grey.

He had a frank and pleasant look,   60
   A cheerful eye and accent bland;
His very speech and manner spoke
   The generous heart, the open hand;
About him all was gay or grand,
   He had the praise of great and small;
He bought, improved, projected, plann'd,
   And reign'd a prince at Greyling Hall.

My lady!—she was all we love;
   All praise (to speak her worth) is faint;
Her manners show'd the yielding dove,   70
   Her morals, the seraphic saint;
She never breathed nor look'd complaint;
   No equal upon earth had she:—
Now, what is this fair thing I paint?
   Alas! as all that live shall be.

There was, beside, a gallant youth,
   And him my bosom's friend I had:—
Oh! I was rich in very truth,
   It made me proud—it made me mad!—
Yes, I was lost—but there was cause!—   80
   Where stood my tale?—I cannot find—
But I had all mankind's applause,
   And all the smiles of womankind.

There were two cherub-things beside,
   A gracious girl, a glorious boy;
Yet more to swell my full-blown pride,
   To varnish higher my fading joy,

SIR EUSTACE GREY

Pleasures were ours without alloy,
  Nay, Paradise,—till my frail Eve
Our bliss was tempted to destroy,
  Deceived and fated to deceive.   90

But I deserved; for all that time,
  When I was loved, admired, caress'd,
There was within each secret crime,
  Unfelt, uncancell'd, unconfess'd:
I never then my God address'd,
  In grateful praise or humble prayer;
And, if His Word was not my jest,
  (Dread thought!) it never was my care.

I doubted—fool I was to doubt!—   100
  If that all-piercing eye could see;
If He who looks all worlds throughout,
  Would so minute and careful be,
As to perceive and punish me:—
  With man I would be great and high,
But with my God so lost, that He,
  In his large view, should pass me by.

Thus bless'd with children, friend, and wife,
  Bless'd far beyond the vulgar lot;
Of all that gladdens human life,   110
  Where was the good, that I had not?
But my vile heart had sinful spot,
  And Heaven beheld its deep'ning stain;
Eternal justice I forgot,
  And mercy sought not to obtain.

Come near—I'll softly speak the rest!—
  Alas! 'tis known to all the crowd,
Her guilty love was all confess'd,
  And his, who so much truth avow'd,
My faithless friend's.—In pleasure proud   120
  I sat, when these cursed tidings came;
Their guilt, their flight was told aloud,
  And Envy smiled to hear my shame!

Crabbe   Q   241

I call'd on Vengeance; at the word
    She came:—Can I the deed forget?
I held the sword, th' accursed sword,
    The blood of his false heart made wet;
And that fair victim paid her debt;
    She pined, she died, she loath'd to live;—
I saw her dying—see her yet: 130
    Fair fallen thing! my rage forgive!

Those cherubs still, my life to bless,
    Were left; could I my fears remove,
Sad fears that check'd each fond caress,
    And poison'd all parental love?
Yet that with jealous feelings strove,
    And would at last have won my will,
Had I not, wretch! been doom'd to prove
    Th' extremes of mortal good and ill.

In youth! health! joy! in beauty's pride!   140
    They droop'd: as flowers when blighted bow,
The dire infection came.—They died,
    And I was cursed—as I am now.—
Nay, frown not, angry friend—allow
    That I was deeply, sorely tried;
Hear then, and you must wonder how
    I could such storms and strifes abide.

Storms!—not that clouds embattled make,
    When they afflict this earthly globe;
But such as with their terrors shake   150
    Man's breast, and to the bottom probe:
They make the hypocrite disrobe,
    They try us all, if false or true;
For this, one devil had pow'r on Job;
    And I was long the slave of two.

PHYSICIAN.

Peace, peace, my friend; these subjects fly;
    Collect thy thoughts—go calmly on.—

SIR EUSTACE GREY

PATIENT.

And shall I then the fact deny?
  I was,—thou know'st—I was begone,
Like him who fill'd the eastern throne,   160
  To whom the Watcher cried aloud [1];
That royal wretch of Babylon,
  Who was so guilty and so proud.

Like him, with haughty, stubborn mind,
  I, in my state, my comforts sought;
Delight and praise I hoped to find,
  In what I builded, planted, bought!
Oh! arrogance! by misery taught—
  Soon came a voice! I felt it come:
"Full be his cup, with evil fraught,   170
  "Demons his guides, and death his doom!"

Then was I cast from out my state;
  Two fiends of darkness led my way;
They waked me early, watch'd me late,
  My dread by night, my plague by day!
Oh! I was made their sport, their play,
  Through many a stormy troubled year;
And how they used their passive prey
  Is sad to tell;—but you shall hear.

And first, before they sent me forth,   180
  Through this unpitying world to run,
They robb'd Sir Eustace of his worth,
  Lands, manors, lordships, every one;
So was that gracious man undone,
  Was spurn'd as vile, was scorn'd as poor,
Whom every former friend would shun,
  And menials drove from every door.

Then those ill-favour'd Ones [2], whom none
  But my unhappy eyes could view,
Led me, with wild emotion, on,   190
  And, with resistless terror, drew.

Q 2   243

GEORGE CRABBE

Through lands we fled, o'er seas we flew,
  And halted on a boundless plain;
Where nothing fed, nor breathed, nor grew,
  But silence ruled the still domain.

Upon that boundless plain, below,
  The setting sun's last rays were shed,
And gave a mild and sober glow,
  Where all were still, asleep, or dead;
Vast ruins in the midst were spread,   200
  Pillars and pediments sublime,
Where the grey moss had form'd a bed,
  And clothed the crumbling spoils of time.

There was I fix'd, I know not how,
  Condemn'd for untold years to stay:
Yet years were not;—one dreadful *now*
  Endured no change of night or day;
The same mild evening's sleeping ray
  Shone softly-solemn and serene,
And all that time I gazed away,   210
  The setting sun's sad rays were seen.

At length a moment's sleep stole on—
  Again came my commission'd foes;
Again through sea and land we're gone,
  No peace, no respite, no repose:
Above the dark broad sea we rose,
  We ran through bleak and frozen land;
I had no strength their strength t' oppose,
  An infant in a giant's hand.

They placed me where those streamers play,   220
  Those nimble beams of brilliant light;
It would the stoutest heart dismay,
  To see, to feel, that dreadful sight:
So swift, so pure, so cold, so bright,
  They pierced my frame with icy wound,
And, all that half-year's polar night,
  Those dancing streamers wrapp'd me round.

SIR EUSTACE GREY

Slowly that darkness pass'd away,
  When down upon the earth I fell;—
Some hurried sleep was mine by day;⁣
  But, soon as toll'd the evening bell,
They forced me on, where ever dwell
  Far-distant men in cities fair,
Cities of whom no trav'lers tell,
  Nor feet but mine were wanderers there.

Their watchmen stare, and stand aghast,
  As on we hurry through the dark;
The watch-light blinks as we go past,
  The watch-dog shrinks and fears to bark;
The watch-tower's bell sounds shrill; and, hark!   240
  The free wind blows—we've left the town—
A wide sepulchral ground I mark,
  And on a tombstone place me down.

What monuments of mighty dead!
  What tombs of various kinds are found!
And stones erect their shadows shed
  On humble graves, with wickers bound;
Some risen fresh, above the ground,
  Some level with the native clay,
What sleeping millions wait the sound,   250
  "Arise, ye dead, and come away!"

Alas! they stay not for that call;
  Spare me this wo! ye demons, spare!—
They come! the shrouded shadows all—
  'Tis more than mortal brain can bear;
Rustling they rise, they sternly glare
  At man, upheld by vital breath;
Who, led by wicked fiends, should dare
  To join the shadowy troops of death!

Yes, I have felt all man can feel,   260
  Till he shall pay his nature's debt:
Ills that no hope has strength to heal,
  No mind the comfort to forget:

Whatever cares the heart can fret,
 The spirits wear, the temper gall,
Wo, want, dread, anguish, all beset
 My sinful soul!—together all!

Those fiends upon a shaking fen
 Fix'd me, in dark tempestuous night;
There never trod the foot of men;   270
 There flock'd the fowl in wint'ry flight;
There danced the moor's deceitful light
 Above the pool where sedges grow;
And, when the morning-sun shone bright,
 It shone upon a field of snow.

They hung me on a bough so small,
 The rook could build her nest no higher;
They fix'd me on the trembling ball
 That crowns the steeple's quiv'ring spire;
They set me where the seas retire,   280
 But drown with their returning tide;
And made me flee the mountain's fire,
 When rolling from its burning side.

I've hung upon the ridgy steep
 Of cliffs, and held the rambling brier;
I've plunged below the billowy deep,
 Where air was sent me to respire;
I've been where hungry wolves retire;
 And (to complete my woes) I've ran
Where Bedlam's crazy crew conspire   290
 Against the life of reasoning man.

I've furl'd in storms the flapping sail,
 By hanging from the topmast-head;
I've served the vilest slaves in jail,
 And pick'd the dunghill's spoil for bread;
I've made the badger's hole my bed,
 I've wander'd with a gipsy crew;
I've dreaded all the guilty dread,
 And done what they would fear to do.

SIR EUSTACE GREY

On sand, where ebbs and flows the flood,   300
  Midway they placed and bade me die;
Propp'd on my staff, I stoutly stood,
  When the swift waves came rolling by;
And high they rose, and still more high,
  Till my lips drank the bitter brine;
I sobb'd convulsed, then cast mine eye,
  And saw the tide's re-flowing sign.

And then, my dreams were such as nought
  Could yield but my unhappy case;
I've been of thousand devils caught,   310
  And thrust into that horrid place,
Where reign dismay, despair, disgrace;
  Furies with iron fangs were there,
To torture that accursed race,
  Doom'd to dismay, disgrace, despair.

Harmless I was, yet hunted down
  For treasons, to my soul unfit;
I've been pursued through many a town,
  For crimes that petty knaves commit;
I've been adjudged t' have lost my wit,   320
  Because I preach'd so loud and well;
And thrown into the dungeon's pit,
  For trampling on the pit of hell.

Such were the evils, man of sin,
  That I was fated to sustain;
And add to all, without—within,
  A soul defiled with every stain
That man's reflecting mind can pain;
  That pride, wrong, rage, despair, can make;
In fact, they'd nearly touch'd my brain,   330
  And reason on her throne would shake.

But pity will the vilest seek,
  If punish'd guilt will not repine ;—
I heard a heavenly teacher speak,
  And felt the SUN OF MERCY shine:

GEORGE CRABBE

I hail'd the light! the birth divine!
And then was seal'd among the few;
Those angry fiends beheld the sign,
And from me in an instant flew.

Come, hear how thus the charmers cry   340
　To wandering sheep, the strays of sin,
While some the wicket-gate pass by,
　And some will knock and enter in:
Full joyful 'tis a soul to win,
　For he that winneth souls is wise;
Now, hark! the holy strains begin,
　And thus the sainted preacher cries [3] :—

　　" Pilgrim, burthen'd with thy sin,
　　" Come the way to Zion's gate,
　　" There, till Mercy let thee in,   350
　　" Knock and weep, and watch and wait.
　　　" Knock!—He knows the sinner's cry;
　　　" Weep!—He loves the mourner's tears;
　　　" Watch!—for saving grace is nigh;
　　　" Wait!—till heavenly light appears.

　　" Hark! it is the Bridegroom's voice;
　　" Welcome, pilgrim, to thy rest;
　　" Now within the gate rejoice,
　　" Safe and seal'd, and bought and bless'd!
　　　" Safe—from all the lures of vice;   360
　　　" Seal'd—by signs the chosen know;
　　　" Bought—by love and life the price;
　　　" Bless'd—the mighty debt to owe.

　　" Holy Pilgrim! what for thee
　　" In a world like this remain?
　　" From thy guarded breast shall flee
　　" Fear and shame, and doubt and pain.
　　　" Fear—the hope of Heaven shall fly;
　　　" Shame—from glory's view retire;
　　　" Doubt—in certain rapture die;   370
　　　" Pain—in endless bliss expire."

SIR EUSTACE GREY

But though my day of grace was come,
   Yet still my days of grief I find ;
The former clouds' collected gloom
   Still sadden the reflecting mind ;
The soul, to evil things consign'd,
   Will of their evil some retain ;
The man will seem to earth inclined,
   And will not look erect again.

Thus, though elect, I feel it hard   380
   To lose what I possess'd before,
To be from all my wealth debarr'd :—
   The brave Sir Eustace is no more.
But old I wax and passing poor,
   Stern, rugged men my conduct view ;
They chide my wish, they bar my door,
   'Tis hard—I weep—you see I do.—

Must you, my friends, no longer stay ?
   Thus quickly all my pleasures end ;
But I'll remember, when I pray,   390
   My kind physician and his friend ;
And those sad hours you deign to spend
   With me, I shall requite them all ;
Sir Eustace for his friends shall send,
   And thank their love at Greyling Hall.

VISITOR.

The poor Sir Eustace !—Yet his hope
   Leads him to think of joys again ;
And when his earthly visions droop,
   His views of heavenly kind remain.—
But whence that meek and humbled strain,   400
   That spirit wounded, lost, resign'd ?
Would not so proud a soul disdain
   The madness of the poorest mind ?

PHYSICIAN.

No ! for the more he swell'd with pride,
   The more he felt misfortune's blow ;

Disgrace and grief he could not hide,
  And poverty had laid him low:
Thus shame and sorrow working slow,
  At length this humble spirit gave;
Madness on these began to grow,   410
  And bound him to his fiends a slave.

Though the wild thoughts had touch'd his brain,
  Then was he free.—So, forth he ran;
To soothe or threat, alike were vain:
  He spake of fiends; look'd wild and wan;
Year after year, the hurried man
  Obey'd those fiends from place to place;
Till his religious change began
  To form a frenzied child of grace.

For, as the fury lost its strength,   420
  The mind reposed; by slow degrees
Came lingering hope, and brought at length,
  To the tormented spirit ease:
This slave of sin, whom fiends could seize,
  Felt or believed their power had end;—
"'Tis faith," he cried, "my bosom frees,
  "And now my SAVIOUR is my friend."

But ah! though time can yield relief,
  And soften woes it cannot cure,
Would we not suffer pain and grief,   430
  To have our reason sound and sure?
Then let us keep our bosoms pure,
  Our fancy's favourite flights suppress;
Prepare the body to endure,
  And bend the mind to meet distress;
And then HIS guardian care implore,
Whom demons dread and men adore.

SIR EUSTACE GREY

NOTES TO SIR EUSTACE GREY.

Note 1, p. 243, line 161.

To whom the Watcher cried aloud.

Prophecy of Daniel, chap. iv. 22 [and 23].

Note 2, page 243, line 188.

Then those ill-favour'd Ones, &c.

Vide Bunyan's Pilgrim's Progress [Part II.].

Note 3, page 248, line 347.

And thus the sainted preacher cries.

It has been suggested to me, that this change from restlessness to repose, in the mind of Sir Eustace, is wrought by a methodistic call ; and it is admitted to be such : a sober and rational conversion could not have happened while the disorder of the brain continued. Yet the verses which follow, in a different measure, are not intended to make any religious persuasion appear ridiculous ; they are to be supposed as the effect of memory in the disordered mind of the speaker, and, though evidently enthusiastic in respect to language, are not meant to convey any impropriety of sentiment.

GEORGE CRABBE

THE HALL OF JUSTICE.

IN TWO PARTS.

PART I.

Confiteor facere hoc annos; sed et altera causa est,
Anxietas animi, continuusque dolor.
Ovid [Epp. ex Ponto Lib. I. Ep. IV. vv. 7—8].

MAGISTRATE, VAGRANT, CONSTABLE, &c.

VAGRANT.

TAKE, take away thy barbarous hand,
  And let me to thy master speak;
Remit awhile the harsh command,
  And hear me, or my heart will break.

MAGISTRATE.

Fond wretch! and what canst thou relate,
  But deeds of sorrow, shame, and sin?
Thy crime is proved, thou know'st thy fate;
  But come, thy tale!—begin, begin!—

VAGRANT.

My crime!——This sick'ning child to feed,
  I seized the food your witness saw;   10
I knew your laws forbade the deed,
  But yielded to a stronger law.

Know'st thou, to Nature's great command
  All human laws are frail and weak?
Nay! frown not—stay his eager hand,
  And hear me, or my heart will break.

252

THE HALL OF JUSTICE

In this, th' adopted babe I hold
  With anxious fondness to my breast,
My heart's sole comfort I behold,
  More dear than life, when life was bless'd ;   20
I saw her pining, fainting, cold,
  I begg'd—but vain was my request.

I saw the tempting food, and seized—
  My infant-sufferer found relief ;
And, in the pilfer'd treasure pleased,
  Smiled on my guilt, and hush'd my grief.

But I have griefs of other kind,
  Troubles and sorrows more severe ;
Give me to ease my tortured mind,
  Lend to my woes a patient ear ;   30
And let me—if I may not find
  A friend to help—find one to hear.

Yet nameless let me plead—my name
  Would only wake the cry of scorn ;
A child of sin, conceived in shame,
  Brought forth in wo, to misery born.

My mother dead, my father lost,
  I wander'd with a vagrant crew ;
A common care, a common cost,
  Their sorrows and their sins I knew ;   40
With them, by want on error forced,
  Like them, I base and guilty grew.

Few are my years, not so my crimes ;
  The age, which these sad looks declare,
Is Sorrow's work, it is not Time's,
  And I am old in shame and care.

Taught to believe the world a place
  Where every stranger was a foe,
Train'd in the arts that mark our race,
  To what new people could I go ?   50
Could I a better life embrace,
  Or live as virtue dictates ? No !—

GEORGE CRABBE

So through the land I wandering went,
  And little found of grief or joy;
But lost my bosom's sweet content
  When first I loved—the Gipsy-Boy.

A sturdy youth he was and tall,
  His looks would all his soul declare;
His piercing eyes were deep and small,
  And strongly curl'd his raven-hair.   60

Yes, Aaron had each manly charm,
  All in the May of youthful pride;
He scarcely fear'd his father's arm,
  And every other arm defied.—
Oft, when they grew in anger warm,
  (Whom will not love and power divide?)
I rose, their wrathful souls to calm,
  Not yet in sinful combat tried.

His father was our party's chief,
  And dark and dreadful was his look;   70
His presence fill'd my heart with grief;
  Although to me he kindly spoke.

With Aaron I delighted went,
  His favour was my bliss and pride;
In growing hope our days we spent,
  Love growing charms in either spied;
It saw them, all which Nature lent,
  It lent them all which she denied.

Could I the father's kindness prize,
  Or grateful looks on him bestow,   80
Whom I beheld in wrath arise,
  When Aaron sunk beneath his blow?

He drove him down with wicked hand,—
  It was a dreadful sight to see;
Then vex'd him, till he left the land,
  And told his cruel love to me;—
The clan were all at his command,
  Whatever his command might be.

254

THE HALL OF JUSTICE

The night was dark, the lanes were deep,
    And one by one they took their way ;   90
He bade me lay me down and sleep,
    I only wept and wish'd for day.

Accursèd be the love he bore,
    Accursèd was the force he used ;
So let him of his God implore
    For mercy, and be so refused !

You frown again ;—to show my wrong,
    Can I in gentle language speak ?
My woes are deep, my words are strong ;—
    And hear me, or my heart will break.   100

MAGISTRATE.

I hear thy words, I feel thy pain ;
    Forbear awhile to speak thy woes ;
Receive our aid, and then again
    The story of thy life disclose.

For, though seduced and led astray,
    Thou'st travell'd far and wander'd long ;
Thy God hath seen thee all the way,
    And all the turns that led thee wrong.

GEORGE CRABBE

THE HALL OF JUSTICE.

PART II.

Quondam ridentes oculi, nunc fonte perenni
  Deplorant pœnas noĉte dieque suas.
Corn. Galli [Maximiniani (Pseudo-Galli)] *Eleg.* [I. vv. 137-8.]

MAGISTRATE.

COME, now again thy woes impart,
  Tell all thy sorrows, all thy sin;
We cannot heal the throbbing heart
  Till we discern the wounds within.

Compunĉtion weeps our guilt away,
  The sinner's safety is his pain;
Such pangs for our offences pay,
  And these severer griefs are gain.

VAGRANT.

The son came back—he found us wed;
  Then dreadful was the oath he swore;—   10
His way through Blackburn Forest led;—
  His father we beheld no more.

Of all our daring clan not one
  Would on the doubtful subjeĉt dwell;
For all esteem'd the injured son,
  And fear'd the tale which he could tell.

But I had mightier cause for fear;
  For slow and mournful round my bed
I saw a dreadful form appear—
  It came when I and Aaron wed.   20

256

THE HALL OF JUSTICE

(Yes! we were wed, I know my crime,—
  We slept beneath the [elmen] tree;
But I was grieving all the time,
  And Aaron frown'd my tears to see.

For he not yet had felt the pain
  That rankles in a wounded breast;
He waked to sin, then slept again,
  Forsook his God, yet took his rest.—

But I was forced to feign delight,
  And joy in mirth and music sought;   30
And mem'ry now recalls the night,
  With such surprise and horror fraught,
That reason felt a moment's flight,
  And left a mind to madness wrought.)

When waking, on my heaving breast
  I felt a hand as cold as death;
A sudden fear my voice suppress'd,
  A chilling terror stopp'd my breath.—

I seem'd—no words can utter how!
  For there my father-husband stood—   40
And thus he said :—" Will God allow,
  " The great avenger, just and good,
" A wife to break her marriage vow,
  " A son to shed his father's blood?"

I trembled at the dismal sounds,
  But vainly strove a word to say;
So, pointing to his bleeding wounds,
  The threat'ning spectre stalk'd away[1].

I brought a lovely daughter forth,
  His father's child, in Aaron's bed;   50
He took her from me in his wrath;—
  "Where is my child?"—"Thy child is dead."

[1] The state of mind here described will account for a vision of this nature, without having recourse to any supernatural appearance.

Crabbe   R   257

GEORGE CRABBE

'Twas false—we wander'd far and wide,
    Through town and country, field and fen,
Till Aaron, fighting, fell and died,
    And I became a wife again.

I then was young:—my husband sold
    My fancied charms for wicked price;
He gave me oft, for sinful gold,
    The slave, but not the friend, of vice—   60
Behold me, Heaven! my pains behold,
    And let them for my sins suffice!

The wretch, who lent me thus for gain,
    Despised me when my youth was fled;
Then came disease, and brought me pain—
    Come, death, and bear me to the dead!
For, though I grieve, my grief is vain,
    And fruitless all the tears I shed.

True, I was not to virtue train'd;
    Yet well I knew my deeds were ill;   70
By each offence my heart was pain'd—
    I wept, but I offended still;
My better thoughts my life disdain'd,
    But yet the viler led my will.

My husband died, and now no more
    My smile was sought, or ask'd my hand—
A widow'd vagrant, vile and poor,
    Beneath a vagrant's vile command.

Ceaseless I roved the country round,
    To win my bread by fraudful arts,   80
And long a poor subsistence found,
    By spreading nets for simple hearts.

Though poor, and abject, and despised,
    Their fortunes to the crowd I told;
I gave the young the love they prized,
    And promised wealth to bless the old;
Schemes for the doubtful I devised,
    And charms for the forsaken sold.

THE HALL OF JUSTICE

At length for arts like these confined
  In prison with a lawless crew,   90
I soon perceived a kindred mind,
  And there my long-lost daughter knew:

His father's child, whom Aaron gave
  To wander with a distant clan,
The miseries of the world to brave,
  And be the slave of vice and man.

She knew my name—we met in pain;
  Our parting pangs can I express?
She sail'd a convict o'er the main,
  And left an heir to her distress.   100

This is that heir to shame and pain,
  For whom I only could descry
A world of trouble and disdain—
  Yet, could I bear to see her die,
Or stretch her feeble hand in vain,
  And, weeping, beg of me supply?

No! though the fate thy mother knew
  Was shameful! shameful though thy race
Have wander'd all, a lawless crew,
  Outcasts, despised in every place: 110

Yet, as the dark and muddy tide,
  When far from its polluted source,
Becomes more pure, and, purified,
  Flows in a clear and happy course—

In thee, dear infant! so may end
  Our shame, in thee our sorrows cease!
And thy pure course will then extend,
  In floods of joy, o'er vales of peace.

GEORGE CRABBE

Oh ! by the GOD who loves to spare,
  Deny me not the boon I crave ;   120
Let this loved child your mercy share,
  And let me find a peaceful grave ;
Make her yet spotless soul your care,
  And let my sins their portion have ;
Her for a better fate prepare,
  And punish whom 'twere sin to save !

MAGISTRATE.

Recall the word, renounce the thought,
  Command thy heart and bend thy knee.
There is to all a pardon brought,
  A ransom rich, assured and free ;   130
'Tis full when found, 'tis found if sought,
  Oh ! seek it, till 'tis seal'd to thee.

VAGRANT.

But how my pardon shall I know ?

MAGISTRATE.

  By feeling dread that 'tis not sent ;
By tears, for sin that freely flow ;
  By grief, that all thy tears are spent ;
By thoughts on that great debt we owe,
  With all the mercy GOD has lent ;
By suffering what thou canst not show,
  Yet showing how thine heart is rent :   140
Till thou canst feel thy bosom glow,
  And say, "MY SAVIOUR, I REPENT ! "

WOMAN!

MR. LEDYARD, AS QUOTED BY M. PARKE IN HIS TRAVELS
INTO AFRIC:

"To a Woman I never addressed myself in the language of decency and
"friendship, without receiving a decent and friendly answer. If I
"was hungry or thirsty, wet or sick, they did not hesitate, like Men,
"to perform a generous action: in so free and kind a manner did they
"contribute to my relief, that if I was dry, I drank the sweetest
"draught; and if hungry, I ate the coarsest morsel with a double
"relish."

PLACE the white man on Afric's coast,
  Whose swarthy sons in blood delight,
Who of their scorn to Europe boast,
  And paint their very demons white:
There, while the sterner sex disdains
  To soothe the woes they cannot feel,
Woman will strive to heal his pains,
  And weep for those she cannot heal.
Hers is warm pity's sacred glow;
  From all her stores she bears a part,   10
And bids the spring of hope re-flow,
  That languish'd in the fainting heart.

"What, though so pale his haggard face,
  "So sunk and sad his looks,"—she cries—
"And far unlike our nobler race,
  "With crispèd locks and rolling eyes:
"Yet misery marks him of our kind;
  "We see him lost, alone, afraid;
"And pangs of body, griefs in mind,
  "Pronounce him man, and ask our aid.   20

"Perhaps, in some far-distant shore,
  "There are who in these forms delight;
"Whose milky features please them more,
  "Than ours of jet thus burnish'd bright.
"Of such may be his weeping wife,
  "Such children for their sire may call;
"And, if we spare his ebbing life,
  "Our kindness may preserve them all."

GEORGE CRABBE

Thus her compassion woman shows,
  Beneath the line her acts are these;
Nor the wide waste of Lapland-snows
  Can her warm flow of pity freeze:—
"From some sad land the stranger comes,
  "Where joys, like ours, are never found;
"Let's soothe him in our happy homes,
  "Where freedom sits, with plenty crown'd.

"'Tis good the fainting soul to cheer,
  "To see the famish'd stranger fed;
"To milk for him the mother-deer,
  "To smooth for him the furry bed.
"The powers above our Lapland bless
  "With good no other people know,
"T' enlarge the joys that we possess,
  "By feeling those that we bestow!"

Thus, in extremes of cold and heat,
  Where wandering man may trace his kind;
Wherever grief and want retreat,
  In Woman they compassion find;
She makes the female breast her seat,
  And dictates mercy to the mind.

Man may the sterner virtues know,
  Determined justice, truth severe;
But female hearts with pity glow,
  And Woman holds affliction dear.
For guiltless woes her sorrows flow,
  And suffering vice compels her tear;
'Tis hers to soothe the ills below,
  And bid life's fairer views appear.
To Woman's gentle kind we owe
  What comforts and delights us here;
They its gay hopes on youth bestow,
  And care they soothe, and age they cheer.

THE BOROUGH.

Paulo majora canamus.—VIRGIL. [*Ecl.* IV. v. I.]

GEORGE CRABBE

TO

HIS GRACE

THE DUKE OF RUTLAND,

MARQUIS OF GRANBY;

RECORDER OF CAMBRIDGE AND SCARBOROUGH;
LORD-LIEUTENANT AND CUSTOS-ROTULORUM OF THE
COUNTY OF LEICESTER; K.G. & LL.D.

My Lord,

THE poem, for which I have ventured to solicit
your Grace's attention, was composed in a situation so near to
Belvoir Castle, that the author had all the advantage to be
derived from prospects extensive and beautiful, and from works
of grandeur and sublimity: and, though nothing of the influence
arising from such situation should be discernible in these verses,
either from want of adequate powers in the writer, or because
his subjects do not assimilate with such views, yet would it be
natural for him to indulge a wish, that he might inscribe his
labours to the lord of a scene which perpetually excited his
admiration, and he would plead the propriety of placing the
titles of the House of Rutland at the entrance of a volume
written in the Vale of Belvoir.

But, my Lord, a motive much more powerful than a sense
of propriety, a grateful remembrance of benefits conferred by
the noble family in which you preside, has been the great in-
ducement for me to wish that I might be permitted to inscribe
this work to your Grace. The honours of that time were to me
unexpected, they were unmerited, and they were transitory;
but since I am thus allowed to make public my gratitude, I am
in some degree restored to the honour of that period; I have
again the happiness to find myself favoured, and my exertions
stimulated, by the condescension of the Duke of Rutland.

It was my fortune, in a poem which yet circulates, to

DEDICATION

write of the virtues, talents, and heroic death of Lord Robert Manners, and to bear witness to the affection of a brother whose grief was poignant, and to be soothed only by remembrance of his worth whom he so deeply deplored. In a patron thus favourably predisposed, my Lord, I might look for much lenity, and could not fear the severity of critical examination : from your Grace, who, happily, have no such impediment to justice, I must not look for the same kind of indulgence. I am assured, by those whose situation gave them opportunity for knowledge, and whose abilities and attention guarded them from error, that I must not expect my failings will escape detection from want of discernment, neither am I to fear that any merit will be undistinguished through deficiency of taste. It is from this information, my Lord, and a consciousness of much which needs forgiveness, that I entreat your Grace to read my verses, with a wish, I had almost added, with a purpose, to be pleased, and to make every possible allowance for subjects not always pleasing, for manners sometimes gross, and for language too frequently incorrect.

With the fullest confidence in your Grace's ability and favour, in the accuracy of your judgment, and the lenity of your decision ; with grateful remembrance of benefits received, and due consciousness of the little I could merit ; with prayers that your Grace may long enjoy the dignities of the House of Rutland, and continue to dictate improvement for the surrounding country—I terminate an address, in which a fear of offending your Grace has made me so cautious in my expressions, that I may justly fear to offend many of my readers, who will think that something more of animation should have been excited by the objects I view, the benevolence I honour, and the gratitude I profess.

I have the honour to be,

My Lord,

Your Grace's

Most obliged

and obedient humble servant,

GEORGE CRABBE.

265

GEORGE CRABBE

PREFACE.

WHETHER, if I had not been encouraged by some proofs of public favour, I should have written the Poem now before the reader, is a question which I cannot positively determine ; but I will venture to assert, that I should not, in that case, have committed the work to the press; I should not have allowed my own opinion of it to have led me into further disappointment, against the voice of judges impartial and indifferent, from whose sentence it had been fruitless to appeal. The success of a late publication, therefore, may be fairly assigned as the principal cause for the appearance of this.

When the ensuing Letters were so far written, that I could form an opinion of them, and when I began to conceive that they might not be unacceptable to the public, I felt myself prompted by duty, as well as interest, to put them to the press ; I considered myself bound by gratitude for the favourable treatment I had already received, to show that I was not unmindful of it ; and, however this might be mixed with other motives, it operated with considerable force upon my mind, acting as a stimulus to exertions naturally tardy, and to expectations easily checked.

It must nevertheless be acknowledged that, although such favourable opinion had been formed, I was not able, with the requisite impartiality, to determine the comparative value of an unpublished manuscript, and a work sent into the world. Books, like children, when established, have doubtless our parental affection and good wishes ; we rejoice to hear that they are doing well, and are received and respected in good company : but it is to manuscripts in the study, as to children in the nursery, that our care, our anxiety, and our tenderness are principally directed : they are fondled as our endearing companions; their faults are corrected with the lenity of partial

PREFACE

love, and their good parts are exaggerated by the strength of parental imagination ; nor is it easy even for the more cool and reasonable among parents, thus circumstanced, to decide upon the comparative merits of their offspring, whether they be children of the bed or issue of the brain.

But, however favourable my own opinion may have been, or may still be, I could not venture to commit so long a Poem to the press without some endeavour to obtain the more valuable opinion of less partial judges. At the same time, I am willing to confess that I have lost some portion of the timidity once so painful, and that I am encouraged to take upon myself the decision of various points, which heretofore I entreated my friends to decide. Those friends were then my council, whose opinion I was implicitly to follow ; they are now advisers, whose ideas I am at liberty to reject. This will not, I hope, seem like arrogance : it would be more safe, it would be more pleasant, still to have that reliance on the judgment of others; but it cannot always be obtained ; nor are they, however friendly disposed, ever ready to lend a helping hand to him whom they consider as one who ought by this time to have cast away the timidity of inexperience, and to have acquired the courage that would enable him to decide for himself.

When it is confessed that I have less assistance from my friends, and that the appearance of this work is, in a great measure, occasioned by the success of a former, some readers will, I fear, entertain the opinion that the book before them was written in haste, and published without due examination and revisal. Should this opinion be formed, there will doubtless occur many faults which may appear as originating in neglect. Now, readers are, I believe, disposed to treat with more than common severity those writers who have been led into presumption by the approbation bestowed on their diffidence, and into idleness and unconcern, by the praises given to their attention. I am therefore even anxious it should be generally known that sufficient time and application were bestowed upon this work, and by this I mean that no material alteration would be effected by delay ; it is true that this confession removes one plea for the errors of the book—want of time ; but, in my opinion, there is not much consolation to be drawn by reasonable minds from this resource : if a work fails, it appears to be poor satisfaction when it is observed, that if the author had taken more care, the event had been less disgraceful.

When the reader enters into the Poem, he will find the author retired from view, and an imaginary personage brought forward to describe his Borough for him. To him it seemed convenient to speak in the first person ; but the inhabitant of a village, in the centre of the kingdom, could not appear in the character of a residing burgess in a large sea-port ; and when, with this point, was considered what relations were to be given, what manners delineated, and what situations described, no method appeared to be so convenient as that of borrowing the assistance of an ideal friend. By this means the reader is in some degree kept from view of any particular place; nor will he perhaps be so likely to determine where those persons reside, and what their connexions, who are so intimately known to this man of straw.

From the title of this Poem, some persons will, I fear, expect a political satire,—an attack upon corrupt principles in a general view, or upon the customs and manners of some particular place ; of these they will find nothing satirized, nothing related. It may be that graver readers would have preferred a more historical account of so considerable a Borough —its charter, privileges, trade, public structures, and subjects of this kind ; but I have an apology for the omission of these things, in the difficulty of describing them, and in the utter repugnancy which subsists between the studies and objects of topography and poetry. What I thought I could best describe, that I attempted :—the sea, and the country in the immediate vicinity ; the dwellings, and the inhabitants ; some incidents and characters, with an exhibition of morals and manners, offensive perhaps to those of extremely delicate feelings, but sometimes, I hope, neither unamiable nor unaffecting. An Election indeed forms a part of one Letter, but the evil there described is one not greatly nor generally deplored, and there are probably many places of this kind where it is not felt.

From the variety of relations, characters, and descriptions which a BOROUGH affords, several were rejected which a reader might reasonably expect to have met with : in this case he is entreated to believe that these, if they occurred to the author,

PREFACE

were considered by him as beyond his ability, as subjects which he could not treat in a manner satisfactory to himself. Possibly the admission of some will be thought to require more apology than the rejection of others. In such variety, it is to be apprehended, that almost every reader will find something not according with his ideas of propriety, or something repulsive to the tone of his feelings; nor could this be avoided but by the sacrifice of every event, opinion, and even expression, which could be thought liable to produce such effect; and this casting away so largely of our cargo, through fears of danger, though it might help us to clear it, would render our vessel of little worth when she came into port. I may likewise entertain a hope, that this very variety, which gives scope to objection and censure, will also afford a better chance for approval and satisfaction.

Of these objectionable parts many must be to me unknown; of others some opinion may be formed, and for their admission some plea may be stated.

In the first Letter is nothing which particularly calls for remark, except possibly the last line—giving a promise to the reader that he should both smile and sigh in the perusal of the following Letters. This may appear vain, and more than an author ought to promise; but let it be considered that the character assumed is that of a friend, who gives an account of objects, persons, and events to his correspondent, and who was therefore at liberty, without any imputation of this kind, to suppose in what manner he would be affected by such descriptions.

Nothing, I trust, in the second Letter, which relates to the imitation of what are called weather-stains on buildings, will seem to any invidious or offensive. I wished to make a comparison between those minute and curious bodies which cover the surface of some edifices, and those kinds of stain which are formed of boles and ochres, and laid on with a brush. Now, as the work of time cannot be anticipated in such cases, it may be very judicious to have recourse to such expedients as will give to a recent structure the venerable appearance of antiquity; and in this case, though I might still observe the vast difference between the living varieties of nature, and the distant imitation of the artist, yet I would not forbear to make use of his dexterity, because he could not clothe my freestone with *mucor*, *lichen*, and *byssus*.

The wants and mortifications of a poor Clergyman are the subjects of one portion of the third Letter ; and, he being represented as a stranger in the Borough, it may be necessary to make some apology for his appearance in the Poem. Previous to a late meeting of a literary society, whose benevolent purpose is well known to the public, I was induced by a friend to compose a few verses, in which, with the general commendation of the design, should be introduced a hint that the bounty might be farther extended; these verses a gentleman did me the honour to recite at the meeting, and they were printed as an extract from the Poem, to which in fact they may be called an appendage.

I am now arrived at that part of my work, which I may expect will bring upon me some animadversion. Religion is a subject deeply interesting to the minds of many ; and, when these minds are weak, they are often led by a warmth of feeling into the violence of causeless resentment. I am therefore anxious that my purpose should be understood ; and I wish to point out what things they are which an author may hold up to ridicule and be blameless. In referring to the two principal divisions of enthusiastical teachers, I have denominated them, as I conceive they are generally called, *Calvinistic* and *Arminian* Methodists. The *Arminians*, though divided and perhaps subdivided, are still, when particular accuracy is not intended, considered as one body, having had, for many years, one head, who is yet held in high respect by the varying members of the present day. But the Calvinistic societies are to be looked upon rather as separate and independent congregations ; and it is to one of these (unconnected, as is supposed, with any other) I more particularly allude. But while I am making use of this division, I must entreat that I may not be considered as one who takes upon him to censure the religious opinions of any society or individual : the reader will find that the spirit of the enthusiast, and not his opinions, his manners, and not his creed, have engaged my attention. I have nothing to observe of the Calvinist and Arminian, considered as such ; but my remarks are pointed at the enthusiast and the bigot, at their folly and their craft.

PREFACE

To those readers who have seen the journals of the first Methodists, or the extracts quoted from them by their opposers[1] in the early times of this spiritual influenza, are sufficiently known all their leading notions and peculiarities ; so that I have no need to enter into such unpleasant inquiries in this place. I have only to observe that their tenets remain the same, and have still the former effect on the minds of the converted. There is yet that imagined contention with the powers of darkness, that is at once so lamentable and so ludicrous ; there is the same offensive familiarity with the Deity, with a full trust and confidence both in the immediate efficacy of their miserably delivered supplications, and in the reality of numberless small miracles wrought at their request and for their convenience ; there still exists that delusion, by which some of the most common diseases of the body are regarded as proofs of the malignity of Satan contending for dominion over the soul ; and there still remains the same wretched jargon, composed of scriptural language, debased by vulgar expressions, which has a kind of mystic influence on the minds of the ignorant. It will be recollected that it is the abuse of those scriptural terms which I conceive to be improper : they are doubtless most significant and efficacious when used with propriety; but it is painful to the mind of a soberly devout person, when he hears every rise and fall of the animal spirits, every whim and notion of enthusiastic ignorance, expressed in the venerable language of the Apostles and Evangelists.

The success of these people is great, but not surprising : as the powers they claim are given, and come not of education, many may, and therefore do, fancy they are endowed with them ; so that they who do not venture to become preachers, yet exert the minor gifts, and gain reputation for the faculty of prayer, as soon as they can address the Creator in daring flights of unpremeditated absurdity. The less indigent gain the praise of hospitality, and the more harmonious become distinguished in their choirs; curiosity is kept alive by succession of ministers, and self-love is flattered by the consideration that they are the persons at whom the world wonders; add to this, that, in many of them, pride is gratified by their consequence as new members

---

[1] Methodists and Papists compared; Treatise on Grace, by Bishop Warburton, &c.

of a sect whom their conversion pleases, and by the liberty, which as seceders they take, of speaking contemptuously of the Church and ministers, whom they have relinquished.

Of those denominated *Calvinistic Methodists*, I had principally one sect in view, or, to adopt the term of its founder, *a church.* This *church* consists of several congregations in town and country, unknown perhaps in many parts of the kingdom, but, where known, the cause of much curiosity and some amusement. To such of my readers as may judge an enthusiastic teacher and his peculiarities to be unworthy any serious attention, I would observe that there is something unusually daring in the boast of this man, who claims the authority of a messenger sent from God, and declares without hesitation that his call was immediate ; that he is assisted by the sensible influence of the Spirit, and that miracles are perpetually wrought in his favour and for his convenience.

As it was and continues to be my desire to give proof that I had advanced nothing respecting this extraordinary person, his operations or assertions, which might not be readily justified by quotations from his own writings, I had collected several of these and disposed them under certain heads. But I found that by this means a very disproportioned share of attention must be given to the subject, and after some consideration, I have determined to relinquish the design ; and, should any have curiosity to search whether my representation of the temper and disposition, the spirit and manners, the knowledge and capacity, of a very popular teacher be correct, he is referred to about fourscore pamphlets, whose titles will be found on the covers of the late editions of the *Bank of Faith*, itself a wonderful performance, which (according to the turn of mind in the reader) will either highly excite, or totally extinguish, curiosity. In these works will be abundantly seen, abuse and contempt of the Church of England and its ministers; vengeance and virulent denunciation against all offenders; scorn for morality and heathen virtue, with that kind of learning which the author possesses, and his peculiar style of composition. A few of the titles placed below will give some information to the reader respecting the merit and design of those performances[1].

[1] Barbar, in two Parts; Bond-Child; Cry of Little Faith; Satan's Lawsuit; Forty Stripes for Satan; Myrrh and Odour of Saints; the

PREFACE

As many of the preacher's subjects are controverted and nice questions in divinity, he has sometimes allowed himself relaxation from the severity of study, and favoured his admirers with the effects of an humbler kind of inspiration, viz. that of the Muse. It must be confessed that these flights of fancy are very humble, and have nothing of that daring and mysterious nature which the prose of the author leads us to expect. *The Dimensions of eternal* Love is a title of one of his more learned productions, with which might have been expected (as a fit companion) *The Bounds of infinite Grace;* but no such work appears, and possibly the author considered one attempt of this kind was sufficient to prove the extent and direction of his abilities.

Of the whole of this mass of inquiry and decision, of denunciation and instruction (could we suppose it read by intelligent persons), different opinions would probably be formed ; the more indignant and severe would condemn the whole as the produce of craft and hypocrisy, while the more lenient would allow that such things might originate in the wandering imagination of a dreaming enthusiast.

None of my readers will, I trust, do me so much injustice as to suppose I have here any other motive than a vindication of what I have advanced in the verses which describe this kind of character, or that I had there any other purpose than to express (what I conceive to be) justifiable indignation against the assurance, the malignity, and (what is of more importance) the pernicious influence of such sentiments on the minds of the simple and ignorant, who, if they give credit to his relations, must be no more than tools and instruments under the control and management of one *called to be their Apostle.*

Nothing would be more easy for me, as I have observed, than to bring forward quotations such as would justify all I have advanced; but, even had I room, I cannot tell whether there be not something degrading in such kind of attack : the reader might smile at those miraculous accounts, but he would consider them and the language of the author as beneath his further attention : I therefore once more refer him to those

Naked Bow of God ; Rule and Riddle ; Way and Fare for Wayfaring Men ; Utility of the Books and Excellency of the Parchments ; Correspondence between *Noctua, Aurita* (the words so separated), and *Philomela,* &c.

pamphlets, which will afford matter for pity and for contempt, by which some would be amused and others astonished—not without sorrow, when they reflect that thousands look up to the writer as a man literally inspired, to whose wants they administer with their substance, and to whose guidance they prostrate their spirit and understanding.

Having been so long detained by this Letter, I must not permit my desire of elucidating what may seem obscure, or of defending what is liable to misconstruction, any further to prevail over a wish for brevity, and the fear of giving an air of importance to subjects which have perhaps little in themselves.

The circumstance recorded in the fifth Letter is a fact ; although it may appear to many almost incredible, that, in this country, and but few years since, a close and successful man should be a stranger to the method of increasing money by the loan of it. The Minister of the place where the honest Fisherman resided has related to me the apprehension and suspicion he witnessed. With trembling hand and dubious look, the careful man received and surveyed the bond given to him; and, after a sigh or two of lingering mistrust, he placed it in the coffer whence he had just before taken his cash ; for which, and for whose increase, he now indulged a belief that it was indeed both promise and security.

If the Letter which treats of Inns should be found to contain nothing interesting or uncommon ; if it describe things which we behold every day, and some which we do not wish to behold at any time : let it be considered that this Letter is one of the shortest, and that from a Poem whose subject was a Borough, populous and wealthy, these places of public accommodation could not, without some impropriety, be excluded.

I entertain the strongest, because the most reasonable, hope that no liberal practitioner in the Law will be offended by the notice taken of dishonourable and crafty attorneys. The increased difficulty of entering into the profession will in time render it much more free than it now is from those who disgrace it ; at present such persons remain, and it would not be difficult to give instances of neglect, ignorance, cruelty, oppression, and chicanery ; nor are they by any means confined

PREFACE

to one part of the country : quacks and impostors are indeed in every profession, as well with a licence as without one. The character and actions of *Swallow* might doubtless be contrasted by the delineation of an able and upright Solicitor ; but this Letter is of sufficient length, and such persons, without question, are already known to my readers.

When I observe, under the article Physic, that the young and less experienced physician will write rather with a view of making himself known, than to investigate and publish some useful fact, I would not be thought to extend this remark to all the publications of such men. I could point out a work, containing experiments the most judicious, and conclusions the most interesting, made by a gentleman, then young, which would have given just celebrity to a man after long practice. The observation is nevertheless generally true : many opinions have been adopted and many books written, not that the theory might be well defended, but that a young physician might be better known.

If I have in one Letter praised the good-humour of a man confessedly too inattentive to business, and, in another, if I have written somewhat sarcastically of " the brick-floored parlour which the butcher lets :" be credit given to me, that in the one case I had no intention to apologize for idleness, nor any design in the other to treat with contempt the resources of the poor. The good-humour is considered as the consolation of disappointment, and the room is so mentioned because the lodger is vain. Most of my readers will perceive this ; but I shall be sorry if by any I am supposed to make pleas for the vices of men, or treat their wants and infirmities with derision or with disdain.

It is probable, that really polite people, with cultivated minds and harmonious tempers, may judge my description of a Card-club conversation to be highly exaggerated, if not totally fictitious ; and I acknowledge that the club must admit a particular kind of members to afford such specimens of acrimony and objurgation. Yet, that such language is spoken, and such manners exhibited, is most certain, chiefly among those who, being successful in life, without previous education, not very nice in their feelings, or very attentive to improprieties, sit down to game with no other view than that of adding the gain

GEORGE CRABBE

of the evening to the profits of the day ; whom therefore disappointment itself makes angry, and, when caused by another, resentful and vindictive.

The Letter on Itinerant Players will to some appear too harshly written, their profligacy exaggerated, and their distresses magnified ; but, though the respectability of a part of these people may give us a more favourable view of the whole body, though some actors be sober, and some managers prudent : still there is vice and misery left, more than sufficient to justify my description. But, if I could find only one woman who (passing forty years on many stages, and sustaining many principal characters) laments in her unrespected old age, that there was no workhouse to which she could legally sue for admission ; if I could produce only one female, seduced upon the boards, and starved in her lodging, compelled by her poverty to sing, and by her sufferings to weep, without any prospect but misery, or any consolation but death ; if I could exhibit only one youth who sought refuge from parental authority in the licentious freedom of a wandering company : yet, with three such examples, I should feel myself justified in the account I have given.—But such characters and sufferings are common, and there are few of these societies which could not show members of this description. To some, indeed, the life has its satisfactions : they never expected to be free from labour, and their present kind, they think, is light; they have no delicate ideas of shame, and therefore duns and hisses give them no other pain than what arises from the fear of not being trusted, joined with the apprehension that they may have nothing to subsist upon except their credit.

For the Alms-House itself, its Governors and Inhabitants, I have not much to offer, in favour of the subject or of the characters. One of these, *Sir Denys Brand*, may be considered as too highly placed for an author (who seldom ventures above middle-life) to delineate; and indeed I had some idea of reserving him for another occasion, where he might have appeared with those in his own rank ; but then it is most uncertain whether he would ever appear, and he has been so many years prepared for the public whenever opportunity might offer, that I have at length given him place, and though with his inferiors, yet as a ruler over them. Of these, one (*Benbow*) may be thought

276

PREFACE

too low and despicable to be admitted here; but he is a Borough-character, and, however disgusting in some respects a picture may be, it will please some, and be tolerated by many, if it can boast that one merit of being a faithful likeness.

Blaney and *Clelia*, a male and female inhabitant of this mansion, are drawn at some length ; and I may be thought to have given them attention which they do not merit. I plead not for the originality, but for the truth, of the character ; and, though it may not be very pleasing, it may be useful to delineate (for certain minds) these mixtures of levity and vice; people who are thus incurably vain and determinately worldly; thus devoted to enjoyment and insensible of shame, and so miserably fond of their pleasures, that they court even the remembrance with eager solicitation, by conjuring up the ghosts of departed indulgences with all the aid that memory can afford them. These characters demand some attention, because they hold out a warning to that numerous class of young people who are too lively to be discreet; to whom the purpose of life is amusement, and who are always in danger of falling into vicious habits, because they have too much activity to be quiet, and too little strength to be steady.

The characters of the Hospital-Directors were written many years since, and, so far as I was capable of judging, are drawn with *fidelity*. I mention this circumstance, that, if any reader should find a difference in the versification or expression, he will be thus enabled to account for it.

The Poor are here almost of necessity introduced, for they must be considered, in every place, as a large and interesting portion of its inhabitants. I am aware of the great difficulty of acquiring just notions on the maintenance and management of this class of our fellow-subjects, and I forbear to express any opinion of the various modes which have been discussed or adopted : of one method only I venture to give my sentiments, that of collecting the poor of a hundred into one building. This admission of a vast number of persons, of all ages and both sexes, of very different inclinations, habits, and capacities, into a society, must, at a first view, I conceive, be looked upon as a cause of both vice and misery; nor does anything which I have heard or read invalidate the opinion ; happily, it is not a prevailing one, as these houses are, I believe, still confined to that part of the kingdom where they originated.

GEORGE CRABBE

To this subject follow several Letters describing the follies and crimes of persons in lower life, with one relation of a happier and more consolatory kind. It has been a subject of greater vexation to me than such trifle ought to be, that I could not, without destroying all appearance of arrangement, separate these melancholy narratives, and place the fallen Clerk in Office at a greater distance from the Clerk of the Parish, especially as they resembled each other in several particulars; both being tempted, seduced, and wretched. Yet are there, I conceive, considerable marks of distinction: their guilt is of different kind; nor would either have committed the offence of the other. The Clerk of the Parish could break the commandment, but he could not have been induced to have disowned an article of that creed for which he had so bravely contended, and on which he fully relied; and the upright mind of the Clerk in Office would have secured him from being guilty of wrong and robbery, though his weak and vacillating intellect could not preserve him from infidelity and profaneness. Their melancholy is nearly alike, but not its consequences. *Jachin* retained his belief, and though he hated life, he could never be induced to quit it voluntarily; but *Abel* was driven to terminate his misery in a way which the unfixedness of his religious opinions rather accelerated than retarded. I am therefore not without hope that the more observant of my readers will perceive many marks of discrimination in these characters.

The Life of *Ellen Orford*, though sufficiently burthened with error and misfortune, has in it little besides, which resembles those of the above unhappy men, and is still more unlike that of *Grimes*, in a subsequent Letter. There is in this character cheerfulness and resignation, a more uniform piety, and an immovable trust in the aid of religion : this, with the light texture of the introductory part, will, I hope, take off from that idea of sameness which the repetition of crimes and distresses is likely to create. The character of *Grimes*, his obduracy and apparent want of feeling, his gloomy kind of misanthropy, the progress of his madness, and the horrors of his imagination, I must leave to the judgment and observation of my readers. The mind here exhibited is one untouched by pity, unstung by remorse, and uncorrected by shame : yet is this hardihood of temper and spirit broken by want, disease,

278

PREFACE

solitude, and disappointment ; and he becomes the victim of a distempered and horror-stricken fancy. It is evident, therefore, that no feeble vision, no half-visible ghost, not the momentary glance of an unbodied being, nor the half-audible voice of an invisible one, would be created by the continual workings of distress on a mind so depraved and flinty. The ruffian of Mr *Scott*[1] has a mind of this nature : he has no shame or remorse : but the corrosion of hopeless want, the wasting of unabating disease, and the gloom of unvaried solitude, will have their effect on every nature ; and, the harder that nature is, and the longer time required to work upon it, so much the more strong and indelible is the impression. This is all the reason I am able to give, why a man of feeling so dull should yet become insane, should be of so horrible a nature.

That a Letter on Prisons should follow those narratives is unfortunate, but not to be easily avoided. I confess it is not pleasant to be detained so long by subjects so repulsive to the feelings of many as the sufferings of mankind ; but, though I assuredly would have altered this arrangement, had I been able to have done it by substituting a better, yet am I not of opinion that my verses, or indeed the verses of any other person, can so represent the evils and distresses of life as to make any material impression on the mind, and much less any of injurious nature. Alas ! sufferings real, evident, continually before us, have not effects very serious or lasting, even in the minds of the more reflecting and compassionate ; nor indeed does it seem right that the pain caused by sympathy should serve for more than a stimulus to benevolence. If, then, the strength and solidity of truth placed before our eyes have effect so feeble and transitory, I need not be very apprehensive that my representations of Poor-houses and Prisons, of wants and sufferings, however faithfully taken, will excite any feelings which can be seriously lamented. It has always been held as a salutary exercise of the mind, to contemplate the evils and miseries of our nature. I am not, therefore, without hope, that even this gloomy subject of Imprisonment, and more especially the Dream of the condemned Highwayman, will excite in some minds that mingled pity and abhorrence, which, while it is not unpleasant to the feelings, is useful in its operation : it ties and

[1] Marmion.

GEORGE CRABBE

binds us to all mankind by sensations common to us all, and in some degree connects us, without degradation, even to the most miserable and guilty of our fellow-men.

Our concluding subject is Education ; and some attempt is made to describe its various seminaries, from that of the Poor Widow, who pronounces the alphabet for infants, to seats whence the light of learning is shed abroad on the world. If, in this Letter, I describe the lives of literary men as embittered by much evil ; if they be often disappointed, and sometimes unfitted for the world they improve : let it be considered that they are described as men who possess that great pleasure, the exercise of their own talents, and the delight which flows from their own exertions ; they have joy in their pursuits, and glory in their acquirements of knowledge. Their victory over difficulties affords the most rational cause of triumph, and the attainment of new ideas leads to incalculable riches, such as gratify the glorious avarice of aspiring and comprehensive minds. Here, then, I place the reward of learning.—Our Universities produce men of the first scholastic attainments, who are heirs to large possessions, or descendants from noble families. Now, to those so favoured, talents and acquirements are, unquestionably, means of arriving at the most elevated and important situations ; but these must be the lot of a few. In general, the diligence, acuteness, and perseverance of a youth at the University, have no other reward than some College honours and emoluments, which they desire to exchange, many of them, for very moderate incomes in the obscurity of some distant village : so that, in stating the reward of an ardent and powerful mind to consist principally (I might have said entirely) in its own views, efforts, and excursions, I place it upon a sure foundation, though not one so elevated as the more ambitious aspire to. It is surely some encouragement to a studious man to reflect, that if he be disappointed, he cannot be without gratification ; and that, if he gets but a very humble portion of what the world can give, he has a continual fruition of unwearying enjoyment, of which it has not power to deprive him.

Long as I have detained the reader, I take leave to add a few words on the subject of imitation, or, more plainly speaking, borrowing. In the course of a long Poem, and

PREFACE

more especially of two long ones, it is very difficult to avoid a recurrence of the same thoughts, and of similar expressions ; and, however careful I have been myself in detecting and removing these kinds of repetitions, my readers, I question not, would, if disposed to seek them, find many remaining. For these I can only plead that common excuse—they are the offences of a bad memory, and not of voluntary inattention ; to which I must add the difficulty (I have already mentioned) of avoiding the error. This kind of plagiarism will therefore, I conceive, be treated with lenity ; and of the more criminal kind, borrowing from others, I plead, with much confidence, "not guilty." But while I claim exemption from guilt, I do not affirm that much of sentiment and much of expression may not be detected in the vast collection of English poetry : it is sufficient for an author, that he uses not the words or ideas of another without acknowledgment ; and this, and no more than this, I mean, by disclaiming debts of the kind. Yet resemblances are sometimes so very striking, that it requires faith in a reader to admit they were undesigned. A line in the second Letter,

" And monuments themselves memorials need,"

was written long before the author, in an accidental recourse to Juvenal, read—

" Quandoquidem data sunt ipsis quoque fata sepulchris."
Sat. x. l. 146.

and for this I believe the reader will readily give me credit. But there is another apparent imitation in the life of *Blaney* (Letter xiv), a simile of so particular a kind, that its occurrence to two writers at the same time must appear as an extraordinary event. For this reason I once determined to exclude it from the relation ; but, as it was truly unborrowed, and suited the place in which it stood, this seemed, on after-consideration, to be an act of cowardice, and the lines are therefore printed as they were written about two months before the very same thought (prosaically drest) appeared in a periodical work of the last summer. It is highly probable, in these cases, that both may derive the idea from a forgotten but common source ; and in this way I must entreat the reader to do me justice, by accounting for other such resemblances, should any be detected.

GEORGE CRABBE

I know not whether to some readers the placing two or three Latin quotations to a Letter may not appear pedantic and ostentatious, while both they and the English ones may be thought unnecessary. For the necessity I have not much to advance ; but if they be allowable (and certainly the best writers have adopted them), then, where two or three different subjects occur, so many of these mottoes seem to be required : nor will a charge of pedantry remain, when it is considered that these things are generally taken from some books familiar to the school-boy, and the selecting them is facilitated by the use of a book of common-place. Yet, with this help, the task of motto-hunting has been so unpleasant to me, that I have in various instances given up the quotation I was in pursuit of, and substituted such English verse or prose as I could find or invent for my purpose.

THE BOROUGH

CONTENTS.

THE BOROUGH.

LETTER I.

GENERAL DESCRIPTION.

These did the ruler of the deep ordain,
To build proud navies, and to rule the main.
Pope's Homer's Iliad, book vi. line 45. [?]

———

Such [place hath] Deptford, navy-building town,
  Woolwich and Wapping, smelling strong of pitch;
Such Lambeth, envy of each band and gown,
  And Twickenham such, which fairer scenes enrich.
Pope's Imitation of Spenser.

———

. . . . Et cum cœlestibus undis
Æquoreæ miscentur aquæ; caret ignibus æther,
Cæcaque nox premitur tenebris hiemisque suisque;
[Discutiunt] tamen has, præbentque micantia lumen
Fulmina; fulmineis ardescunt ignibus undæ.
Ovid. Metamorph. lib. xi. [vv. 519-523].

The Difficulty of describing Town Scenery—·A Comparison with certain
  Views in the Country—The River and Quay—The Shipping and
  Business—Ship-Building—Sea-Boys and Port-Views—Village and
  Town Scenery again compared—Walks from Town—Cottage and
  adjoining Heath, &c.—House of Sunday Entertainment—The Sea:
  a Summer and Winter View—A Shipwreck at Night, and its Effects
  on Shore—Evening Amusements in the Borough—An Apology for
  the imperfect View which can be given of these Subjects.

THE BOROUGH.

LETTER I.

GENERAL DESCRIPTION.

" DESCRIBE the Borough."—Though our idle tribe
    May love description, can we so describe,
That you shall fairly streets and buildings trace,
And all that gives distinction to a place?
This cannot be; yet, moved by your request,
A part I paint—let fancy form the rest.
  Cities and towns, the various haunts of men,
Require the pencil; they defy the pen.
Could he, who sang so well the Grecian fleet,
So well have sung of alley, lane, or street?   10
Can measured lines these various buildings show,
The Town-Hall Turning, or the Prospect Row?
Can I the seats of wealth and want explore,
And lengthen out my lays from door to door?
  Then, let thy fancy aid me.—I repair
From this tall mansion of our last-year's mayor,
Till we the outskirts of the Borough reach,
And these half-buried buildings next the beach;
Where hang at open doors the net and cork,
While squalid sea-dames mend the meshy work;   20
Till comes the hour, when, fishing through the tide,
The weary husband throws his freight aside—
A living mass, which now demands the wife,
Th' alternate labours of their humble life.
  Can scenes like these withdraw thee from thy wood,
Thy upland forest or thy valley's flood?

285

GEORGE CRABBE

Seek, then, thy garden's shrubby bound, and look,
As it steals by, upon the bordering brook :
That winding streamlet, limpid, lingering, slow,
Where the reeds whisper when the zephyrs blow ;   30
Where in the midst, upon her throne of green,
Sits the large lily [1] as the water's queen ;
And makes the current, forced awhile to stay,
Murmur and bubble as it shoots away ;
Draw then the strongest contrast to that stream,
And our broad river will before thee seem.
   With ceaseless motion comes and goes the tide,
Flowing, it fills the channel vast and wide ;
Then back to sea, with strong majestic sweep
It rolls, in ebb yet terrible and deep ;   40
Here sampire-banks [2] and salt-wort [3] bound the flood;
There stakes and sea-weeds, withering on the mud ;
And, higher up, a ridge of all things base,
Which some strong tide has roll'd upon the place.
   Thy gentle river boasts its pigmy boat,
Urged on by pains, half grounded, half afloat ;
While at her stern an angler takes his stand,
And marks the fish he purposes to land ;
From that clear space, where, in the cheerful ray
Of the warm sun, the scaly people play.   50
   Far other craft our prouder river shows,
Hoys, pinks and sloops ; brigs, brigantines and snows :
Nor angler we on our wide stream descry,
But one poor dredger where his oysters lie :
He, cold and wet, and driving with the tide,
Beats his weak arms against his tarry side,
Then drains the remnant of diluted gin,
To aid the warmth that languishes within ;
Renewing oft his poor attempts to beat
His tingling fingers into gathering heat.   60
   He shall again be seen when evening comes,
And social parties crowd their favourite rooms ;
Where on the table pipes and papers lie,
The steaming bowl or foaming tankard by.
'Tis then, with all these comforts spread around,
They hear the painful dredger's welcome sound ;

THE BOROUGH

And few themselves the savoury boon deny,
The food that feeds, the living luxury.
  Yon is our quay! those smaller hoys from town,
Its various wares, for country-use, bring down;   70
Those laden waggons, in return, impart
The country-produce to the city mart;
Hark to the clamour in that miry road,
Bounded and narrow'd by yon vessels' load;
The lumbering wealth she empties round the place,
Package, and parcel, hogshead, chest, and case;
While the loud seaman and the angry hind,
Mingling in business, bellow to the wind.
  Near these a crew amphibious, in the docks,
Rear, for the sea, those castles on the stocks: 80
See the long keel, which soon the waves must hide;
See the strong ribs which form the roomy side;
Bolts yielding slowly to the sturdiest stroke,
And planks [4] which curve and crackle in the smoke.
Around the whole rise cloudy wreaths, and far
Bear the warm pungence of o'er-boiling tar.
  Dabbling on shore half-naked sea-boys crowd,
Swim round a ship, or swing upon the shroud;
Or, in a boat purloin'd, with paddles play,
And grow familiar with the watery way.   90
Young though they be, they feel whose sons they are;
They know what British seamen do and dare;
Proud of that fame, they raise and they enjoy
The rustic wonder of the village-boy.
  Before you bid these busy scenes adieu,
Behold the wealth that lies in public view,
Those far-extended heaps of coal and coke,
Where fresh-fill'd lime-kilns breathe their stifling smoke.
This shall pass off, and you behold, instead,
The night-fire gleaming on its chalky bed;   100
When from the light-house brighter beams will rise,
To show the shipman where the shallow lies.
  Thy walks are ever pleasant; every scene
Is rich in beauty, lively, or serene:
Rich—is that varied view with woods around,
Seen from the seat, within the shrubb'ry bound;

287

GEORGE CRABBE

Where shines the distant lake, and where appear
From ruins bolting, unmolested deer;
Lively—the village-green, the inn, the place
Where the good widow schools her infant race;   110
Shops, whence are heard the hammer and the saw,
And village-pleasures unreproved by law.
Then, how serene—when in your favourite room,
Gales from your jasmines soothe the evening gloom;
When from your upland paddock you look down,
And just perceive the smoke which hides the town;
When weary peasants at the close of day
Walk to their cots, and part upon the way;
When cattle slowly cross the shallow brook,
And shepherds pen their folds, and rest upon their crook.   120
   We prune our hedges, prime our slender trees,
And nothing looks untutor'd and at ease;
On the wide heath, or in the flow'ry vale,
We scent the vapours of the sea-born gale;
Broad-beaten paths lead on from stile to stile,
And sewers from streets the road-side banks defile;
Our guarded fields a sense of danger show,
Where garden-crops with corn and clover grow;
Fences are form'd of wreck and placed around
(With tenters tipp'd), a strong repulsive bound;   130
Wide and deep ditches by the gardens run,
And there in ambush lie the trap and gun;
Or yon broad board, which guards each tempting prize,
"Like a tall bully, lifts its head and lies."
   There stands a cottage with an open door,
Its garden undefended blooms before;
Her wheel is still, and overturn'd her stool,
While the lone widow seeks the neighb'ring pool.
This gives us hope all views of town to shun—
No! here are tokens of the sailor-son: 140
That old blue jacket, and that shirt of check,
And silken kerchief for the seaman's neck;
Sea-spoils and shells from many a distant shore,
And furry robe from frozen Labrador.
   Our busy streets and sylvan-walks between,
Fen, marshes, bog and heath all intervene;

THE BOROUGH

Here pits of crag, with spongy, plashy base,
To some enrich th' uncultivated space :
For there are blossoms rare, and curious rush,
The gale's rich balm, and sun-dew's crimson blush,   150
Whose velvet leaf, with radiant beauty dress'd,
Forms a gay pillow for the plover's breast.
    Not distant far, a house, commodious made,
Lonely yet public stands, for Sunday-trade ;
Thither, for this day free, gay parties go,
Their tea-house walk, their tippling rendezvous ;
There humble couples sit in corner-bowers,
Or gaily ramble for th' allotted hours ;
Sailors and lasses from the town attend,
The servant-lover, the apprentice-friend ;   160
With all the idle social tribes who seek
And find their humble pleasures once a week.
    Turn to the watery world !—but who to thee
(A wonder yet unview'd) shall paint—the sea ?
Various and vast, sublime in all its forms,
When lull'd by zephyrs, or when roused by storms ;
Its colours changing, when from clouds and sun
Shades after shades upon the surface run ;
Embrown'd and horrid now, and now serene,
In limpid blue, and evanescent green ;   170
And oft the foggy banks on ocean lie,
Lift the fair sail, and cheat th' experienced eye [6].
    Be it the summer-noon : a sandy space
The ebbing tide has left upon its place ;
Then, just the hot and stony beach above,
Light twinkling streams in bright confusion move
(For heated thus, the warmer air ascends,
And with the cooler in its fall contends) ;
Then the broad bosom of the ocean keeps
An equal motion, swelling as it sleeps,   180
Then slowly sinking ; curling to the strand,
Faint, lazy waves o'ercreep the ridgy sand,
Or tap the tarry boat with gentle blow,
And back return in silence, smooth and slow.
Ships in the calm seem anchor'd ; for they glide
On the still sea, urged solely by the tide ;

Crabbe   T   289

GEORGE CRABBE

Art thou not present, this calm scene before,
Where all beside is pebbly length of shore,
And far as eye can reach, it can discern no more? [*J*]
Yet sometimes comes a ruffling cloud, to make 190
The quiet surface of the ocean shake;
As an awaken'd giant with a frown
Might show his wrath, and then to sleep sink down.
 View now the winter-storm, above, one cloud,
Black and unbroken, all the skies o'ershroud.
Th' unwieldy porpoise through the day before
Had roll'd in view of boding men on shore;
And sometimes hid, and sometimes show'd, his form,
Dark as the cloud, and furious as the storm.
 All where the eye delights, yet dreads, to roam, 200
The breaking billows cast the flying foam
Upon the billows rising—all the deep
Is restless change; the waves so swell'd and steep,
Breaking and sinking, and the sunken swells,
Nor one, one moment, in its station dwells.
But, nearer land, you may the billows trace,
As if contending in their watery chase;
May watch the mightiest till the shoal they reach,
Then break and hurry to their utmost stretch;
Curl'd as they come, they strike with furious force, 210
And then, re-flowing, take their grating course,
Raking the rounded flints, which ages past
Roll'd by their rage, and shall to ages last.
 Far off, the petrel in the troubled way
Swims with her brood, or flutters in the spray;
She rises often, often drops again,
And sports at ease on the tempestuous main.
 High o'er the restless deep, above the reach
Of gunner's hope, vast flights of wild-ducks stretch;
Far as the eye can glance on either side, 220
In a broad space and level line they glide;
All in their wedge-like figures from the north,
Day after day, flight after flight, go forth.
 In-shore their passage tribes of sea-gulls urge,
And drop for prey within the sweeping surge;

THE BOROUGH

Oft in the rough opposing blast they fly
Far back, then turn, and all their force apply,
While to the storm they give their weak complaining cry ; [ ]]
Or clap the sleek white pinion to the breast,
And in the restless ocean dip for rest.   230
  Darkness begins to reign ; the louder wind
Appals the weak and awes the firmer mind ;
But frights not him, whom evening and the spray
In part conceal—yon prowler on his way.
Lo ! he has something seen ; he runs apace,
As if he fear'd companion in the chase ;
He sees his prize, and now he turns again,
Slowly and sorrowing—"Was your search in vain ? "
Gruffly he answers, " 'Tis a sorry sight !
" A seaman's body ; there'll be more to-night ! "   240
  Hark to those sounds ! they're from distress at sea :
How quick they come ! What terrors may there be !
Yes, 'tis a driven vessel : I discern
Lights, signs of terror, gleaming from the stern ;
Others behold them too, and from the town
In various parties seamen hurry down ;
Their wives pursue, and damsels urged by dread,
Lest men so dear be into danger led ;
Their head the gown has hooded, and their call
In this sad night is piercing like the squall ;   250
They feel their kinds of power, and when they meet,
Chide, fondle, weep, dare, threaten, or entreat.
  See one poor girl, all terror and alarm,
Has fondly seized upon her lover's arm ;
"Thou shalt not venture ; " and he answers "No !
" I will not "—still she cries, " Thou shalt not go."
  No need of this ; not here the stoutest boat
Can through such breakers, o'er such billows float ;
Yet may they view these lights upon the beach,
Which yield them hope, whom help can never reach.   260
  From parted clouds the moon her radiance throws
On the wild waves, and all the danger shows ;
But shows them beaming in her shining vest,
Terrific splendour ! gloom in glory dress'd !
This for a moment, and then clouds again

T 2

GEORGE CRABBE

Hide every beam, and fear and darkness reign.
But hear we now those sounds? Do lights appear?
I see them not! the storm alone I hear:
And lo! the sailors homeward take their way;
Man must endure—let us submit and pray.   270
Such are our winter-views; but night comes on—
Now business sleeps, and daily cares are gone;
Now parties form, and some their friends assist
To waste the idle hours at sober whist;
The tavern's pleasure or the concert's charm
Unnumber'd moments of their sting disarm;
Play-bills and open doors a crowd invite,
To pass off one dread portion of the night;
And show and song and luxury combined
Lift off from man this burthen of mankind.   280
Others advent'rous walk abroad and meet
Returning parties pacing through the street;
When various voices, in the dying day,
Hum in our walks, and greet us in our way;
When tavern-lights flit on from room to room,
And guide the tippling sailor, staggering home:
There as we pass, the jingling bells betray
How business rises with the closing day:
Now walking silent, by the river's side,
The ear perceives the rippling of the tide;   290
Or measured cadence of the lads who tow
Some enter'd hoy, to fix her in her row;
Or hollow sound, which from the parish-bell
To some departed spirit bids farewell!
Thus shall you something of our BOROUGH know,
Far as a verse, with Fancy's aid, can show;
Of sea or river, of a quay or street,
The best description must be incomplete;
But when a happier theme [succeeds], and when
Men are our subjects and the deeds of men;   300
Then may we find the Muse in happier style,
And we may sometimes sigh and sometimes smile.

THE BOROUGH

NOTES TO LETTER I.

Note 1, page 286, line 32.

Sits the large lily as the water's queen.

The white water-lily. Nymphæa alba.

Note 2, page 286, line 41.

Sampire-banks.

The jointed glasswort. *Salicornia* is here meant, not the true sampire, the *crithmum maritimum.*

Note 3, page 286, line 41.

Salt-wort.

The salsola of botanists.

Note 4, page 287, line 84.

And planks which curve and crackle in the smoke.

The curvature of planks for the sides of a ship, &c. is, I am informed, now generally made by the power of steam. Fire is nevertheless still used for boats and vessels of the smaller kind.

Note 5, page 289, lines 171 and 172.

And oft the foggy banks on ocean lie,
Lift the fair sail, and cheat th' experienced eye.

Of the effect of these mists, known by the name of fog-banks, wonderful and indeed incredible relations are given; but their property of appearing to elevate ships at sea, and to bring them in view, is, I believe, generally acknowledged.

GEORGE CRABBE

THE BOROUGH.

LETTER II.

THE CHURCH.

. . . . Festinat enim decurrere velox
Flosculus angustæ miseræque brevissima vitæ
Portio! dum bibimus, dum serta, unguenta, puellas
Poscimus, obrepit non intellecta senectus.
Juvenal. Satir. ix. lin. 126.

And when at last thy love shall die,
  Wilt thou receive his parting breath?
Wilt thou repress each struggling sigh,
  And cheer with smiles the bed of death?

Percy [?].

Several Meanings of the word *Church*—The Building so called, here
intended—Its Antiquity and Grandeur—Columns and Ailes—The
Tower: the Stains made by Time compared with the mock Antiquity
of the Artist—Progress of Vegetation on such Buildings—Bells—
Tombs: one in decay—Mural Monuments, and the Nature of their
Inscriptions—An Instance in a departed Burgess—Churchyard Graves
—Mourners for the Dead—A Story of a betrothed Pair in humble
Life, and Effects of Grief in the Survivor.

THE BOROUGH.

LETTER II.

THE CHURCH.

" WHAT is a Church? "—Let Truth and Reason speak,
    They would reply, " The faithful, pure, and meek;
" From Christian folds the one selected race,
" Of all professions, and in every place."
    " What is a Church? "—" A flock," our vicar cries,
" Whom bishops govern and whom priests advise;
" Wherein are various states and due degrees,
" The bench for honour, and the stall for ease;
" That ease be mine, which, after all his cares,
" The pious, peaceful prebendary shares."   10
    " What is a Church? "—Our honest sexton tells,
" 'Tis a tall building, with a tower and bells;
" Where priest and clerk with joint exertion strive
" To keep the ardour of their flock alive:
" That, by his periods eloquent and grave;
" This, by responses, and a well-set stave.
" These for the living; but, when life be fled,
" I toll myself the requiem for the dead."
    'Tis to this Church I call thee, and that place
Where slept our fathers, when they'd run their race.   20
We too shall rest, and then our children keep
Their road in life, and then, forgotten, sleep;
Meanwhile the building slowly falls away,
And, like the builders, will in time decay.
    The old foundation—but it is not clear
When it was laid—you care not for the year:
On this, as parts decay'd by time and storms,
Arose these various disproportion'd forms;
Yet Gothic, all the learn'd who visit us
(And our small wonders) have decided thus: 30
" Yon noble Gothic arch;" "That Gothic door;"

GEORGE CRABBE

So have they said ; of proof you'll need no more.
Here large plain columns rise in solemn style :
You'd love the gloom they make in either aile,
When the sun's rays, enfeebled as they pass
(And shorn of splendour) through the storied glass,
Faintly display the figures on the floor,
Which pleased distinctly in their place before.
But, ere you enter, yon bold tower survey,
Tall and entire, and venerably gray ;   40
For time has soften'd what was harsh when new,
And now the stains are all of sober hue—
The living stains which Nature's hand alone,
Profuse of life, pours forth upon the stone,
For ever growing ; where the common eye
Can but the bare and rocky bed descry,
There Science loves to trace her tribes minute,
The juiceless foliage, and the tasteless fruit ;
There she perceives them round the surface creep,
And, while they meet, their due distinction keep,   50
Mix'd but not blended ; each its name retains,
And these are Nature's ever-during stains.
And would'st thou, artist, with thy tints and brush,
Form shades like these ? Pretender, where thy blush ?
In three short hours shall thy presuming hand
Th' effect of three slow centuries command [1] ?
Thou may'st thy various greens and grays contrive :
They are not lichens, nor like aught alive.—
But yet proceed, and when thy tints are lost,
Fled in the shower, or crumbled by the frost ;   60
When all thy work is done away as clean
As if thou never spread'st thy gray and green :
Then may'st thou see how Nature's work is done,
How slowly true she lays her colours on ;
When her least speck upon the hardest flint
Has mark and form and is a living tint,
And so embodied with the rock, that few
Can the small germ upon the substance view [2].
Seeds, to our eye invisible, will find
On the rude rock the bed that fits their kind ;   70
There, in the rugged soil, they safely dwell,

THE BOROUGH

Till showers and snows the subtle atoms swell,
And spread th' enduring foliage ;—then we trace
The freckled flower upon the flinty base ;
These all increase, till in unnoticed years
The stony tower as gray with age appears ;
With coats of vegetation, thinly spread,
Coat above coat, the living on the dead.
These then dissolve to dust, and make a way
For bolder foliage, nursed by their decay ;   80
The long-enduring ferns in time will all
Die and depose their dust upon the wall,
Where the wing'd seed may rest, till many a flower
Show Flora's triumph o'er the falling tower.
   But ours yet stands, and has its bells renown'd
For size magnificent and solemn sound.
Each has its motto : some contrived to tell,
In monkish rhyme, the uses of a bell [3]—
Such wond'rous good, as few conceive could spring
From ten loud coppers when their clappers swing.   90
Enter'd the Church, we to a tomb proceed,
Whose names and titles few attempt to read ;
Old English letters, and those half pick'd out,
Leave us, unskilful readers, much in doubt.
Our sons shall see its more degraded state ;
The tomb of grandeur hastens to its fate ;
That marble arch, our sexton's favourite show,
With all those ruff'd and painted pairs below—
The noble lady and the lord who rest
Supine, as courtly dame and warrior dress'd—   100
All are departed from their state sublime,
Mangled and wounded in their war with time,
Colleagued with mischief ; here a leg is fled,
And lo ! the baron with but half a head ;
Midway is cleft the arch ; the very base
Is batter'd round and shifted from its place.
   Wonder not, mortal, at thy quick decay—
See ! men of marble piece-meal melt away ;
When whose the image we no longer read,
But monuments themselves memorials need [4].   110
   With few such stately proofs of grief or pride,

By wealth erected, is our Church supplied;
But we have mural tablets, every size,
That wo could wish, or vanity devise.
  Death levels man,—the wicked and the just,
The wise, the weak, lie blended in the dust;
And by the honours dealt to every name,
The king of terrors seems to level fame.
—See here lamented wives, and every wife
The pride and comfort of her husband's life;   120
Here to her spouse, with every virtue graced,
His mournful widow has a trophy placed;
And here 'tis doubtful if the duteous son,
Or the good father, be in praise outdone.
  This may be nature; when our friends we lose,
Our alter'd feelings alter too our views;
What in their tempers teased us or distress'd,
Is, with our anger and the dead, at rest;
And much we grieve, no longer trial made,
For that impatience which we then display'd;   130
Now to their love and worth of every kind
A soft compunction turns th' afflicted mind;
Virtues, neglected then, adored become,
And graces slighted blossom on the tomb.
  'Tis well; but let not love nor grief believe
That we assent (who neither loved nor grieve)
To all that praise which on the tomb is read,
To all that passion dictates for the dead;
But, more indignant, we the tomb deride,
Whose bold inscription flattery sells to pride.   140
  Read of this Burgess—on the stone appear,
How worthy he! how virtuous! and how dear!
What wailing was there when his spirit fled,
How mourn'd his lady for her lord when dead,
And tears abundant through the town were shed;   [ ]]
See! he was liberal, kind, religious, wise,
And free from all disgrace and all disguise;
His sterling worth, which words cannot express,
Lives with his friends, their pride and their distress.
  All this of Jacob Holmes? for his the name;   150
He thus kind, liberal, just, religious?—shame!

THE BOROUGH

What is the truth? Old Jacob married thrice;
He dealt in coals, and av'rice was his vice;
He ruled the Borough when his year came on,
And some forget, and some are glad he's gone;
For never yet with shilling could he part,
But when it left his hand, it struck his heart.
   Yet, here will love its last attentions pay,
And place memorials on these beds of clay.
Large level stones lie flat upon the grave,   160
And half a century's sun and tempest brave;
But many an honest tear and heartfelt sigh
Have follow'd those who now unnoticed lie;
Of these what numbers rest on every side!
Without one token left by grief or pride;
Their graves soon levell'd to the earth, and then
Will other hillocks rise o'er other men;
Daily the dead on the decay'd are thrust,
And generations follow, "dust to dust."
   Yes! there are real mourners—I have seen   170
A fair, sad girl, mild, suffering, and serene;
Attention (through the day) her duties claim'd,
And to be useful as resign'd she aim'd;
Neatly she dress'd, nor vainly seem'd t' expect
Pity for grief, or pardon for neglect.
But, when her wearied parents sunk to sleep,
She sought her place to meditate and weep:
Then to her mind was all the past display'd,
That faithful memory brings to sorrow's aid:
For then she thought on one regretted youth,   180
Her tender trust, and his unquestion'd truth;
In ev'ry place she wander'd where they'd been,
And sadly-sacred held the parting-scene,
Where last for sea he took his leave—that place
With double interest would she nightly trace;
For long the courtship was, and he would say,
Each time he sail'd,—"This once, and then the day."
Yet prudence tarried; but, when last he went,
He drew from pitying love a full consent.
   Happy he sail'd, and great the care she took,   190
That he should softly sleep, and smartly look;

GEORGE CRABBE

White was his better linen, and his check
Was made more trim than any on the deck;
And every comfort men at sea can know
Was hers to buy, to make, and to bestow:
For he to Greenland sail'd, and much she told,
How he should guard against the climate's cold;
Yet saw not danger; dangers he'd withstood,
Nor could she trace the fever in his blood.
His messmates smiled at flushings in his cheek,   200
And he too smiled, but seldom would he speak;
For now he found the danger, felt the pain,
With grievous symptoms he could not explain;
Hope was awaken'd, as for home he sail'd,
But quickly sank, and never more prevail'd.
He call'd his friend, and prefaced with a sigh
A lover's message—"Thomas, I must die.
"Would I could see my Sally, and could rest
"My throbbing temples on her faithful breast,
"And gazing go!—if not, this trifle take,   210
"And say, till death I wore it for her sake.
"Yes! I must die—blow on, sweet breeze, blow on!
"Give me one look, before my life be gone,
"Oh! give me that, and let me not despair,
"One last fond look—and now repeat the prayer."
He had his wish, had more; I will not paint
The lovers' meeting: she beheld him faint—
With tender fears she took a nearer view,
Her terrors doubling as her hopes withdrew;
He tried to smile, and, half succeeding, said,   220
"Yes! I must die;" and hope for ever fled.
Still long she nursed him: tender thoughts meantime
Were interchanged, and hopes and views sublime.
To her he came to die, and every day
She took some portion of the dread away;
With him she pray'd, to him his Bible read,
Soothed the faint heart, and held the aching head.
She came with smiles the hour of pain to cheer;
Apart, she sigh'd; alone, she shed the tear;
Then, as if breaking from a cloud, she gave   230
Fresh light, and gilt the prospect of the grave.

300

THE BOROUGH

One day he lighter seem'd, and they forgot
The care, the dread, the anguish of their lot ;
They spoke with cheerfulness, and seem'd to think,
Yet said not so—"Perhaps he will not sink."
A sudden brightness in his look appear'd,
A sudden vigour in his voice was heard ;—
She had been reading in the Book of Prayer,
And led him forth, and placed him in his chair ;
Lively he seem'd, and spoke of all he knew,   240
The friendly many, and the favourite few ;
Nor one that day did he to mind recall
But she has treasured, and she loves them all ;
When in her way she meets them, they appear
Peculiar people—death has made them dear.
He named his friend, but then his hand she press'd,
And fondly whisper'd, "Thou must go to rest ; "
"I go," he said ; but, as he spoke, she found
His hand more cold, and fluttering was the sound !
Then gazed affrighten'd ; but she caught a last,   250
A dying look of love—and all was past !
   She placed a decent stone his grave above,
Neatly engraved—an offering of her love ;
For that she wrought, for that forsook her bed,
Awake alike to duty and the dead ;
She would have grieved, had friends presumed to spare
The least assistance—'twas her proper care.
   Here will she come, and on the grave will sit,
Folding her arms, in long abstracted fit ;
But if observer pass, will take her round,   260
And careless seem, for she would not be found ;
Then go again, and thus her hour employ,
While visions please her, and while woes destroy.
   Forbear, sweet maid ! nor be by fancy led
To hold mysterious converse with the dead ;
For sure at length thy [thoughts'], thy [spirit's] pain
In this sad conflict will disturb thy brain.
All have their tasks and trials ; thine are hard,
But short the time, and glorious the reward :
Thy patient spirit to thy duties give ;   270
Regard the dead, but to the living live [5].

301

GEORGE CRABBE

NOTES TO LETTER II.

Note 1, page 296, lines 55 and 56.

In three short hours shall thy presuming hand
Th' effect of three slow centuries command?

If it should be objected, that centuries are not slower than hours, because the speed of time must be uniform, I would answer, that I understand so much, and mean that they are slower in no other sense, than because they are not finished so soon.

Note 2, page 296, line 68.

Can the small germ upon the substance view.

This kind of vegetation, as it begins upon siliceous stones, is very thin, and frequently not to be distinguished from the surface of the flint. The byssus jolithus (lepraria jolithus of the present system), an adhesive carmine crust on rocks and old buildings, was, even by scientific persons, taken for the substance on which it spread. A great variety of these minute vegetables are to be found in some parts of the coast, where the beach, formed of stones of various kinds, is undisturbed, and exposed to every change of weather; in this situation the different species of lichen, in their different stages of growth, have an appearance interesting and agreeable even to those who are ignorant of, and indifferent to, the cause.

Note 3, page 297, lines 87 and 88.

Each has its motto: some contrived to tell,
In monkish rhyme, the uses of a bell.

The several purposes for which bells are used are expressed in two Latin verses of this kind.

Note 4, page 297, line 110.

But monuments themselves memorials need.

Quandoquidem data sunt ipsis quoque fata sepulchris.
Juvenal. Sat. x. l. 146.

Note 5, page 301, last line.

Regard the dead, but to the living live.

It has been observed to me, that in the first part of the story I have represented this young woman as resigned and attentive to her duties; from which it should appear that the concluding advice is unnecessary; but if the reader will construe the expression " to the living live," into the sense—"live entirely for them, attend to duties only which are real, and not those imposed by the imagination," I shall have no need to alter the line which terminates the story.

THE BOROUGH.

LETTER III.

THE VICAR—THE CURATE, &c.

And telling me the sov'reign'st thing on earth
Was parmacity for an inward bruise.
Shakspeare.—Henry IV. Part I. Aĉt 1 [Sc. 3, v. 58].

So gentle, yet so brisk, so wond'rous sweet,
So fit to prattle at a lady's feet.
Churchill [, *The Author*].

Much are the precious hours of youth mispent
In climbing learning's rugged, steep ascent:
When to the top the bold adventurer's got,
He reigns, vain monarch [, o'er] a barren spot;
[Whilst] in the vale of ignorance below
Folly and vice to rank luxuriance grow;
Honours and wealth pour in on every side,
And proud preferment rolls her golden tide.
Churchill [, *The Author*].

VICAR.

The lately departed Minister of the Borough—His soothing and suppli-
catory Manners—His cool and timid Affeĉtions—No Praise due to
such negative Virtue—Address to Charaĉters of this Kind—The
Vicar's Employments—His Talents and moderate Ambition—His
Dislike of Innovation—His mild but ineffeĉtual Benevolence—A
Summary of his Charaĉter.

CURATE.

Mode of paying the Borough-Minister—The Curate has no such Resources
—His Learning and Poverty—Erroneous Idea of his Parent—His
Feelings as a Husband and Father—The dutiful Regard of his
numerous Family—His Pleasure as a Writer, how interrupted—
No Resource in the Press—Vulgar Insult—His Account of a Literary
Society, and a Fund for the Relief of indigent Authors, &c.

GEORGE CRABBE

THE BOROUGH.

LETTER III.

THE VICAR—THE CURATE, &c.

WHERE ends our chancel in a vaulted space,
    Sleep the departed vicars of the place;
Of most, all mention, memory, thought are past—
But take a slight memorial of the last.
To what famed college we our Vicar owe,
To what fair county, let historians show.
Few now remember when the mild young man,
Ruddy and fair, his Sunday-task began;
Few live to speak of that soft soothing look
He cast around, as he prepared his book;   10
It was a kind of supplicating smile,
But nothing hopeless of applause, the while;
And when he finish'd, his corrected pride
Felt the desert, and yet the praise denied.
Thus he his race began, and to the end
His constant care was, no man to offend;
No haughty virtues stirr'd his peaceful mind,
Nor urged the priest to leave the flock behind;
He was his Master's soldier, but not one
To lead an army of his martyrs on: 20
Fear was his ruling passion; yet was love,
Of timid kind, once known his heart to move;
It led his patient spirit where it paid
Its languid offerings to a listening maid;
She, with her widow'd mother, heard him speak,
And sought awhile to find what he would seek.

304

THE BOROUGH

Smiling he came, he smiled when he withdrew,
And paid the same attention to the two;
Meeting and parting without joy or pain,
He seem'd to come that he might go again. 30
The wondering girl, no prude, but something nice,
At length was chill'd by his unmelting ice;
She found her tortoise held such sluggish pace,
That she must turn and meet him in the chase.
This not approving, she withdrew till one
Came who appear'd with livelier hope to run;
Who sought a readier way the heart to move,
Than by faint dalliance of unfixing love.
  Accuse me not that I approving paint
Impatient hope or love without restraint; 40
Or think the passions, a tumultuous throng,
Strong as they are, ungovernably strong:
But is the laurel to the soldier due,
Who cautious comes not into danger's view?
What worth has virtue by desire untried,
When Nature's self enlists on duty's side?
  The married dame in vain assail'd the truth
And guarded bosom of the Hebrew youth;
But with the daughter of the Priest of On
The love was lawful, and the guard was gone; 50
But Joseph's fame had lessen'd in our view,
Had he, refusing, fled the maiden too.
  Yet our good priest to Joseph's praise aspired,
As once rejecting what his heart desired;
"I am escaped," he said, when none pursued;
When none attack'd him, "I am unsubdued;"
"Oh pleasing pangs of love," he sang again,
Cold to the joy, and stranger to the pain.
Ev'n in his age would he address the young,
"I too have felt these fires, and they are strong;" 60
But from the time he left his favourite maid,
To ancient females his devoirs were paid;
And still they miss him after morning prayer;
Nor yet successor fills the Vicar's chair,
Where kindred spirits in his praise agree,
A happy few, as mild and cool as he—

Crabbe   U   305

GEORGE CRABBE

The easy followers in the female train,
Led without love, and captives without chain.
Ye lilies male ! think (as your tea you sip,
While the town small-talk flows from lip to lip ;   70
Intrigues half-gather'd, conversation-scraps,
Kitchen-cabals, and nursery-mishaps)
If the vast world may not some scene produce,
Some state, where your small talents might have use.
Within seraglios you might harmless move,
'Mid ranks of beauty, and in haunts of love ;
There from too daring man the treasures guard,
An easy duty, and its own reward ;
Nature's soft substitutes, you there might save
From crime the tyrant, and from wrong the slave.   80
But let applause be dealt in all we may :
Our priest was cheerful, and in season gay ;
His frequent visits seldom fail'd to please ;
Easy himself, he sought his neighbour's ease.
To a small garden with delight he came,
And gave successive flowers a summer's fame ;
These he presented with a grace his own
To his fair friends, and made their beauties known,
Not without moral compliment : how they
" Like flowers were sweet, and must like flowers decay."   90
Simple he was, and loved the simple truth,
Yet had some useful cunning from his youth ;
A cunning never to dishonour lent,
And rather for defence than conquest meant ;
'Twas fear of power, with some desire to rise,
But not enough to make him enemies ;
He ever aim'd to please ; and to offend
Was ever cautious ; for he sought a friend ;
Yet for the friendship never much would pay,
Content to bow, be silent, and obey,   100
And by a soothing suff'rance find his way.   [ ]
Fiddling and fishing were his arts ; at times
He alter'd sermons, and he aim'd at rhymes ;
And his fair friends, not yet intent on cards,
Oft he amused with riddles and charades.
Mild were his doctrines, and not one discourse

THE BOROUGH

But gain'd in softness what it lost in force:
Kind his opinions; he would not receive
An ill report, nor evil act believe;
"If true, 'twas wrong; but blemish great or small   110
"Have all mankind; yea, sinners are we all."
   If ever fretful thought disturb'd his breast,
If aught of gloom that cheerful mind oppress'd,
It sprang from innovation; it was then
He spake of mischief made by restless men,
Not by new doctrines: never in his life
Would he attend to controversial strife;
For sects he cared not; "They are not of us,
"Nor need we, brethren, their concerns discuss;
"But 'tis the change, the schism at home I feel;   120
"Ills few perceive, and none have skill to heal:
"Not at the altar our young brethren read
"(Facing their flock) the decalogue and creed;
"But at their duty, in their desks they stand,
"With naked surplice, lacking hood and band:
"Churches are now of holy song bereft,
"And half our ancient customs changed or left;
"Few sprigs of ivy are at Christmas seen,
"Nor crimson berry tips the holly's green;
"Mistaken choirs refuse the solemn strain   130
"Of ancient Sternhold, which from ours amain
"[Comes] flying forth, from aile to aile about,
"Sweet links of harmony and long drawn out."
   These were to him essentials; all things new
He deem'd superfluous, useless, or untrue;
To all beside indifferent, easy, cold,
Here the fire kindled, and the wo was told.
   Habit with him was all the test of truth,
"It must be right: I've done it from my youth."
Questions he answer'd in as brief a way,   140
"It must be wrong—it was of yesterday."
   Though mild benevolence our priest possess'd,
'Twas but by wishes or by words express'd:
Circles in water, as they wider flow,
The less conspicuous in their progress grow;
And when at last they touch upon the shore,

U 2

307

Distinction ceases, and they're view'd no more.
His love, like that last circle, all embraced,
But with effect that never could be traced.
  Now rests our Vicar. They who knew him best 150
Proclaim his life t' have been entirely rest—
Free from all evils which disturb his mind
Whom studies vex and controversies blind.
  The rich approved—of them in awe he stood;
The poor admired—they all believed him good;
The old and serious of his habits spoke;
The frank and youthful loved his pleasant joke;
Mothers approved a safe contented guest,
And daughters one who back'd each small request:
In him his flock found nothing to condemn; 160
Him sectaries liked—he never troubled them;
No trifles fail'd his yielding mind to please,
And all his passions sunk in early ease;
Nor one so old has left this world of sin,
More like the being that he enter'd in.

THE CURATE.

ASK you what lands our pastor tithes?—Alas!
  But few our acres, and but short our grass:
In some fat pastures of the rich, indeed,
May roll the single cow or favourite steed,
Who, stable-fed, is here for pleasure seen, 170
His sleek sides bathing in the dewy green:
But these, our hilly heath and common wide,
Yield a slight portion for the parish-guide;
No crops luxuriant in our borders stand,
For here we plough the ocean, not the land;
Still reason wills that we our pastor pay,
And custom does it on a certain day.
Much is the duty, small the legal due,
And this with grateful minds we keep in view;
Each makes his off'ring, some by habit led, 180
Some by the thought, that all men must be fed;

THE BOROUGH

Duty and love, and piety and pride,
Have each their force, and for the priest provide.
  Not thus our Curate, one whom all believe
Pious and just, and for whose fate they grieve;
All see him poor, but ev'n the vulgar know
He merits love, and their respect bestow.
A man so learn'd you shall but seldom see,
Nor one so honour'd, so aggrieved as he—
Not grieved by years alone; though his appear   190
Dark and more dark, severer on severe:
Not in his need,—and yet we all must grant
How painful 'tis for feeling age to want;
Nor in his body's sufferings—yet we know
Where time has plough'd, there misery loves to sow:
But in the wearied mind, that all in vain
Wars with distress, and struggles with its pain.
  His father saw his powers—" I'll give," quoth he,
" My first-born learning; 'twill a portion be."
Unhappy gift! a portion for a son!   200
But all he had :—he learn'd, and was undone!
  Better, apprenticed to an humble trade,
Had he the cassock for the priesthood made,
Or thrown the shuttle, or the saddle shaped,
And all these pangs of feeling souls escaped.
  He once had hope—hope ardent, lively, light;
His feelings pleasant, and his prospects bright:
Eager of fame, he read, he thought, he wrote,
Weigh'd the Greek page, and added note on note;
At morn, at evening at his work was he,   210
And dream'd what his Euripides would be.
  Then care began;—he loved, he woo'd, he wed;
Hope cheer'd him still, and Hymen bless'd his bed—
A Curate's bed! then came the woful years,
The husband's terrors, and the father's tears;
A wife grown feeble, mourning, pining, vex'd,
With wants and woes—by daily cares perplex'd;
No more a help, a smiling, soothing aid,
But boding, drooping, sickly, and afraid.
  A kind physician, and without a fee,   220
Gave his opinion—" Send her to the sea."

"Alas!" the good man answer'd, "can I send
"A friendless woman? Can I find a friend?
"No; I must with her, in her need, repair
"To that new place; the poor lie everywhere;—
"Some priest will pay me for my pious pains:"—
He said, he came, and here he yet remains.
   Behold his dwelling; this poor hut he hires,
Where he from view, though not from want, retires;
Where four fair daughters, and five sorrowing sons,   230
Partake his sufferings, and dismiss his duns.
All join their efforts, and in patience learn
To want the comforts they aspire to earn;
For the sick mother something they'd obtain,
To soothe her grief and mitigate her pain;
For the sad father something they'd procure,
To ease the burthen they themselves endure.
   Virtues like these at once delight and press
On the fond father with a proud distress;
On all around he looks with care and love,   240
Grieved to behold, but happy to approve.
   Then from his care, his love, his grief he steals,
And by himself an author's pleasure feels;
Each line detains him; he omits not one,
And all the sorrows of his state are gone.—
Alas! ev'n then, in that delicious hour,
He feels his fortune, and laments its power.
   Some tradesman's bill his wandering eyes engage,
Some scrawl for payment, thrust 'twixt page and page;
Some bold, loud rapping at his humble door,   250
Some surly message he has heard before,
Awake, alarm, and tell him he is poor.   [ ]
   An angry dealer, vulgar, rich, and proud,
Thinks of his bill, and passing, raps aloud;
The elder daughter meekly makes him way—
"I want my money, and I cannot stay:
"My mill is stopp'd; what, Miss! I cannot grind;
"Go tell your father he must raise the wind."
Still trembling, troubled, the dejected maid
Says, "Sir! my father!—" and then stops afraid: 260
Ev'n his hard heart is soften'd, and he hears

THE BOROUGH

Her voice with pity; he respects her tears;
His stubborn features half admit a smile,
And his tone softens—"Well! I'll wait awhile."
 Pity, a man so good, so mild, so meek,
At such an age, should have his bread to seek;
And all those rude and fierce attacks to dread,
That are more harrowing than the want of bread;
Ah! who shall whisper to that misery peace,
And say that want and insolence shall cease?   270
 "But why not publish?"—those who know too well,
Dealers in Greek, are fearful 'twill not sell;
Then he himself is timid, troubled, slow,
Nor likes his labours nor his griefs to show;
The hope of fame may in his heart have place,
But he has dread and horror of disgrace;
Nor has he that confiding, easy way,
That might his learning and himself display;
But to his work he from the world retreats,
And frets and glories o'er the favourite sheets.   280
 But see the man himself; and sure I trace
Signs of new joy exulting in that face
O'er care that sleeps—we err, or we discern
Life in thy looks—the reason may we learn?
 "Yes," he replied, "I'm happy, I confess,
"To learn that some are pleased with happiness
"Which others feel—there are who now combine
"The worthiest natures in the best design,
"To aid the letter'd poor, and soothe such ills as mine: [ʃ]
"We who more keenly feel the world's contempt,   290
"And from its miseries are the least exempt;
"Now hope shall whisper to the wounded breast,
"And grief, in soothing expectation, rest.
 "Yes, I am taught that men who think, who feel,
"Unite the pains of thoughtful men to heal;
"Not with disdainful pride, whose bounties make
"The needy curse the benefits they take;
"Not with the idle vanity that knows
"Only a selfish joy when it bestows;
"Not with o'erbearing wealth, that, in disdain,   300
"Hurls the superfluous bliss at groaning pain;

311

"But these are men who yield such bless'd relief
"That with the grievance they destroy the grief;
"Their timely aid the needy sufferers find,
"Their generous manner soothes the suffering mind;
"Theirs is a gracious bounty, form'd to raise
"Him whom it aids; their charity is praise;
"A common bounty may relieve distress,
"But whom the vulgar succour, they oppress;
"This, though a favour, is an honour too;   310
"Though mercy's duty, yet 'tis merit's due:
"When our relief from such resources rise,
"All painful sense of obligation dies;
"And grateful feelings in the bosom wake,
"For 'tis their offerings, not their alms, we take.
  "Long may these founts of charity remain,
"And never shrink but to be fill'd again;
"True! to the author they are now confined,
"To him who gave the treasure of his mind,
"His time, his health, and thankless found mankind: 320[ ]]
"But there is hope that from these founts may flow
"A sideway stream, and equal good bestow—
"Good that may reach us, whom the day's distress
"Keeps from the fame and perils of the press;
"Whom study beckons from the ills of life,
"And they from study—melancholy strife!
"Who then can say but bounty now so free,
"And so diffused, may find its way to me?
  "Yes! I may see my decent table yet
"Cheer'd with the meal that adds not to my debt;   330
"May talk of those to whom so much we owe,
"And guess their names whom yet we may not know;
"Bless'd we shall say are those who thus can give,
"And next who thus upon the bounty live;
"Then shall I close with thanks my humble meal,
"And feel so well—Oh! God! how I shall feel!"

THE BOROUGH.

LETTER IV.

SECTS AND PROFESSIONS IN RELIGION.

> . . . . . But cast your eyes again,
> And view those errors which new sects maintain,
> Or which of old disturb'd the [Church's] peaceful reign :
> And we can point each period of the time
> When they began and who begat the crime ;
> Can calculate how long th' eclipse endured ;
> Who interposed ; what digits were obscured ;
> Of all which are already pass'd away,
> We [know] the rise, the progress, and decay.
> *Dryden.—Hind and Panther*, Part II.

> [Ah !] said the Hind, how many sons have you
> Who call you mother, whom you never knew ?
> But most of them who that relation plead
> Are such ungracious youths as wish you dead ;
> They gape at rich revenues which you hold,
> And fain would nibble at your grandame gold.
> *Hind and Panther* [Part III].

Sects and Professions in Religion are numerous and successive—General
   Effect of false Zeal—Deists—Fanatical Idea of Church Reformers—
   The Church of Rome--Baptists—Swedenborgians—Universalists—
   Jews.
Methodists of two Kinds ; Calvinistic and Arminian.
The Preaching of a Calvinistic Enthusiast—His Contempt of Learning—
   Dislike to sound Morality : why—His Idea of Conversion—His
   Success and Pretensions to Humility.
The Arminian Teacher of the older Flock—Their Notions of the
   Operations and Power of Satan—Description of his Devices—Their
   Opinion of regular Ministers—Comparison of these with the Preacher
   himself—A Rebuke to his Hearers ; introduces a Description of the
   powerful Effects of the Word in the early and awakening Days of
   Methodism.

313

GEORGE CRABBE

THE BOROUGH.

LETTER IV.

SECTS AND PROFESSIONS IN RELIGION.

" SECTS in Religion? "—Yes, of every race
   We nurse some portion in our favour'd place ;
Not one warm preacher of one growing sect
Can say our Borough treats him with neglect ;
Frequent as fashions they with us appear,
And you might ask, " how think we for the year ? "
They come to us as riders in a trade,
And with much art exhibit and persuade.
   Minds are for sects of various kinds decreed,
As diff'rent soils are form'd for diff'rent seed ;   10
Some, when converted, sigh in sore amaze,
And some are wrapt in joy's ecstatic blaze ;
Others again will change to each extreme,
They know not why—as hurried in a dream ;
Unstable they, like water, take all forms,
Are quick and stagnant, have their calms and storms ;
High on the hills, they in the sunbeams glow ;
Then muddily they move debased and slow,
Or cold and frozen rest, and neither rise nor flow.   [ ]
   Yet none the cool and prudent teacher prize ;   20
On him they dote who wakes their ecstasies ;
With passions ready primed such guide they meet,
And warm and kindle with th' imparted heat ;
'Tis he who wakes the nameless strong desire,
The melting rapture, and the glowing fire ;
'Tis he who pierces deep the tortured breast,
And stirs the terrors, never more to rest.

Opposed to these we have a prouder kind,
Rash without heat, and without raptures blind ;
These our *Glad Tidings* unconcern'd peruse,   30
Search without awe, and without fear refuse ;
The truths, the blessings found in Sacred Writ,
Call forth their spleen, and exercise their wit ;
Respect from these nor saints nor martyrs gain;
The zeal they scorn, and they deride the pain ;
And take their transient, cool, contemptuous view,
Of that which must be tried, and doubtless—*may be true.*

Friends of our faith we have, whom doubts like these,
And keen remarks, and bold objections please ;
They grant such doubts have weaker minds oppress'd,   40
Till sound conviction gave the troubled rest.

" But still," they cry, " let none their censures spare;
" They but confirm the glorious hopes we share ;
" From doubt, disdain, derision, scorn, and lies,
" With five-fold triumph sacred truth shall rise."

Yes ! I allow, so truth shall stand at last,
And gain fresh glory by the conflict past—
As Solway-Moss (a barren mass and cold,
Death to the seed, and poison to the fold,)
The smiling plain and fertile vale o'erlaid,   50
Choked the green sod, and kill'd the springing blade ;
That, changed by culture, may in time be seen,
Enrich'd by golden grain, and pasture green ;
And these fair acres, rented and enjoy'd,
May those excel by Solway-Moss destroy'd [1].

Still must have mourn'd the tenant of the day,
For hopes destroy'd and harvests swept away ;
To him the gain of future years unknown,
The instant grief and suffering were his own.
So must I grieve for many a wounded heart,   60
Chill'd by those doubts which bolder minds impart :
Truth in the end shall shine divinely clear,
But sad the darkness till those times appear ;
Contests for truth, as wars for freedom, yield
Glory and joy to those who gain the field ;
But still the Christian must in pity sigh
For all who suffer, and uncertain die.

Here are, who all the Church maintains approve,
But yet the Church herself they will not love ;
In angry speech, they blame the carnal tie,   70
Which pure Religion lost her spirit by ;
What time from prisons, flames, and tortures led,
She slumber'd careless in a royal bed ;
To make, they add, the Churches' glory shine,
Should Diocletian reign, not Constantine.
   "In pomp," they cry, "is England's Church array'd ;
" Her cool reformers wrought like men afraid.
" We would have pull'd her gorgeous temples down,
" And spurn'd her mitre, and defiled her gown ;
" We would have trodden low both bench and stall,   80
" Nor left a tithe remaining, great or small."
   Let us be serious.—Should such trials come,
Are they themselves prepared for martyrdom ?
It seems to us that our reformers knew
Th' important work they undertook to do ;
An equal priesthood they were loth to try,
Lest zeal and care should with ambition die ;
To them it seem'd that, take the tenth away,
Yet priests must eat, and you must feed or pay :
Would they indeed, who hold such pay in scorn,   90
Put on the muzzle when they tread the corn ?
Would they, all gratis, watch and tend the fold,
Nor take one fleece to keep them from the cold ?
   Men are not equal, and 'tis meet and right
That robes and titles our respect excite ;
Order requires it ; 'tis by vulgar pride
That such regard is censured and denied,
Or by that false enthusiastic zeal,
That thinks the spirit will the priest reveal,
And show to all men, by their powerful speech,   100
Who are appointed and inspired to teach.
Alas ! could we the dangerous rule believe,
Whom for their teacher should the crowd receive ?
Since all the varying kinds demand respect,
All press you on to join their chosen sect,
Although but in this single point agreed,
" Desert your churches and adopt our creed."

THE BOROUGH

We know full well how much our forms offend
The burthen'd Papist and the simple Friend—
Him who new robes for every service takes,   110
And who in drab and beaver sighs and shakes.
He on the priest, whom hood and band adorn,
Looks with the sleepy eye of silent scorn ;
But him I would not for my friend and guide,
Who views such things with spleen, or wears with pride.
  See next our several sects—but first behold
The Church of Rome, who here is poor and old :
Use not triumphant rail'ry, or, at least,
Let not thy mother be a whore and beast.
Great was her pride indeed in ancient times ;   120
Yet shall we think of nothing but her crimes ?
Exalted high above all earthly things,
She placed her foot upon the neck of kings ;
But some have deeply since avenged the crown,
And thrown her glory and her honours down ;
Nor neck nor ear can she of kings command,
Nor place a foot upon her own fair land.
  Among her sons, with us a quiet few,
Obscure themselves, her ancient state review ;
And fond and melancholy glances cast   130
On power insulted, and on triumph pass'd :
They look, they can but look, with many a sigh,
On sacred buildings doom'd in dust to lie ;
" On seats," they tell, " where priests 'mid tapers dim
" Breathed the warm prayer, or tuned the midnight hymn ;
" Where trembling penitents their guilt confess'd ;
" Where want had succour, and contrition rest.
" There weary men from trouble found relief,
" There men in sorrow found repose from grief ;
" To scenes like these the fainting soul retired ;   140
" Revenge and anger in these cells expired ;
" By pity soothed, remorse lost half her fears,
" And soften'd pride dropp'd penitential tears.
  " Then convent-walls and nunnery-spires arose,
" In pleasant spots which monk or abbot chose ;
" When counts and barons saints devoted fed,
" And, making cheap exchange, had pray'r for bread.

"Now all is lost; the earth where abbeys stood
"Is layman's land, the glebe, the stream, the wood;
"His oxen low where monks retired to eat;   150
"His cows repose upon the prior's seat;
"And wanton doves within the cloisters bill,
"Where the chaste votary warr'd with wanton will."
Such is the change they mourn, but they restrain
The rage of grief, and passively complain.
We've Baptists old and new; forbear to ask
What the distinction—I decline the task.
This I perceive, that, when a sect grows old,
Converts are few, and the converted cold:
First comes the hot-bed heat, and, while it glows,   160
The plants spring up, and each with vigour grows;
Then comes the cooler day, and, though awhile
The verdure prospers and the blossoms smile,
Yet poor the fruit, and form'd by long delay,
Nor will the profits for the culture pay;
The skilful gard'ner then no longer stops,
But turns to other beds for bearing crops.
Some Swedenborgians in our streets are found,
Those wandering walkers on enchanted ground;
Who in our world can other worlds survey,   170
And speak with spirits, though confined in clay:
Of Bible-mysteries they the keys possess,
Assured themselves, where wiser men but guess:
'Tis theirs to see—around, about, above—
How spirits mingle thoughts, and angels move;
Those whom our grosser views from us exclude,
To them appear a heavenly multitude;
While the dark sayings, seal'd to men like us,
Their priests interpret, and their flocks discuss.
But while these gifted men, a favour'd fold,   180
New powers exhibit and new worlds behold;
Is there not danger lest their minds confound
The pure above them with the gross around?
May not these Phaetons, who thus contrive
'Twixt heaven above and earth beneath to drive,
When from their flaming chariots they descend,
The worlds they visit in their fancies blend?

318

THE BOROUGH

Alas! too sure on both they bring disgrace;
Their earth is crazy, and their heav'n is base.
  We have, it seems, who treat, and doubtless well,   190
Of a chastising, not awarding hell;
Who are assured that an offended God
Will cease to use the thunder and the rod;
A soul on earth, by crime and folly stain'd,
When here corrected, has improvement gain'd—
In other state still more improved to grow,
And nobler powers in happier world to know;
New strength to use in each divine employ,
And, more enjoying, looking to more joy.
  A pleasing vision! could we thus be sure   200
Polluted souls would be at length so pure;
The view is happy, we may think it just,
It may be true—but who shall add it must?
To the plain words and sense of sacred writ,
With all my heart I reverently submit;
But, where it leaves me doubtful, I'm afraid
To call conjecture to my reason's aid;
Thy thoughts, thy ways, great God! are not as mine,
And to thy mercy I my soul resign.
  Jews are with us, but far unlike to those,   210
Who, led by David, warr'd with Israel's foes;
Unlike to those whom his imperial son
Taught truths divine—the preacher Solomon:
Nor war nor wisdom yield our Jews delight;
They will not study, and they dare not fight [2].
  These are, with us, a slavish, knavish crew,
Shame and dishonour to the name of Jew;
The poorest masters of the meanest arts,
With cunning heads, and cold and cautious hearts;
They grope their dirty way to petty gains,   220
While poorly paid for their nefarious pains.
  Amazing race! deprived of land and laws,
A general language, and a public cause;
With a religion none can now obey,
With a reproach that none can take away:
A people still, whose common ties are gone;
Who, mix'd with every race, are lost in none.

GEORGE CRABBE

What said their prophet?—"Shouldst thou disobey,
"The Lord shall take thee from thy land away;
"Thou shalt a by-word and a proverb be,   230
"And all shall wonder at thy woes and thee;
"Daughter and son shalt thou, while captive, have,
"And see them made the bond-maid and the slave;
"He, whom thou leav'st, the Lord thy God, shall bring
"War to thy country on an eagle-wing:
"A people strong and dreadful to behold,
"Stern to the young, remorseless to the old;
"Masters, whose speech thou canst not understand,
"By cruel signs shall give the harsh command;
"Doubtful of life shalt thou by night, by day,   240
"For grief, and dread, and trouble pine away;
"Thy evening-wish,—'Would God I saw the sun!'
"Thy morning-sigh,—'Would God the day were done!'
"Thus shalt thou suffer, and to distant times
"Regret thy misery, and lament thy crimes(3)."
   A part there are, whom doubtless man might trust,
Worthy as wealthy, pure, religious, just;
They who with patience, yet with rapture look
On the strong promise of the sacred book:
As unfulfill'd th' endearing words they view,   250
And blind to truth, yet own their prophets true;
Well pleased they look for Sion's coming state,
Nor think of Julian's boast and Julian's fate(4).
   More might I add; I might describe the flocks
Made by seceders from the ancient stocks;
Those who will not to any guide submit,
Nor find one creed to their conceptions fit.
Each sect, they judge, in something goes astray,
And every church has lost the certain way;
Then for themselves they carve out creed and laws,   260
And weigh their atoms, and divide their straws.
   A sect remains, which though divided long
In hostile parties, both are fierce and strong,
And into each enlists a warm and zealous throng.   [ʃ]
Soon as they rose in fame, the strife arose,
The Calvinistic these, th' Arminian those;
With Wesley some remain'd, the remnant Whitfield chose. [ʃ]

THE BOROUGH

Now various leaders both the parties take,
And the divided hosts their new divisions make.
  See yonder preacher to his people pass,   270
Borne up and swell'd by tabernacle-gas ;
Much he discourses, and of various points,
All unconnected, void of limbs and joints ;
He rails, persuades, explains, and moves the will,
By fierce bold words, and strong mechanic skill.
  " That Gospel Paul with zeal and love maintain'd,
" To others lost, to you is now explain'd ;
" No worldly learning can these points discuss,
" Books teach them not as they are taught to us.
" Illiterate call us ! let their wisest man   280
" Draw forth his thousands as your teacher can :
" They give their moral precepts ; so, they say,
" Did Epictetus once, and Seneca ;
" One was a slave, and slaves we all must be,
" Until the Spirit comes and sets us free.
" Yet hear you nothing from such men but works ;
" They make the Christian service like the Turks'.
  " Hark to the churchman : day by day he cries,—
" ' Children of men, be virtuous and be wise ;
" ' Seek patience, justice, temp'rance, meekness, truth ;   290
" ' In age be courteous, be sedate in youth.'—
" So they advise, and when such things be read,
" How can we wonder that their flocks are dead ?
  " The heathens wrote of virtue, they could dwell
" On such light points—in them it might be well,
" They might for virtue strive ; but I maintain,
" Our strife for virtue would be proud and vain.
" When Samson carried Gaza's gates so far,
" Lack'd he a helping hand to bear the bar ?
" Thus the most virtuous must in bondage groan :   300
" Samson is grace, and carries all alone [5].
  " Hear you not priests their feeble spirits spend
" In bidding sinners turn to God, and mend ;
" To check their passions, and to walk aright;
" To run the race, and fight the glorious fight ?
" Nay more—to pray, to study, to improve,
" To grow in goodness, to advance in love ?

  Crabbe   x

"Oh! babes and sucklings, dull of heart and slow,
"Can grace be gradual? Can conversion grow?
"The work is done by instantaneous call;   310
"Converts at once are made, or not at all;
"Nothing is left to grow, reform, amend;
"The first emotion is the movement's end:
"If once forgiven, debt can be no more;
"If once adopted, will the heir be poor?
"The man who gains the twenty-thousand prize,
"Does he by little and by little rise?
"There can no fortune for the soul be made
"By peddling cares and savings in her trade.
 "Why are our sins forgiven?—Priests reply, 320
"—'Because by faith on mercy we rely;
"'Because, believing, we repent and pray.'—
"Is this their doctrine?—then, they go astray:
"We're pardon'd neither for belief nor deed,
"For faith nor practice, principle nor creed;
"Nor for our sorrow for our former sin,
"Nor for our fears when better thoughts begin;
"Nor prayers nor penance in the cause avail;
"All strong remorse, all soft contrition fail:—
"It is the *call!* till that proclaims us free, 330
"In darkness, doubt, and bondage we must be;
"Till that *assures* us, we've in vain endured,
"And all is over when we're once assured.
 "This is conversion:—First, there comes a cry
"Which utters, 'Sinner, thou'rt condemn'd to die;'
"Then the struck soul to every aid repairs,
"To church and altar, ministers and prayers;
"In vain she strives—involved, ingulf'd in sin,
"She looks for hell, and seems already in:
"When in this travail, the new birth comes on, 340
"And in an instant every pang is gone;
"The mighty work is done without our pains—
"Claim but a part, and not a part remains.
 "All this experience tells the soul, and yet ⎫
"These moral men their pence and farthings set ⎬ [♪]
"Against the terrors of the countless debt. ⎭
"But such compounders, when they come to jail,

322

"Will find that virtues never serve as bail.
"So much to duties; now to learning look,
"And see their priesthood piling book on book; 350
"Yea, books of infidels, we're told, and plays,
"Put out by heathens in the wink'd-on days;
"The very letters are of crooked kind,
"And show the strange perverseness of their mind.
"Have I this learning? When the Lord would speak,
"Think ye he needs the Latin or the Greek?
"And lo! with all their learning, when they rise
"To preach, in view the ready sermon lies;
"Some low-prized stuff they purchased at the stalls,
"And more like Seneca's than mine or Paul's. 360
"Children of bondage, how should they explain
"The spirit's freedom, while they wear a chain?
"They study words, for meanings grow perplex'd,
"And slowly hunt for truth, from text to text,
"Through Greek and Hebrew—we the meaning seek
"Of that within, who every tongue can speak.
"This all can witness; yet the more I know,
"The more a meek and humble mind I show.
"No; let the Pope, the high and mighty priest,
"Lord to the poor, and servant to the Beast, 370
"Let bishops, deans, and prebendaries swell
"With pride and fatness till their hearts rebel:
"I'm meek and modest.—If I could be proud,
"This crowded meeting, lo! th' amazing crowd!
"Your mute attention, and your meek respect,
"My spirit's fervour, and my words' effect,
"Might stir th' unguarded soul; and oft to me
"The tempter speaks, whom I compel to flee;
"He goes in fear, for he my force has tried—
"Such is my power! but can you call it pride? 380
"No, fellow-pilgrims! of the things I've shown
"I might be proud, were they indeed my own!
"But they are lent; and well you know the source
"Of all that's mine, and must confide of course;
"Mine! no, I err; 'tis but consign'd to me,
"And I am nought but steward and trustee."

x 2

GEORGE CRABBE

FAR other doctrines yon Arminian speaks;
"Seek grace," he cries; "for he shall find who seeks."
This is the ancient stock by Wesley led—
They the pure body, he the reverend head; 390
All innovation they with dread decline;
Their John the elder was the John divine.
Hence still their moving prayer, the melting hymn,
The varied accent, and the active limb;
Hence that implicit faith in Satan's might,
And their own matchless prowess in the fight.
In every act they see that lurking foe,
Let loose awhile, about the world to go:—
A dragon, flying round the earth, to kill
The heavenly hope, and prompt the carnal will; 400
Whom sainted knights attack in sinners' cause,
And force the wounded victim from his paws;
Who but for them would man's whole race subdue;
For not a hireling will the foe pursue.
 "Show me one Churchman who will rise and pray
"Through half the night, though lab'ring all the day,
"Always abounding—show me him, I say."—
Thus cries the preacher, and he adds, "their sheep
"Satan devours at leisure as they sleep.
"Not so with us; we drive him from the fold, 410
"For ever barking and for ever bold;
"While they securely slumber, all his schemes
"Take full effect—the devil never dreams:
"Watchful and changeful through the world he goes,
"And few can trace this deadliest of their foes;
"But I detect, and at his work surprise,
"The subtle serpent under all disguise.
 "Thus to man's soul the foe of souls will speak,
"—'A saint elect, you can have nought to seek;
"'Why all this labour in so plain a case— 420
"'Such care to run, when certain of the race?'
"All this he urges to the carnal will;
"He knows you're slothful, and would have you still.
"Be this your answer,—'Satan, I will keep
"'Still on the watch till you are laid asleep.'
"Thus too the Christian's progress he'll retard:—

324

"'The gates of mercy are for ever barr'd,
"'And that with bolts so driven and so stout,
"'Ten thousand workmen cannot wrench them out.'
"To this deceit you have but one reply—   430
"Give to the father of all lies, the lie.
    "A sister's weakness he'll by fits surprise—
"His her wild laughter, his her piteous cries;
"And, should a pastor at her side attend,
"He'll use her organs to abuse her friend.
"These are possessions—unbelieving wits
"Impute them all to nature: 'They're her fits,
"'Caused by commotions in the nerves and brains.'—
"Vain talk! but they'll be fitted for their pains.
    "These are in part the ills the foe has wrought,   440
"And these the churchman thinks not worth his thought;
"They bid the troubled try for peace and rest,
"Compose their minds, and be no more distress'd;
"As well might they command the passive shore
"To keep secure, and be o'erflow'd no more;
"To the wrong subject is their skill applied—
"To act like workmen, they should stem the tide.
    "These are the church-physicians; they are paid
"With noble fees for their advice and aid;
"Yet know they not the inward pulse to feel,   450
"To ease the anguish, or the wound to heal.
"With the sick sinner thus their work begins:
"'Do you repent you of your former sins?
"'Will you amend if you revive and live,
"'And, pardon seeking, will you pardon give?
"'Have you belief in what your Lord has done,
"'And are you thankful?—all is well, my son.'
    "A way far different ours—we thus surprise
"A soul with questions, and demand replies;
"'How dropp'd you first,' I ask, 'the legal yoke?   460
"'What the first word the living Witness spoke?
"'Perceived you thunders roar and lightnings shine,
"'And tempests gathering ere the birth divine?
"'Did fire, and storm, and earthquake all appear
"'Before that still small voice, *What dost thou here?*
"'Hast thou by day and night, and soon and late,

GEORGE CRABBE

"'Waited and watch'd before Admission-gate;
"'And so, a pilgrim and a soldier, pass'd
"'To Sion's hill through battle and through blast?
"'Then, in thy way didst thou thy foe attack,   470
"'And mad'st thou proud Apollyon turn his back?'
  "Heart-searching things are these, and shake the mind,
"Yea, like the rustling of a mighty wind.
  "Thus would I ask:—'Nay, let me question now,
"'How sink my sayings in your bosoms? how?
"'Feel you a quickening? drops the subject deep?
"'Stupid and stony, no! you're all asleep;
"'Listless and lazy, waiting for a close,
"'As if at church—Do I allow repose?
"'Am I a legal minister? do I   480
"'With form or rubrick, rule or rite, comply?
"''Then, whence this quiet, tell me, I beseech?
"''One might believe you heard your rector preach,
"''Or his assistant dreamer:—Oh! return,
"''Ye times of burning, when the heart would burn.
"''Now hearts are ice, and you, my freezing fold,
"''Have spirits sunk and sad, and bosoms stony-cold.'
  "Oh! now again for those prevailing powers,
"Which once began this mighty work of ours;
"When the wide field, God's temple, was the place,   490
"And birds flew by to catch a breath of grace;
"When 'mid his timid friends and threat'ning foes,
"Our zealous chief as Paul at Athens rose:
"When with infernal spite and knotty clubs
"The ill-one arm'd his scoundrels and his scrubs;
"And there were flying all around the spot
"Brands at the preacher, but they touch'd him not;
"Stakes brought to smite him, threaten'd in his cause,
"And tongues, attuned to curses, roar'd applause;
"Louder and louder grew his awful tones,   500
"Sobbing and sighs were heard, and rueful groans;
"Soft women fainted, prouder man express'd
"Wonder and wo, and butchers smote the breast;
"Eyes wept, ears tingled; stiff'ning on each head,
"The hair drew back, and Satan howl'd and fled.
  "In that soft season, when the gentle breeze

" Rises all round, and swells by slow degrees ;
" Till tempests gather, when through all the sky
" The thunders rattle, and the lightnings fly ;
" When rain in torrents wood and vale deform,   510
" And all is horror, hurricane, and storm :
" So, when the preacher in that glorious time,
" Than clouds more melting, more than storm sublime,
" Dropp'd the new word, there came a charm around ;
" Tremors and terrors rose upon the sound ;
" The stubborn spirits by his force he broke,
" As the fork'd lightning rives the knotted oak.
" Fear, hope, dismay, all signs of shame or grace,
" Chain'd every foot, or featured every face ;
" Then took his sacred trump a louder swell,   520
" And now they groan'd, they sicken'd, and they fell ;
" Again he sounded, and we heard the cry
" Of the word-wounded, as about to die ;
" Further and further spread the conquering word,
" As loud he cried—' the battle of the Lord.'
" Ev'n those apart who were the sound denied,
" Fell down instinctive, and in spirit died.
" Nor [stay'd] he yet—his eye, his frown, his speech,
" His very gesture had a power to teach ;
" With outstretch'd arms, strong voice and piercing call, 530
" He won the field, and made the Dagons fall ;
" And thus in triumph took his glorious way,
" Through scenes of horror, terror, and dismay.",

GEORGE CRABBE

NOTES TO LETTER IV.

Note 1, page 315, line 55.

May those excel by Solway-Moss destroy'd.

For an account of this extraordinary and interesting event, I refer my readers to the Journals of the year 1772.

Note 2, page 319, line 215.

They will not study, and they dare not fight.

Some may object to this assertion; to whom I beg leave to answer, that I do not use the word *fight* in the sense of the Jew Mendoza.

Note 3, page 320, line 245.

Regret thy misery, and lament thy crimes.

See the Book of Deuteronomy, chapter [xxviii.] and various other places.

Note 4, page 320, line 253.

Nor think of Julian's boast and Julian's fate.

His boast, that he would rebuild the Temple at Jerusalem; his fate (whatever becomes of the miraculous part of the story), that he died before the foundation was laid.

Note 5, page 321, line 301

Samson is grace, and carries all alone.

Whoever has attended to the books or preaching of these enthusiastic people, must have observed much of this kind of absurd and foolish application of scripture history; it seems to them as reasoning.

THE BOROUGH.

LETTER V.

ELECTIONS.

Say then which class to greater folly stoop,
The great in promise, or the poor in hope?

Be brave, for your [captain] is brave, and vows reformation ; there shall be
in England seven halfpenny loaves sold for a penny ; the three-hooped
pot shall have ten hoops[; and] I will make it felony to drink small
beer[.....] all shall eat and drink on my score, and I will apparel
them all in one livery, that they may agree like brothers, and
worship me their lord.
Shakspeare's Henry VI. [Part I. Act IV. Sc. 2.]

The Evils of the Contest, and how in part to be avoided—The Miseries
endured by a Friend of the Candidate—The various Liberties taken
with him, who has no personal Interest in the Success—The unreason-
able Expectations of Voters—The Censures of the opposing Party—
The Vices as well as Follies shown in such Time of Contest—Plans
and Cunning of Electors—Evils which remain after the Decision,
opposed in vain by the Efforts of the Friendly, and of the Successful ;
among whom is the Mayor—Story of his Advancement till he was
raised to the Government of the Borough—These Evils not to be
placed in Balance with the Liberty of the People, but are yet Subjects
of just Complaint.

329

GEORGE CRABBE

THE BOROUGH.

LETTER V.

THE ELECTION.

YES, our Election's past, and we've been free,
   Somewhat as madmen without keepers be;
And such desire of freedom has been shown,
That both the parties wish'd her all their own:
All our free smiths and cobblers in the town
Were loth to lay such pleasant freedom down—
To put the bludgeon and cockade aside,
And let us pass unhurt and undefied.
   True! you might then your party's sign produce,
And so escape with only half th' abuse— 10
With half the danger as you walk'd along,
With rage and threat'ning but from half the throng.
This you might do, and not your fortune mend;
For where you lost a foe, you gain'd a friend;
And, to distress you, vex you, and expose,
Election-friends are worse than any foes;
The party-curse is with the canvass past,
But party-friendship, for your grief, will last.
   Friends of all kinds, the civil and the rude,
Who humbly wish, or boldly dare t' intrude: 20
These beg or take a liberty to come
(Friends should be free), and make your house their home;
They know that warmly you their cause espouse,
And come to make their boastings and their bows.
You scorn their manners, you their words mistrust;
But you must hear them, and they know you must.

THE BOROUGH

One plainly sees a friendship firm and true
Between the noble candidate and you ;
So humbly begs (and states at large the case),
"You'll think of Bobby and the little place."   30
    Stifling his shame by drink, a wretch will come,
And prate your wife and daughter from the room :
In pain you hear him, and at heart despise,
Yet with heroic mind your pangs disguise ;
And still in patience to the sot attend,
To show what man can bear to serve a friend.
    One enters hungry—not to be denied,
And takes his place and jokes—"We're of a side."
Yet worse, the proser who, upon the strength
Of his one vote, has tales of three hours' length—   40
This sorry rogue you bear, yet with surprise
Start at his oaths, and sicken at his lies.
    Then comes there one, and tells in friendly way,
What the opponents in their anger say ;
All that through life has vex'd you, all abuse,
Will this kind friend in pure regard produce ;
And, having through your own offences run,
Adds (as appendage) what your friends have done.
    Has any female cousin made a trip
To Gretna-Green, or more vexatious slip ?   50
Has your wife's brother, or your uncle's son,
Done aught amiss, or is he thought t' have done ?
Is there of all your kindred some who lack
Vision direct, or have a gibbous back ?
From your unlucky name may quips and puns
Be made by these upbraiding Goths and Huns ?
To some great public character have you
Assign'd the fame to worth and talents due,
Proud of your praise ?—In this, in any case,
Where the brute-spirit may affix disgrace,   60
These friends will smiling bring it, and the while
You silent sit, and practise for a smile.
    Vain of their power, and of their value sure,
They nearly guess the tortures you endure ;
Nor spare one pang—for they perceive your heart
Goes with the cause ; you'd die before you'd start ;

Do what they may, they're sure you'll not offend
Men who have pledged their honours to your friend.
  Those friends indeed, who start as in a race,
May love the sport, and laugh at this disgrace;   70
They have in view the glory and the prize,
Nor heed the dirty steps by which they rise:
But we, their poor associates, lose the fame,
Though more than partners in the toil and shame.
  Were this the whole, and did the time produce
But shame and toil, but riot and abuse:
We might be then from serious griefs exempt,
And view the whole with pity and contempt.
Alas! but here the vilest passions rule;
It is Seduction's, is Temptation's school: 80
Where vices mingle in the oddest ways,
The grossest slander and the dirtiest praise;
Flattery enough to make the vainest sick,
And clumsy stratagem, and scoundrel trick.
Nay more, your anger and contempt to cause,
These, while they fish for profit, claim applause;
Bribed, bought and bound, they banish shame and fear;
Tell you they're stanch, and have a soul sincere;
Then talk of honour, and, if doubt's express'd,
Show where it lies, and smite upon the breast.   90
  Among these worthies, some at first declare
For whom they vote; he then has most to spare.
Others hang off—when coming to the post
Is spurring time, and then he'll spare the most;
While some, demurring, wait, and find at last
The bidding languish, and the market pass'd;
These will affect all bribery to condemn,
And, be it Satan laughs, he laughs at them.
  Some too are pious—one desired the Lord
To teach him where "to drop his little word;   100
"To lend his vote, where it will profit best;
"Promotion came not from the east or west;
"But as their freedom had promoted some,
"He should be glad to know which way 'twould come.
"It was a naughty world, and, where to sell
"His precious charge, was more than he could tell."

THE BOROUGH

"But you succeeded?"—true, at mighty cost;
And our good friend, I fear, will think he's lost.
Inns, horses, chaises, dinners, balls and notes;
What fill'd their purses, and what drench'd their throats;   110
The private pension, and indulgent lease,
Have all been granted to these friends who fleece—
Friends who will hang like burs upon his coat,
And boundless judge the value of a vote.
    And, though the terrors of the time be pass'd,
There still remain the scatterings of the blast.
The boughs are parted that entwined before,
And ancient harmony exists no more ;
The gusts of wrath our peaceful seats deform,
And sadly flows the sighing of the storm :   120
Those who have gain'd are sorry for the gloom,
But they who lost unwilling peace should come ;
There open envy, here suppress'd delight,
Yet live till time shall better thoughts excite,
And so prepare us, by a six-years' truce,
Again for riot, insult, and abuse.
    Our worthy mayor, on the victorious part,
Cries out for peace, and cries with all his heart ;
He, civil creature ! ever does his best,
To banish wrath from every voter's breast ;   130
"For where," says he, with reason strong and plain,
"Where is the profit? what will anger gain?"
His short stout person he is wont to brace
In good brown broad-cloth, edged with two-inch lace,
When in his seat ; and still the coat seems new,
Preserved by common use of seaman's blue.
    He was a fisher from his earliest day,
And placed his nets within the Borough's bay ;
Where by his skates, his herrings, and his soles,
He lived, nor dream'd of corporation-doles [1] ;   140
But, toiling, saved and, saving, never ceased
Till he had box'd up twelve score pounds at least.
He knew not money's power, but judged it best
Safe in his trunk to let his treasure rest ;
Yet to a friend complain'd : "Sad charge, to keep
"So many pounds, and then I cannot sleep."

GEORGE CRABBE

"Then put it out," replied the friend.—"What, give
"My money up? why, then I could not live."—
"Nay, but for interest place it in his hands,
"Who'll give you mortgage on his house or lands."—
"Oh but," said Daniel, "that's a dangerous plan;
"He may be robb'd like any other man."—
"Still he is bound, and you may be at rest,
"More safe the money than within your chest;
"And you'll receive, from all deductions clear,
"Five pounds for every hundred, every year."—
"What good in that?" quoth Daniel, "for 'tis plain,
"If part I take, there can but part remain."—
"What! you, my friend, so skill'd in gainful things,
"Have you to learn what interest money brings?"—
"Not so," said Daniel, "perfectly I know,
"He's the most interest who has most to show."—
"True! and he'll show the more, the more he lends;
"Thus he his weight and consequence extends;
"For they who borrow must restore each sum,
"And pay for use—What, Daniel, art thou dumb?"
For much amazed was that good man—"Indeed!"
Said he, with glad'ning eye, "will money breed?
"How have I lived? I grieve, with all my heart,
"For my late knowledge in this precious art:—
"Five pounds for every hundred will he give?
"And then the hundred?——I begin to live."—
So he began, and other means he found,
As he went on, to multiply a pound:
Though blind so long to interest, all allow
That no man better understands it now.
Him in our body-corporate we chose,
And, once among us, he above us rose;
Stepping from post to post, he reach'd the chair,
And there he now reposes—that's the mayor.
But 'tis not he, 'tis not the kinder few,
The mild, the good, who can our peace renew;
A peevish humour swells in every eye,
The warm are angry, and the cool are shy;
There is no more the social board at whist,
The good old partners are with scorn dismiss'd;

150

160

170

180

334

THE BOROUGH

No more with dog and lantern comes the maid,
To guide the mistress when the rubber's play'd;
Sad shifts are made, lest ribbons blue and green
Should at one table, at one time be seen.   190
On care and merit none will now rely,
'Tis party sells what party-friends must buy;
The warmest burgess wears a bodger's coat,
And fashion gains less int'rest than a vote;
Uncheck'd, the vintner still his poison vends;
For he too votes, and can command his friends.
   But, this admitted, be it still agreed,
These ill effects from noble cause proceed;
Though like some vile excrescences they be,
The tree they spring from is a sacred tree,   200
And its true produce, strength and liberty.   [J]
   Yet if we could th' attendant ills suppress;
If we could make the sum of mischief less;
If we could warm and angry men persuade
No more man's common comforts to invade;
And that old ease and harmony re-seat
In all our meetings, so in joy to meet:
Much would of glory to the Muse ensue,
And our good vicar would have less to do.

NOTE TO LETTER V.

Note 1, page 333, line 140.

He lived, nor dream'd of corporation-doles.

   I am informed that some explanation is here necessary, though I am
ignorant for what class of my readers it can be required.   Some corporate
bodies have actual property, as appears by their receiving rents; and they
obtain money on the admission of members into their society: this they
may lawfully share perhaps.   There are, moreover, other doles, of still
greater value, of which it is not necessary for me to explain the nature, or
to inquire into the legality.

THE BOROUGH.

LETTER VI.

PROFESSIONS—LAW.

Quid leges sine moribus
Vanæ proficiunt?
Horace [Lib. III. *Od.* XXIV. vv. 35–6].

———————

Væ misero mihi!
Mea nunc facinora aperiuntur, clam quæ speravi fore.
[Plaut. *Trucul.* Act IV. Sc. 3, vv. 20–1].

———————

Trades and Professions of every Kind to be found in the Borough—Its
Seamen and Soldiers—Law, the Danger of the Subject—Coddrington's
Offence—Attorneys increased; their splendid Appearance, how sup-
ported—Some worthy Exceptions—Spirit of Litigation, how stirred
up—A Boy articled as a Clerk; his Ideas—How this Profession
perverts the Judgment—Actions appear through this Medium in a
false Light—Success from honest Application—Archer a worthy
Character—Swallow a Character of different Kind—His Origin,
Progress, Success, &c.

THE BOROUGH

THE BOROUGH.

LETTER VI.

PROFESSIONS—LAW.

" TRADES and Professions "—these are themes the Muse,
  Left to her freedom, would forbear to choose ;
But to our Borough they in truth belong,
And we, perforce, must take them in our song.
  Be it then known that we can boast of these
In all denominations, ranks, degrees ;
All who our numerous wants through life supply,
Who soothe us sick, attend us when we die,
Or for the dead their various talents try.   [}]
Then have we those who live by secret arts,   10
By hunting fortunes, and by stealing hearts ;
Or who by nobler means themselves advance ;
Or who subsist by charity and chance.
  Say, of our native heroes shall I boast,
Born in our streets, to thunder on our coast—
Our Borough-seamen ? Could the timid Muse
More patriot-ardour in their breasts infuse ;
Or could she paint their merit or their skill,
She wants not love, alacrity, or will ;
But needless all : that ardour is their own,   20
And, for their deeds, themselves have made them known.
  Soldiers in arms ! Defenders of our soil !
Who from destruction save us ; who from spoil
Protect the sons of peace who traffic, or who toil :   [}]
Would I could duly praise you ; ₂that each deed
Your foes might honour, and your friends might read :

Crabbe   Y   337

GEORGE CRABBE

This too is needless; you've imprinted well
Your powers, and told what I should feebly tell.
Beside, a Muse like mine, to satire prone,
Would fail in themes where there is praise alone.   30
—Law shall I sing, or what to Law belongs?
Alas! there may be danger in such songs;
A foolish rhyme, 'tis said, a trifling thing,
The law found treason, for it touch'd the king.
But kings have mercy in these happy times,
Or surely *one* had suffer'd for his rhymes;
Our glorious Edwards and our Henrys bold,
So touch'd, had kept the reprobate in hold;
But he escaped—nor fear, thank Heav'n, have I,
Who love my king, for such offence to die.   40
But I am taught the danger would be much,
If these poor lines should one attorney touch—
(One of those *limbs* of law who're always here;
The *heads* come down to guide them twice a year.)
I might not swing indeed; but he in sport
Would whip a rhymer on from court to court;
Stop him in each, and make him pay for all
The long proceedings in that dreaded Hall.—
Then let my numbers flow discreetly on,
Warn'd by the fate of luckless Coddrington[1];   50
Lest some *attorney* (pardon me the name)
Should wound a poor *solicitor* for fame.
  One man of law in George the Second's reign
Was all our frugal fathers would maintain;
He too was kept for forms; a man of peace,
To frame a contract, or to draw a lease:
He had a clerk, with whom he used to write
All the day long, with whom he drank at night;
Spare was his visage, moderate his bill,
And he so kind, men doubted of his skill.   60
  Who thinks of this, with some amazement sees,
For one so poor, three flourishing at ease—
Nay, one in splendour!—See that mansion tall,
That lofty door, the far-resounding hall;

[1] The account of Coddrington [Collingbourne] occurs in "*The Mirrour for Magistrates*"; he suffered in the reign of Richard III.

THE BOROUGH

Well-furnish'd rooms, plate shining on the board,
Gay liveried lads, and cellar proudly stored :
Then say how comes it that such fortunes crown
These sons of strife, these terrors of the town?
   Lo ! that small office ! there th' incautious guest
Goes blindfold in, and that maintains the rest ;   70
There in his web th' observant spider lies,
And peers about for fat intruding flies ;
Doubtful at first, he hears the distant hum,
And feels them flutt'ring as they nearer come.
They buzz and blink, and doubtfully they tread
On the strong birdlime of the utmost thread ;
But, when they're once entangled by the gin,
With what an eager clasp he draws them in ;
Nor shall they 'scape till after long delay,
And all that sweetens life is drawn away.   80
   "Nay, this," you cry, "is common-place, the tale
" Of petty tradesmen o'er their evening-ale.
" There are who, living by the legal pen,
" Are held in honour—'honourable men.'"
   Doubtless—there are, who hold manorial courts,
Or whom the trust of powerful friends supports ;
Or who, by labouring through a length of time,
Have pick'd their way, unsullied by a crime.
These are the few—in this, in every place,
Fix the litigious rupture-stirring race :   90
Who to contention as to trade are led,
To whom dispute and strife are bliss and bread.
   There is a doubtful pauper, and we think
'Tis not with us to give him meat and drink ;
There is a child, and 'tis not mighty clear
Whether the mother lived with us a year ;
A road's indicted, and our seniors doubt
If in our proper boundary or without :
But what says our attorney? He our friend
Tells us 'tis just and manly to contend.   100
   "What ! to a neighbouring parish yield your cause,
" While you have money, and the nation laws?
" What ! lose without a trial, that which tried,
" May—nay it must—be given on our side?

"All men of spirit would contend ; such men
"Than lose a pound would rather hazard ten.
"What! be imposed on? No! a British soul
"Despises imposition, hates control ;
"The law is open ; let them, if they dare,
"Support their cause ; the Borough need not spare.   110
"All I advise is vigour and good-will :
"Is it agreed then?—Shall I file a bill?"
 The trader, grazier, merchant, priest, and all
Whose sons aspiring to [professions'] call,
Choose from their lads some bold and subtle boy,
And judge him fitted for this grave employ.
Him a keen old practitioner admits,
To write five years and exercise his wits :
The youth has heard—it is in fact his creed—
Mankind dispute, that lawyers may be fee'd :   120
Jails, bailiffs, writs, all terms and threats of law,
Grow now familiar as once top and taw ;
Rage, hatred, fear, the mind's severer ills,
All bring employment, all augment his bills ;
As feels the surgeon for the mangled limb,
The mangled mind is but a job for him ;
Thus taught to think, these legal reasoners draw
Morals and maxims from their views of law ;
They cease to judge by precepts taught in schools,
By man's plain sense, or by religious rules ;   130
No! nor by law itself, in truth discern'd,
But as its statutes may be warp'd and turn'd.
How they should judge of man, his word and deed,
They in their books and not their bosoms read :
Of some good act you speak with just applause,
"No! no!" says he, "'twould be a losing cause."
Blame you some tyrant's deed?—he answers, "Nay,
"He'll get a verdict ; heed you what you say."
Thus, to conclusions from examples led,
The heart resigns all judgment to the head ;   140
Law, law alone, for ever kept in view,
His measures guides, and rules his conscience too ;
Of ten commandments, he confesses three
Are yet in force, and tells you which they be,

THE BOROUGH

As law instructs him, thus: "Your neighbour's wife
"You must not take, his chattels, nor his life;
"Break these decrees, for damage you must pay;
"These you must reverence, and the rest—you may."
    Law was design'd to keep a state in peace;
To punish robbery, that wrong might cease;   150
To be impregnable—a constant fort,
To which the weak and injured might resort.
But these perverted minds its force employ,
Not to protect mankind, but to annoy;
And, long as ammunition can be found,
Its lightning flashes and its thunders sound.
    Or, law with lawyers is an ample still,
Wrought by the passions' heat with chymic skill;
While the fire burns, the gains are quickly made,
And freely flow the profits of the trade;   160
Nay, when the fierceness fails, these artists blow
The dying fire, and make the embers glow,   [ʃ]
As long as they can make the smaller profits flow;
At length the process of itself will stop,
When they perceive they've drawn out every drop.
    Yet, I repeat, there are, who nobly strive
To keep the sense of moral worth alive:
Men who would starve, ere meanly deign to live
On what deception and chican'ry give;
And these at length succeed: they have their strife,   170
Their apprehensions, stops, and rubs in life;
But honour, application, care, and skill,
Shall bend opposing fortune to their will.
    Of such is Archer, he who keeps in awe
Contending parties by his threats of law.
He, roughly honest, has been long a guide
In Borough-business, on the conquering side;
And seen so much of both sides, and so long,
He thinks the bias of man's mind goes wrong.
Thus, though he's friendly, he is still severe,   180
Surly though kind, suspiciously sincere:
So much he's seen of baseness in the mind,
That, while a friend to man, he scorns mankind;
He knows the human heart, and sees with dread,

341

By slight temptation, how the strong are led;
He knows how interest can asunder rend
The bond of parent, master, guardian, friend,
To form a new and a degrading tie
'Twixt needy vice and tempting villany.
Sound in himself, yet, when such flaws appear,   190
He doubts of all, and learns that self to fear:
For, where so dark the moral view is grown,
A timid conscience trembles for her own;
The pitchy taint of general vice is such
As daubs the fancy, and you dread the touch.
    Far unlike him was one in former times,
Famed for the spoil he gather'd by his crimes;
Who, while his brethren nibbling held their prey,
He like an eagle seized and bore the whole away.
    Swallow, a poor attorney, brought his boy   200
Up at his desk, and gave him his employ;
He would have bound him to an honest trade,
Could preparations have been duly made.
The clerkship ended, both the sire and son
Together did what business could be done;
Sometimes they'd luck to stir up small disputes
Among their friends, and raise them into suits.
Though close and hard, the father was content
With this resource, now old and indolent;
But his young Swallow, gaping and alive   210
To fiercer feelings, was resolved to thrive:—
"Father," he said, "but little can they win
"Who hunt in couples, where the game is thin;
"Let's part in peace, and each pursue his gain
"Where it may start—our love may yet remain."
The parent growl'd, he couldn't think that love
Made the young cockatrice his den remove;
But, taught by habit, he the truth suppress'd,
Forced a frank look, and said he "thought it best."
Not long they'd parted ere dispute arose;   220
The game they hunted quickly made them foes.
Some house the father by his art had won
Seem'd a fit cause of contest to the son:
Who raised a claimant, and then found a way

By a stanch witness to secure his prey.
The people cursed him, but in times of need
Trusted in one so certain to succeed:
By law's dark by-ways he had stored his mind
With wicked knowledge, how to cheat mankind.
Few are the freeholds in our ancient town;   230
A copy-right from heir to heir came down,
From whence some heat arose, when there was doubt
In point of heirship; but the fire went out,
Till our attorney had the art to raise
The dying spark, and blow it to a blaze.
For this he now began his friends to treat;
His way to starve them was to make them eat,
And drink oblivious draughts—to his applause
It must be said, he never starved a cause;
He'd roast and boil'd upon his board—the boast   240
Of half his victims was his boil'd and roast—
And these at every hour: he seldom took
Aside his client, till he'd praised his cook;
Nor to an office led him, there in pain
To give his story and go out again,
But first the brandy and the chine were seen,
And then the business came by starts between.
  "Well, if 'tis so, the house to you belongs;
" But have you money to redress these wrongs?
" Nay, look not sad, my friend; if you're correct,   250
" You'll find the friendship that you'd not expect."
  If right the man, the house was Swallow's own;
If wrong, his kindness and good-will were shown.
" Rogue!" "Villain!" "Scoundrel!" cried the losers all;
He let them cry, for what would that recall?
At length he left us, took a village seat,
And like a vulture look'd abroad for meat;
The Borough-booty, give it all its praise,
Had only served the appetite to raise;
But, if from simple heirs he drew their land,   260
He might a noble feast at will command;
Still he proceeded by his former rules,
His bait their pleasures, when he fish'd for fools;—
Flagons and haunches on his board were placed,

And subtle avarice look'd like thoughtless waste.
Most of his friends, though youth from him had fled,
Were young, were minors, of their sires in dread;
Or those whom widow'd mothers kept in bounds,
And check'd their generous rage for steeds and hounds;
Or such as travell'd 'cross the land to view   270
A Christian's conflict with a boxing Jew.
Some too had run upon Newmarket heath
With so much speed that they were out of breath;
Others had tasted claret, till they now
To humbler port would turn, and knew not how.
All these for favours would to Swallow run,
Who never sought their thanks for all he'd done;
He kindly took them by the hand, then bow'd
Politely low, and thus his love avow'd—
(For he'd a way that many judged polite;   280
A cunning dog, he'd fawn before he'd bite):—
"Observe, my friends, the frailty of our race
"When age unmans us—let me state a case:
"There's our friend Rupert; we shall soon redress
"His present evil—drink to our success—
"I flatter not, but did you ever see
"Limbs better turn'd? a prettier boy than he?
"His senses all acute, his passions such
"As nature gave—she never does too much;
"His the bold wish the cup of joy to drain,   290
"And strength to bear it without qualm or pain.
"Now view his father as he dozing lies,
"Whose senses wake not when he opes his eyes;
"Who slips and shuffles when he means to walk,
"And lisps and gabbles if he tries to talk;
"Feeling he's none: he could as soon destroy
"The earth itself, as aught it holds enjoy;
"A nurse attends him to lay straight his limbs,
"Present his gruel, and respect his whims.
"Now, shall this dotard from our hero hold   300
"His lands and lordships? Shall he hide his gold?
"That which he cannot use, and dare not show,
"And will not give—why longer should he owe?
"Yet, 'twould be murder should we snap the locks,

"And take the thing he worships from the box ;
"So let him dote and dream : but, till he die,
"Shall not our generous heir receive supply ?
"For ever sitting on the river's brink,
"And ever thirsty, shall he fear to drink ?
"The means are simple : let him only wish,   310
"Then say he's willing, and I'll fill his dish."
   They all applauded, and not least the boy,
Who now replied, "It fill'd his heart with joy
"To find he needed not deliv'rance crave
"Of death, or wish the justice in the grave ;
"Who, while he spent, would every art retain,
"Of luring home the scatter'd gold again ;
"Just as a fountain gaily spirts and plays
"With what returns in still and secret ways."
   Short was the dream of bliss ; he quickly found,   320
His father's acres all were Swallow's ground.
Yet to those arts would other heroes lend
A willing ear, and Swallow was their friend ;
Ever successful, some began to think
That Satan help'd him to his pen and ink ;
And shrewd suspicions ran about the place,
"There was a compact"—I must leave the case.
But of the parties, had the fiend been one,
The business could not have been speedier done.
Still, when a man has angled day and night,   330
The silliest gudgeons will refuse to bite :
So Swallow tried no more ; but if they came
To seek his friendship, that remain'd the same.
Thus he retired in peace, and some would say,
He balk'd his partner, and had learn'd to pray.
To this some zealots lent an ear, and sought
How Swallow felt, then said "a change is wrought."
'Twas true there wanted all the signs of grace,
But there were strong professions in their place ;
Then, too, the less that men from him expect,   340
The more the praise to the converting sect ;
He had not yet subscribed to all their creed,
Nor own'd a call ; but he confess'd the need.
His acquiescent speech, his gracious look,

That pure attention, when the brethren spoke,
Was all contrition,—he had felt the wound,
And with confession would again be sound.
  True, Swallow's board had still the sumptuous treat;
But could they blame? the warmest zealots eat.
He drank—'twas needful his poor nerves to brace;   350
He swore—'twas habit; he was grieved—'twas grace.
What could they do a new-born zeal to nurse?
"His wealth's undoubted—let him hold our purse;
"He'll add his bounty, and the house we'll raise
"Hard by the church, and gather all her strays;
"We'll watch her sinners as they home retire,
"And pluck the brands from the devouring fire."
  Alas! such speech was but an empty boast;
The good men reckon'd, but without their host;
Swallow, delighted, took the trusted store,   360
And own'd the sum: they did not ask for more,
Till more was needed; when they call'd for aid—
And had it?—No, their agent was afraid;
"Could he but know to whom he should refund,
"He would most gladly—nay, he'd go beyond;
"But, when such numbers claim'd, when some were gone,
"And others going—he must hold it on;
"The Lord would help them."—Loud their anger grew,
And while they threat'ning from his door withdrew,
He bow'd politely low, and bade them all adieu.   370[ ]]
  But lives the man by whom such deeds are done?
Yes, many such—but Swallow's race is run;
His name is lost;—for, though his sons have name,
It is not his, they all escape the shame;
Nor is there vestige now of all he had,
His means are wasted, for his heir was mad.
Still we of Swallow as a monster speak,
A hard, bad man, who prey'd upon the weak.

THE BOROUGH.

LETTER VII.

PROFESSIONS—PHYSIC.

[Jam mala finissem letho; sed credula vitam
    Spes fovet, et fore cras semper ait melius.]
                Tibullus [Lib. II. vi. vv. 19-20].

He fell to juggle, cant, and cheat——
For as those fowls that live in water
Are never wet, he did but smatter;
Whate'er he labour'd to appear,
His understanding still was clear.
A paltry wretch he had, half-starved,
That him in place of zany served.
            Butler's Hudibras [Part II. Canto III].

The Worth and Excellence of the true Physician—Merit not the sole
Cause of Success—Modes of advancing Reputation—Motives of
medical Men for publishing their Works—The great Evil of
Quackery—Present State of advertising Quacks—Their Hazard—
Some fail, and why—Causes of Success—How Men of Understanding
are prevailed upon to have Recourse to Empirics, and to permit their
Names to be advertised—Evils of Quackery: to nervous Females; to
Youth; to Infants—History of an advertising Empiric, &c.

GEORGE CRABBE

THE BOROUGH.

LETTER VII.

PROFESSIONS—PHYSIC.

NEXT, to a graver tribe we turn our view,
And yield the praise to worth and science due;
But this with serious words and sober style,
For these are friends with whom we seldom smile:
Helpers of men[1] they're call'd, and we confess
Theirs the deep study, theirs the lucky guess.
We own that numbers join with care and skill
A temperate judgment, a devoted will:
Men who suppress their feelings, but who feel
The painful symptoms they delight to heal;   10
Patient in all their trials, they sustain
The starts of passion, the reproach of pain;
With hearts affected, but with looks serene,
Intent they wait through all the solemn scene;
Glad, if a hope should rise from nature's strife,
To aid their skill and save the lingering life.
But this must virtue's generous effort be,
And spring from nobler motives than a fee:
To the physicians of the soul, and these,
Turn the distress'd for safety, hope, and ease.   20
  But as physicians of that nobler kind
Have their warm zealots, and their sectaries blind;
So among these for knowledge most renown'd,
Are dreamers strange, and stubborn bigots found.
Some, too, admitted to this honour'd name,
Have, without learning, found a way to fame;

---

[1] Opiferque per orbem
Dicor.
   [Ovid, *Metam.* Lib. I. vv. 521-2.]

348

THE BOROUGH

And some by learning :—young physicians write,
To set their merit in the fairest light ;
With them a treatise is a bait that draws
Approving voices; 'tis to gain applause,   30
And to exalt them in the public view,
More than a life of worthy toil could do.
When 'tis proposed to make the man renown'd,
In every age convenient doubts abound ;
Convenient themes in every period start,
Which he may treat with all the pomp of art ;
Curious conjectures he may always make,
And either side of dubious questions take.
He may a system broach, or, if he please,
Start new opinions of an old disease ;   40
Or may some simple in the woodland trace,
And be its patron, till it runs its race ;
As rustic damsels from their woods are won,
And live in splendour till their race be run ;
It weighs not much on what their powers be shown,
When all his purpose is to make them known.
    To show the world what long experience gains,
Requires not courage, though it calls for pains ;
But, at life's outset to inform mankind,
Is a bold effort of a valiant mind.   50
    The great good man, for noblest cause, displays
What many labours taught, and many days ;
These sound instruction from experience give,
The others show us how they mean to live ;
That they have genius, and they hope mankind
Will to its efforts be no longer blind.
    There are, beside, whom powerful friends advance,
Whom fashion favours, person, patrons, chance ;
And merit sighs to see a fortune made
By daring rashness or by dull parade.   60
    But these are trifling evils; there is one
Which walks uncheck'd, and triumphs in the sun :
There was a time, when we beheld the quack,
On public stage, the licensed trade attack ;
He made his labour'd speech with poor parade ;
And then a laughing zany lent him aid.

349

GEORGE CRABBE

Smiling we pass'd him, but we felt the while
Pity so much, that soon we ceased to smile;
Assured that fluent speeeh and flow'ry vest
Disguised the troubles of a man distress'd.　　　70
　But now our quacks are gamesters, and they play
With craft and skill to ruin and betray;
With monstrous promise they delude the mind,
And thrive on all that tortures human-kind.
　Void of all honour, avaricious, rash,
The daring tribe compound their boasted trash—
Tincture or syrup, lotion, drop or pill;
All tempt the sick to trust the lying bill;
And twenty names of cobblers turn'd to squires,
Aid the bold language of these blushless liars.　　80
There are among them those who cannot read,
And yet they'll buy a patent, and succeed;
Will dare to promise dying sufferers aid,—
For who, when dead, can threaten or upbraid?
With cruel avarice still they recommend
More draughts, more syrup, to the journey's end:
" I feel it not; "—" Then take it every hour."—
" It makes me worse; "—"Why, then it shows its power."—
" I fear to die; "—" Let not your spirits sink,
" You're always safe, while you believe and drink."　　90
　How strange to add, in this nefarious trade,
That men of parts are dupes by dunces made:
That creatures nature meant should clean our streets
Have purchased lands and mansions, parks and seats;
Wretches with conscience so obtuse, they leave
Their untaught sons their parents to deceive;
And, when they're laid upon their dying-bed,
No thought of murder comes into their head;
Nor one revengeful ghost to them appears,
To fill the soul with penitential fears.　　100
　Yet not the whole of this imposing train
Their gardens, seats, and carriages obtain;
Chiefly, indeed, they to the robbers fall,
Who are most fitted to disgrace them all.
But there is hazard—patents must be bought,
Venders and puffers for the poison sought;

THE BOROUGH

And then in many a paper through the year
Must cures and cases, oaths and proofs appear;
Men snatch'd from graves, as they were dropping in,
Their lungs cough'd up, their bones pierced through their
    skin;   110
Their liver all one scirrhus, and the frame
Poison'd with evils which they dare not name;
Men who spent all upon physicians' fees,   ⎫
Who never slept, nor had a moment's ease,   ⎬
Are now as roaches sound, and all as brisk as bees. [∫]
    If the sick gudgeons to the bait attend,
And come in shoals, the angler gains his end;
But, should the advertising cash be spent,
Ere yet the town has due attention lent,
Then bursts the bubble, and the hungry cheat   120
Pines for the bread he ill deserves to eat:
It is a lottery, and he shares perhaps
The rich man's feast, or begs the pauper's scraps.
    From powerful causes spring th' empiric's gains,
Man's love of life, his weakness, and his pains;
These first induce him the vile trash to try,
Then lend his name, that other men may buy.
This love of life, which in our nature rules,
To vile imposture makes us dupes and tools;
Then pain compels th' impatient soul to seize   130
On promised hopes of instantaneous ease;
And weakness too with every wish complies,
Worn out and won by importunities.
    Troubled with something in your bile or blood,
You think your doctor does you little good;
And, grown impatient, you require in haste
The nervous cordial, nor dislike the taste;
It comforts, heals, and strengthens; nay, you think
It makes you better every time you drink;
"Then lend your name"—you're loth, but yet confess 140
Its powers are great, and so you acquiesce.
Yet, think a moment, ere your name you lend,
With whose 'tis placed, and what you recommend;
Who tipples brandy will some comfort feel,
But will he to the med'cine set his seal?

GEORGE CRABBE

Wait, and you'll find the cordial you admire
Has added fuel to your fever's fire.
Say, should a robber chance your purse to spare,
Would you the honour of the man declare?
Would you assist his purpose? swell his crime?   150
Besides, he might not spare a second time.
Compassion sometimes sets the fatal sign;
The man was poor, and humbly begg'd a line;
Else how should noble names and titles back
The spreading praise of some advent'rous quack?
But he the moment watches, and entreats
Your honour's name—your honour joins the cheats;
You judged the med'cine harmless, and you lent
What help you could, and with the best intent;
But can it please you, thus to league with all   160
Whom he can beg or bribe to swell the scrawl?
Would you these wrappers with your name adorn,
Which hold the poison for the yet unborn?
No class escapes them—from the poor man's pay
The nostrum takes no trifling part away;
See! those square patent bottles from the shop,
Now decoration to the cupboard's top;
And there a favourite hoard you'll find within,
Companions meet! the julep and the gin.
Time too with cash is wasted; 'tis the fate   170
Of real helpers to be call'd too late;
This find the sick, when (time and patience gone)
Death with a tenfold terror hurries on.
Suppose the case surpasses human skill,
There comes a quack to flatter weakness still;
What greater evil can a flatterer do,
Than from himself to take the sufferer's view?
To turn from sacred thoughts his reasoning powers,
And rob a sinner of his dying hours?
Yet this they, dare and, craving to the last,   180
In hope's strong bondage hold their victim fast:
For soul or body no concern have they,
All their inquiry, "Can the patient pay?
"And will he swallow draughts until his dying day?"   [*]
    Observe what ills to nervous females flow,

352

THE BOROUGH

When the heart flutters, and the pulse is low;
If once induced these cordial sips to try,
All feel the ease, and few the danger fly;
For, while obtain'd, of drams they've all the force,
And when denied, then drams are the resource.   190
  Nor these the only evils—there are those
Who for the troubled mind prepare repose;
They write: the young are tenderly address'd,
Much danger hinted, much concern express'd;
They dwell on freedoms lads are prone to take,
Which makes the doctor tremble for their sake;
Still, if the youthful patient will but trust
In one so kind, so pitiful, and just;
If he will take the tonic all the time,
And hold but moderate intercourse with crime: 200
The sage will gravely give his honest word,
That strength and spirits shall be both restored;
In plainer English—if you mean to sin,
Fly to the drops, and instantly begin.
  Who would not lend a sympathizing sigh,
To hear yon infant's pity-moving cry?
That feeble sob, unlike the new-born note,
Which came with vigour from the op'ning throat;
When air and light first rush'd on lungs and eyes,
And there was life and spirit in the cries;   210
Now an abortive, faint attempt to weep
Is all we hear; sensation is asleep.
The boy was healthy, and at first express'd
His feelings loudly, when he fail'd to rest;
When cramm'd with food, and tighten'd every limb,
To cry aloud, was what pertain'd to him;
Then the good nurse, (who, had she borne a brain,
Had sought the cause that made her babe complain,)
Has all her efforts, loving soul! applied,
To set the cry, and not the cause, aside;   220
She gave her powerful sweet without remorse,
The sleeping cordial—she had tried its force,
Repeating oft: the infant, freed from pain,
Rejected food, but took the dose again,
Sinking to sleep; while she her joy express'd,

Crabbe   z

That her dear charge could sweetly take his rest :
Soon may she spare her cordial ; not a doubt
Remains but quickly he will rest without.

This moves our grief and pity, and we sigh
To think what numbers from these causes die ;   230
But what contempt and anger should we show,
Did we the lives of these impostors know !

Ere for the world's I left the cares of school,
One I remember who assumed the fool :
A part well suited—when the idler boys
Would shout around him, and he loved the noise ;
They call'd him Neddy ;—Neddy had the art
To play with skill his ignominious part ;
When he his trifles would for sale display,
And act the mimic for a schoolboy's pay.   240
For many years he plied his humble trade,
And used his tricks and talents to persuade ;
The fellow barely read, but chanced to look
Among the fragments of a tatter'd book ;
Where, after many efforts made to spell
One puzzling word, he found it *oxymel* :
A potent thing, 'twas said, to cure the ills
Of ailing lungs—the *oxymel of squills.*
Squills he procured, but found the bitter strong,
And most unpleasant ; none would take it long ;   250
But the pure acid and the sweet would make
A med'cine numbers would for pleasure take.

There was a fellow near, an artful knave,
Who knew the plan, and much assistance gave ;
He wrote the puffs, and every talent plied
To make it sell : it sold, and then he died.

Now all the profit fell to Ned's control,
And Pride and Avarice quarrell'd for his soul ;
When mighty profits by the trash were made,
Pride built a palace, Avarice groan'd and paid ;   260
Pride placed the signs of grandeur all about,
And Avarice barr'd his friends and children out.

Now see him doctor ! yes, the idle fool,
The butt, the robber of the lads at school ;
Who then knew nothing, nothing since acquired,

THE BOROUGH

Became a doctor, honour'd and admired ;
His dress, his frown, his dignity were such,
Some who had known him thought his knowledge much ;
Nay, men of skill, of apprehension quick,
Spite of their knowledge, trusted him when sick.   270
Though he could never reason, write, nor spell,
They yet had hope his trash would make them well ;
And while they scorn'd his parts, they took his oxymel. [ ]
Oh ! when his nerves had once received a shock,
Sir Isaac Newton might have gone to Rock[1]:
Hence impositions of the grossest kind ;
Hence thought is feeble, understanding blind ;
Hence sums enormous by those cheats are made,
And deaths unnumber'd by their dreadful trade.

Alas ! in vain is my contempt express'd ;   280
To stronger passions are their words address'd :
To pain, to fear, to terror their appeal,
To those who, weakly reasoning, strongly feel.
What then our hopes ?—perhaps there may by law
Be method found, these pests to curb and awe ;
Yet in this land of freedom, law is slack
With any being to commence attack ;
Then let us trust to science—there are those
Who can their falsehoods and their frauds disclose,
All their vile trash detect, and their low tricks expose.   290[ ]
Perhaps their numbers may in time confound
Their arts—as scorpions give themselves the wound :
For, when these curers dwell in every place,
While of the cured we not a man can trace,
Strong truth may then the public mind persuade,
And spoil the fruits of this nefarious trade.

[1] An empiric who *flourished* at the same time with this great man.

THE BOROUGH.

LETTER VIII.

TRADES.

Non possidentem multa vocaveris
Recte beatum : rectius occupat
Nomen Beati, qui Deorum
Muneribus sapienter uti,
Duramque callet pauperiem pati.
Hor. lib. iv. od. 9 [vv. 45-9].

———

Non uxor salvum te vult, non filius : omnes
Vicini oderunt; noti, pueri atque puellæ.
Miraris, cum tu argento post omnia ponas,
Si nemo præstet, quem non merearis, amorem?
Hor. Sat. lib. i. [Sat. i. vv. 84-7].

———

Non propter vitam faciunt patrimonia quidam,
Sed vitio cæci propter patrimonia vivunt.
Juvenal. Sat. 12. [vv. 50-1].

———

No extensive Manufactories in the Borough : yet considerable Fortunes
made there—Ill Judgment of Parents in disposing of their Sons—The
best educated not the most likely to succeed—Instance—Want of
Success compensated by the lenient Power of some Avocations—The
Naturalist—The Weaver an Entomologist, &c.—A Prize-Flower—
Story of Walter and William.

THE BOROUGH.

LETTER VIII.

TRADES.

OF manufactures, trade, inventions rare,
Steam-towers and looms, you'd know our Borough's share—
'Tis small : we boast not these rich subjects here,
Who hazard thrice ten thousand pounds a year;
We've no huge buildings, where incessant noise
Is made by springs and spindles, girls and boys;
Where, 'mid such thundering sounds, the maiden's song
Is "Harmony in Uproar" [1] all day long.
  Still, common minds with us, in common trade,
Have gain'd more wealth than ever student made;   10
And yet a merchant, when he gives his son
His college-learning, thinks his duty done;
A way to wealth he leaves his boy to find,
Just when he's made for the discovery blind.
  Jones and his wife perceived their elder boy
Took to his learning, and it gave them joy;
This they encouraged, and were bless'd to see
Their son a Fellow with a high degree;
A living fell, he married, and his sire
Declared 'twas all a father could require;   20
Children then bless'd them, and when letters came,
The parents proudly told each grandchild's name.
  Meantime the sons at home in trade were placed,
Money their object—just the father's taste;
Saving he lived and long, and when he died,
He gave them all his fortune to divide.

357

GEORGE CRABBE

"Martin," said he, "at vast expense was taught;
"He gain'd his wish, and has the ease he sought."
Thus the good priest (the Christian-scholar!) finds
What estimate is made by vulgar minds;   30
He sees his brothers, who had every gift
Of thriving, now assisted in their thrift;
While he whom learning, habits, all prevent,
Is largely mulct for each impediment.
Yet, let us own that trade has much of chance :
Not all the careful by their care advance ;
With the same parts and prospects, one a seat
Builds for himself; one finds it in the Fleet.
Then, to the wealthy you will see denied
Comforts and joys that with the poor abide :   40
There are who labour through the year, and yet
No more have gain'd than—not to be in debt ;
Who still maintain the same laborious course,
Yet pleasure hails them from some favourite source ;
And health, amusements, children, wife or friend,
With life's dull views their consolations blend.
Nor these alone possess the lenient power
Of soothing life in the desponding hour ;
Some favourite studies, some delightful care,
The mind with trouble and distresses share ;   50
And by a coin, a flower, a verse, a boat,
The stagnant spirits have been set afloat ;
They pleased at first, and then the habit grew,
Till the fond heart no higher pleasure knew ;
Till, from all cares and other comforts freed,
Th' important nothing took in life the lead.
With all his phlegm, it broke a Dutchman's heart,
At a vast price with one loved root to part ;
And toys like these fill many a British mind,
Although their hearts are found of firmer kind.   60
Oft have I smiled the happy pride to see
Of humble tradesmen, in their evening glee ;
When, of some pleasing, fancied good possess'd,
Each grew alert, was busy, and was bless'd ;
Whether the call-bird yield the hour's delight,
Or, magnified in microscope, the mite ;

358

THE BOROUGH

Or whether tumblers, croppers, carriers seize
The gentle mind, they rule it and they please.
   There is my friend the Weaver; strong desires
Reign in his breast; 'tis beauty he admires: 70
See! to the shady grove he wings his way,
And feels in hope the raptures of the day—
Eager he looks; and soon, to glad his eyes,
From the sweet bower, by nature form'd, arise
Bright troops of virgin moths and fresh-born butterflies; [}]
Who broke that morning from their half-year's sleep,
To fly o'er flow'rs where they were wont to creep.
   Above the sovereign oak a sovereign skims,
The purple Emp'ror, strong in wing and limbs:
There fair Camilla takes her flight serene,   80
Adonis blue, and Paphia, silver-queen;
With every filmy fly from mead or bower,
And hungry Sphinx, who threads the honey'd flower;
She o'er the Larkspur's bed, where sweets abound,
Views ev'ry bell, and hums th' approving sound;
Poised on her busy plumes, with feeling nice
She draws from every flower, nor tries a floret twice.
   He fears no bailiff's wrath, no baron's blame,
His is untax'd and undisputed game;
Nor less the place of curious plant he knows [2];   90
He both his Flora and his Fauna shows;
For him is blooming in its rich array
The glorious flower which bore the palm away;
In vain a rival tried his utmost art,
His was the prize, and joy o'erflow'd his heart.
   "This, this is beauty! cast, I pray, your eyes
"On this my glory! see the grace! the size!
"Was ever stem so tall, so stout, so strong,
"Exact in breadth, in just proportion, long!
"These brilliant hues are all distinct and clean,   100
"No kindred tint, no blending streaks between;
"This is no shaded, run-off [3], pin-eyed [4] thing,
"A king of flowers, a flower for England's king:
"I own my pride, and thank the favouring star,
"Which shed such beauty on my fair Bizarre [5]."
   Thus may the poor the cheap indulgence seize,

GEORGE CRABBE

While the most wealthy pine and pray for ease;
Content not always waits upon success,
And more may he enjoy who profits less.
Walter and William took (their father dead)   110
Jointly the trade to which they both were bred;
When fix'd, they married, and they quickly found
With due success their honest labours crown'd:
Few were their losses, but, although a few,
Walter was vex'd, and somewhat peevish grew:
"You put your trust in every pleading fool,"
Said he to William, and grew strange and cool.
"Brother, forbear," he answer'd; "take your due,
"Nor let my lack of caution injure you:"
Half friends they parted,—better so to close,   120
Than longer wait to part entirely foes.
Walter had knowledge, prudence, jealous care;
He let no idle views his bosom share;
He never thought nor felt for other men—
"Let one mind one, and all are minded then."
Friends he respected, and believed them just;
But they were men, and he would no man trust;
He tried and watch'd his people day and night,—
The good it harm'd not; for the bad 'twas right:
He could their humours bear, nay disrespect,   130
But he could yield no pardon to neglect;
That all about him were of him afraid,
"Was right," he said—"so should we be obey'd."
These merchant-maxims, much good-fortune too,
And ever keeping one grand point in view,
To vast amount his once small portion drew.   [ ]]
William was kind and easy; he complied
With all requests, or grieved when he denied;
To please his wife he made a costly trip,
To please his child he let a bargain slip;   140
Prone to compassion, mild with the distress'd,
He bore with all who poverty profess'd,
And some would he assist, nor one would he arrest.   [ ]]
He had some loss at sea, bad debts at land,
His clerk absconded with some bills in hand,
And plans so often fail'd that he no longer plann'd.   [ ]]

THE BOROUGH

To a small house (his brother's) he withdrew,
At easy rent—the man was not a Jew;
And there his losses and his cares he bore,
Nor found that want of wealth could make him poor.　150
　No, he in fact was rich; nor could he move,
But he was follow'd by the looks of love;
All he had suffer'd, every former grief,
Made those around more studious in relief;
He saw a cheerful smile in every face,
And lost all thoughts of error and disgrace.
　Pleasant it was to see them in their walk
Round their small garden, and to hear them talk;
Free are their children, but their love refrains
From all offence—none murmurs, none complains;　160
Whether a book amused them, speech or play,
Their looks were lively, and their hearts were gay;
There no forced efforts for delight were made,
Joy came with prudence, and without parade;
Their common comforts they had all in view,
Light were their troubles, and their wishes few;
Thrift made them easy for the coming day;
Religion took the dread of death away;
A cheerful spirit still insured content,
And love smiled round them wheresoe'er they went.　170
　Walter, meantime, with all his wealth's increase,
Gain'd many points, but could not purchase peace;
When he withdrew from business for an hour,
Some fled his presence, all confess'd his power;
He sought affection, but received instead
Fear undisguised, and love-repelling dread;
He look'd around him—"Harriet, dost thou love?"—
"I do my duty," said the timid dove;—
"Good Heav'n, your duty! prithee, tell me now—
"To love and honour—was not that your vow?　180
"Come, my good Harriet, I would gladly seek
"Your inmost thought—Why can't the woman speak?
"Have you not all things?"—"Sir, do I complain?"—
"No, that's my part, which I perform in vain;
"I want a simple answer, and direct—
"But you evade; yes! 'tis as I suspect.

GEORGE CRABBE

"Come then, my children! Watt! upon your knees
"Vow that you love me."—"Yes, sir, if you please."—
"Again! by Heav'n, it mads me; I require
"Love, and they'll do whatever I desire.   190
"Thus too my people shun me; I would spend
"A thousand pounds to get a single friend;
"I would he happy—I have means to pay
"For love and friendship, and you run away;
"Ungrateful creatures! why, you seem to dread
"My very looks; I know you wish me dead.
"Come hither, Nancy! you must hold me dear;
"Hither, I say; why! what have you to fear?
"You see I'm gentle—Come, you trifler, come;
"My God! she trembles! Idiot, leave the room!   200
"Madam! your children hate me; I suppose
"They know their cue; you make them all my foes;
"I've not a friend in all the world—not one:
"I'd be a bankrupt sooner; nay, 'tis done;
"In every better hope of life I fail;
"You're all tormentors, and my house a jail;
"Out of my sight! I'll sit and make my will—
"What, glad to go? stay, devils, and be still;
"'Tis to your uncle's cot you wish to run,
"To learn to live at ease and be undone;   210
"Him you can love, who lost his whole estate,
"And I, who gain you fortunes, have your hate;
"'Tis in my absence you yourselves enjoy:
"Tom! are you glad to lose me? tell me, boy:
"'Yes!' does he answer?"—"'Yes!' upon my soul;"
"No awe, no fear, no duty, no control!
"Away! away! ten thousand devils seize
"All I possess, and plunder where they please!
"What's wealth to me?—yes, yes! it gives me sway,
"And you shall feel it—Go! begone, I say."   220

THE BOROUGH

NOTES TO LETTER VIII.

Note 1, page 358, line 8.

Is "Harmony in Uproar" all day long.

The title of a short piece of humour by Arbuthnot.

Note 2, page 360, line 90.

Nor less the place of curious plant he knows.

In botanical language, "*the habitat*," the favourite soil or situation of the more scarce species.

Note 3, page 360, line 102.

This is no shaded, run-off, pin-eyed thing.

This, it must be acknowledged, is contrary to the opinion of Thomson, and I believe of some other poets, who, in describing the varying hues of our most beautiful flowers, have considered them as lost and blended with each other ; whereas their beauty, in the eye of a florist (and I conceive in that of the uninitiated also), depends upon the distinctness of their colours : the stronger the bounding line, and the less they break into the neighbouring tint, so much the richer and more valuable is the flower esteemed.

Note 4, page 360, line 102.

Pin-eyed.

An auricula, or any other single flower, is so called when the *stigma* (the part which arises from the seed-vessel) is protruded beyond the tube of the flower, and becomes visible.

Note 5, page 360, line 105.

Which shed such beauty on my faire Bizarre.

This word, so far as it relates to flowers, means those variegated with three or more colours irregularly and indeterminately.

363

THE BOROUGH.

LETTER IX.

AMUSEMENTS.

Interpone tuis interdum gaudia curis,
Ut possis animo quemvis sufferre laborem.
[(*Dionys.*) *Cato de Moribus.* III. 7.]

. . . . . . nostra [fatiscit]
Laxaturque chelys ; vires instigat alitque
Tempestiva quies, major post otia virtus.
Statius, Sylv. lib. IV. [4, vv. 32–3].

Jamque mare et tellus nullum discrimen habebant;
Omnia pontus [erat]: deerant quoque littora ponto.
Ovid. Metamorph. lib. I [vv. 291–2].

Common Amusements of a Bathing-place—Morning Rides, Walks, &c.—
Company resorting to the Town—Different Choice of Lodgings—
Cheap Indulgences—Sea-side Walks—Wealthy Invalid—Summer-
Evening on the Sands—Sea Productions—"Water parted from the
Sea "—Winter Views serene—In what Cases to be avoided—Sailing
upon the River—A small Islet of Sand off the Coast—Visited by
Company—Covered by the Flowing of the Tide—Adventure in that
Place.

364

THE BOROUGH.

LETTER IX.

AMUSEMENTS.

OF our amusements ask you?—We amuse
Ourselves and friends with sea-side walks and views,
Or take a morning ride, a novel, or the news;   [}]
Or, seeking nothing, glide about the street,
And, so engaged, with various parties meet;
Awhile we stop, discourse of wind and tide,
Bathing and books, the raffle, and the ride:
Thus, with the aid which shops and sailing give,
Life passes on; 'tis labour, but we live.
  When evening comes, our invalids awake,   10
Nerves cease to tremble, heads forbear to ache;
Then cheerful meals the sunken spirits raise,
Cards or the dance, wine, visiting, or plays.
  Soon as the season comes, and crowds arrive,
To their superior rooms the wealthy drive;
Others look round for lodging snug and small,
Such is their taste—they've hatred to a hall;
Hence one his fav'rite habitation gets,
The brick-floor'd parlour which the butcher lets;
Where, through his single light, he may regard   20
The various business of a common yard,
Bounded by backs of buildings form'd of clay,
By stable, sties, and coops, et-cætera.
  The needy-vain, themselves awhile to shun,
For dissipation to these dog-holes run;
Where each (assuming petty pomp) appears,
And quite forgets the shopboard and the shears.

365

GEORGE CRABBE

For them are cheap amusements : they may slip
Beyond the town and take a private dip ;
When they may urge that to be safe they mean: 30
They've heard there's danger in a light machine ;
They too can gratis move the quays about,
And gather kind replies to every doubt ;
There they a pacing, lounging tribe may view,
The stranger's guides, who've little else to do ;
The Borough's placemen, where no more they gain
Than keeps them idle, civil, poor, and vain.
Then may the poorest with the wealthy look
On ocean, glorious page of Nature's book !
May see its varying views in every hour,   40⎫
All softness now, then rising with all power,   ⎬
As sleeping to invite, or threat'ning to devour :   [∫]
'Tis this which gives us all our choicest views ;
Its waters heal us, and its shores amuse.
    See those fair nymphs upon that rising strand,
Yon long salt lake has parted from the land ;
Well pleased to press that path, so clean, so pure,
To seem in danger, yet to feel secure ;
Trifling with terror, while they strive to shun
The curling billows ; laughing as they run ;   50
They know the neck that joins the shore and sea,
Or, ah ! how changed that fearless laugh would be.
    Observe how various parties take their way,
By sea-side walks, or make the sand-hills gay ;
There group'd are laughing maids and sighing swains,
And some apart who feel unpitied pains :
Pains from diseases, pains which those who feel
To the physician, not the fair, reveal ;
For nymphs (propitious to the lover's sigh)
Leave these poor patients to complain and die.   60
    Lo ! where on that huge anchor sadly leans
That sick tall figure, lost in other scenes ;
He late from India's clime impatient sail'd,
There, as his fortune grew, his spirits fail'd ;
For each delight, in search of wealth he went,
For ease alone, the wealth acquired is spent—
And spent in vain ; enrich'd, aggriev'd, he sees

366

THE BOROUGH

The envied poor possess'd of joy and ease ;
And now he flies from place to place, to gain
Strength for enjoyment, and still flies in vain.⠀⠀⠀⠀⠀70
Mark, with what sadness, of that pleasant crew,
Boist'rous in mirth, he takes a transient view,
And, fixing then his eye upon the sea,
Thinks what has been and what must shortly be :
Is it not strange that man should health destroy,
For joys that come when he is dead to joy ?
⠀Now is it pleasant in the summer-eve,
When a broad shore retiring waters leave,
Awhile to wait upon the firm fair sand,
When all is calm at sea, all still at land ;⠀⠀⠀⠀80
And there the ocean's produce to explore,
As floating by, or rolling on the shore ;
Those living jellies [1] which the flesh inflame,
Fierce as a nettle, and from that its name ;
Some in huge masses, some that you may bring
In the small compass of a lady's ring ;
Figured by hand divine—there's not a gem
Wrought by man's art to be compared to them ;
Soft, brilliant, tender, through the wave they glow,
And make the moonbeam brighter where they flow.⠀⠀90
Involved in sea-wrack, here you find a race,
Which science, doubting, knows not where to place ;
On shell or stone is dropp'd the embryo-seed,
And quickly vegetates a vital breed [2].
⠀While thus with pleasing wonder you inspect
Treasures the vulgar in their scorn reject,
See as they float along th' entangled weeds
Slowly approach, upborne on bladdery beads ;
Wait till they land, and you shall then behold
The fiery sparks those tangled frons' infold,⠀⠀⠀⠀100
Myriads of living points [3] ; th' unaided eye
Can but the fire and not the form descry.
And now your view upon the ocean turn,
And there the splendour of the waves discern ;
Cast but a stone, or strike them with an oar,
And you shall flames within the deep explore ;
Or scoop the stream phosphoric as you stand,

367

And the cold flames shall flash along your hand;
When, lost in wonder, you shall walk and gaze
On weeds that sparkle, and on waves that blaze [4].   110
The ocean too has winter-views serene,
When all you see through densest fog is seen;
When you can hear the fishers near at hand
Distinctly speak, yet see not where they stand;
Or sometimes them and not their boat discern,
Or half-conceal'd some figure at the stern;
The view's all bounded, and from side to side
Your utmost prospect but a few ells wide;
Boys who, on shore, to sea the pebble cast,
Will hear it strike against the viewless mast;   120
While the stern boatman growls his fierce disdain,
At whom he knows not, whom he threats in vain.
'Tis pleasant then to view the nets float past,
Net after net till you have seen the last;
And as you wait till all beyond you slip,
A boat comes gliding from an anchor'd ship,
Breaking the silence with the dipping oar
And their own tones, as labouring for the shore—
Those measured tones which with the scene agree,
And give a sadness to serenity.   130
All scenes like these the tender maid should shun,
Nor to a misty beach in autumn run;
Much should she guard against the evening cold,
And her slight shape with fleecy warmth infold;
This she admits, but not with so much ease
Gives up the night-walk when th' attendants please.
Her have I seen, pale, vapour'd through the day,
With crowded parties at the midnight play;
Faint in the morn, no powers could she exert;
At night with Pam delighted and alert;   140
In a small shop she's raffled with a crowd,
Breathed the thick air, and cough'd and laugh'd aloud;
She, who will tremble if her eye explore
"The smallest monstrous mouse that creeps on floor;"
Whom the kind doctor charged, with shaking head,
At early hour to quit the beaux for bed:
She has, contemning fear, gone down the dance,

THE BOROUGH

Till she perceived the rosy morn advance;
Then has she wonder'd, fainting o'er her tea,
Her drops and juleps should so useless be :   150
Ah! sure her joys must ravish every sense,
Who buys a portion at so vast expense.
  Among those joys, 'tis one at eve to sail
On the broad river with a favourite gale;
When no rough waves upon the bosom ride,
But the keel cuts, nor rises on the tide;
Safe from the stream the nearer gunwale stands,
Where playful children trail their idle hands,
Or strive to catch long grassy leaves that float
On either side of the impeded boat :   160
What time the moon, arising, shows the mud
A shining border to the silver flood;
When, by her dubious light, the meanest views,
Chalk, stones, and stakes, obtain the richest hues;
And when the cattle, as they gazing stand,
Seem nobler objects than when view'd from land.
Then anchor'd vessels in the way appear,
And sea-boys greet them as they pass—"What cheer?"
The sleeping shell-ducks at the sound arise,
And utter loud their unharmonious cries;   170
Fluttering, they move their weedy beds among,
Or, instant diving, hide their plumeless young.
  Along the wall, returning from the town,
The weary rustic homeward wanders down;
Who stops and gazes at such joyous crew,
And feels his envy rising at the view;
He the light speech and laugh indignant hears,
And feels more press'd by want, more vex'd by fears.
  Ah! go in peace, good fellow, to thine home,
Nor fancy these escape the general doom;   180
Gay as they seem, be sure with them are hearts
With sorrow tried; there's sadness in their parts.
If thou couldst see them when they think alone,
Mirth, music, friends, and these amusements gone;
Couldst thou discover every secret ill
That pains their spirit, or resists their will;
Couldst thou behold forsaken Love's distress,

Crabbe   AA   369

Or Envy's pang at glory and success,
Or Beauty, conscious of the spoils of Time,
Or Guilt, alarm'd when Memory shows the crime—   190
All that gives sorrow, terror, grief, and gloom :
Content would cheer thee, trudging to thine home [5].
　　There are, 'tis true, who lay their cares aside,
And bid some hours in calm enjoyment glide ;
Perchance some fair-one to the sober night
Adds (by the sweetness of her song) delight ;
And, as the music on the water floats,
Some bolder shore returns the soften'd notes ;
Then, youth, beware, for all around conspire
To banish caution and to wake desire ;   200
The day's amusement, feasting, beauty, wine, ⎫
These accents sweet and this soft hour combine, ⎬ [⌡]
When most unguarded, then to win that heart of thine : ⎭
But see, they land ! the fond enchantment flies,
And in its place life's common views arise.
　　Sometimes a party, row'd from town, will land
On a small islet form'd of shelly sand,
Left by the water when the tides are low,
But which the floods in their return o'erflow :
There will they anchor, pleased awhile to view   210
The watery waste, a prospect wild and new ;
The now receding billows give them space
On either side the growing shores to pace ;
And then, returning, they contract the scene,
Till small and smaller grows the walk between,
As sea to sea approaches, shore to shores,
Till the next ebb the sandy isle restores.
　　Then what alarm ! what danger and dismay,
If all their trust, their boat should drift away ;
And once it happen'd—gay the friends advanced ;   220
They walk'd, they ran, they play'd, they sang, they danced ;
The urns were boiling, and the cups went round,
And not a grave or thoughtful face was found ;
On the bright sand they trod with nimble feet,
Dry shelly sand that made the summer-seat ;
The wondering mews flew fluttering o'er the head,
And waves ran softly up their shining bed.

THE BOROUGH

Some form'd a party from the rest to stray,
Pleased to collect the trifles in their way ;
These to behold, they call their friends around—   230
No friends can hear, or hear another sound ;
Alarm'd, they hasten, yet perceive not why,
But catch the fear that quickens as they fly.
   For lo ! a lady sage, who paced the sand
With her fair children, one in either hand,
Intent on home, had turn'd, and saw the boat
Slipp'd from her moorings, and now far afloat ;
She gazed, she trembled, and though faint her call,
It seem'd, like thunder, to confound them all.
Their sailor-guides, the boatman and his mate,   240
Had drank, and slept regardless of their state ;
" Awake ! " they cried aloud ; " Alarm the shore !
" Shout all, or never shall we reach it more ! "
Alas ! no shout the distant land can reach,
Nor eye behold them from the foggy beach.
Again they join in one loud, powerful cry,
Then cease, and eager listen for reply ;
None came—the rising wind blew sadly by.
They shout once more, and then they turn aside,
To see how quickly flow'd the coming tide ;   250
Between each cry they find the waters steal
On their strange prison, and new horrors feel ;
Foot after foot on the contracted ground
The billows fall, and dreadful is the sound ;
Less and yet less the sinking isle became,
And there was wailing, weeping, wrath, and blame.
   Had one been there, with spirit strong and high,
Who could observe, as he prepared to die :
He might have seen of hearts the varying kind,
And traced the movement of each different mind ;   260
He might have seen, that not the gentle maid
Was more than stern and haughty man afraid ;
Such calmly grieving, will their fears suppress,
And silent prayers to Mercy's throne address ;
While fiercer minds, impatient, angry, loud,
Force their vain grief on the reluctant crowd.
The party's patron, sorely sighing, cried,

"Why would you urge me? I at first denied."
Fiercely they answer'd, "Why will you complain,
"Who saw no danger, or was warn'd in vain?"   270
A few essay'd the troubled soul to calm;
But dread prevail'd, and anguish and alarm.
  Now rose the water through the lessening sand,
And they seem'd sinking while they yet could stand;
The sun went down, they look'd from side to side,
Nor aught except the gathering sea descried;
Dark and more dark, more wet, more cold it grew,
And the most lively bade to hope adieu;
Children, by love then lifted from the seas,
Felt not the waters at the parents' knees,   280
But wept aloud; the wind increased the sound,
And the cold billows as they broke around.
  "Once more, yet once again, with all our strength,
"Cry to the land—we may be heard at length."
Vain hope, if yet unseen! but hark! an oar,
That sound of bliss! comes dashing to their shore;
Still, still the water rises; "Haste!" they cry,
"Oh! hurry, seamen; in delay we die;"
(Seamen were these, who in their ship perceived
The drifted boat, and thus her crew relieved.)   290
And now the keel just cuts the cover'd sand,
Now to the gunwale stretches every hand;
With trembling pleasure all confused embark,
And kiss the tackling of their welcome ark;
While the most giddy, as they reach the shore,
Think of their danger, and their GOD adore.

THE BOROUGH

NOTES TO LETTER IX.

Note 1, page 368, line 83.

Those living jellies which the flesh inflame.

Some of the smaller species of the Medusa (sea-nettle) are exquisitely beautiful: their form is nearly oval, varied with serrated longitudinal lines; they are extremely tender, and by no means which I am acquainted with can be preserved, for they soon dissolve in either spirit of wine or water, and lose every vestige of their shape, and indeed of their substance: the larger species are found in mis-shapen masses of many pounds weight; these, when handled, have the effect of the nettle, and the stinging is often accompanied or succeeded by the more unpleasant feeling, perhaps in a slight degree resembling that caused by the torpedo.

Note 2, page 368, line 94.

And quickly vegetates a vital breed.

Various tribes and species of marine vermes are here meant: that which so nearly resembles a vegetable in its form, and perhaps, in some degree, manner of growth, is the coralline called by naturalists Sertularia, of which there are many species in almost every part of the coast. The animal protrudes its many claws (apparently in search of prey) from certain pellucid vesicles which proceed from a horny, tenacious, branchy stem.

Note 3, page 368, line 101.

Myriads of living points; th' unaided eye
Can but the fire and not the form descry.

These are said to be a minute kind of animal of the same class; when it does not shine, it is invisible to the naked eye.

Note 4, page 369, line 110.

On weeds that sparkle, and on waves that blaze.

For the cause or causes of this phenomenon, which is sometimes, though rarely, observed on our coasts, I must refer the reader to the writers on natural philosophy and natural history.

Note 5, page 371, line 192.

Content would cheer thee, trudging to thine home.

This is not offered as a reasonable source of contentment, but as one motive for resignation: there would not be so much envy if there were more discernment.

THE BOROUGH.

LETTER X.

CLUBS AND SOCIAL MEETINGS.

Non inter lances mensasque nitentes,
Cum stupet insanis acies fulgoribus, et cum
Acclinis falsis animus meliora recusat;
Verum hîc impransi mecum disquirite.
Hor. Sat. lib. ii. [Sat. 2. vv. 4–7].

O prodiga rerum
Luxuries, nunquam parvo contenta paratu,
Et quæsitorum terrâ pelagoque ciborum
Ambitiosa fames et lautæ gloria mensæ.
Lucan. lib. iv. [vv. 373–6].

[Sed] quæ non prosunt singula, [multa] juvant.
[Ovid. Remed. Amor. v. 420.]

Rusticus agricolam, miles fera bella gerentem,
Rectorem dubiæ navita puppis amat.
Ovid. Pont. lib. ii. [Ep. 2. vv. 61–2].

Desire of Country Gentlemen for Town Associations—Book-clubs—Too
much of literary Character expected from them—Literary Conversation
prevented: by Feasting: by Cards—Good, notwithstanding, results—
Card-club with Eagerness resorted to—Players—Umpires at the
Whist Table—Petulances of Temper there discovered—Free-and-easy
Club: not perfectly easy or free—Freedom, how interrupted—The
superior Member—Termination of the Evening—Drinking and Smok-
ing Clubs—The Midnight Conversation of the Delaying Members—
Society of the poorer Inhabitants: its Use: gives Pride and Con-
sequence to the humble Character—Pleasant Habitations of the frugal
Poor—Sailor returning to his Family—Freemasons' Club—The
Mystery—What its Origin—Its professed Advantages—Griggs and
Gregorians—A Kind of Masons—Reflections on these various
Societies.

THE BOROUGH.

LETTER X.

CLUBS AND SOCIAL MEETINGS.

YOU say you envy in your calm retreat
   Our social meetings;—'tis with joy we meet.
In these our parties you are pleased to find
Good sense and wit, with intercourse of mind;
Composed of men, who read, reflect, and write;
Who, when they meet, must yield and share delight.
To you our Book-club has peculiar charm,
For which you sicken in your quiet farm;
Here you suppose us at our leisure placed,
Enjoying freedom, and displaying taste;   10
With wisdom cheerful, temperately gay,
Pleased to enjoy, and willing to display.
  If thus your envy gives your ease its gloom,
Give wings to fancy, and among us come.
We're now assembled; you may soon attend—
I'll introduce you—"Gentlemen, my friend."—
  "Now are you happy? you have pass'd a night
"In gay discourse, and rational delight."—
  "Alas! not so; for how can mortals think,
"Or thoughts exchange, if thus they eat and drink?   20
"No! I confess, when we had fairly dined,
"That was no time for intercourse of mind;
"There was each dish prepared with skill t' invite,
"And to detain the struggling appetite;
"On such occasions minds with one consent
"Are to the comforts of the body lent;
"There was no pause—the wine went quickly round,

375

GEORGE CRABBE

"Till struggling Fancy was by Bacchus bound;
"Wine is to wit as water thrown on fire:
"By duly sprinkling, both are raised the higher;   30
"Thus largely dealt, the vivid blaze they choke,
"And all the genial flame goes off in smoke."—
    "But when no more your boards these loads contain,
"When wine no more o'erwhelms the labouring brain,
"But serves, a gentle stimulus: we know
"How wit must sparkle, and how fancy flow."—
It might be so, but no such club-days come;
We always find these dampers in the room.
If to converse were all that brought us here,
A few odd members would in turn appear;   40
Who, dwelling nigh, would saunter in and out,
O'erlook the list, and toss the books about;
Or, yawning, read them, walking up and down,
Just as the loungers in the shops in town;
Till, fancying nothing would their minds amuse,
They'd push them by, and go in search of news.
    But our attractions are a stronger sort,
The earliest dainties and the oldest port;
All enter then with glee in every look,
And not a member thinks about a book.   50
    Still let me own, there are some vacant hours,
When minds might work, and men exert their powers:
Ere wine to folly spurs the giddy guest,
But gives to wit its vigour and its zest;
Then might we reason, might in turn display
Our several talents, and be wisely gay;
We might—but who a tame discourse regards,
When whist is named, and we behold the cards?
    We from that time are neither grave nor gay;
Our thought, our care, our business is to play: 60
Fix'd on these spots and figures, each attends
Much to his partners, nothing to his friends.
    Our public cares, the long, the warm debate,
That kept our patriots from their beds so late;
War, peace, invasion, all we hope or dread,
Vanish like dreams when men forsake their bed;
And groaning nations and contending kings

376

THE BOROUGH

Are all forgotten for these painted things :
Paper and paste, vile figures and poor spots,
Level all minds, philosophers and sots ;   70
And give an equal spirit, pause, and force,
Join'd with peculiar diction, to discourse :
" Who deals ?—you led—we're three by cards—had you
" Honour in hand ? "—" Upon my honour, two."
Hour after hour, men thus contending sit,
Grave without sense, and pointed without wit.
    Thus it appears these envied clubs possess
No certain means of social happiness ;
Yet there's a good that flows from scenes like these—
Man meets with man at leisure and at ease ;   80
We to our neighbours and our equals come,
And rub off pride that man contracts at home ;
For there, admitted master, he is prone
To claim attention and to talk alone :
But here he meets with neither son nor spouse ;
No humble cousin to his bidding bows ;
To his raised voice his neighbours' voices rise ;
To his high look as lofty look replies ;
When much he speaks, he finds that ears are closed,
And certain signs inform him when he's prosed ;   90
Here all the value of a listener know,
And claim, in turn, the favour they bestow.
    No pleasure gives the speech, when all would speak,
And all in vain a civil hearer seek.
To chance alone we owe the free discourse,
In vain you purpose what you cannot force ;
'Tis when the favourite themes unbidden spring,
That fancy soars with such unwearied wing ;
Then may you call in aid the moderate glass,
But let it slowly and unprompted pass ;   100
So shall there all things for the end unite,
And give that hour of rational delight.
    Men to their clubs repair, themselves to please,
To care for nothing, and to take their ease ;
In fact, for play, for wine, for news they come ;
Discourse is shared with friends, or found at home.

GEORGE CRABBE

But cards with books are incidental things;
We've nights devoted to these queens and kings.
Then, if we choose the social game, we may;
Now, 'tis a duty, and we're bound to play;   110
Nor ever meeting of the social kind
Was more engaging, yet had less of mind.
Our eager parties, when the lunar light
Throws its full radiance on the festive night,
Of either sex, with punctual hurry come,
And fill, with one accord, an ample room.
Pleased, the fresh packs on cloth of green they see,
And, seizing, handle with preluding glee;
They draw, they sit, they shuffle, cut and deal;
Like friends assembled, but like foes to feel: 120
But yet not all—a happier few have joys
Of mere amusement, and their cards are toys;
No skill nor art, nor fretful hopes have they,
But while their friends are gaming, laugh and play.
  Others there are, the veterans of the game,
Who owe their pleasure to their envied fame;
Through many a year, with hard-contested strife,
Have they attain'd this glory of their life.
Such is that ancient burgess, whom in vain
Would gout and fever on his couch detain;   130
And that large lady, who resolves to come,
Though a first fit has warn'd her of her doom!
These are as oracles: in every cause
They settle doubts, and their decrees are laws;
But all are troubled, when, with dubious look,
Diana questions what Apollo spoke.
  Here avarice first, the keen desire of gain,
Rules in each heart, and works in every brain;
Alike the veteran-dames and virgins feel,
Nor care what gray-beards or what striplings deal;   140
Sex, age, and station, vanish from their view,
And gold, their sov'reign good, the mingled crowd pursue.
  Hence they are jealous, and as rivals, keep
A watchful eye on the beloved heap;
Meantime discretion bids the tongue be still,
And mild good-humour strives with strong ill-will;

378

THE BOROUGH

Till prudence fails; when, all impatient grown,
They make their grief, by their suspicions, known.
  " Sir, I protest, were Job himself at play,
" He'd rave to see you throw your cards away;   150
" Not that I care a button—not a pin
" For what I lose; but we had cards to win:
" A saint in heaven would grieve to see such hand
" Cut up by one who will not understand."—
  " Complain of me! and so you might indeed,
" If I had ventured on that foolish lead,
" That fatal heart—but I forgot your play—
" Some folk have ever thrown their hearts away."—
  " Yes, and their diamonds; I have heard of one
" Who made a beggar of an only son."—   160
  " Better a beggar, than to see him tied
" To art and spite, to insolence and pride."—
  " Sir, were I you, I'd strive to be polite,
" Against my nature, for a single night."—
  " So did you strive, and, madam! with success;
" I knew no being we could censure less! "—
Is this too much? alas! my peaceful muse
Cannot with half their virulence abuse.
And hark! at other tables discord reigns,
With feign'd contempt for losses and for gains;   170
Passions awhile are bridled; then they rage,
In waspish youth, and in resentful age;
With scraps of insult—" Sir, when next you play,
" Reflect whose money 'tis you throw away.
" No one on earth can less such things regard,
" But when one's partner doesn't know a card——"
  " I scorn suspicion, ma'am, but while you stand
" Behind that lady, pray keep down your hand."—
  " Good heav'n, revoke! remember, if the set
" Be lost, in honour you should pay the debt."—   180
  " There, there's your money; but, while I have life,
" I'll never more sit down with man and wife;
" They snap and snarl indeed, but in the heat
" Of all their spleen, their understandings meet;
" They are Freemasons, and have many a sign,
" That we, poor devils! never can divine:

379

GEORGE CRABBE

"May it be told, do ye divide th' amount,
"Or goes it all to family account?"

Next is the club, where to their friends in town
Our country neighbours once a month come down;   190
We term it Free-and-easy, and yet we
Find it no easy matter to be free:
Ev'n in our small assembly, friends among,
Are minds perverse, there's something will be wrong;
Men are not equal; some will claim a right
To be the kings and heroes of the night;
Will their own favourite themes and notions start,
And you must hear, offend them, or depart.
There comes Sir Thomas from his village-seat,
Happy, he tells us, all his friends to meet;   200
He brings the ruin'd brother of his wife,
Whom he supports, and makes him sick of life:
A ready witness whom he can produce
Of all his deeds—a butt for his abuse.
Soon as he enters, has the guests espied,
Drawn to the fire, and to the glass applied—
"Well, what's the subject?—what are you about?
"The news, I take it—come, I'll help you out;"—
And then, without one answer, he bestows
Freely upon us all he hears and knows;   210
Gives us opinions, tells us how he votes,
Recites the speeches, adds to them his notes,
And gives old ill-told tales for new-born anecdotes;   [ ]]
Yet cares he nothing what we judge or think,
Our only duty's to attend and drink.
At length, admonish'd by his gout, he ends
The various speech, and leaves at peace his friends;
But now, alas! we've lost the pleasant hour,
And wisdom flies from wine's superior power.
Wine, like the rising sun, possession gains,   220
And drives the mist of dulness from the brains;
The gloomy vapour from the spirit flies,
And views of gaiety and gladness rise.
Still it proceeds; till from the glowing heat,

380

THE BOROUGH

The prudent calmly to their shades retreat;—
Then is the mind o'ercast—in wordy rage
And loud contention angry men engage;
Then spleen and pique, like fire-works thrown in spite,
To mischief turn the pleasures of the night;
Anger abuses, Malice loudly rails,   230
Revenge awakes, and Anarchy prevails:
Till wine, that raised the tempest, makes it cease,
And maudlin Love insists on instant peace;
He noisy mirth and roaring song commands,
Gives idle toasts, and joins unfriendly hands;
Till fuddled Friendship vows esteem and weeps,
And jovial Folly drinks and sings and sleeps.

———

A club there is of Smokers.—Dare you come
To that close, clouded, hot, narcotic room?
When, midnight past, the very candles seem   240
Dying for air, and give a ghastly gleam;
When curling fumes in lazy wreaths arise,
And prosing topers rub their winking eyes;
When the long tale, renew'd when last they met,
Is spliced anew, and is unfinish'd yet;
When but a few are left the house to tire,
And they half-sleeping by the sleepy fire;
Ev'n the poor ventilating vane, that flew
Of late so fast, is now grown drowsy too;
When sweet, cold, clammy punch its aid bestows,   250
Then thus the midnight conversation flows:—
    "Then, as I said, and—mind me—as I say,
"At our last meeting—you remember"—"Ay;"
"Well, very well—then freely as I drink
"I spoke my thought—you take me—what I think:
"And sir, said I, if I a freeman be,
"It is my bounden duty to be free."—
    "Ay, there you posed him; I respect the chair,
"But man is man, although the man's a mayor.
"If Muggins live—no, no!—if Muggins die,   260
"He'll quit his office—neighbour, shall I try?"—
    "I'll speak my mind, for here are none but friends:

381

GEORGE CRABBE

"They're all contending for their private ends;
"No public spirit, once a vote would bring;
"I say a vote was then a pretty thing;   }
"It made a man to serve his country and his king.   [∫]
"But for that place, that Muggins must resign,
"You've my advice—'tis no affair of mine."

The poor man has his club; he comes and spends
His hoarded pittance with his chosen friends;   270
Nor this alone—a monthly dole he pays,
To be assisted when his health decays;
Some part his prudence, from the day's supply,
For cares and troubles in his age, lays by;
The printed rules he guards with painted frame,
And shows his children where to read his name:
Those simple words his honest nature move,
That bond of union tied by laws of love.
This is his pride, it gives to his employ
New value, to his home another joy;   280
While a religious hope its balm applies
For all his fate inflicts and all his state denies.
    Much would it please you, sometimes to explore
The peaceful dwellings of our borough poor;
To view a sailor just return'd from sea;
His wife beside; a child on either knee,
And others crowding near, that none may lose
The smallest portion of the welcome news:
What dangers pass'd, "when seas ran mountains high,
"When tempests raved, and horrors veil'd the sky;   290
"When prudence fail'd, when courage grew dismay'd
"When the strong fainted, and the wicked pray'd,—
"Then in the yawning gulf far down we drove,
"And gazed upon the billowy mount above;
"Till up that mountain, swinging with the gale,
"We view'd the horrors of the watery vale."
    The trembling children look with stedfast eyes,
And panting, sob involuntary sighs:
Soft sleep awhile his torpid touch delays,
And all is joy and piety and praise.   300

382

THE BOROUGH

Masons are ours, Freemasons—but, alas!
To their own bards I leave the mystic class;
In vain shall one, and not a gifted man,
Attempt to sing of this enlighten'd clan:
I know no word, boast no directing sign,
And not one token of the race is mine;
Whether with Hiram, that wise widow's son,
They came from Tyre to royal Solomon,
Two pillars raising by their skill profound,
Boaz and Jachin through the East renown'd: 310
Whether the sacred books their rise express,
Or books profane, 'tis vain for me to guess.
It may be, lost in date remote and high,
They know not what their own antiquity;
It may be too, derived from cause so low,
They have no wish their origin to show.
If, as crusaders, they combined to wrest
From heathen lords the land they long possess'd,
Or were at first some harmless club, who made
Their idle meetings solemn by parade,   320
Is but conjecture—for the task unfit,
Awe-struck and mute, the puzzling theme I quit.
Yet, if such blessings from their order flow,
We should be glad their moral code to know;
Trowels of silver are but simple things,
And aprons worthless as their apron-strings;
But, if indeed you have the skill to teach
A social spirit, now beyond our reach;
If man's warm passions you can guide and bind,
And plant the virtues in the wayward mind;   330
If you can wake to christian-love the heart—
In mercy, something of your powers impart.
    But, as it seems, we Masons must become
To know the secret, and must then be dumb;
And, as we venture for uncertain gains,
Perhaps the profit is not worth the pains.
    When Bruce, the dauntless traveller, thought he stood
On Nile's first rise, the fountain of the flood,
And drank exulting in the sacred spring,
The critics told him it was no such thing;   340

That springs unnumber'd round the country ran,
But none could show him where they first began :
So might we feel, should we our time bestow
To gain these secrets and these signs to know ;
Might question still if all the truth we found,
And firmly stood upon the certain ground ;
We might our title to the mystery dread,
And fear we drank not at the river-head.

Griggs and Gregorians here their meetings hold,
Convivial sects, and Bucks alert and bold :   350
A kind of Masons, but without their sign ;
The bonds of union—pleasure, song, and wine.
Man, a gregarious creature, loves to fly
Where he the trackings of the herd can spy ;
Still to be one with many he desires,
Although it leads him through the thorns and briers.
A few—but few—there are, who in the mind
Perpetual source of consolation find ;
The weaker many to the world will come,
For comforts seldom to be found from home.   360
When the faint hands no more a brimmer hold ;
When flannel-wreaths the useless limbs infold,
The breath impeded, and the bosom cold ;   [ )]
When half the pillow'd man the palsy chains,
And the blood falters in the bloated veins—
Then, as our friends no further aid supply
Than hope's cold phrase and courtesy's soft sigh,
We should that comfort for ourselves ensure,
Which friends could not, if we could friends procure.
Early in life, when we can laugh aloud,   370
There's something pleasant in a social crowd,
Who laugh with us—but will such joy remain,
When we lie struggling on the bed of pain ?
When our physician tells us with a sigh,
No more on hope and science to rely,
Life's staff is useless then ; with labouring breath
We pray for hope divine—the staff of death.
This is a scene which few companions grace,

THE BOROUGH

And where the heart's first favourites yield their place.
   Here all the aid of man to man must end,   380
Here mounts the soul to her eternal Friend ;
The tenderest love must here its tie resign,
And give th' aspiring heart to love divine.
   Men feel their weakness, and to numbers run,
Themselves to strengthen, or themselves to shun ;
But though to this our weakness may be prone,
Let's learn to live, for we must die, alone.

THE BOROUGH.

LETTER XI.

INNS.

All the comforts of life in a tavern are known,
'Tis his home who possesses not one of his own;
And to him who has rather too much of that one,
'Tis the house of a friend where he's welcome to run:
The instant you enter my door you're my lord,
With whose taste and whose pleasure I'm proud to accord;
And the louder you call and the longer you stay,
The more I am happy to serve and obey.

To the house of a friend if you're pleased to retire,
You must all things admit, you must all things admire;
You must pay with observance the price of your treat,
You must eat what is praised, and must praise what you eat:
But here you may come, and no tax we require,
You may loudly condemn what you greatly admire;
You may growl at our wishes and pains to excel,
And may snarl at the rascals who please you so well.

At your wish we attend, and confess that your speech
On the nation's affairs might the minister teach;
His views you may blame, and his measures oppose,
There's no tavern-treason—you're under the Rose:
Should rebellions arise in your own little state,
With me you may safely their consequence wait;
To recruit your lost spirits 'tis prudent to come,
And to fly to a friend when the devil's at home.

That I've faults is confess'd; but it won't be denied,
'Tis my interest the faults of my neighbours to hide;
If I've sometimes lent Scandal occasion to prate,
I've often conceal'd what she'd love to relate;
If to Justice's bar some have wander'd from mine,
'Twas because the dull rogues wouldn't stay by their wine;
And for brawls at my house, well the poet explains,
That men drink *shallow draughts*, and so madden their brains.

A difficult Subject for Poetry—Invocation of the Muse—Description of
the principal Inn and those of the first Class The large deserted
Tavern—Those of a second Order—Their Company—One of particular Description—A lower Kind of Public-Houses; yet distinguished among themselves—Houses on the Quays for Sailors—The
Green-Man: its Landlord, and the Adventure of his Marriage, &c.

THE BOROUGH.

LETTER XI.

INNS.

MUCH do I need, and therefore will I ask,
    A Muse to aid me in my present task ;
For then with special cause we beg for aid,
When of our subject we are most afraid :
Inns are this subject—'tis an ill-drawn lot ;
So, thou who gravely triflest, fail me not.
Fail not, but haste, and to my memory bring
Scenes yet unsung, which few would choose to sing :
Thou mad'st a Shilling splendid ; thou hast thrown
On humble themes the graces all thine own ;   10
By thee the Mistress of a village-school
Became a queen, enthroned upon her stool ;
And far beyond the rest thou gav'st to shine
Belinda's Lock—that deathless work was thine.
    Come, lend thy cheerful light, and give to please
These seats of revelry, these scenes of ease ;
Who sings of Inns much danger has to dread,
And needs assistance from the fountain-head.
    High in the street, o'erlooking all the place,
The rampant Lion shows his kingly face ;   20
His ample jaws extend from side to side,
His eyes are glaring, and his nostrils wide ;
In silver shag the sovereign form is dress'd ;
A mane horrific sweeps his ample chest ;
Elate with pride, he seems t' assert his reign,
And stands, the glory of his wide domain.

GEORGE CRABBE

Yet nothing dreadful to his friends the sight,
But sign and pledge of welcome and delight:
To him the noblest guest the town detains
Flies for repast, and in his court remains;　　　30
Him too the crowd with longing looks admire,
Sigh for his joys, and modestly retire;
Here not a comfort shall to them be lost
Who never ask or never feel the cost.
The ample yards on either side contain
Buildings where order and distinction reign;—
The splendid carriage of the wealthier guest,
The ready chaise and driver smartly dress'd;
Whiskeys and gigs and curricles are there,
And high-fed prancers, many a raw-boned pair.　　40
On all without a lordly host sustains
The care of empire, and observant reigns;
The parting guest beholds him at his side,
With pomp obsequious, bending in his pride;
Round all the place his eyes all objects meet,
Attentive, silent, civil, and discreet.
O'er all within the lady-hostess rules,
Her bar she governs, and her kitchen schools;
To every guest th' appropriate speech is made,
And every duty with distinction paid:　　50
Respectful, easy, pleasant, or polite—
"Your honour's servant—Mister Smith, good night."
Next, but not near, yet honour'd through the town,
There swing, incongruous pair! the Bear and Crown;
That Crown suspended gems and ribands deck,
A golden chain hangs o'er that furry neck.
Unlike the nobler beast, the Bear is bound,
And with the Crown so near him, scowls uncrown'd;
Less his dominion, but alert are all
Without, within, and ready for the call;　　60
Smart lads and light run nimbly here and there,
Nor for neglected duties mourns the Bear.
To his retreats, on the election-day,
The losing party found their silent way;
There they partook of each consoling good,
Like him uncrown'd, like him in sullen mood—

THE BOROUGH

Threat'ning, but bound.—Here meet a social kind,
Our various clubs, for various cause combined;
Nor has he pride, but thankful takes as gain
The dew-drops shaken from the Lion's mane: 70
A thriving couple here their skill display,
And share the profits of no vulgar sway.
  Third in our Borough's list appears the sign
Of a fair queen—the gracious Caroline;
But in decay—each feature in the face
Has stain of Time, and token of disgrace.
The storm of winter, and the summer-sun,
Have on that form their equal mischief done;
The features now are all disfigured seen,
And not one charm adorns th' insulted queen: 80
To this poor face was never paint applied,
Th' unseemly work of cruel Time to hide;
Here we may rightly such neglect upbraid;
Paint on such faces is by prudence laid.
Large the domain, but all within combine
To correspond with the dishonour'd sign;
And all around dilapidates; you call—
But none replies—they're inattentive all.
At length a ruin'd stable holds your steed,
While you through large and dirty rooms proceed,   90
Spacious and cold; a proof they once had been
In honour—now magnificently mean;
Till in some small half-furnish'd room you rest,
Whose dying fire denotes it had a guest.
In those you pass'd where former splendour reign'd,
You saw the carpets torn, the paper stain'd;
Squares of discordant glass in windows fix'd,
And paper oil'd in many a space betwixt;
A soil'd and broken sconce; a mirror crack'd,
With table underpropp'd, and chairs new-back'd;   100
A marble side-slab with ten thousand stains,
And all an ancient tavern's poor remains.
  With much entreaty, they your food prepare,
And acid wine afford, with meagre fare;
Heartless you sup; and when a dozen times
You've read the fractured window's senseless rhymes;

GEORGE CRABBE

Have been assured that Phœbe Green was fair,
And Peter Jackson took his supper there :
You reach a chilling chamber, where you dread
Damps, hot or cold, from a tremendous bed ;   110
Late comes your sleep, and you are waken'd soon
By rustling tatters of the old festoon.
O'er this large building, thus by time defaced,
A servile couple has its owner placed,
Who, not unmindful that its style is large,
To lost magnificence adapt their charge.
Thus an old beauty, who has long declined,
Keeps former dues and dignity in mind ;
And wills that all attention should be paid
For graces vanish'd and for charms decay'd.   120
Few years have pass'd, since brightly 'cross the way
Lights from each window shot the lengthen'd ray,
And busy looks in every face were seen,
Through the warm precincts of the reigning Queen.
There fires inviting blazed, and all around
Was heard the tinkling bells' seducing sound ;
The nimble waiters to that sound from far
Sprang to the call, then hasten'd to the bar ;
Where a glad priestess of the temple sway'd,
The most obedient, and the most obey'd ;   130
Rosy and round, adorn'd in crimson vest,
And flaming ribands at her ample breast,
She, skill'd like Circe, tried her guests to move
With looks of welcome and with words of love ;
And such her potent charms, that men unwise
Were soon transform'd and fitted for the sties.
Her port in bottles stood, a well-stain'd row,
Drawn for the evening from the pipe below ;
Three powerful spirits fill'd a parted case ;
Some cordial-bottles stood in secret place ;   140
Fair acid fruits in nets above were seen ;
Her plate was splendid, and her glasses clean ;
Basins and bowls were ready on the stand,
And measures clatter'd in her powerful hand.
Inferior houses now our notice claim,
But who shall deal them their appropriate fame ?

390

THE BOROUGH

Who shall the nice, yet known distinction, tell,
Between the peal complete and single bell?
Determine, ye, who on your shining nags
Wear oil-skin beavers and bear seal-skin bags;   150
Or ye, grave topers, who with coy delight
Snugly enjoy the sweetness of the night;
Ye travellers all, superior inns denied
By moderate purse, the low by decent pride:
Come and determine,—will ye take your place
At the *full* orb, or *half* the lunar face?
With the Black-Boy or Angel will ye dine?
Will ye approve the Fountain or the Vine?
Horses the *white* or *black* will ye prefer?
The Silver-Swan, or swan opposed to her—   160
Rare bird! whose form the raven-plumage decks,
And graceful curve her three alluring necks?
All these a decent entertainment give,
And by their comforts comfortably live.
Shall I pass by the Boar?—there are who cry,
"Beware the Boar," and pass determined by:
Those dreadful tusks, those little peering eyes
And churning chaps, are tokens to the wise.
There dwells a kind old aunt, and there you see
Some kind young nieces in her company—   170
Poor village nieces, whom the tender dame
Invites to town, and gives their beauty fame;
The grateful sisters feel th' important aid,
And the good aunt is flatter'd and repaid.
What though it may some cool observers strike,
That such fair sisters should be so unlike;
That still another and another comes,
And at the matron's table smiles and blooms;
That all appear as if they meant to stay
Time undefined, nor name a parting day;   180
And yet, though all are valued, all are dear,
Causeless, they go, and seldom more appear:
Yet—let Suspicion hide her odious. head,
And Scandal vengeance from a burgess dread—
A pious friend, who with the ancient dame
At sober cribbage takes an evening game;

GEORGE CRABBE

His cup beside him, through their play he quaffs,
And oft renews, and innocently laughs;
Or, growing serious, to the text resorts,
And from the Sunday-sermon makes reports; 190
While all, with grateful glee, his wish attend,
A grave protector and a powerful friend.
But Slander says, who indistinctly sees,
Once he was caught with Silvia on his knees—
A cautious burgess with a careful wife
To be so caught!—'tis false, upon my life.
  Next are a lower kind, yet not so low
But they, among them, their distinctions know;
And, when a thriving landlord aims so high
As to exchange the Chequer for the Pye, 200
Or from Duke William to the Dog repairs,
He takes a finer coat and fiercer airs.
  Pleased with his power, the poor man loves to say
What favourite inn shall share his evening's pay;
Where he shall sit the social hour, and lose
His past day's labours and his next day's views.
Our seamen too have choice: one takes a trip
In the warm cabin of his favourite ship;
And on the morrow in the humbler boat
He rows, till fancy feels herself afloat; 210
Can he the sign—Three Jolly Sailors pass,
Who hears a fiddle and who sees a lass?
The Anchor too affords the seaman joys,
In small smoked room, all clamour, crowd, and noise;
Where a curved settle half surrounds the fire,
Where fifty voices purl and punch require.
They come for pleasure in their leisure hour,
And they enjoy it to their utmost power;
Standing they drink, they swearing smoke, while all
Call or make ready for a second call: 220
There is no time for trifling—" Do ye see?
"We drink and drub the French extempore."
  See! round the room, on every beam and balk,
Are mingled scrolls of hieroglyphic chalk;
Yet nothing heeded—would one stroke suffice
To blot out all, here honour is too nice—

392

THE BOROUGH

"Let knavish landsmen think such dirty things,
"We're British tars, and British tars are kings."
But the Green-Man shall I pass by unsung,
Which mine own James upon his sign-post hung?   230
His sign, his image,—for he once was seen
A squire's attendant, clad in keeper's green;
Ere yet, with wages more, and honour less,
He stood behind me in a graver dress.
 James in an evil hour went forth to woo
Young Juliet Hart, and was her Romeo:
They'd seen the play, and thought it vastly sweet
For two young lovers by the moon to meet;
The nymph was gentle, of her favours free,
Ev'n at a word—no Rosalind was she;   240
Nor, like that other Juliet, tried his truth
With—"Be thy purpose marriage, gentle youth?"
But him received, and heard his tender tale,
When sang the lark, and when the nightingale:
So in few months the generous lass was seen
I' the way that all the Capulets had been.
 Then first repentance sèized the amorous man,
And—shame on love—he reason'd and he ran;
The thoughtful Romeo trembled for his purse,
And the sad sounds, "for better and for worse."   250
 Yet could the lover not so far withdraw,
But he was haunted both by love and law:
Now law dismay'd him as he view'd its fangs,
Now pity seized him for his Juliet's pangs;
Then thoughts of justice and some dread of jail,
Where all would blame him and where none might bail;
These drew him back, till Juliet's hut appear'd,
Where love had drawn him when he should have fear'd.
 There sat the father in his wicker throne,
Uttering his curses in tremendous tone;   260
With foulest names his daughter he reviled,
And look'd a very Herod at the child:
Nor was she patient, but with equal scorn,
Bade him remember when his Joe was born:
Then rose the mother, eager to begin
Her plea for frailty, when the swain came in.

393

GEORGE CRABBE

To him she turn'd, and other theme began,
Show'd him his boy, and bade him be a man—
"An honest man, who, when he breaks the laws,
"Will make a woman honest if there's cause." 270
With lengthen'd speech she proved what came to pass
Was no reflection on a loving lass:
"If she your love as wife and mother claim,
"What can it matter which was first the name?
"But 'tis most base, 'tis perjury and theft,
"When a lost girl is like a widow left;
"The rogue who ruins"—here the father found
His spouse was treading on forbidden ground.
    "That's not the point," quoth he,—"I don't suppose
"My good friend Fletcher to be one of those; 280
"What's done amiss he'll mend in proper time—
"I hate to hear of villany and crime.
"'Twas my misfortune, in the days of youth,
"To find two lasses pleading for my truth;
"The case was hard, I would with all my soul
"Have wedded both, but law is our control;
"So one I took, and when we gain'd a home,
"Her friend agreed—what could she more?—to come;
"And when she found that I'd a widow'd bed,
"Me she desired—what could I less?—to wed. 290
"An easier case is yours: you've not the smart
"That two fond pleaders cause in one man's heart;
"You've not to wait from year to year distress'd,
"Before your conscience can be laid at rest;
"There smiles your bride, there sprawls your new-born son,
"—A ring, a licence, and the thing is done."
    "My loving James,"—the lass began her plea,
"I'll make thy reason take a part with me.
"Had I been froward, skittish, or unkind,
"Or to thy person or thy passion blind; 300
"Had I refused, when 'twas thy part to pray,
"Or put thee off with promise and delay;
"Thou might'st in justice and in conscience fly,
"Denying her who taught thee to deny:
"But, James, with me thou hadst an easier task,
"Bonds and conditions I forbore to ask;

394

THE BOROUGH

"I laid no traps for thee, no plots or plans,
"Nor marriage named by licence or by banns;
"Nor would I now the parson's aid employ,
"But for this cause"—and up she held her boy.   310
  Motives like these could heart of flesh resist?
James took the infant and in triumph kiss'd;
Then to his mother's arms the child restored,
Made his proud speech, and pledged his worthy word.
  "Three times at church our banns shall publish'd be,
"Thy health be drunk in bumpers three times three;
"And thou shalt grace (bedeck'd in garments gay)
"The christening-dinner on the wedding day."
  James at my door then made his parting bow,
Took the Green-Man, and is a master now.   320

THE BOROUGH.

LETTER XII.

PLAYERS.

These are monarchs none respect;
   Heroes, yet an humbled crew;
Nobles, whom the crowd correct;
   Wealthy men, whom duns pursue;
Beauties, shrinking from the view
   Of the day's detecting eye;
Lovers, who with much ado
   Long-forsaken damsels woo,
And heave the ill-feign'd sigh.

These are misers, craving means
   Of existence through the day;
Famous scholars, conning scenes
   Of a dull bewildering play;
Ragged beaux and misses grey,
   Whom the rabble praise and blame;
Proud and mean, and sad and gay,
   Toiling after ease, are they,
Infamous[1], and boasting fame.

Players arrive in the Borough—Welcomed by their former Friends—Are better fitted for Comic than Tragic Scenes: yet better approved in the latter by one Part of their Audience—Their general Character and Pleasantry—Particular Distresses and Labours—Their Fortitude and Patience—A private Rehearsal—The Vanity of the aged Actress —A Heroine from the Milliner's Shop—A deluded Tradesman—Of what Persons the Company is composed—Character and Adventures of Frederick Thompson.

[1] Strolling players are thus held in a legal sense.

THE BOROUGH.

LETTER XII.

PLAYERS.

DRAWN by the annual call, we now behold
    Our troop dramatic, heroes known of old,
And those, since last they march'd, inlisted and enroll'd :   [ ]]
Mounted on hacks or borne in waggons some,
The rest on foot (the humbler brethren) come.
Three favour'd places, an unequal time,
Join to support this company sublime :
Ours for the longer period—see how light
Yon parties move, their former friends in sight,
Whose claims are all allow'd, and friendship glads the
    night.   10 [ ]]
Now public rooms shall sound with words divine,
And private lodgings hear how heroes shine ;
No talk of pay shall yet on pleasure steal,
But kindest welcome bless the friendly meal ;
While o'er the social jug and decent cheer,
Shall be described the fortunes of the year.
    Peruse these bills, and see what each can do,—
Behold ! the prince, the slave, the monk, the Jew ;
Change but the garment, and they'll all engage
To take each part, and act in every age.   20
Cull'd from all houses, what a house are they !
Swept from all barns, our borough-critics say ;
But with some portion of a critic's ire,
We all endure them ; there are some admire :
They might have praise, confined to farce alone ;

GEORGE CRABBE

Full well they grin—they should not try to groan;
But then our servants' and our seamen's wives
Love all that rant and rapture as their lives;
He who 'Squire Richard's part could well sustain,
Finds as King Richard he must roar amain,   30
"My horse! my horse!"—Lo! now to their abodes,
Come lords and lovers, empresses and gods.
The master-mover of these scenes has made
No trifling gain in this adventurous trade;—
Trade we may term it, for he duly buys
Arms out of use and undirected eyes;
These he instructs, and guides them as he can,
And vends each night the manufactured man.
Long as our custom lasts, they gladly stay,
Then strike their tents, like Tartars! and away!   40
The place grows bare where they too long remain,
But grass will rise ere they return again.
    Children of Thespis, welcome! knights and queens!
Counts! barons! beauties! when before your scenes,
And mighty monarchs thund'ring from your throne;
Then step behind, and all your glory's gone:
Of crown and palace, throne and guards bereft,
The pomp is vanish'd, and the care is left.
Yet strong and lively is the joy they feel,
When the full house secures the plenteous meal;   50
Flatt'ring and flatter'd, each attempts to raise
A brother's merits for a brother's praise:
For never hero shows a prouder heart,
Than he who proudly acts a hero's part—
Nor without cause; the boards, we know, can yield
Place for fierce contest, like the tented field.
    Graceful to tread the stage, to be in turn
The prince we honour, and the knave we spurn;
Bravely to bear the tumult of the crowd,
The hiss tremendous, and the censure loud: 60
These are their parts—and he who these sustains
Deserves some praise and profit for his pains.
Heroes at least of gentler kind are they,
Against whose swords no weeping widows pray,
No blood their fury sheds, nor havoc marks their way. [ ]]

398

THE BOROUGH

Sad happy race! soon raised and soon depress'd;
Your days all pass'd in jeopardy and jest;
Poor without prudence, with afflictions vain,
Not warn'd by misery, not enrich'd by gain;
Whom justice pitying, chides from place to place,　　70
A wandering, careless, wretched, merry race;
Who cheerful looks assume, and play the parts
Of happy rovers with repining hearts;
Then cast off care, and in the mimic pain
Of tragic wo, feel spirits light and vain,
Distress and hope—the mind's, the body's wear,
The man's affliction, and the actor's tear:
Alternate times of fasting and excess
Are yours, ye smiling children of distress.
　　Slaves though ye be, your wandering freedom seems,　80)
And with your varying views and restless schemes,　　}
Your griefs are transient, as your joys are dreams.　　[ )]
　　Yet keen those griefs—ah! what avail thy charms,
Fair Juliet! what that infant in thine arms;
What those heroic lines thy patience learns,
What all the aid thy present Romeo earns,
Whilst thou art crowded in that lumbering wain,
With all thy plaintive sisters to complain?
　　Nor is there lack of labour.—To rehearse,
Day after day, poor scraps of prose and verse;　　90
To bear each other's spirit, pride, and spite;
To hide in rant the heart-ache of the night;
To dress in gaudy patch-work, and to force
The mind to think on the appointed course:
This is laborious, and may be defined
The bootless labour of the thriftless mind.
　　There is a veteran dame—I see her stand
Intent and pensive with her book in hand;
Awhile her thoughts she forces on her part,
Then dwells on objects nearer to the heart;　　100
Across the room she paces, gets her tone,
And fits her features for the Danish throne;
To-night a queen—I mark her motion slow,
I hear her speech, and Hamlet's mother know.
　　Methinks 'tis pitiful to see her try

GEORGE CRABBE

For strength of arms and energy of eye;
With vigour lost, and spirits worn away,
Her pomp and pride she labours to display;
And when awhile she 's tried her part to act,
To find her thoughts arrested by some fact;
When struggles more and more severe are seen
In the plain actress than the Danish queen;—
At length she feels her part, she finds delight,
And fancies all the plaudits of the night:
Old as she is, she smiles at every speech,
And thinks no youthful part beyond her reach.
But, as the mist of vanity again
Is blown away by press of present pain,
Sad and in doubt she to her purse applies
For cause of comfort, where no comfort lies;
Then to her task she sighing turns again,—
"Oh! Hamlet, thou hast cleft my heart in twain!"
    And who that poor, consumptive, wither'd thing,
Who strains her slender throat and strives to sing?
Panting for breath, and forced her voice to drop,
And far unlike the inmate of the shop,
Where she, in youth and health, alert and gay,
Laugh'd off at night the labours of the day;
With novels, verses, fancy's fertile powers,
And sister-converse pass'd the evening-hours;
But Cynthia's soul was soft, her wishes strong,
Her judgment weak, and her conclusions wrong.
The morning-call and counter were her dread,
And her contempt the needle and the thread;
But, when she read a gentle damsel's part,
Her wo, her wish—she had them all by heart.
    At length the hero of the boards drew nigh,
Who spake of love till sigh re-echo'd sigh;
He told in honey'd words his deathless flame,
And she his own by tender vows became;
Nor ring nor licence needed souls so fond,
Alphonso's passion was his Cynthia's bond:
And thus the simple girl, to shame betray'd,
Sinks to the grave forsaken and dismay'd.
    Sick without pity, sorrowing without hope,

110

120

130

140

THE BOROUGH

See her, the grief and scandal of the troop;
A wretched martyr to a childish pride,
Her wo insulted, and her praise denied;
Her humble talents, though derided, used,
Her prospects lost, her confidence abused;   150
All that remains—for she not long can brave
Increase of evils—is an early grave.
   Ye gentle Cynthias of the shop, take heed
What dreams ye cherish, and what books ye read.
   A decent sum had Peter Nottage made,
By joining bricks—to him a thriving trade.
Of his employment master and his wife,
This humble tradesman led a lordly life;
The house of kings and heroes lack'd repairs,
And Peter, though reluctant, served the players: 160
Connected thus, he heard in way polite,—
"Come, Master Nottage, see us play to-night."
At first 'twas folly, nonsense, idle stuff,
But seen for nothing it grew well enough;
And better now—now best, and every night
In this fool's paradise he drank delight;
And, as he felt the bliss, he wish'd to know
Whence all this rapture and these joys could flow;
For, if the seeing could such pleasure bring,
What must the feeling?—feeling like a king?   170
   In vain his wife, his uncle, and his friend,
Cried—"Peter! Peter! let such follies end;
" 'Tis well enough these vagabonds to see,
" But would you partner with a showman be?"
   "Showman!" said Peter, "did not Quin and Clive,
" And Roscius-Garrick, by the science thrive?
"Showman!—'tis scandal; I'm by genius led
" To join a class who've Shakspeare at their head."
   Poor Peter thus by easy steps became
A dreaming candidate for scenic fame;   180
And, after years consumed, infirm and poor,
He sits and takes the tickets at the door.
   Of various men these marching troops are made—
Pen-spurning clerks, and lads contemning trade;
Waiters and servants by confinement teased,

Crabbe   cc   401

And youths of wealth by dissipation eased;
With feeling nymphs, who, such resource at hand,
Scorn to obey the rigour of command;
Some, who from higher views by vice are won,
And some of either sex by love undone;   190
The greater part lamenting as their fall
What some an honour and advancement call.

There are who names in shame or fear assume,
And hence our Bevilles and our Savilles come:
It honours him, from tailor's board kick'd down,
As Mister Dormer to amuse the town;
Falling, he rises: but a kind there are
Who dwell on former prospects, and despair;
Justly, but vainly, they their fate deplore,
And mourn their fall who fell to rise no more.   200
Our merchant Thompson, with his sons around,
Most mind and talent in his Frederick found:
He was so lively, that his mother knew,
If he were taught, that honour must ensue;
The father's views were in a different line;
But if at college he were sure to shine,
Then should he go—to prosper, who could doubt—
When school-boy stigmas would be all wash'd out;
For there were marks upon his youthful face,
'Twixt vice and error—a neglected case: 210
These would submit to skill; a little time,
And none could trace the error or the crime;
Then let him go, and once at college, he
Might choose his station—what would Frederick be?
'Twas soon determined.—He could not descend
To pedant-laws and lectures without end;
And then the chapel—night and morn to pray,
Or mulct and threaten'd if he kept away;
No! not to be a bishop—so he swore,
And at his college he was seen no more.   220
His debts all paid, the father with a sigh,
Placed him in office—"Do, my Frederick, try;
"Confine thyself a few short months, and then——"
He tried a fortnight, and threw down the pen.
Again demands were hush'd: "My son, you're free,

THE BOROUGH

"But you're unsettled ; take your chance at sea : "
So in few days the midshipman equipp'd,
Received the mother's blessing and was shipp'd.
  Hard was her fortune ! soon compell'd to meet
The wretched stripling staggering through the street ;   230
For, rash, impetuous, insolent and vain,
The captain sent him to his friends again.
About the borough roved th' unhappy boy,
And ate the bread of every chance-employ ;
Of friends he borrow'd, and the parents yet
In secret fondness authorised the debt ;
The younger sister, still a child, was taught
To give with feign'd affright the pittance sought ;
For now the father cried—"It is too late
"For trial more—I leave him to his fate "—   240
Yet left him not ; and with a kind of joy
The mother heard of her desponding boy :
At length he sicken'd, and he found, when sick,
All aid was ready, all attendance quick ;
A fever seized him, and at once was lost
The thought of trespass, error, crime and cost ;
Th' indulgent parents knelt beside the youth ;
They heard his promise and believed his truth ;
And, when the danger lessen'd on their view,
They cast off doubt, and hope assurance grew ;—   250
Nursed by his sisters, cherish'd by his sire,
Begg'd to be glad, encouraged to aspire,
His life, they said, would now all care repay,
And he might date his prospects from that day ;
A son, a brother to his home received,
They hoped for all things, and in all believed.
  And now will pardon, comfort, kindness, draw
The youth from vice ? will honour, duty, law ?
Alas ! not all : the more the trials lent,
The less he seem'd to ponder and repent ;   260
Headstrong, determined in his own career,
He thought reproof unjust and truth severe ;
The soul's disease was to its crisis come,
He first abused and then abjured his home ;
And when he chose a vagabond to be,

GEORGE CRABBE

He made his shame his glory—"I'll be free."
Friends, parents, relatives, hope, reason, love,
With anxious ardour for that empire strove;
In vain their strife, in vain the means applied,
They had no comfort, but that all were tried;   270
One strong vain trial made, the mind to move,
Was the last effort of parental love.
Ev'n then he watch'd his father from his home,
And to his mother would for pity come,
Where, as he made her tender terrors rise,
He talk'd of death, and threaten'd for supplies.
Against a youth so vicious and undone
All hearts were closed, and every door but one:
The players received him; they with open heart
Gave him his portion and assign'd his part;   280
And ere three days were added to his life,
He found a home, a duty, and a wife.
His present friends, though they were nothing nice,
Nor ask'd how vicious he, or what his vice,
Still they expected he should now attend
To the joint duty as an useful friend;
The leader too declared, with frown severe,
That none should pawn a robe that kings might wear;
And much it moved him, when he Hamlet play'd,
To see his Father's Ghost so drunken made.   290
Then too the temper, the unbending pride
Of this ally would no reproof abide:—
So, leaving these, he march'd away and join'd
Another troop, and other goods purloin'd;
And other characters, both gay and sage,
Sober and sad, made stagger on the stage;
Then to rebuke, with arrogant disdain,
He gave abuse, and sought a home again.
Thus changing scenes, but with unchanging vice,
Engaged by many, but with no one twice: 300
Of this, a last and poor resource, bereft,
He to himself, unhappy guide! was left—
And who shall say where guided? to what seats
Of starving villany? of thieves and cheats?
In that sad time, of many a dismal scene

404

Had he a witness (not inactive) been;
Had leagued with petty pilferers, and had crept,
Where of each sex degraded numbers slept.
With such associates he was long allied,
Where his capacity for ill was tried,   310
And, that once lost, the wretch was cast aside;   [ ]
For now, though willing with the worst to act,
He wanted powers for an important fact;
And, while he felt as lawless spirits feel,
His hand was palsied, and he couldn't steal.
  By these rejected, is there lot so strange,
So low, that he could suffer by the change?
Yes! the new station as a fall we judge—
He now became the harlot's humble drudge,
Their drudge in common: they combined to save   320
Awhile from starving their submissive slave;
For now his spirit left him, and his pride,
His scorn, his rancour, and resentment died;
Few were his feelings—but the keenest these,
The rage of hunger, and the sigh for ease;
He who abused indulgence, now became
By want subservient and by misery tame;
A slave, he begg'd forbearance; bent with pain,
He shunn'd the blow—"Ah! strike me not again."
  Thus was he found: the master of a hoy   330
Saw the sad wretch, whom he had known a boy
At first in doubt; but Frederick laid aside
All shame, and humbly for his aid applied.
He, tamed and smitten with the storms gone by,
Look'd for compassion through one living eye,
And stretch'd th' unpalsied hand; the seaman felt
His honest heart with gentle pity melt,   [ ]
And his small boon with cheerful frankness dealt;
Then made inquiries of th' unhappy youth,
Who told, nor shame forbade him, all the truth.   340
  "Young Frederick Thompson to a chandler's shop
"By harlots order'd and afraid to stop!—
"What! our good merchant's favourite to be seen
"In state so loathsome and in dress so mean?"—
  So thought the seaman as he bade adieu,

And, when in port, related all he knew.
But time was lost, inquiry came too late,
Those whom he served knew nothing of his fate;
No! they had seized on what the sailor gave,
Nor bore resistance from their abject slave;   350
The spoil obtain'd, they cast him from the door,
Robb'd, beaten, hungry, pain'd, diseased and poor.
Then nature (pointing to the only spot
Which still had comfort for so dire a lot,)
Although so feeble, led him on the way,
And hope look'd forward to a happier day.
He thought, poor prodigal! a father yet
His woes would pity and his crimes forget;
Nor had he brother who with speech severe
Would check the pity or refrain the tear: 360
A lighter spirit in his bosom rose,
As near the road he sought an hour's repose.
And there he found it: he had left the town,
But buildings yet were scatter'd up and down;
To one of these, half-ruin'd and half-built,
Was traced this child of wretchedness and guilt;
There on the remnant of a beggar's vest,
Thrown by in scorn, the sufferer sought for rest;
There was this scene of vice and wo to close,
And there the wretched body found repose.   370

THE BOROUGH.

LETTER XIII.

THE ALMS-HOUSE AND TRUSTEES.

Do good by stealth, and blush to find it fame.
  [*Pope, Epilogue to the Satires*, Dialogue I., v. 136.]

There are a sort of men whose visages
Do cream and mantle like a standing [pond,]
And do a wilful stillness entertain,
With purpose to be dress'd in an opinion[. . .]
As who should say, "I am Sir Oracle,
"And when I ope my lips, let no dog bark!"
    Merchant of Venice [Act I. Sc. i. vv. 88–94].

Sum felix; quis enim neget? felixque manebo;
Hoc quoque quis dubitet? Tutum me copia fecit.

The frugal Merchant—Rivalship in Modes of Frugality—Private Exceptions to the general Manners—Alms-House built—Its Description —Founder dies—Six Trustees—Sir Denys Brand, a Principal—His Eulogium in the Chronicles of the Day—Truth reckoned invidious on these Occasions—An Explanation of the Magnanimity and Wisdom of Sir Denys—His Kinds of Moderation and Humility—Laughton, his Successor, a planning, ambitious, wealthy Man—Advancement in Life his perpetual Object, and all Things made the Means of it— His Idea of Falsehood—His Resentment dangerous: how removed— Success produces Love of Flattery: his daily Gratification—His Merits and Acts of Kindness—His proper Choice of Alms-Men—In this Respect meritorious—His Predecessor not so cautious.

THE BOROUGH.

LETTER XIII.

THE ALMS-HOUSE AND TRUSTEES.

LEAVE now our streets, and in yon plain behold
   Those pleasant seats for the reduced and old ;
A merchant's gift, whose wife and children died,
When he to saving all his powers applied ;
He wore his coat till bare was every thread,
And with the meanest fare his body fed.
He had a female cousin, who with care
Walk'd in his steps and learn'd of him to spare ;
With emulation and success they strove,
Improving still, still seeking to improve,   10
As if that useful knowledge they would gain—
How little food would human life sustain :
No pauper came their table's crums to crave ;
Scraping they lived, but not a scrap they gave :
When beggars saw the frugal merchant pass,
It moved their pity, and they said, " Alas !
" Hard is thy fate, my brother," and they felt
A beggar's pride as they that pity dealt :
The dogs, who learn of man to scorn the poor,
Bark'd him away from ev'ry decent door ;   20
While they who saw him bare, but thought him rich,
To show respect or scorn, they knew not which.
  But while our merchant seem'd so base and mean,
He had his wanderings, sometimes, " not unseen ; "
To give in secret was a favourite act,
Yet more than once they took him in the fact.
To scenes of various wo he nightly went,

And serious sums in healing misery spent;
Oft has he cheer'd the wretched, at a rate
For which he daily might have dined on plate;   30
He has been seen—his hair all silver-white,
Shaking and shining—as he stole by night,
To feed unenvied on his still delight.   [ ]
A two-fold taste he had: to give and spare,
Both were his duties, and had equal care;
It was his joy, to sit alone and fast,
Then send a widow and her boys repast.
Tears in his eyes would, spite of him, appear,
But he from other eyes has kept the tear:
All in a wint'ry night from far he came,   40
To soothe the sorrows of a suff'ring dame;
Whose husband robb'd him, and to whom he meant
A ling'ring, but reforming punishment.
Home then he walk'd, and found his anger rise,
When fire and rush-light met his troubled eyes;
But, these extinguish'd, and his prayer address'd
To Heaven in hope, he calmly sank to rest.
    His seventieth year was pass'd, and then was seen
A building rising on the northern green;
There was no blinding all his neighbours' eyes,   50
Or surely no one would have seen it rise.
Twelve rooms contiguous stood, and six were near;
There men were placed, and sober matrons here;
There were behind small useful gardens made,
Benches before, and trees to give them shade;
In the first room were seen, above, below,
Some marks of taste, a few attempts at show;
The founder's picture and his arms were there
(Not till he left us), and an elbow'd chair;
There, 'mid these signs of his superior place,   60
Sat the mild ruler of this humble race.
    Within the row are men who strove in vain,
Through years of trouble, wealth and ease to gain;
Less must they have than an appointed sum,
And freemen been, or hither must not come;
They should be decent and command respect
(Though needing fortune,) whom these doors protect,

And should for thirty dismal years have tried
For peace unfelt and competence denied.
   Strange, that o'er men thus train'd in sorrow's school,   70
Power must be held, and they must live by rule !
Infirm, corrected by misfortunes, old,
Their habits settled and their passions cold ;
Of health, wealth, power, and worldly cares, bereft,
Still must they not at liberty be left ;
There must be one to rule them, to restrain
And guide the movements of his erring train.
   If then control imperious, check severe,
Be needed where such reverend men appear ;
To what would youth, without such checks, aspire,   80
Free the wild wish, uncurb'd the strong desire ?
And where (in college or in camp) they found
The heart ungovern'd and the hand unbound ?
   His house endow'd, the generous man resign'd
All power to rule, nay power of choice declined ;
He and the female saint survived to view
Their work complete, and bade the world adieu !
   Six are the guardians of this happy seat,
And one presides when they on business meet ;
As each expires, the five a brother choose ;   90
Nor would Sir Denys Brand the charge refuse ;
True, 'twas beneath him, "but to do men good
"Was motive never by his heart withstood."
He too is gone, and they again must strive
To find a man in whom his gifts survive.
   Now, in the various records of the dead,
Thy worth, Sir Denys, shall be weigh'd and read ;
There we the glory of thy house shall trace,
With each alliance of thy noble race.
   Yes ! here we have him !—"Came in William's reign   100
" The Norman-Brand, the blood without a stain ;
"From the fierce Dane and ruder Saxon clear,
"Pict, Irish, Scot, or Cambrian mountaineer ;
"But the pure Norman was the sacred spring,
"And he, Sir Denys, was in heart a king :
"Erect in person and so firm in soul,
"Fortune he seem'd to govern and control ;

THE BOROUGH

"Generous as he who gives his all away,
"Prudent as one who toils for weekly pay;
"In him all merits were decreed to meet—   110
"Sincere though cautious, frank and yet discreet;
"Just all his dealings, faithful every word;
"His passions' master, and his temper's lord."
    Yet more, kind dealers in decaying fame?
His magnanimity you next proclaim;
You give him learning, join'd with sound good sense,
And match his wealth with his benevolence;
What hides the multitude of sins, you add—
Yet seem to doubt if sins he ever had.
    Poor honest Truth! thou writ'st of living men,   120
And art a railer and detractor then;
They die, again to be described, and now
A foe to merit and mankind art thou!
    Why banish truth? it injures not the dead;
It aids not them with flattery to be fed;
And, when mankind such perfect pictures view,
They copy less, the more they think them true.
Let us a mortal as he was behold,
And see the dross adhering to the gold;
When we the errors of the virtuous state,   130
Then erring men their worth may emulate.
    View then this picture of a noble mind:
Let him be wise, magnanimous, and kind;
What was the wisdom? Was it not the frown
That keeps all question, all inquiry down?
His words were powerful and decisive all;
But his slow reasons came for no man's call.
"'Tis thus," he cried, no doubt with kind intent,
To give results and spare all argument.—
    "Let it be spared—all men at least agree   140
"Sir Denys Brand had magnanimity:
"His were no vulgar charities; none saw
"Him like the merchant to the hut withdraw;
"He left to meaner minds the simple deed,
"By which the houseless rest, the hungry feed;
"His was a public bounty vast and grand;
"'Twas not in him to work with viewless hand;

"He raised the room that towers above the street,
"A public room where grateful parties meet;
"He first the life-boat plann'd; to him the place   150
"Is deep in debt—'twas he reviv'd the race;
"To every public act this hearty friend
"Would give with freedom or with frankness lend;
"His money built the jail, nor prisoner yet
"Sits at his ease, but he must feel the debt;
"To these let candour add his vast display—
"Around his mansion all is grand and gay,
"And this is bounty with the name of pay."   [ ]]
    I grant the whole, nor from one deed retract,
But wish recorded too the private act;   160
All these were great, but still our hearts approve
Those simpler tokens of the christian love;
'Twould give me joy some gracious deed to meet,
That has not call'd for glory through the street.
Who felt for many, could not always shun,
In some soft moment, to be kind to one;
And yet they tell us, when Sir Denys died,
That not a widow in the Borough sigh'd;
Great were his gifts, his mighty heart I own,
But why describe what all the world has known?   170
    The rest is petty pride, the useless art
Of a vain mind to hide a swelling heart.
Small was his private room; men found him there
By a plain table, on a paltry chair;
A wretched floor-cloth, and some prints around,
The easy purchase of a single pound:
These humble trifles and that study small
Make a strong contrast with the servants' hall;
There barely comfort, here a proud excess,
The pompous seat of pamper'd idleness,   180
Where the sleek rogues with one consent declare,
They would not live upon his honour's fare.
He daily took but one half-hour to dine,
On one poor dish and some three sips of wine;
Then he'd abuse them for their sumptuous feasts,
And say, "My friends! you make yourselves like beasts;
"One dish suffices any man to dine,

THE BOROUGH

"But you are greedy as a herd of swine;
"Learn to be temperate."—Had they dared t' obey,
He would have praised and turn'd them all away.　190
　Friends met Sir Denys riding in his ground,
And there the meekness of his spirit found :
For that grey coat, not new for many a year,
Hides all that would like decent dress appear;
An old brown pony 'twas his will to ride,
Who shuffled onward, and from side to side;
A five-pound purchase, but so fat and sleek,
His very plenty made the creature weak.
　"Sir Denys Brand! and on so poor a steed!"—
"Poor! it may be—such things I never heed:"　200
And who that youth behind, of pleasant mien,
Equipp'd as one who wishes to be seen,
Upon a horse, twice victor for a plate,
A noble hunter, bought at dearest rate?—
Him the lad, fearing, yet resolved to guide,
He curbs his spirit, while he strokes his pride.
　"A handsome youth, Sir Denys; and a horse
"Of finer figure never trod the course—
"Yours, without question?"—"Yes! I think, a groom
"Bought me the beast; I cannot say the sum:　210
"I ride him not, it is a foolish pride
"Men have in cattle—but my people ride;
"The boy is—hark ye, sirrah! what's your name?
"Ay, Jacob, yes! I recollect—the same,
"As I bethink me now, a tenant's son—
"I think a tenant—is your father one?"
　There was an idle boy who ran about,
And found his master's humble spirit out;
He would at awful distance snatch a look,
Then run away and hide him in some nook;　220
"For oh!" quoth he, "I dare not fix my sight
"On him, his grandeur puts me in a fright;
"Oh! Mister Jacob, when you wait on him,
"Do you not quake and tremble every limb?"
The steward soon had orders—"Summers, see
"That Sam be clothed, and let him wait on me."

413

Sir Denys died, bequeathing all affairs
In trust to Laughton's long experienced cares,
Before a guardian; and, Sir Denys dead,
All rule and power devolved upon his head.   230
Numbers are call'd to govern, but in fact
Only the powerful and assuming act.
　Laughton, too wise to be a dupe to fame,
Cared not a whit of what descent he came,
Till he was rich; he then conceived the thought
To fish for pedigree, but never caught.
All his desire, when he was young and poor,
Was to advance; he never cared for more:
"Let me buy, sell, be factor, take a wife,
"Take any road to get along in life."   240
　Was he a miser then? a robber? foe
To those who trusted? a deceiver?—No!
He was ambitious; all his powers of mind
Were to one end controll'd, improved, combined;
Wit, learning, judgment, were, by his account,
Steps for the ladder he design'd to mount.
Such step was money: wealth was but his slave,
For power he gain'd it, and for power he gave;
Full well the Borough knows that he'd the art
Of bringing money to the surest mart;   250
Friends too were aids, they led to certain ends,
Increase of power and claim on other friends.
A favourite step was marriage: then he gain'd
Seat in our hall, and o'er his party reign'd;
Houses and lands he bought, and long'd to buy,
But never drew the springs of purchase dry;
And thus at last they answer'd every call,
The failing found him ready for their fall.
He walks along the street, the mart, the quay,
And looks and mutters, "This belongs to me."   260
His passions all partook the general bent;
Interest inform'd him when he should resent,
How long resist, and on what terms relent.
In points where he determined to succeed,
In vain might reason or compassion plead;
But gain'd his point, he was the best of men,

THE BOROUGH

'Twas loss of time to be vexatious then :
Hence he was mild to all men whom he led,
Of all who dared resist the scourge and dread.
  Falsehood in him was not the useless lie   270
Of boasting pride or laughing vanity ;
It was the gainful, the persuading art,
That made its way and won the doubting heart,
Which argued, soften'd, humbled, and prevail'd ;
Nor was it tried till ev'ry truth had fail'd ;
No sage on earth could more than he despise
Degrading, poor, unprofitable lies.
  Though fond of gain, and grieved by wanton waste,
To social parties he had no distaste ;
With one presiding purpose in his view,   280
He sometimes could descend to trifle too !
Yet, in these moments, he had still the art
To ope the looks and close the guarded heart ;
And, like the public host, has sometimes made
A grand repast, for which the guests have paid.
  At length, with power endued and wealthy grown,
Frailties and passions, long suppress'd, were shown ;
Then, to provoke him was a dangerous thing ;
His pride would punish, and his temper sting ;
His powerful hatred sought th' avenging hour,   290
And his proud vengeance struck with all his power—
Save when th' offender took a prudent way
The rising storm of fury to allay.
This might he do, and so in safety sleep,
By largely casting to the angry deep ;
Or, better yet (its swelling force t' assuage,)
By pouring oil of flattery on its rage.
  And now, of all the heart approved, possess'd,
Fear'd, favour'd, follow'd, dreaded, and caress'd,
He gently yields to one mellifluous joy,   300
The only sweet that is not found to cloy,
Bland adulation ! Other pleasures pall
On the sick taste, and transient are they all ;
But this one sweet has such enchanting power,
The more we take, the faster we devour ;
Nauseous to those who must the dose apply,

And most disgusting to the standers-by ;
Yet in all companies will Laughton feed,
Nor care how grossly men perform the deed.
　　As gapes the nursling, or, what comes more near,　　310
Some Friendly-island chief, for hourly cheer—
When wives and slaves, attending round his seat,
Prepare by turns the masticated meat :
So for this master, husband, parent, friend,
His ready slaves their various efforts blend,
And, to their lord still eagerly inclined,
Pour the crude trash of a dependent mind.
　　But let the muse assign the man his due :
Worth he possess'd, nor were his virtues few ;—
He sometimes help'd the injured in their cause ;　　320
His power and purse have back'd the failing laws ;
He for religion has a due respect,
And all his serious notions are correct ;
Although he pray'd and languish'd for a son,
He grew resign'd when Heaven denied him one ;
He never to this quiet mansion sends
Subject unfit, in compliment to friends.
Not so Sir Denys, who would yet protest
He always chose the worthiest and the best :
Not men in trade by various loss brought down,　　330
But those whose glory once amazed the town ;
Who their last guinea in their pleasures spent,
Yet never fell so low as to repent ;
To these his pity he could largely deal,
Wealth they had known, and therefore want could feel.
　　Three seats were vacant while Sir Denys reign'd,
And three such favourites their admission gain'd ;
These let us view, still more to understand
The moral feelings of Sir Denys Brand.

THE BOROUGH.

LETTER XIV.

INHABITANTS OF THE ALMS-HOUSE.

BLANEY.

Sed [quam] cæcus inest vitiis amor, omne futurum
Despicitur; suadent brevem præsentia fruĉtum,
Et ruit in vetitum damni secura libido.
Claudian. in Eutrop. [Lib. II. vv. 50–2].

—

Nunquam parvo contenta peraĉta
Et quæsitorum terrâ pelagoque ciborum
Ambitiosa fames et lautæ gloria mensæ.

—

Et Luxus, populator Opum, [cui] semper adhærens,
Infelix humili gressu comitatur Egestas.
Claudian. in Rufinum [Lib. I. vv. 35–6].

—

Behold what blessing[s] wealth to life can lend!
Pope [Moral Essays, Ep. III. v. 297].

—

Blaney, a wealthy Heir, dissipated, and reduced to Poverty—His Fortune restored by Marriage: again consumed—His Manner of living in the West Indies—Recalled to a larger Inheritance—His more refined and expensive Luxuries—His Method of quieting Conscience—Death of his Wife—Again become poor—His Method of supporting Existence—His Ideas of Religion—His Habits and Connexions when old —Admitted into the Alms-House.

THE BOROUGH.

LETTER XIV.

LIFE OF BLANEY.

OBSERVE that tall pale veteran! what a look
  Of shame and guilt! who cannot read that book?
Misery and mirth are blended in his face,
Much innate vileness and some outward grace;
There wishes strong and stronger griefs are seen,
Looks ever changed, and never one serene:
Show not that manner, and these features all,
The serpent's cunning and the sinner's fall?
  Hark to that laughter!—'tis the way he takes
To force applause for each vile jest he makes;   10
Such is yon man, by partial favour sent
To these calm seats to ponder and repent.
  Blaney, a wealthy heir at twenty-one,
At twenty-five was ruin'd and undone:
These years with grievous crimes we need not load,
He found his ruin in the common road;—
Gamed without skill, without inquiry bought,
Lent without love, and borrow'd without thought.
But, gay and handsome, he had soon the dower
Of a kind wealthy widow in his power;   20
Then he aspired to loftier flights of vice,
To singing harlots of enormous price;
He took a jockey in his gig to buy
A horse, so valued that a duke was shy;
To gain the plaudits of the knowing few,
Gamblers and grooms, what would not Blaney do?

418

THE BOROUGH

His dearest friend, at that improving age,
Was Hounslow Dick, who drove the western stage.
Cruel he was not.—If he left his wife,
He left her to her own pursuits in life ;   30
Deaf to reports, to all expenses blind ;
Profuse, not just, and careless, but not kind.
  Yet, thus assisted, ten long winters pass'd
In wasting guineas ere he saw his last ;
Then he began to reason, and to feel
He could not dig, nor had he learn'd to steal ;
And should he beg as long as he might live,
He justly fear'd that nobody would give.
But he could charge a pistol, and, at will,
All that was mortal by a bullet kill :   40
And he was taught, by those whom he would call
Man's surest guides—that he was mortal all.
  While thus he thought, still waiting for the day,
When he should dare to blow his brains away,
A place for him a kind relation found,
Where England's monarch ruled, but far from English ground ;
He gave employ that might for bread suffice,
Correct his habits and restrain his vice.
  Here Blaney tried (what such man's miseries teach)
To find what pleasures were within his reach ;   50
These he enjoy'd, though not in just the style
He once possess'd them in his native isle ;
Congenial souls he found in every place,
Vice in all soils, and charms in every race :
His lady took the same amusing way,
And laugh'd at Time till he had turn'd them grey :
At length for England once again they steer'd,
By ancient views and new designs endear'd ;
His kindred died, and Blaney now became
An heir to one who never heard his name.   60
  What could he now ?—The man had tried before
The joys of youth, and they were joys no more ;
To vicious pleasure he was still inclined,
But vice must now be season'd and refined ;
Then as a swine he would on pleasure seize,
Now common pleasures had no power to please :

GEORGE CRABBE

Beauty alone has for the vulgar charms,
He wanted beauty trembling with alarms;
His was no more a youthful dream of joy,
The wretch desired to ruin and destroy;   70
He bought indulgence with a boundless price,
Most pleased when decency bow'd down to vice,
When a fair dame her husband's honour sold,
And a frail Countess play'd for Blaney's gold.
  "But did not conscience in her anger rise?"
Yes! and he learn'd her terrors to despise;
When stung by thought, to soothing books he fled,
And grew composed and harden'd as he read;
Tales of Voltaire, and essays gay and slight,
Pleased him and shone with their phosphoric light;   80
Which, though it rose from objects vile and base,
Where'er it came threw splendour on the place,
And was that light which the deluded youth,
And this grey sinner, deem'd the light of truth.
  He different works for different cause admired—
Some fix'd his judgment, some his passions fired;
To cheer the mind and raise a dormant flame,
He had the books, decreed to lasting shame,
Which those who read are careful not to name:
These won to vicious act the yielding heart,   90
And then the cooler reasoners soothed the smart.
  He heard of Blount, and Mandeville, and Chubb,
How they the doctors of their day would drub;
How Hume had dwelt on miracles so well,
That none would now believe a miracle;
And though he cared not works so grave to read,
He caught their faith and sign'd the sinner's creed.
  Thus was he pleased to join the laughing side;
Nor ceased the laughter when his lady died.
Yet was he kind and careful of her fame,   100
And on her tomb inscribed a virtuous name:
"A tender wife, respected, and so forth."—
The marble still bears witness to the worth.
  He has some children, but he knows not where;
Something they cost, but neither love nor care;
A father's feelings he has never known,

His joys, his sorrows, have been all his own.
He now would build—and lofty seat he built,
And sought, in various ways, relief from guilt.
Restless, for ever anxious to obtain   110
Ease for the heart by ramblings of the brain,
He would have pictures, and of course a taste,
And found a thousand means his wealth to waste.
Newmarket steeds he bought at mighty cost;
They sometimes won, but Blaney always lost.
  Quick came his ruin, came when he had still
For life a relish, and in pleasure skill:
By his own idle reckoning he supposed
His wealth would last him till his life was closed;
But no! he found his final hoard was spent,   120
While he had years to suffer and repent.
Yet at the last, his noble mind to show,
And in his misery how he bore the blow,
He view'd his only guinea, then suppress'd
For a short time, the tumults in his breast,
And, moved by pride, by habit and despair,
Gave it an opera-bird to hum an air.
  Come ye! who live for pleasure, come, behold
A man of pleasure when he's poor and old;
When he looks back through life, and cannot find   130
A single action to relieve his mind;
When he looks forward, striving still to keep
A steady prospect of eternal sleep;
When not one friend is left, of all the train
Whom 'twas his pride and boast to entertain—
Friends now employ'd from house to house to run
And say, "Alas! poor Blaney is undone!"—
Those whom he shook with ardour by the hand,
By whom he stood as long as he could stand,
Who seem'd to him from all deception clear,   140
And who, more strange! might think themselves sincere.
  Lo! now the hero shuffling through the town,
To hunt a dinner and to beg a crown;
To tell an idle tale, that boys may smile;
To bear a strumpet's billet-doux a mile;
To cull a wanton for a youth of wealth,

GEORGE CRABBE

(With [reverent] view to both his taste and health);
To be a useful, needy thing between
Fear and desire—the pander and the screen;
To flatter pictures, houses, horses, dress,   150
The wildest fashion or the worst excess;
To be the grey seducer, and entice
Unbearded folly into acts of vice;
And then, to level every fence which law
And virtue fix to keep the mind in awe,
He first inveigles youth to walk astray,   ⎫
Next prompts and soothes them in their fatal way,   [}]
Then vindicates the deed, and makes the mind his prey.   ⎭
    Unhappy man! what pains he takes to state
(Proof of his fear!) that all below is fate;   160
That all proceed in one appointed track,
Where none can stop, or take their journey back!
Then what is vice or virtue?—Yet he'll rail
At priests till memory and quotation fail;
He reads, to learn the various ills they've done,
And calls them vipers, every mother's son.
    He is the harlot's aid, who wheedling tries
To move her friend for vanity's supplies;
To weak indulgence he allures the mind,
Loth to be duped, but willing to be kind;   170
And if successful—what the labour pays?
He gets the friend's contempt and Chloe's praise,
Who, in her triumph, condescends to say,
"What a good creature Blaney was to-day!"
    Hear the poor dæmon when the young attend,
And willing ear to vile experience lend;
When he relates (with laughing, leering eye)
The tale licentious, mix'd with blasphemy:
No genuine gladness his narrations cause,
The frailest heart denies sincere applause;   180
And many a youth has turn'd him half aside,
And laugh'd aloud, the sign of shame to hide.
    Blaney, no aid in his vile cause to lose,
Buys pictures, prints, and a licentious muse;
He borrows every help from every art,
To stir the passions and mislead the heart.

THE BOROUGH

But from the subject let us soon escape,
Nor give this feature all its ugly shape:
Some to their crimes escape from satire owe;
Who shall describe what Blaney dares to show?   190
    While thus the man, to vice and passion slave,
Was, with his follies, moving to the grave,
The ancient ruler of this mansion died,
And Blaney boldly for the seat applied.
Sir Denys Brand, then guardian, join'd his suit;
"'Tis true," said he, "the fellow's quite a brute—
"A very beast; but yet, with all his sin,
"He has a manner—let the devil in."
    They half complied, they gave the wish'd retreat,
But raised a worthier to the vacant seat.   200
    Thus forced on ways unlike each former way,
Thus led to prayer without a heart to pray,
He quits the gay and rich, the young and free,
Among the badge-men with a badge to be.
He sees an humble tradesman raised to rule
The grey-beard pupils of this moral school;
Where he himself, an old licentious boy,
Will nothing learn, and nothing can enjoy;
In temp'rate measures he must eat and drink,
And, pain of pains! must live alone and think.   210
    In vain, by fortune's smiles, thrice affluent made,
Still has he debts of ancient date unpaid;
Thrice into penury by error thrown,
Not one right maxim has he made his own;
The old men shun him—some his vices hate,
And all abhor his principles and prate;
Nor love nor care for him will mortal show,
Save a frail sister in the female row.

THE BOROUGH.

LETTER XV.

INHABITANTS OF THE ALMS-HOUSE.

CLELIA.

> She early found herself mistress of herself. All she did was right: all she said was admired. Early, very early, did she dismiss blushes from her cheek: she could not blush, because she could not doubt; and silence, whatever was the subject, was as much a stranger to her as diffidence.
>
> *Richardson.*

> Quo fugit Venus? heu! Quove color? decens
> Quo motus? Quid habes illius, illius,
> Quæ spirabat amores,
> Quæ me surpuerat mihi?
> *Horatius*, lib. iv. od. 13 [vv. 17-20].

Her lively and pleasant Manners—Her Reading and Decision—Her Intercourse with different Classes of Society—Her Kind of Character—The favoured Lover—Her Management of him: his of her—After one Period, Clelia with an Attorney: her Manner and Situation there—Another such Period, when her Fortune still declines—Mistress of an Inn—A Widow—Another such Interval: she becomes poor and infirm, but still vain and frivolous—The fallen Vanity—Admitted into the House; meets Blaney.

THE BOROUGH.

LETTER XV.

CLELIA.

WE had a sprightly nymph—in every town
Are some such sprights, who wander up and down;
She had her useful arts, and could contrive,
In time's despite, to stay at twenty-five;—
"Here will I rest; move on, thou lying year,
"This is mine age, and I will rest me here."
Arch was her look, and she had pleasant ways
Your good opinion of her heart to raise;
Her speech was lively, and with ease express'd,
And well she judged the tempers she address'd :   10
If some soft stripling had her keenness felt,
She knew the way to make his anger melt;
Wit was allow'd her, though but few could bring
Direct example of a witty thing;
'Twas that gay, pleasant, smart, engaging speech,
Her beaux admired, and just within their reach;
Not indiscreet, perhaps, but yet more free
Than prudish nymphs allow their wit to be.
Novels and plays, with poems, old and new,
Were all the books our nymph attended to;   20
Yet from the press no treatise issued forth,
But she would speak precisely of its worth.
She with the London stage familiar grew,
And every actor's name and merit knew;
She told how this or that their part mistook,
And of the rival Romeos gave the look;
Of either house 'twas hers the strength to see,
Then judge with candour—"Drury-Lane for me."
What made this knowledge, what this skill complete?

425

GEORGE CRABBE

A fortnight's visit in Whitechapel-street.　30
Her place in life was rich and poor between,
With those a favourite, and with these a queen ;
She could her parts assume, and condescend
To friends more humble while an humble friend ;
And thus a welcome, lively guest could pass,
Threading her pleasant way from class to class.
　"Her reputation ? "—That was like her wit,
And seem'd her manner and her state to fit ;
Something there was—what, none presumed to say :
Clouds lightly passing on a smiling day—　40
Whispers and hints which went from ear to ear,
And mix'd reports no judge on earth could clear.
　But of each sex a friendly number press'd
To joyous banquets this alluring guest.
There, if, indulging mirth and freed from awe,
If, pleasing all and pleased with all she saw,
Her speech were free, and such as freely dwelt
On the same feelings all around her felt ;
Or if some fond presuming favourite tried
To come so near as once to be denied ;　50
Yet not with brow so stern or speech so nice,
But that he ventured on denial twice :—
If these have been, and so has scandal taught,
Yet malice never found the proof she sought.
　But then came one, the Lovelace of his day,
Rich, proud, and crafty, handsome, brave, and gay ;
Yet loved he not those labour'd plans and arts,
But left the business to the ladies' hearts,
And, when he found them in a proper train,
He thought all else superfluous and vain.　60
But in that training he was deeply taught,
And rarely fail'd of gaining all he sought ;
He knew how far directly on to go ;
How to recede and dally to and fro ;
How to make all the passions his allies,
And, when he saw them in contention rise,
To watch the wrought-up heart, and conquer by surprise.　[}]
　Our heroine fear'd him not ; it was her part,
To make sure conquest of such gentle heart—
426

THE BOROUGH

Of one so mild and humble ; for she saw   70
In Henry's eye a love chastised by awe.
Her thoughts of virtue were not all sublime,
Nor virtuous all her thoughts ; 'twas now her time
To bait each hook, in every way to please,
And the rich prize with dext'rous hand to seize.
She had no virgin-terrors ; she could stray
In all love's maze, nor fear to lose her way ;
Nay, could go near the precipice, nor dread
A failing caution or a giddy head ;
She'd fix her eyes upon the roaring flood,   80
And dance upon the brink where danger stood.
    'Twas nature all, she judged, in one so young,
To drop the eye and falter in the tongue ;
To be about to take, and then command
His daring wish, and only view the hand :
Yes ! all was nature ; it became a maid
Of gentle soul t' encourage love afraid.—
He, so unlike the confident and bold,
Would fly in mute despair to find her cold :
The young and tender germ requires the sun   90
To make it spread ; it must be smiled upon.
Thus the kind virgin gentle means devised
To gain a heart so fond, a hand so prized ;
More gentle still she grew ; to change her way
Would cause confusion, danger and delay :
Thus, (an increase of gentleness her mode,)
She took a plain, unvaried, certain road,
And every hour believed success was near,
Till there was nothing left to hope or fear.
    It must be own'd that in this strife of hearts,   100
Man has advantage—has superior arts.
The lover's aim is to the nymph unknown,
Nor is she always certain of her own ;
Or has her fears, nor these can so disguise,
But he who searches, reads them in her eyes,
In the avenging frown, in the regretting sighs :
These are his signals, and he learns to steer
The straighter course whenever they appear.

427

"Pass we ten years, and what was Clelia's fate?"
At an attorney's board alert she sate,   110
Not legal mistress: he with other men
Once sought her hand, but other views were then;
And when he knew he might the bliss command,
He other [blessing] sought, without the hand;
For still he felt alive the lambent flame,
And offer'd her a home—and home she came.
    There, though her higher friendships lived no more,
She loved to speak of what she shared before—
"Of the dear Lucy, heiress of the hall—
"Of good Sir Peter—of their annual ball,   120
"And the fair countess!—Oh! she loved them all!"   [ ]
The humbler clients of her friend would stare,
The knowing smile—but neither caused her care;
She brought her spirits to her humble state,
And soothed with idle dreams her frowning fate.

    "Ten summers pass'd, and how was Clelia then?"
Alas! she suffer'd in this trying ten;
The pair had parted: who to him attend,
Must judge the nymph unfaithful to her friend;
But who on her would equal faith bestow,   130
Would think him rash—and surely she must know.
    Then as a matron Clelia taught a school,
But nature gave not talents fit for rule.
Yet now, though marks of wasting years were seen,
Some touch of sorrow, some attack of spleen;
Still there was life, a spirit quick and gay,
And lively speech and elegant array.
    The Griffin's landlord these allured so far,
He made her mistress of his heart and bar;
He had no idle retrospective whim,   140
Till she was his, her deeds concern'd not him.
So far was well,—but Clelia thought not fit
(In all the Griffin needed) to submit:
Gaily to dress and in the bar preside,
Soothed the poor spirit of degraded pride;
But cooking, waiting, welcoming a crew

428

THE BOROUGH

Of noisy guests, were arts she never knew:
Hence daily wars, with temporary truce,
His vulgar insult, and her keen abuse;
And as their spirits wasted in the strife,   150
Both took the Griffin's ready aid of life;
But she with greater prudence—Harry tried
More powerful aid, and in the trial died;
Yet drew down vengeance: in no distant time,
Th' insolvent Griffin struck his wings sublime;—
Forth from her palace walk'd th' ejected queen,
And show'd to frowning fate a look serene;
Gay spite of time, though poor, yet well attired,
Kind without love, and vain if not admired.

    Another term is past; ten other years   160
In various trials, troubles, views, and fears.
Of these some pass'd in small attempts at trade;
Houses she kept for widowers lately made;
For now she said, " They'll miss th' endearing friend,
" And I'll be there the soften'd heart to bend."
And true a part was done as Clelia plann'd—
The heart was soften'd, but she miss'd the hand.
She wrote a novel, and Sir Denys said,
The dedication, was the best he read;
But Edgeworths, Smiths, and Radcliffes so engross'd   170
The public ear, that all her pains were lost.
To keep a toy-shop was attempt the last,
There too she fail'd, and schemes and hopes were past.
    Now friendless, sick and old, and wanting bread,
The first-born tears of fallen pride were shed—
True, bitter tears; and yet that wounded pride,
Among the poor, for poor distinctions sigh'd.
Though now her tales were to her audience fit;
Though loud her tones, and vulgar grown her wit;
Though now her dress—(but let me not explain   180
The piteous patch-work of the needy-vain,
The flirtish form to coarse materials lent,
And one poor robe through fifty fashions sent;)
Though all within was sad, without was mean—

Still 'twas her wish, her comfort to be seen :
She would to plays on lowest terms resort,
Where once her box was to the beaux a court;
And, strange delight ! to that same house where she
Join'd in the dance, all gaiety and glee,
Now, with the menials crowding to the wall,   190
She'd see, not share, the pleasures of the ball,
And with degraded vanity unfold,
How she too triumphed in the years of old.
To her poor friends 'tis now her pride to tell
On what a height she stood before she fell ;
At church she points to one tall seat, and " There
" We sat," she cries, " when my papa was mayor."
Not quite correct in what she now relates,
She alters persons, and she forges dates ;
And, finding memory's weaker help decay'd,   200
She boldly calls invention to her aid.
    Touch'd by the pity he had felt before,
For her Sir Denys op'd the alms-house door.
" With all her faults," he said, " the woman knew
" How to distinguish—had a manner too;
" And, as they say she is allied to some
" In decent station—let the creature come."
    Here she and Blaney meet, and take their view
Of all the pleasures they would still pursue.
Hour after hour they sit, and nothing hide   210
Of vices past ; their follies are their pride ;
What to the sober and the cool are crimes,
They boast—exulting in those happy times ;
The darkest deeds no indignation raise,
The purest virtue never wins their praise ;
But still they on their ancient joys dilate,
Still with regret departed glories state,
And mourn their grievous fall, and curse their rigorous fate. [ ]]

THE BOROUGH.

LETTER XVI.

INHABITANTS OF THE ALMS-HOUSE.

BENBOW.

Thou art the Knight of the Burning Lamp[....]...If thou [wert] any
way given to virtue, I would swear by thy face; my oath should be by
this fire. [....] a perpetual triumph, [....] Thou hast saved me a thousand
marks in links and torches, walking [with thee in the] night betwixt tavern
and tavern...

> *Shakspeare* [Henry IV. Part I. Act III. Sc. 3].

Ebrietas tibi fida comes, tibi Luxus, et atris
Circa te semper volitans Infamia pennis.
Silius Italicus [Punica, Lib. v. vv. 96-7].

Benbow, an improper Companion for the Badgemen of the Alms-house—
He resembles Bardolph—Left in Trade by his Father—Contracts
useless Friendships—His Friends drink with him, and employ others—
Called worthy and honest! Why—Effect of Wine on the Mind of
Man—Benbow's common Subject—the Praise of departed Friends
and Patrons—'Squire Asgill, at the Grange: his Manners, Servants,
Friends—True to his Church: ought therefore to be spared—His
Son's different Conduct—Vexation of the Father's Spirit if admitted
to see the Alteration—Captain Dowling, a boon Companion, ready
to drink at all Times, and with any Company; famous in his Club-
room—His easy Departure—Dolley Murrey, a Maiden advanced in
Years: abides by Ratafia and Cards—Her free Manners—Her Skill
in the Game—Her Preparation and Death—Benbow, how interrupted;
his Submission.

THE BOROUGH.

LETTER XVI.

BENBOW.

SEE yonder badgeman, with that glowing face,
  A meteor shining in this sober place !
Vast sums were paid, and many years were past,
Ere gems so rich around their radiance cast !
Such was the fiery front that Bardolph wore,
Guiding his master to the tavern-door;
There first that meteor rose, and there alone,
In its due place, the rich effulgence shone.
But this strange fire the seat of peace invades,
And shines portentous in these solemn shades.   10
  Benbow, a boon companion, long approved
By jovial sets, and (as he thought) beloved,
Was judged as one to joy and friendship prone,
And deem'd injurious to himself alone ;
Gen'rous and free, he paid but small regard
To trade, and fail'd; and some declared " 'twas hard."
These were his friends—his foes conceived the case
Of common kind; he sought and found disgrace;
The reasoning few, who neither scorn'd nor loved,
His feelings pitied and his faults reproved.   20
  Benbow, the father, left possessions fair,
A worthy name and business to his heir;
Benbow, the son, those fair possessions sold,
And lost his credit, while he spent the gold.

432

THE BOROUGH

He was a jovial trader: men enjoy'd
The night with him; his day was unemploy'd;
So, when his credit and his cash were spent,
Here, by mistaken pity, he was sent;
Of late he came, with passions unsubdued,
And shared and cursed the hated solitude,   30
Where gloomy thoughts arise, where grievous cares intrude.[ ]]
 Known but in drink—he found an easy friend,
Well pleased his worth and honour to commend;
And, thus inform'd, the guardian of the trust
Heard the applause and said the claim was just;
A worthy soul! unfitted for the strife,
Care and contention of a busy life ;—
Worthy, and why?—that o'er the midnight bowl
He made his friend the partner of his soul,
And any man his friend;—then thus in glee,   40
"I speak my mind; I love the truth," quoth he;
Till 'twas his fate that useful truth to find,
'Tis sometimes prudent not to speak the mind.
 With wine inflated, man is all upblown,
And feels a power which he believes his own;
With fancy soaring to the skies, he thinks
His all the virtues all the while he drinks;
But when the gas from the balloon is gone,
When sober thoughts and serious cares come on,
Where then the worth that in himself he found?—   50
Vanish'd—and he sank grov'ling on the ground.
 Still some conceit will Benbow's mind inflate;
Poor as he is—'tis pleasant to relate
The joys he once possess'd : it soothes his present state.   [ ]]
 Seated with some grey beadsman, he regrets
His former feasting, though it swell'd his debts;
Topers once famed, his friends in earlier days,
Well he describes, and thinks description praise :
Each hero's worth with much delight he paints;
Martyrs they were, and he would make them saints.   60
 "Alas! alas!" Old England now may say,
"My glory withers; it has had its day :
"We're fallen on evil times; men read and think;
"Our bold forefathers loved to fight and drink.

GEORGE CRABBE

"Then lived the good 'Squire Asgill—what a change
"Has death and fashion shown us at the Grange!
"He bravely thought it best became his rank,
"That all his tenants and his tradesmen drank;
"He was delighted from his favourite room
"To see them 'cross the park go daily home,   70
"Praising aloud the liquor and the host,
"And striving who should venerate him most.
  "No pride had he, and there was difference small
"Between the master's and the servants' hall;
"And here or there the guests were welcome all.   [ ]
"Of Heaven's free gifts he took no special care;
"He never quarrel'd for a simple hare;
"But sought, by giving sport, a sportsman's name,
"Himself a poacher, though at other game.
"He never planted nor inclosed—his trees   80
"Grew like himself, untroubled and at ease;
"Bounds of all kinds he hated, and had felt
"Choked and imprison'd in a modern belt,
"Which some rare genius now has twined about
"The good old house, to keep old neighbours out;
"Along his valleys, in the evening hours,
"The borough-damsels stray'd to gather flowers,
"Or by the brakes and brushwood of the park,
"To take their pleasant rambles in the dark.
  "Some prudes, of rigid kind, forbore to call   90
"On the kind females—favourites at the hall;
"But better natures saw, with much delight,
"The different orders of mankind unite;
"'Twas schooling pride to see the footman wait,
"Smile on his sister and receive her plate.
  "His worship ever was a churchman true,
"He held in scorn the methodistic crew;
"'May God defend the Church, and save the King,'
"He'd pray devoutly and divinely sing.
"Admit that he the holy day would spend   100
"As priests approved not—still he was a friend.
"Much then I blame the preacher, as too nice,
"To call such trifles by the name of vice,
"Hinting, though gently and with cautious speech,

434

"Of good example—'tis their trade to preach;
"But still 'twas pity, when the worthy 'squire
"Stuck to the church: what more could they require?
"'Twas almost joining that fanatic crew,
"To throw such morals at his honour's pew;
"A weaker man, had he been so reviled,   110
"Had left the place—he only swore and smiled.
  "But think, ye rectors and ye curates, think,
"Who are your friends, and at their frailties wink;
"Conceive not—mounted on your Sunday-throne,
"Your fire-brands fall upon your foes alone;
"They strike your patrons—and, should all withdraw
"In whom your wisdoms may discern a flaw,
"You would the flower of all your audience lose,
"And spend your crackers on their empty pews.
  "The father dead, the son has found a wife,   120
"And lives a formal, proud, unsocial life;—
"The lands are now enclosed; the tenants all,
"Save at a rent-day, never see the hall;
"No lass is suffer'd o'er the walks to come,
"And, if there's love, they have it all at home.
  "Oh! could the ghost of our good 'squire arise,
"And see such change, would it believe its eyes?
"Would it not glide about from place to place,
"And mourn the manners of a feebler race?
"At that long table, where the servants found   130
"Mirth and abundance while the year went round;
"Where a huge pollard on the winter-fire
"At a huge distance made them all retire;
"Where not a measure in the room was kept,
"And but one rule—they tippled till they slept:
"There would it see a pale old hag preside,
"A thing made up of stinginess and pride;
"Who carves the meat, as if the flesh could feel,
"Careless whose flesh must miss the plenteous meal.
"Here would the ghost a small coal-fire behold,   140
"Not fit to keep one body from the cold;
"Then would it flit to higher rooms, and stay
"To view a dull, dress'd company at play;
"All the old comfort, all the genial fare

GEORGE CRABBE

"For ever gone! how sternly would it stare;
"And, though it might not to their view appear,
"'Twould cause among them lassitude and fear;
"Then wait to see—where he delight has seen—
"The dire effect of fretfulness and spleen.
  "Such were the worthies of these better days;   150
"We had their blessings—they shall have our praise.—
  "Of Captain Dowling would you hear me speak?
"I'd sit and sing his praises for a week:
"He was a man, and man-like all his joy,—
"I'm led to question, was he ever boy?
"Beef was his breakfast;—if from sea and salt,
"It relish'd better with his wine of malt;
"Then, till he dined, if walking in or out,
"Whether the gravel teased him or the gout,
"Though short in wind and flannel'd every limb,   160
"He drank with all who had concerns with him:
"Whatever trader, agent, merchant, came,
"They found him ready, every hour the same;
"Whatever liquors might between them pass,
"He took them all, and never balk'd his glass;
"Nay, with the seamen working in the ship,
"At their request, he'd share the grog and flip.
"But in the club-room was his chief delight,
"And punch the favourite liquor of the night;
"Man after man they from the trial shrank,   170
"And Dowling ever was the last who drank.
"Arrived at home, he, ere he sought his bed,
"With pipe and brandy would compose his head;
"Then half an hour was o'er the news beguiled,
"When he retired as harmless as a child.
"Set but aside the gravel and the gout,
"And breathing short—his sand ran fairly out.
  "At fifty-five we lost him—after that
"Life grows insipid and its pleasures flat;
"He had indulged in all that man can have,   180
"He did not drop a dotard to his grave;
"Still to the last, his feet upon the chair,
"With rattling lungs now gone beyond repair;
"When on each feature death had fix'd his stamp,

436

"And not a doctor could the body vamp;
"Still at the last, to his beloved bowl
"He clung, and cheer'd the sadness of his soul;
"For, though a man may not have much to fear,
"Yet death looks ugly, when the view is near.
"—'I go,' he said, ' but still my friends shall say,   190
"' 'Twas as a man—I did not sneak away;
"' An honest life with worthy souls I've spent—
"' Come, fill my glass;'—he took it, and he went.—
  "Poor Dolly Murrey!—I might live to see
"My hundredth year, but no such lass as she.
"Easy by nature, in her humour gay,
"She chose her comforts, ratafia and play:
"She loved the social game, the decent glass;
"And was a jovial, friendly, laughing lass.
"We sat not then at Whist demure and still,   200
"But pass'd the pleasant hours at gay Quadrille;
"Lame in her side, we placed her in her seat,
"Her hands were free, she cared not for her feet;
"As the game ended, came the glass around,
"(So was the loser cheer'd, the winner crown'd.)
"Mistress of secrets, both the young and old
"In her confided—not a tale she told;
"Love never made impression on her mind,
"She held him weak, and all his captives blind;
"She suffer'd no man her free soul to vex,   210
"Free from the weakness of her gentle sex;
"One with whom ours unmoved conversing sate,
"In cool discussion or in free debate.
  "Once in her chair we'd placed the good old lass,
"Where first she took her preparation glass;
"By lucky thought she'd been that day at prayers,
"And long before had fix'd her small affairs;
"So all was easy—on her cards she cast
"A smiling look; I saw the thought that pass'd:
"' A king,' she call'd;—though conscious of her skill,   220
"' Do more,' I answer'd—' More?' she said; 'I will;'"
"And more she did—cards answer'd to her call,
"She saw the mighty to her mightier fall:
"' A vole! a vole!' she cried, "'tis fairly won,

GEORGE CRABBE

"'My game is ended and my work is done.'—
"This said, she gently, with a single sigh,
"Died as one taught and practised how to die.
 "Such were the dead-departed; I survive,
"To breathe in pain among the dead-alive."
 The bell then call'd these ancient men to pray ;   230
"Again !" said Benbow—"tolls it every day ?
"Where is the life I led ? "—He sigh'd, and walk'd his way. [ ]]

THE BOROUGH.

LETTER XVII.

THE HOSPITAL AND GOVERNORS.

Blessed be the man [that] provideth for the sick and needy : the Lord
shall deliver him in [the] time of trouble.
[Communion Service, [Ps. xli. v. Prayer Book Version].

Quas dederis, solas semper habebis opes.
Martial [Lib. v. Epigr. xliii.].

Nil negat, et sese vel non poscentibus offert.
Claudian [*in Eutrop*. Lib. i. v. 365].

Decipias alios verbis voltuque benigno ;
Nam mihi jam notus dissimulator eris.
Martial [Lib. iv. Epigr. lxxxix.].

Christian Charity anxious to provide for future as well as present Miseries
—Hence the Hospital for the Diseased—Description of a recovered
Patient—The Building: how erected—The Patrons and Governors—
Eusebius—The more active Manager of Business a moral and correct
Contributor—One of different Description—Good the Result, how-
ever intermixed with Imperfection.

439

THE BOROUGH.

LETTER XVII.

THE HOSPITAL AND GOVERNORS.

AN ardent spirit dwells with christian love,
   The eagle's vigour in the pitying dove;
'Tis not enough that we with sorrow sigh,
That we the wants of pleading man supply;
That we in sympathy with sufferers feel,
Nor hear a grief without a wish to heal.
Not these suffice—to sickness, pain, and wo,
The christian spirit loves with aid to go;
Will not be sought, waits not for want to plead,
But seeks the duty—nay, prevents the need;   10
Her utmost aid to every ill applies,
And plans relief for coming miseries.
  Hence yonder building rose: on either side
Far stretch'd the wards, all airy, warm, and wide;
And every ward has beds by comfort spread,
And smooth'd for him who suffers on the bed.
There have all kindness, most relief—for some
Is cure complete—it is the sufferer's home:
Fevers and chronic ills, corroding pains,
Each accidental mischief man sustains;   20
Fractures and wounds, and wither'd limbs and lame,
With all that, slow or sudden, vex our frame,
Have here attendance—here the sufferers lie   )
(Where love and science every aid apply),   }
And heal'd with rapture live, or soothed by comfort die. [ )]
  See one relieved from anguish, and to-day
Allow'd to walk and look an hour away;

440

THE BOROUGH

Two months confined by fever, frenzy, pain,
He comes abroad and is himself again :
'Twas in the spring, when carried to the place,   30
The snow fell down and melted in his face.
  'Tis summer now ; all objects gay and new ;
Smiling alike the viewer and the view :
He stops as one unwilling to advance,
Without another and another glance ;
With what a pure and simple joy he sees
Those sheep and cattle browzing at their ease ;
Easy himself, there's nothing breathes or moves
But he would cherish—all that lives he loves :
Observing every ward as round he goes,   40
He thinks what pain, what danger they enclose ;
Warm in his wish for all who suffer there,
At every view he meditates a prayer :
No evil counsels in his breast abide,
There joy, and love, and gratitude reside.
  The wish that Roman necks in one were found,
That he who form'd the wish might deal the wound,
This man had never heard ; but of the kind,
Is that desire which rises in his mind ;
He'd have all English hands (for further he   50
Cannot conceive extends our charity),
All but his own, in one right-hand to grow,
And then what hearty shake would he bestow !
  "How rose the building ? "—Piety first laid
A strong foundation, but she wanted aid ;
To Wealth unwieldy was her prayer address'd,
Who largely gave, and she the donor bless'd.
Unwieldy Wealth then to his couch withdrew,
And took the sweetest sleep he ever knew.
  Then busy Vanity sustain'd her part,   60
"And much," she said, " it moved her tender heart ;
"To her all kinds of man's distress were known,
"And all her heart adopted as its own."
  Then Science came—his talents he display'd,
And Charity with joy the dome survey'd ;
Skill, Wealth, and Vanity, obtain the fame,
And Piety, the joy that makes no claim.

GEORGE CRABBE

Patrons there are, and governors, from whom
The greater aid and guiding orders come;
Who voluntary cares and labours take,   70
The sufferers' servants for the service' sake.
Of these a part I give you—but a part—
Some hearts are hidden; some have not a heart.
First let me praise—for so I best shall paint—
That pious moralist, that reasoning saint!
Can I of worth like thine, Eusebius, speak?
The man is willing, but the muse is weak;—
'Tis thine to wait on wo! to soothe! to heal!
With learning social, and polite with zeal:
In thy pure breast although the passions dwell,   80
They're train'd by virtue and no more rebel;
But have so long been active on her side,
That passion now might be itself the guide.
    Law, conscience, honour, all obey'd; all give
Th' approving voice, and make it bliss to live;
While faith, when life can nothing more supply,
Shall strengthen hope, and make it bliss to die.
    He preaches, speaks and writes with manly sense—
No weak neglect, no labour'd eloquence;
Goodness and wisdom are in all his ways,   90
The rude revere him and the wicked praise.
    Upon humility his virtues grow,
And tower so high because so fix'd below;
As wider spreads the oak his boughs around,
When deeper with his roots he digs the solid ground.
    By him, from ward to ward, is every aid
The sufferer needs with every care convey'd.
Like the good tree he brings his treasure forth,
And, like the tree, unconscious of his worth;
Meek as the poorest Publican is he,   100
And strict as lives the straitest Pharisee;
Of both, in him unite the better part—
The blameless conduct and the humble heart.
    Yet he escapes not; he, with some, is wise
In carnal things, and loves to moralize;
Others can doubt, if all that christian care
Has not its price—there's something he may share.

But this, and ill severer, he sustains,
As gold the fire, and as unhurt remains;
When most reviled, although he feels the smart, 110
It wakes to nobler deeds the wounded heart,
As the rich olive, beaten for its fruit,
Puts forth at every bruise a bearing shoot.
   A second friend we have, whose care and zeal
But few can equal—few indeed can feel.
He lived a life obscure, and profits made
In the coarse habits of a vulgar trade.
His brother, master of a hoy, he loved
So well, that he the calling disapproved:
"Alas! poor Tom!" the landman oft would sigh, 120
When the gale freshen'd and the waves ran high;
And when they parted, with a tear he'd say,
"No more adventure!—here in safety stay."
Nor did he feign; with more than half he had,
He would have kept the seaman, and been glad.
   Alas! how few resist, when strongly tried!—
A rich relation's nearer kinsman died;
He sicken'd, and to him the landman went,
And all his hours with cousin Ephraim spent.
This Thomas heard, and cared not: "I," quoth he, 130
"Have one in port upon the watch for me."
So Ephraim died, and, when the will was shown,
Isaac, the landman, had the whole his own:
Who to his brother sent a moderate purse,
Which he return'd, in anger, with his curse;
Then went to sea, and made his grog so strong,
He died before he could forgive the wrong.
   The rich man built a house, both large and high,
He enter'd in and set him down to sigh;
He planted ample woods and gardens fair, 140
And walk'd with anguish and compunction there:
The rich man's pines, to every friend a treat,
He saw with pain, and he refused to eat;
His daintiest food, his richest wines, were all
Turn'd by remorse to vinegar and gall:
The softest down, by living body press'd,
The rich man bought, and tried to take his rest;

But care had thorns upon his pillow spread,
And scatter'd sand and nettles in his bed.
Nervous he grew—would often sigh and groan,   150
He talk'd but little, and he walk'd alone ;
Till by his priest convinced, that from one deed
Of genuine love would joy and health proceed ;
He from that time with care and zeal began
To seek and soothe the grievous ills of man ;
And, as his hands their aid to grief apply,
He learns to smile and he forgets to sigh.
Now he can drink his wine and taste his food,
And feel the blessings Heav'n has dealt are good ;
And, since the suffering seek the rich man's door,   160
He sleeps as soundly as when young and poor.
Here much he gives—is urgent more to gain ;
He begs—rich beggars seldom sue in vain ;
Preachers most famed he moves, the crowd to move,
And never wearies in the work of love ;
He rules all business, settles all affairs,
He makes collections, he directs repairs ;
And if he wrong'd one brother—Heav'n forgive
The man by whom so many brethren live !

Then, 'mid our signatures, a name appears   170
Of one for wisdom famed above his years ;
And these were forty : he was from his youth
A patient searcher after useful truth :
To language little of his time he gave,
To science less, nor was the muse's slave ;
Sober and grave, his college sent him down,
A fair example for his native town.
Slowly he speaks, and with such solemn air,
You'd think a Socrates or Solon there ;
For though a Christian, he's disposed to draw   180
His rules from reason's and from nature's law.
"Know," he exclaims, "my fellow mortals, know,
"Virtue alone is happiness below ;
"And what is virtue ? Prudence, first to choose
"Life's real good—the evil to refuse ;

444

THE BOROUGH

" Add justice then, the eager hand to hold,
" To curb the lust of power and thirst of gold;
" Join temp'rance next, that cheerful health insures,
" And fortitude unmoved, that conquers or endures."
   He speaks, and lo !—the very man you see: 190
Prudent and temperate, just and patient he;
By prudence taught his worldly wealth to keep,
No folly wastes, no avarice swells the heap:
He no man's debtor, no man's patron lives;
Save sound advice, he neither asks nor gives;
By no vain thoughts or erring fancy sway'd,
His words are weighty, or at least are weigh'd;
Temp'rate in every place—abroad, at home,
Thence will applause, and hence will profit come;
And health from either he in time prepares   200
For sickness, age, and their attendant cares,
But not for fancy's ills;—he never grieves
For love that wounds or friendship that deceives;
His patient soul endures what Heav'n ordains,
But neither feels nor fears ideal pains.
   "Is aught then wanted in a man so wise?"—
Alas!—I think he wants infirmities;
He wants the ties that knit us to our kind—
The cheerful, tender, soft, complacent mind,
That would the feelings, which he dreads, excite,   210
And make the virtues he approves delight;
What dying martyrs, saints, and patriots feel—
The strength of action and the warmth of zeal.
   Again attend!—and see a man whose cares
Are nicely placed on either world's affairs.—
Merchant and saint, 'tis doubtful if he knows
To which account he most regard bestows;
Of both he keeps his ledger:—there he reads
Of gainful ventures and of godly deeds;
There all he gets or loses find a place—   220
A lucky bargain and a lack of grace.
   The joys above this prudent man invite
To pay his tax—devotion!—day and night;
The pains of hell his timid bosom awe,
And force obedience to the church's law:

Hence that continual thought, that solemn air,
Those sad good works, and that laborious prayer.
All these (when conscience, waken'd and afraid
To think how avarice calls and is obey'd)
He in his journal finds, and for his grief   230
Obtains the transient opium of relief.
  "Sink not, my soul!—my spirit, rise and look
" O'er the fair entries of this precious book :
" Here are the sins, our debts;—this fairer side
" Has what to carnal wish our strength denied ;
" Has those religious duties every day
" Paid—which so few upon the sabbath pay ;
" Here too are conquests over frail desires,
" Attendance due on all the church requires ;
" Then alms I give—for I believe the word   240
" Of holy writ, and lend unto the Lord—
" And, if not all th' importunate demand,
" The fear of want restrains my ready hand ;
" —Behold what sums I to the poor resign,
" Sums placed in Heaven's own book, as well as mine!
" Rest, then, my spirit!—fastings, prayers, and alms,
" Will soon suppress these idly-raised alarms,
" And, weigh'd against our frailties, set in view
" A noble balance in our favour due.
" Add that I yearly here affix my name,   250
" Pledge for large payment—not from love of fame,
" But to make peace within ;—that peace to make,
" What sums I lavish! and what gains forsake !
" Cheer up, my heart!—let's cast off every doubt,
" Pray without dread, and place our money out."
  Such the religion of a mind that steers
Its way to bliss, between its hopes and fears ;
Whose passions in due bounds each other keep,
And, thus subdued, they murmur till they sleep ;
Whose virtues all their certain limits know,   260
Like well-dried herbs that neither fade nor grow ;
Who for success and safety ever tries,
And with both worlds alternately complies.
  Such are the guardians of this bless'd estate ;
Whate'er without, they're praised within the gate ;

446

THE BOROUGH

That they are men, and have their faults, is true,
But here their worth alone appears in view :
The Muse indeed, who reads the very breast,
Has something of the secrets there express'd,
But yet in charity ;—and, when she sees   270
Such means for joy or comfort, health or ease,
And knows how much united minds effect,
She almost dreads their failings to detect ;
But truth commands :—in man's erroneous kind,
Virtues and frailties mingle in the mind ;
Happy, when fears to public spirit move,
And even vices to the work of love !

THE BOROUGH.

LETTER XVIII.

THE POOR AND THEIR DWELLINGS.

Bene paupertas
Humili tecto contenta latet.
Seneca [Octavia, Act v. vv. 895–6].

Omnes quibu' res sunt minu' secundæ, magi' sunt, nescio quo modo,
Suspiciosi ; ad contumeliam omnia accipiunt magis ;
Propter suam impotentiam se semper credunt negligi.
Terent. in Adelph. Act 4. Sc. 3 [vv. 12–4].

Show not to the poor thy pride,
   Let their home a cottage be ;
Nor the feeble body hide
   In a palace fit for thee ;
Let him not about him see
Lofty ceilings, ample halls,
   Or a gate his boundary be,
Where nor friend or kinsman calls.

Let him not one walk behold,
   That only one which he must tread,
Nor a chamber large and cold,
   Better far his humble shed,
   Where the aged and sick are led ;
Humble sheds of neighbours by,
   And the old and tatter'd bed,
   Where he sleeps and hopes to die.

To quit of torpid sluggishness the [lair],
And from the pow'rful arms of sloth [get] free,
'Tis rising from the dead—Alas ! it cannot be.
Thomson's Castle of Indolence [Canto II. ll. 59–61].

The Method of treating the Borough Paupers—Many maintained at their
own Dwellings—Some Characters of the Poor—The School-mistress,
when aged—The Idiot—The poor Sailor—The declined Tradesman
and his Companion—This contrasted with the Maintenance of the
Poor in a common Mansion erected by the Hundred—The Objections
to this Method : not Want, nor Cruelty, but the necessary Evils of
this Mode—What they are—Instances of the Evil—A Return to the
Borough Poor—The Dwellings of these—The Lanes and By-ways—
No Attention here paid to Convenience—The Pools in the Path-ways
—Amusements of Sea-port Children—The Town-Flora—Herbs on
Walls and vacant Spaces—A female Inhabitant of an Alley—A large
Building let to several poor Inhabitants—Their Manners and Habits.

448

THE BOROUGH.

LETTER XVIII.

THE POOR AND THEIR DWELLINGS.

YES! we've our Borough-vices, and I know
   How far they spread, how rapidly they grow;
Yet think not virtue quits the busy place,
Nor charity, the virtues' crown and grace.
  "Our poor how feed we?"—To the most we give
A weekly dole, and at their homes they live;—
Others together dwell—but when they come
To the low roof, they see a kind of home,
A social people whom they've ever known,
With their own thoughts and manners like their own.   10
  At her old house, her dress, her air the same,
I see mine ancient letter-loving dame:
"Learning, my child," said she, "shall fame command;
"Learning is better worth than house or land—
"For houses perish, lands are gone and spent;
"In learning then excel, for that's most excellent."
  "And what her learning?"—'Tis with awe to look
In every verse throughout one sacred book;
From this her joy, her hope, her peace is sought:
This she has learn'd, and she is nobly taught.   20
  If aught of mine have gain'd the public ear;
If RUTLAND deigns these humble Tales to hear;
If critics pardon what my friends approved,
Can I mine ancient widow pass unmoved?
Shall I not think what pains the matron took,
When first I trembled o'er the gilded book?

Crabbe   FF   **449**

GEORGE CRABBE

How she, all patient, both at eve and morn,
Her needle pointed at the guarding horn;
And how she soothed me, when, with study sad,
I labour'd on to reach the final zad?   30
Shall I not grateful still the dame survey,
And ask the muse the poet's debt to pay?
Nor I alone, who hold a trifler's pen,
But half our bench of wealthy, weighty men,
Who rule our Borough, who enforce our laws,   )
They own the matron as the leading cause,   }
And feel the pleasing debt, and pay the just applause: [)]
To her own house is borne the week's supply;
There she in credit lives, there hopes in peace to die.
With her a harmless idiot we behold,   40
Who hoards up silver shells for shining gold;
These he preserves, with unremitted care,
To buy a seat, and reign the Borough's mayor:
Alas!—who could th' ambitious changeling tell,
That what he sought our rulers dared to sell?
Near these a sailor in that hut of thatch
(A fish-boat's cabin is its nearest match)
Dwells, and the dungeon is to him a seat,
Large as he wishes—in his view complete.
A lockless coffer and a lidless hutch   50
That hold his stores, have room for twice as much;
His one spare shirt, long glass, and iron box,
Lie all in view; no need has he for locks.
Here he abides, and, as our strangers pass,
He shows the shipping, he presents the glass;
He makes (unask'd) their ports and business known,
And (kindly heard) turns quickly to his own.
Of noble captains—heroes every one—
You might as soon have made the steeple run:
And then his messmates, if you're pleased to stay,   60
He'll one by one the gallant souls display;
And as the story verges to an end,
He'll wind from deed to deed, from friend to friend;
He'll speak of those long lost, the brave of old,
As princes gen'rous and as heroes bold;
Then will his feelings rise, till you may trace

THE BOROUGH

Gloom, like a cloud, frown o'er his manly face—
And then a tear or two, which sting his pride,
These he will dash indignantly aside,
And splice his tale ;—now take him from his cot,   70
And for some cleaner [berth] exchange his lot,
How will he all that cruel aid deplore ?
His heart will break, and he will fight no more.
   Here is the poor old merchant : he declined,
And, as they say, is not in perfect mind ;
In his poor house, with one poor maiden friend,
Quiet he paces to his journey's end.
   Rich in his youth, he traded and he fail'd ;
Again he tried, again his fate prevail'd ;
His spirits low and his exertions small,   80
He fell perforce, he seem'd decreed to fall :
Like the gay knight, unapt to rise was he,
But downward sank with sad alacrity.
A borough-place we gain'd him—in disgrace
For gross neglect, he quickly lost the place ;
But still he kept a kind of sullen pride,
Striving his wants to hinder or to hide.
At length, compell'd by very need, in grief
He wrote a proud petition for relief.
   "He did suppose a fall, like his, would prove   90
"Of force to wake their sympathy and love ;
"Would make them feel the changes all may know,
"And stir them up a new regard to show."
   His suit was granted ;—to an ancient maid,
Relieved herself, relief for him was paid.
Here they together (meet companions) dwell,
And dismal tales of man's misfortunes tell :
"'Twas not a world for them, God help them ! they
"Could not deceive, nor flatter, nor betray ;
"But there's a happy change, a scene to come,   100
"And they, God help them ! shall be soon at home."
   If these no pleasures nor enjoyments gain,
Still none their spirits nor their speech restrain ;
They sigh at ease, 'mid comforts they complain.   [ ]
The poor will grieve, the poor will weep and sigh,
Both when they know, and when they know not why ;

FF 2   451

GEORGE CRABBE

But we our bounty with such care bestow,
That cause for grieving they shall seldom know.
 Your plan I love not;—with a number you
Have placed your poor, your pitiable few;   110
There, in one house, throughout their lives to be—
The pauper-palace which they hate to see;
That giant-building, that high-bounding wall,
Those bare-worn walks, that lofty thund'ring hall!
That large loud clock, which tolls each dreaded hour;
Those gates and locks, and all those signs of power:
It is a prison, with a milder name,
Which few inhabit without dread or shame.
 Be it agreed—the poor who hither come
Partake of plenty, seldom found at home;   120
That airy rooms and decent beds are meant
To give the poor by day, by night, content;
That none are frighten'd, once admitted here,
By the stern looks of lordly overseer;
Grant that the guardians of the place attend,
And ready ear to each petition lend;
That they desire the grieving poor to show
What ills they feel, what partial acts they know,
Not without promise, nay desire to heal
Each wrong they suffer and each wo they feel.—   130
 Alas! their sorrows in their bosoms dwell;
They've much to suffer, but have nought to tell;
They have no evil in the place to state,
And dare not say, it is the house they hate:
They own, there's granted all such place can give,
But live repining, for 'tis there they live.
 Grandsires are there, who now no more must see,
No more must nurse upon the trembling knee,
The lost loved daughter's infant progeny:
Like death's dread mansion, this allows not place   140
For joyful meetings of a kindred race.
 Is not the matron there, to whom the son
Was wont at each declining day to run;
He (when his toil was over) gave delight,
By lifting up the latch, and one "good night"?
Yes, she is here; but nightly to her door

452

THE BOROUGH

The son, still lab'ring, can return no more.
Widows are here, who in their huts were left,
Of husbands, children, plenty, ease bereft;
Yet all that grief within the humble shed   150
Was soften'd, soften'd in the humble bed;—
But here, in all its force, remains the grief,
And not one soft'ning object for relief.
  Who can, when here, the social neighbour meet?
Who learn the story current in the street?
Who to the long-known intimate impart
Facts they have learn'd or feelings of the heart?—
They talk indeed; but who can choose a friend,
Or seek companions at their journey's end?
  Here are not those whom they, when infants, knew; 160
Who, with like fortune, up to manhood grew;
Who, with like troubles, at old age arrived;
Who, like themselves, the joy of life survived;
Whom time and custom so familiar made,
That looks the meaning in the mind convey'd:
But here, to strangers, words nor looks impart
The various movements of the suffering heart;
Nor will that heart with those alliance own,
To whom its views and hopes are all unknown.
  What, if no grievous fears their lives annoy, 170
Is it not worse no prospects to enjoy?
'Tis cheerless living in such bounded view,
With nothing dreadful, but with nothing new;
Nothing to bring them joy, to make them weep—
The day itself is, like the night, asleep;
Or, on the sameness if a break be made,
'Tis by some pauper to his grave convey'd;
By smuggled news from neighb'ring village told,
News never true, or truth a twelvemonth old;
By some new inmate doom'd with them to dwell, 180
Or justice come to see that all goes well;
Or change of room, or hour of leave to crawl
On the black footway winding with the wall,
Till the stern bell forbids, or master's sterner call. [}]
  Here too the mother sees her children train'd,
Her voice excluded and her feelings pain'd.

Who govern here, by general rules must move,
Where ruthless custom rends the bond of love.
Nations, we know, have nature's law transgress'd,
And snatch'd the infant from the parent's breast;   190
But still for public good the boy was train'd,
The mother suffer'd, but the matron gain'd:
Here nature's outrage serves no cause to aid;
The ill is felt, but not the Spartan made.
Then too, I own, it grieves me to behold
Those ever virtuous, helpless now and old,
By all for care and industry approved,
For truth respected, and for temper loved;
And who, by sickness and misfortune tried,
Gave want its worth and poverty its pride: 200
I own it grieves me to behold them sent
From their old home; 'tis pain, 'tis punishment,
To leave each scene familiar, every face,
For a new people and a stranger race;
For those who, sunk in sloth and dead to shame,
From scenes of guilt with daring spirits came;
Men, just and guileless, at such manners start,
And bless their God that time has fenced their heart,
Confirm'd their virtue, and expell'd the fear
Of vice in minds so simple and sincere.   210
Here the good pauper, losing all the praise
By worthy deeds acquired in better days,
Breathes a few months; then, to his chamber led,
Expires, while strangers prattle round his bed.
The grateful hunter, when his horse is old,
Wills not the useless favourite to be sold;
He knows his former worth, and gives him place
In some fair pasture, till he runs his race.
But has the labourer, has the seaman done
Less worthy service, thought not dealt to one?   220
Shall we not, then, contribute to their ease,
In their old haunts, where ancient objects please;
That, till their sight shall fail them, they may trace
The well-known prospect and the long-loved face?
The noble oak, in distant ages seen,
With far-stretch'd boughs and foliage fresh and green,

THE BOROUGH

Though now its bare and forky branches show
How much it lacks the vital warmth below—
The stately ruin yet our wonder gains,
Nay, moves our pity, without thought of pains ;   230
Much more shall real wants and cares of age
Our gentler passions in their cause engage.—
Drooping and burthen'd with a weight of years,
What venerable ruin man appears !
How worthy pity, love, respect, and grief—
He claims protection—he compels relief ;—
And shall we send him from our view, to brave
The storms abroad, whom we at home might save,
And let a stranger dig our ancient brother's grave ?   [ ]]
No !—we will shield him from the storm he fears,   240
And when he falls, embalm him with our tears.

Farewell to these ; but all our poor to know,
Let's seek the winding lane, the narrow row—
Suburbian prospects, where the traveller stops
To see the sloping tenement on props,
With building yards immix'd, and humble sheds and shops ;[ ]]
Where the Cross-Keys and Plumber's-Arms invite
Laborious men to taste their coarse delight ;
Where the low porches, stretching from the door,
Gave some distinction in the days of yore—   250
Yet now, neglected, more offend the eye
By gloom and ruin than the cottage by.
Places like these the noblest town endures,
The gayest palace has its sinks and sewers.
Here is no pavement, no inviting shop,
To give us shelter when compell'd to stop ;
But plashy puddles stand along the way,
Fill'd by the rain of one tempestuous day ;
And these so closely to the buildings run,
That you must ford them, for you cannot shun ;   260
Though here and there convenient bricks are laid,
And door-side heaps afford their dubious aid.
Lo ! yonder shed ; observe its garden-ground,
With the low paling, form'd of wreck, around :

455

GEORGE CRABBE

There dwells a fisher ; if you view his boat,
With bed and barrel—'tis his house afloat ;
Look at his house, where ropes, nets, blocks, abound,
Tar, pitch, and oakum—'tis his boat aground :
That space enclosed but little he regards,
Spread o'er with relics of masts, sails, and yards ;   270
Fish by the wall on spit of elder rest,
Of all his food the cheapest and the best,
By his own labour caught, for his own hunger dress'd.   [ ]]
  Here our reformers come not ; none object
To paths polluted, or upbraid neglect ;
None care that ashy heaps at doors are cast,
That coal-dust flies along the blinding blast ;
None heed the stagnant pools on either side,
Where new-launch'd ships of infant sailors ride :
Rodneys in rags here British valour boast,   280
And lisping Nelsons fright the Gallic coast.
They fix the rudder, set the swelling sail,
They point the bowsprit, and they blow the gale.
True to her port, the frigate scuds away,
And o'er that frowning ocean finds her bay :
Her owner-rigg'd her, and he knows her worth,
And sees her, fearless, gunwale-deep go forth ;
Dreadless he views his sea, by breezes curl'd,
When inch-high billows vex the watery world.
  There, fed by food they love, to rankest size   290
Around the dwellings docks and wormwood rise ;
Here the strong mallow strikes her slimy root,
Here the dull night-shade hangs her deadly fruit ;
On hills of dust the henbane's faded green,
And pencil'd flower of sickly scent is seen ;
At the wall's base the fiery nettle springs,
With fruit globose and fierce with poison'd stings ;
Above (the growth of many a year) is spread
The yellow level of the stone-crop's bed ;
In every chink delights the fern to grow,   300
With glossy leaf and tawny bloom below [1] :
These, with our sea-weeds, rolling up and down,
Form the contracted Flora [2] of the town.
  Say, wilt thou more of scenes so sordid know ?

THE BOROUGH

Then will I lead thee down the dusty row,
By the warm alley and the long close lane—
There mark the fractured door and paper'd pane,
Where flags the noon-tide air, and, as we pass,
We fear to breathe the putrefying mass.
But fearless yonder matron; she disdains   310
To sigh for zephyrs from ambrosial plains;
But mends her meshes torn, and pours her lay
All in the stifling fervour of the day.
  Her naked children round the alley run,
And, roll'd in dust, are bronzed beneath the sun;
Or gambol round the dame, who, loosely dress'd,
Woos the coy breeze, to fan the open breast.
She, once a handmaid, strove by decent art
To charm her sailor's eye and touch his heart;
Her bosom then was veil'd in kerchief clean,   320
And fancy left to form the charms unseen.
  But, when a wife, she lost her former care,
Nor thought on charms, nor time for dress could spare;
Careless she found her friends who dwelt beside;
No rival beauty kept alive her pride:
Still in her bosom virtue keeps her place;
But decency is gone, the virtues' guard and grace.
  See that long boarded building!—By these stairs
Each humble tenant to that home repairs—
By one large window lighted; it was made   330
For some bold project, some design in trade.
This fail'd—and one, a humorist in his way,
(Ill was the humour), bought it in decay;
Nor will he sell, repair, or take it down;
'Tis his—what cares he for the talk of town?
" No! he will let it to the poor—a home
"Where he delights to see the creatures come."
" They may be thieves; "—" Well, so are richer men; "—
" Or idlers, cheats, or prostitutes; "—" What then? "—
" Outcasts pursued by justice, vile and base; "— 340
" They need the more his pity and the place."
Convert to system his vain mind has built,
He gives asylum to deceit and guilt.
  In this vast room, each place by habit fix'd,

GEORGE CRABBE

Are sexes, families, and ages mix'd—
To union forced by crime, by fear, by need,
And all in morals and in modes agreed :
Some ruin'd men, who from mankind remove ;
Some ruin'd females, who yet talk of love ;
And some grown old in idleness—the prey   350
To vicious spleen, still railing through the day ;
And need and misery, vice and danger bind
In sad alliance each degraded mind.
    That window view !—oil'd paper and old glass
Stain the strong rays, which, though impeded, pass,
And give a dusty warmth to that huge room,
The conquer'd sunshine's melancholy gloom ;
When all those western rays, without so bright,
Within become a ghastly glimmering light,
As pale and faint upon the floor they fall,   360
Or feebly gleam on the opposing wall.
That floor, once oak, now pieced with fir unplaned,
Or, where not pieced, in places bored and stain'd ;
That wall, once whiten'd, now an odious sight,
Stain'd with all hues, except its ancient white ;
The only door is fasten'd by a pin
Or stubborn bar, that none may hurry in :
For this poor room, like rooms of greater pride,
At times contains what prudent men would hide.
    Where'er the floor allows an even space,   370
Chalking and marks of various games have place ;
Boys, without foresight, pleased in halters swing ;
On a fix'd hook men cast a flying ring ;
While gin and snuff their female neighbours share,
And the black beverage in the fractured ware.
    On swinging shelf are things incongruous stored—
Scraps of their food ; the cards and cribbage-board,
With pipes and pouches ; while on peg below
Hang a lost member's fiddle and its bow,
That still reminds them how he'd dance and play,   380
Ere sent untimely to the convicts' bay.
    Here by a curtain, by a blanket there,
Are various beds conceal'd, but none with care ;
Where some by day and some by night, as best

458

THE BOROUGH

Suit their employments, seek uncertain rest ;
The drowsy children at their pleasure creep
To the known crib, and there securely sleep.
  Each end contains a grate, and these beside
Are hung utensils for their boil'd and fried—
All used at any hour, by night, by day,   390
As suit the purse, the person, or the prey.
  Above the fire, the mantel-shelf contains
Of china-ware some poor unmatch'd remains ;
There many a tea-cup's gaudy fragment stands,
All placed by vanity's unwearied hands ;
For here she lives, e'en here she looks about,
To find some small consoling objects out.
Nor heed these Spartan dames their house, nor sit
'Mid cares domestic—they nor sew nor knit ;
But of their fate discourse, their ways, their wars,   400
With arm'd authorities, their 'scapes and scars :
These lead to present evils, and a cup,
If fortune grant it, winds description up.
  High hung at either end, and next the wall,
Two ancient mirrors show the forms of all,
In all their force ;—these aid them in their dress,
But, with the good, the evils too express,
Doubling each look of care, each token of distress. [ ]

NOTES TO LETTER XVIII.

Note 1, p. 456, line 301.

With glossy leaf and tawny bloom below.

This scenery is, I must acknowledge, in a certain degree like that heretofore described in the Village; but that also was a maritime country :— if the objects be similar, the pictures must (in their principal features) be alike, or be bad pictures. I have varied them as much as I could, consistently with my wish to be accurate.

Note 2, page 456, line 303.

Form the contracted Flora of the town.

The reader unacquainted with the language of botany is informed, that the Flora of a place means the vegetable species it contains, and is the title of a book which describes them.

459

THE BOROUGH.

LETTER XIX.

THE POOR OF THE BOROUGH.

THE PARISH-CLERK.

Nam dives qui fieri vult,
Et citò vult fieri; sed quæ reverentia legum,
Quis metus aut pudor est unquam properantis avari?
Juvenal. Sat. 14 [vv. 176–8].

Nocte brevem si forte indulsit cura soporem,
Et toto versata thoro jam membra quiescunt,
Continuò templum et violati Numinis aras,
Et, quod præcipuis mentem sudoribus urget,
Te videt in somnis; tua sacra et major imago
Humanâ turbat pavidum, cogitque fateri.
Juvenal. Sat. 13 [vv. 217–22].

The Parish-Clerk began his Duties with the late Vicar, a grave and austere Man; one fully orthodox; a Detecter and Opposer of the Wiles of Satan—His Opinion of his own Fortitude—The more frail offended by these Professions—His good Advice gives further Provocation—They invent Stratagems to overcome his Virtue—His Triumph—He is yet not invulnerable: is assaulted by Fear of Want, and Avarice—He gradually yields to the Seduction—He reasons with himself and is persuaded—He offends, but with Terror; repeats his Offence; grows familiar with Crime; is detected—His Sufferings and Death.

THE BOROUGH.

LETTER XIX.

THE PARISH-CLERK.

WITH our late vicar, and his age the same,   }
    His clerk, hight Jachin, to his office came: }
The like slow speech was his, the like tall slender frame. [}]
But Jachin was the gravest man on ground,
And heard his master's jokes with look profound;
For worldly wealth this man of letters sigh'd,
And had a sprinkling of the spirit's pride;
But he was sober, chaste, devout, and just,
One whom his neighbours could believe and trust:
Of none suspected, neither man nor maid   10
By him were wrong'd, or were of him afraid.
  There was indeed a frown, a trick of state
In Jachin;—formal was his air and gait;
But if he seem'd more solemn and less kind
Than some light men to light affairs confined,
Still 'twas allow'd that he should so behave
As in high seat, and be severely grave.
  This book-taught man to man's first foe profess'd
Defiance stern, and hate that knew not rest;
He held that Satan, since the world began,   20
In every act had strife with every man;
That never evil deed on earth was done,
But of the acting parties he was one:
The flattering guide to make ill prospects clear;
To smooth rough ways the constant pioneer;
The ever-tempting, soothing, softening power,
Ready to cheat, seduce, deceive, devour.

GEORGE CRABBE

"Me has the sly seducer oft withstood,"
Said pious Jachin,—"but he gets no good;
"I pass the house where swings the tempting sign,   30
"And, pointing, tell him, 'Satan, that is thine;'
"I pass the damsels pacing down the street,
"And look more grave and solemn when we meet;
"Nor doth it irk me to rebuke their smiles,
"Their wanton ambling and their watchful wiles.
"Nay, like the good John Bunyan, when I view
"Those forms, I'm angry at the ills they do;
"That I could pinch and spoil, in sin's despite,
"Beauties, which frail and evil thoughts excite[1]!
  "At feasts and banquets seldom am I found,   40
"And (save at church) abhor a tuneful sound;
"To plays and shows I run not to and fro,
"And where my master goes forbear to go."
  No wonder Satan took the thing amiss,
To be opposed by such a man as this—
A man so grave, important, cautious, wise,
Who dared not trust his feeling or his eyes;
No wonder he should lurk and lie in wait,
Should fit his hooks and ponder on his bait;
Should on his movements keep a watchful eye;   50
For he pursued a fish who led the fry.
  With his own peace our clerk was not content;
He tried, good man! to make his friends repent.
  "Nay, nay, my friends, from inns and taverns fly;
"You may suppress your thirst, but not supply.
"A foolish proverb says, 'the devil's at home;'
"But he is there, and tempts in every room:
"Men feel, they know not why, such places please;
"His are the spells—they're idleness and ease;
"Magic of fatal kind he throws around,   60
"Where care is banish'd but the heart is bound.
  "Think not of beauty; when a maid you meet,
"Turn from her view, and step across the street;
"Dread all the sex: their looks create a charm,

---

[1] John Bunyan, in one of the many productions of his zeal, has ventured to make public this extraordinary sentiment, which the frigid piety of our clerk so readily adopted.

THE BOROUGH

"A smile should fright you and a word alarm.
"E'en I myself, with all my watchful care,
"Have for an instant felt th' insidious snare,
"And caught my sinful eyes at th' endangering stare;   [ ]]
"Till I was forced to smite my bounding breast
"With forceful blow and bid the bold-one rest.   70
    "Go not with crowds when they to pleasure run,
"But public joy in private safety shun.
"When bells, diverted from their true intent,
"Ring loud for some deluded mortal sent
"To hear or make long speech in parliament;   [ ]]
"What time the many, that unruly beast,
"Roars its rough joy and shares the final feast:
"Then heed my counsel, shut thine ears and eyes;
"A few will hear me—for the few are wise."
    Not Satan's friends, nor Satan's self could bear   80
The cautious man who took of souls such care:
An interloper—one who, out of place,
Had volunteer'd upon the side of grace.
There was his master ready once a week
To give advice; what further need he seek?
"Amen, so be it:"—what had he to do
With more than this?—'twas insolent and new;
And some determined on a way to see
How frail he was, that so it might not be.
    First they essay'd to tempt our saint to sin,   90
By points of doctrine argued at an inn;
Where he might warmly reason, deeply drink,
Then lose all power to argue and to think.
    In vain they tried; he took the question up,
Clear'd every doubt, and barely touch'd the cup;
By many a text he proved his doctrine sound,
And look'd in triumph on the tempters round.
    Next 'twas their care an artful lass to find,
Who might consult him, as perplex'd in mind;
She, they conceived, might put her case with fears,   100
With tender tremblings and seducing tears;
She might such charms of various kind display,
That he would feel their force and melt away:
For why of nymphs such caution and such dread,

GEORGE CRABBE

Unless he felt and fear'd to be misled?
She came, she spake: he calmly heard her case,
And plainly told her 'twas a want of grace;
Bade her "such fancies and affections check,
"And wear a thicker muslin on her neck."
Abased, his human foes the combat fled,   110
And the stern clerk yet higher held his head.
They were indeed a weak, impatient set;
But their shrewd prompter had his engines yet;
Had various means to make a mortal trip,
Who shunn'd a flowing bowl and rosy lip;
And knew a thousand ways his heart to move,
Who flies from banquets and who laughs at love.
Thus far the playful Muse has lent her aid,
But now departs, of graver theme afraid;
Her may we seek in more appropriate time—   120
There is no jesting with distress and crime.
Our worthy clerk had now arrived at fame,
Such as but few in his degree might claim;
But he was poor, and wanted not the sense
That lowly rates the praise without the pence:
He saw the common herd with reverence treat
The weakest burgess whom they chanced to meet;
While few respected his exalted views,
And all beheld his doublet and his shoes;
None, when they meet, would to his parts allow   130
(Save his poor boys) a hearing or a bow.
To this false judgment of the vulgar mind
He was not fully, as a saint, resign'd;
He found it much his jealous soul affect,
To fear derision and to find neglect.
The year was bad, the christening-fees were small,
The weddings few, the parties paupers all:
Desire of gain, with fear of want combined,
Raised sad commotion in his wounded mind;
Wealth was in all his thoughts, his views, his dreams, 140
And prompted base desires and baseless schemes.
Alas! how often erring mortals keep
The strongest watch against the foes who sleep;
While the more wakeful, bold and artful foe

464

Is suffer'd guardless and unmark'd to go.
Once in a month the sacramental bread
Our clerk with wine upon the table spread;
The custom this, that, as the vicar reads,
He for our off'rings round the church proceeds.
Tall, spacious seats the wealthier people hid,   150
And none had view of what his neighbour did;
Laid on the box and mingled when they fell,
Who should the worth of each oblation tell?
Now as poor Jachin took the usual round,
And saw the alms and heard the metal sound,
He had a thought;—at first it was no more
Than—"these have cash and give it to the poor."
A second thought from this to work began—
"And can they give it to a poorer man?"
Proceeding thus—"My merit could they know,   160
"And knew my need, how freely they'd bestow;
"But though they know not, these remain the same;
"And are a strong, although a secret claim:
"To me, alas! the want and worth are known;—
"Why then, in fact, 'tis but to take my own."
Thought after thought pour'd in, a tempting train—
"Suppose it done, who is it could complain?
"How could the poor? for they such trifles share
"As add no comfort, as suppress no care;
"But many a pittance makes a worthy heap—   170
"What says the law? that silence puts to sleep;—
"Nought then forbids, the danger could we shun;
"And sure the business may be safely done.
"But am I earnest?—earnest? No.—I say,
"If such my mind, that I could plan a way;
"Let me reflect;—I've not allow'd me time
"To purse the pieces, and if dropp'd they'd chime."
Fertile is evil in the soul of man—
He paused—said Jachin, "They may drop on bran.
"Why then 'tis safe and (all consider'd) just;   180
"The poor receive it—'tis no breach of trust;
"The old and widows may their trifles miss,
"There must be evil in a good like this.
"But I'll be kind—the sick I'll visit twice,

Crabbe   GG   465

"When now but once, and freely give advice.
"Yet let me think again."—Again he tried
For stronger reasons on his passion's side;
And quickly these were found, yet slowly he complied.
    The morning came: the common service done—
Shut every door—the solemn rite begun;   190
And, as the priest the sacred sayings read,
The clerk went forward, trembling as he tread;
O'er the tall pew he held the box, and heard
The offer'd piece, rejoicing as he fear'd.
Just by the pillar, as he cautious tripp'd,
And turn'd the aile, he then a portion slipp'd
From the full store, and to the pocket sent,
But held a moment—and then down it went.
    The priest read on; on walk'd the man afraid,
Till a gold offering in the plate was laid;   200
Trembling he took it, for a moment stopp'd,
Then down it fell, and sounded as it dropp'd;
Amazed he started, for th' affrighted man,
Lost and bewilder'd, thought not of the bran;
But all were silent, all on things intent
Of high concern; none ear to money lent;
So on he walk'd, more cautious than before,
And gain'd the purposed sum, and one piece more.
    Practice makes perfect;—when the month came round,
He dropp'd the cash, nor listen'd for a sound;   210
But yet, when, last of all th' assembled flock,
He ate and drank—it gave th' electric shock.
Oft was he forced his reasons to repeat,
Ere he could kneel in quiet at his seat;
But custom soothed him.—Ere a single year
All this was done without restraint or fear:
Cool and collected, easy and composed,
He was correct till all the service closed;
Then to his home, without a groan or sigh,
Gravely he went, and laid his treasure by.   220
    Want will complain: some widows had express'd
A doubt if they were favour'd like the rest;
The rest described with like regret their dole,
And thus from parts they reason'd to the whole;

THE BOROUGH

When all agreed some evil must be done,
Or rich men's hearts grew harder than a stone.
Our easy vicar cut the matter short;
He would not listen to such vile report.
    All were not thus—there govern'd in that year
A stern stout churl, an angry overseer;   230
A tyrant fond of power, loud, lewd, and most severe.   [ ]]
Him the mild vicar, him the graver clerk,
Advised, reproved, but nothing would he mark,
Save the disgrace; "and that, my friends," said he,
"Will I avenge, whenever time may be."
And now, alas! 'twas time;—from man to man
Doubt and alarm and shrewd suspicions ran.
    With angry spirit and with sly intent,
This parish ruler to the altar went;
A private mark he fix'd on shillings three,   240
And but one mark could in the money see;
Besides, in peering round, he chanced to note
A sprinkling slight on Jachin's Sunday-coat.
All doubt was over:—when the flock were bless'd,
In wrath he rose, and thus his mind express'd.
    "Foul deeds are here!" and, saying this, he took
The clerk, whose conscience, in her cold-fit, shook.
His pocket then was emptied on the place;
All saw his guilt; all witness'd his disgrace:
He fell, he fainted; not a groan, a look,   250
Escaped the culprit; 'twas a final stroke—
A death-wound never to be heal'd—a fall
That all had witness'd, and amazed were all.
    As he recover'd, to his mind it came,
"I owe to Satan this disgrace and shame."
All the seduction now appear'd in view;
"Let me withdraw," he said, and he withdrew;
No one withheld him, all in union cried,
E'en the avenger—"We are satisfied;"
For what has death in any form to give,   260
Equal to that man's terrors, if he live?
    He lived in freedom, but he hourly saw
How much more fatal justice is than law;
He saw another in his office reign,

And his mild master treat him with disdain;
He saw that all men shunn'd him, some reviled;
The harsh pass'd frowning, and the simple smiled;
The town maintain'd him, but with some reproof;
"And clerks and scholars proudly kept aloof."
   In each lone place, dejected and dismay'd,   270
Shrinking from view, his wasting form he laid;
Or to the restless sea and roaring wind
Gave the strong yearnings of a ruin'd mind.
On the broad beach, the silent summer-day,
Stretch'd on some wreck, he wore his life away;
Or where the river mingles with the sea,
Or on the mud-bank by the elder-tree,
Or by the bounding marsh-dyke, there was he;   [ ]]
And when unable to forsake the town,
In the blind courts he sate desponding down—   280
Always alone; then feebly would he crawl
The church-way walk, and lean upon the wall.
Too ill for this, he lay beside the door,
Compell'd to hear the reasoning of the poor:
He look'd so pale, so weak, the pitying crowd
Their firm belief of his repentance vow'd;
They saw him then so ghastly and so thin,
That they exclaim'd, "Is this the work of sin?"
   "Yes," in his better moments, he replied,
"Of sinful avarice and the spirit's pride;—   290
"While yet untempted, I was safe and well;
"Temptation came; I reason'd, and I fell.
"To be man's guide and glory I design'd,
"A rare example for our sinful kind;
"But now my weakness and my guilt I see,
"And am a warning—man, be warn'd by me!"
   He said, and saw no more the human face;
To a lone loft he went, his dying place,
And, as the vicar of his state inquired,
Turn'd to the wall and silently expired!   300

THE BOROUGH.

LETTER XX.

THE POOR OF THE BOROUGH.

ELLEN ORFORD.

> Patience and sorrow strove
> Who should express her goodliest.
> *Shakspeare. Lear* [Act iv. Sc. 3, ll. 16-7].

"No charms she now can boast,"—'tis true,
But other charmers wither too:
"And she is old,"—the fact I know,
And old will other heroines grow;
But not like them has she been laid,
In ruin'd castle, sore dismay'd;
Where naughty man and ghostly spright
    Fill'd her pure mind with awe and dread,
Stalk'd round the room, put out the light,
    And shook the curtains round the bed.
No cruel uncle kept her land;
No tyrant father forced her hand;
    She had no vixen virgin-aunt,
Without whose aid she could not eat,
And yet who poison'd all her meat,
    With gibe and sneer and taunt.
Yet of the heroine she'd a share:
She saved a lover from despair,
And granted all his wish, in spite
Of what she knew and felt was right;
    But heroine then no more,
She own'd the fault, and wept and pray'd,
And humbly took the parish aid,
    And dwelt among the poor.

The Widow's Cottage—Blind Ellen one—Hers not the Sorrows or Adventures of Heroines—What these are, first described—Deserted Wives; rash Lovers; courageous Damsels: in desolated Mansions; in grievous Perplexity—These Evils, however severe, of short Duration—Ellen's Story—Her Employment in Childhood—First Love; first Adventure; its miserable Termination—An idiot Daughter—A Husband—Care in Business without Success—The Man's Despondency and its Effect—Their Children: how disposed of—One particularly unfortunate—Fate of the Daughter—Ellen keeps a School and is happy—Becomes blind; loses her School—Her Consolations.

THE BOROUGH.

LETTER XX.

ELLEN ORFORD.

OBSERVE yon tenement, apart and small,
  Where the wet pebbles shine upon the wall;
Where the low benches lean beside the door,
And the red paling bounds the space before;
Where thrift and lavender and lad's-love [1] bloom—
That humble dwelling is the widow's home.
There live a pair, for various fortunes known,
But the Blind Ellen will relate her own ;—
Yet, ere we hear the story she can tell,
On prouder sorrows let us briefly dwell.   10
  I've often marvel'd, when by night, by day,
I've mark'd the manners moving in my way,
And heard the language and beheld the lives
Of lass and lover, goddesses and wives :
That books, which promise much of life to give,
Should show so little how we truly live.
  To me it seems, their females and their men
Are but the creatures of the author's pen ;
Nay, creatures borrow'd and again convey'd
From book to book—the shadows of a shade.   20
Life, if they'd search, would show them many a change,
The ruin sudden and the misery strange !
With more of grievous, base, and dreadful things,
Than novelists relate or poet sings.
But they, who ought to look the world around,
Spy out a single spot in fairy-ground ;
Where all, in turn, ideal forms behold,
And plots are laid and histories are told.

THE BOROUGH

Time have I lent—I would their debt were less—
To flow'ry pages of sublime distress;
And to the heroine's soul-distracting fears
I early gave my sixpences and tears:
Oft have I travell'd in these tender tales,
To Darnley-Cottages and Maple-Vales,
And watch'd the fair-one from the first-born sigh,
When Henry pass'd and gazed in passing by;
Till I beheld them pacing in the park,
Close by a coppice where 'twas cold and dark;
When such affection with such fate appear'd,
Want and a father to be shunn'd and fear'd,
Without employment, prospect, cot, or cash,
That I have judged th' heroic souls were rash.
  Now shifts the scene—the fair, in tower confined,
In all things suffers but in change of mind;
Now woo'd by greatness to a bed of state,
Now deeply threaten'd with a dungeon's grate;
Till, suffering much and being tried enough,
She shines, triumphant maid!—temptation-proof.
  Then was I led to vengeful monks, who mix
With nymphs and swains, and play unpriestly tricks;
Then view'd banditti, who in forest wide,
And cavern vast, indignant virgins hide;
Who, hemm'd with bands of sturdiest rogues about,
Find some strange succour, and come virgins out.
  I've watch'd a wint'ry night on castle-walls;
I've stalk'd by moonlight through deserted halls;
And, when the weary world was sunk to rest,
I've had such sights as—may not be express'd.
  Lo! that chateau, the western tower decay'd,
The peasants shun it—they are all afraid;
For there was done a deed!—could walls reveal,
Or timbers tell it, how the heart would feel!
Most horrid was it:—for, behold, the floor
Has stain of blood, and will be clean no more.
Hark to the winds! which through the wide saloon
And the long passage send a dismal tune—
Music that ghosts delight in;—and now heed
Yon beauteous nymph, who must unmask the deed.

GEORGE CRABBE

See! with majestic sweep she swims alone
Through rooms, all dreary, guided by a groan;   70
Though windows rattle, and though tap'stries shake,
And the feet falter every step they take,
'Mid groans and gibing sprights she silent goes,
To find a something, which will soon expose
The villanies and wiles of her determined foes;   [}]
And, having thus adventured, thus endured,
Fame, wealth, and lover, are for life secured.
  Much have I fear'd, but am no more afraid,
When some chaste beauty, by some wretch betray'd,
Is drawn away with such distracted speed,   80
That she anticipates a dreadful deed;—
Not so do I.—Let solid walls impound
The captive fair, and dig a moat around;
Let there be brazen locks and bars of steel,
And keepers cruel, such as never feel;
With not a single note the purse supply,
And when she begs, let men and maids deny;
Be windows those from which she dares not fall,
And help so distant, 'tis in vain to call;
Still means of freedom will some power devise,   90
And from the baffled ruffian snatch his prize.
  To Northern Wales, in some sequester'd spot,
I've follow'd fair Louisa to her cot;
Where, then a wretched and deserted bride,
The injured fair-one wish'd from man to hide;
Till by her fond repenting Belville found,
By some kind chance—the straying of a hound—
He at her feet craved mercy, nor in vain;
For the relenting dove flew back again.
  There's something rapturous in distress, or, oh!   100
Could Clementina bear her lot of wo?
Or what she underwent could maiden undergo?   [}]
The day was fix'd; for so the lover sigh'd,
So knelt and craved, he couldn't be denied;
When, tale most dreadful! every hope adieu—
For the fond lover is the brother too:
All other griefs abate; this monstrous grief
Has no remission, comfort, or relief;

472

THE BOROUGH

Four ample volumes, through each page disclose—
Good Heaven protect us!—only woes on woes;   110
Till some strange means afford a sudden view
Of some vile plot, and every wo adieu! [2]
    Now, should we grant these beauties all endure
Severest pangs, they've still the speediest cure,
Before one charm be wither'd from the face,   ⎫
Except the bloom, which shall again have place,   ⎬ [ ]
In wedlock ends each wish, in triumph all disgrace;   ⎭
And life to come we fairly may suppose
One light, bright contrast to these wild dark woes.
    These let us leave, and at her sorrows look,   120
Too often seen, but seldom in a book;
Let her who felt, relate them.—On her chair
The heroine sits—in former years the fair,
Now aged and poor; but Ellen Orford knows,
That we should humbly take what Heav'n bestows.
    "My father died—again my mother wed,
" And found the comforts of her life were fled;
" Her angry husband, vex'd through half his years
" By loss and troubles, fill'd her soul with fears;
" Their children many, and 'twas my poor place   130
" To nurse and wait on all the infant-race;
" Labour and hunger were indeed my part,
" And should have strengthen'd an erroneous heart.
    " Sore was the grief to see him angry come,
" And, teased with business, make distress at home;
" The father's fury and the children's cries
" I soon could bear, but not my mother's sighs;
" For she look'd back on comforts, and would say,
" ' I wrong'd thee, Ellen,' and then turn away.
" Thus for my age's good, my youth was tried,   140
" And this my fortune till my mother died.
    " So, amid sorrow much and little cheer—
" A common case—I pass'd my twentieth year;
" For these are frequent evils; thousands share
" An equal grief—the like domestic care.
    " Then in my days of bloom, of health and youth,
" One, much above me, vow'd his love and truth.
" We often met, he dreading to be seen,

GEORGE CRABBE

"And much I question'd what such dread might mean ;
"Yet I believed him true ; my simple heart   150
"And undirected reason took his part.
    "Can he who loves me, whom I love, deceive?   )
"Can I such wrong of one so kind believe,   }
"Who lives but in my smile, who trembles when I grieve? [ ]]
    "He dared not marry, but we met to prove
"What sad encroachments and deceits has love :
"Weak that I was, when he, rebuked, withdrew,
"I let him see that I was wretched too ;
"When less my caution, I had still the pain
"Of his or mine own weakness to complain.   160
    "Happy the lovers class'd alike in life,
"Or happier yet the rich endowing wife ;
"But most aggrieved the fond believing maid,
"Of her rich lover tenderly afraid.
"You judge th' event ; for grievous was my fate,
"Painful to feel, and shameful to relate :
"Ah! sad it was my burthen to sustain,
"When the least misery was the dread of pain ;
"When I have grieving told him my disgrace,
"And plainly mark'd indifference in his face.   170
    "Hard! with these fears and terrors to behold
"The cause of all, the faithless lover cold ;
"Impatient grown at every wish denied,
"And barely civil, soothed and gratified ;
"Peevish when urged to think of vows so strong,
"And angry when I spake of crime and wrong.
    "All this I felt, and still the sorrow grew,
"Because I felt that I deserved it too,
"And begg'd my infant stranger to forgive
"The mother's shame, which in herself must live.   180
    "When known that shame, I, soon expell'd from home,
"With a frail sister shared a hovel's gloom ;
"There barely fed—(what could I more request?)—
"My infant slumberer sleeping at my breast ;
"I from my window saw his blooming bride,
"And my seducer smiling at her side ;
"Hope lived till then ; I sank upon the floor,
"And grief and thought and feeling were no more.

474

"Although revived, I judged that life would close,
"And went to rest, to wonder that I rose: 190
"My dreams were dismal; wheresoe'er I stray'd,
"I seem'd ashamed, alarm'd, despised, betray'd;
"Always in grief, in guilt, disgraced, forlorn,
"Mourning that one so weak, so vile, was born;
"The earth a desert, tumult in the sea,
"The birds affrighted fled from tree to tree,
"Obscured the setting sun, and every thing like me;   [}]
"But Heav'n had mercy, and my need at length
"Urged me to labour and renew'd my strength.
"I strove for patience as a sinner must,   200
"Yet felt th' opinion of the world unjust:
"There was my lover, in his joy, esteem'd,
"And I, in my distress, as guilty deem'd;
"Yet sure, not all the guilt and shame belong
"To her who feels and suffers for the wrong.
"The cheat at play may use the wealth he's won,
"But is not honour'd for the mischief done;
"The cheat in love may use each villain-art,
"And boast the deed that breaks the victim's heart.
"Four years were past; I might again have found   210
"Some erring wish, but for another wound:
"Lovely my daughter grew, her face was fair;
"But no expression ever brighten'd there.
"I doubted long, and vainly strove to make
"Some certain meaning of the words she spake;
"But meaning there was none, and I survey'd
"With dread the beauties of my idiot-maid.
"Still I submitted;—Oh! 'tis meet and fit
"In all we feel to make the heart submit;
"Gloomy and calm my days, but I had then,   220
"It seem'd, attractions for the eyes of men.
"The sober master of a decent trade
"O'erlook'd my errors, and his offer made;
"Reason assented;—true, my heart denied,
"'But thou,' I said, 'shalt be no more my guide.'
"When wed, our toil and trouble, pains and care,
"Of means to live procured us humble share;
"Five were our sons,—and we, though careful, found

"Our hopes declining as the year came round;
"For I perceived, yet would not soon perceive,   230
"My husband stealing from my view to grieve;
"Silent he grew, and when he spoke he sigh'd,
"And surly look'd and peevishly replied.
"Pensive by nature, he had gone of late
"To those who preach'd of destiny and fate,
"Of things fore-doom'd, and of election-grace,
"And how in vain we strive to run our race;
"That all by works and moral worth we gain
"Is to perceive our care and labour vain;
"That still the more we pay, our debts the more remain; 240[ ]]
"That he who feels not the mysterious call,
"Lies bound in sin, still grov'ling from the fall.
"My husband felt not;—our persuasion, prayer,
"And our best reason darken'd his despair;
"His very nature changed; he now reviled
"My former conduct—he reproach'd my child;
"He talk'd of bastard slips, and cursed his bed,
"And from our kindness to concealment fled;
"For ever to some evil change inclined,
"To every gloomy thought he lent his mind, 250
"Nor rest would give to us, nor rest himself could find; [ ]]
"His son suspended saw him, long bereft
"Of life, nor prospect of revival left.
  "With him died all our prospects, and once more
"I shared th' allotments of the parish poor;
"They took my children too, and this I know
"Was just and lawful, but I felt the blow;
"My idiot-maid and one unhealthy boy
"Were left, a mother's misery and her joy.
  "Three sons I follow'd to the grave, and one— 260
"Oh! can I speak of that unhappy son?
"Would all the memory of that time were fled,
"And all those horrors, with my child, were dead!
"Before the world seduced him, what a grace
"And smile of gladness shone upon his face!
"Then he had knowledge; finely would he write;
"Study to him was pleasure and delight;
"Great was his courage, and but few could stand

THE BOROUGH

"Against the sleight and vigour of his hand;
"The maidens loved him;—when he came to die,   270
"No, not the coldest could suppress a sigh.
"Here I must cease—how can I say, my child
"Was by the bad of either sex beguiled?
"Worst of the bad—they taught him that the laws
"Made wrong and right; there was no other cause;
"That all religion was the trade of priests,
"And men, when dead, must perish like the beasts;—
"And he, so lively and so gay before——
"Ah! spare a mother—I can tell no more.
      "Int'rest was made that they should not destroy   280
"The comely form of my deluded boy—
"But pardon came not; damp the place and deep
"Where he was kept, as they'd a tiger keep;
"For he, unhappy! had before them all
"Vow'd he'd escape, whatever might befall.
      "He'd means of dress, and dress'd beyond his means,
"And, so to see him in such dismal scenes,
"I cannot speak it—cannot bear to tell
"Of that sad hour—I heard the passing-bell!
      "Slowly they went; he smiled and look'd so smart,   290
"Yet sure he shudder'd when he saw the cart,
"And gave a look—until my dying-day,
"That look will never from my mind away;
"Oft as I sit, and ever in my dreams,
"I see that look, and they have heard my screams.
      "Now let me speak no more—yet all declared
"That one so young, in pity should be spared,
"And one so manly;—on his graceful neck,
"That chains of jewels may be proud to deck,
"To a small mole a mother's lips have press'd—   300
"And there the cord—my breath is sore oppress'd.
      "I now can speak again:—my elder boy
"Was that year drown'd—a seaman in a hoy.
"He left a numerous race; of these would some
"In their young troubles to my cottage come;
"And these I taught—an humble teacher I—
"Upon their heavenly Parent to rely.
      "Alas! I needed such reliance more:

477

"My idiot-girl, so simply gay before,
"Now wept in pain; some wretch had found a time,   310
"Depraved and wicked, for that coward-crime;
"I had indeed my doubt, but I suppress'd
"The thought that day and night disturb'd my rest;
"She and that sick-pale brother—but why strive
"To keep the terrors of that time alive?
  "The hour arrived, the new, th' undreaded pain,
"That came with violence and yet came in vain.
"I saw her die; her brother too is dead,
"Nor own'd such crime—what is it that I dread?
  "The parish-aid withdrawn, I look'd around,   320
"And in my school a bless'd subsistence found—
"My winter-calm of life: to be of use
"Would pleasant thoughts and heavenly hopes produce;
"I loved them all; it soothed me to presage
"The various trials of their riper age,
"Then dwell on mine, and bless the Power who gave
"Pains to correct us, and remorse to save.
  "Yes! these were days of peace, but they are past—
"A trial came, I will believe, a last;
"I lost my sight, and my employment gone,   330
"Useless I live, but to the day live on;
"Those eyes, which long the light of heaven enjoy'd,
"Were not by pain, by agony destroy'd;
"My senses fail not all; I speak, I pray;
"By night my rest, my food I take by day;
"And as my mind looks cheerful to my end,
"I love mankind and call my GOD my friend."

THE BOROUGH

NOTES TO LETTER XX.

Note 1, page 470, line 5.

Where thrift and lavender and lad's-love bloom.

The lad's or boy's love of some counties is the plant southernwood, the artemisia abrotanum of botanists.

Note 2, page 473, line 112.

Of some vile plot, and every two adieu!

As this incident points out the work alluded to, I wish it to be remembered, that the gloomy tenour, the querulous melancholy of the story, is all I censure. The language of the writer is often animated, and is, I believe, correct; the characters well drawn, and the manners described from real life; but the perpetual occurrence of sad events, the protracted list of teasing and perplexing mischances, joined with much waspish invective, unallayed by pleasantry or sprightliness, and these continued through many hundred pages, render publications, intended for amusement and executed with ability, heavy and displeasing;—you find your favourite persons happy in the end; but they have teased you so much with their perplexities by the way, that you were frequently disposed to quit them in their distresses.

479

THE BOROUGH.

LETTER XXI.

THE POOR OF THE BOROUGH.

ABEL KEENE.

[Cœpisti] melius quam [desinis] : ultima primis
Cedunt. Dissimiles : hic vir et ille puer.
Ovid. Deïanira Herculi [Heroid. VIII. vv. 23-4].

Now the Spirit speaketh expressly, that, in the latter times, some shall
depart from the faith, giving heed to seducing spirits and doctrines of
devils.   [1] *Epistle to Timothy*, [ch. IV. v. 1].

Abel, a poor Man, Teacher of a School of the lower Order ; is placed in
    the Office of a Merchant ; is alarmed by Discourses of the Clerks;
    unable to reply ; becomes a Convert; dresses, drinks, and ridicules
    his former Conduct—The Remonstrance of his Sister, a devout
    Maiden—Its Effect—The Merchant dies—Abel returns to Poverty
    unpitied ; but relieved—His abject Condition—His Melancholy—He
    wanders about : is found—His own Account of himself, and the
    Revolutions in his Mind.

THE BOROUGH.

LETTER XXI.

ABEL KEENE.

A QUIET simple man was Abel Keene ;
   He meant no harm, nor did he often mean.
He kept a school of loud rebellious boys,
And growing old, grew nervous with the noise ;
When a kind merchant hired his useful pen,
And made him happiest of accompting men ;
With glee he rose to every easy day,
When half the labour brought him twice the pay.
   There were young clerks, and there the merchant's son,
Choice spirits all, who wish'd him to be one ;   10
It must, no question, give them lively joy,
Hopes long indulged, to combat and destroy ;
At these they level'd all their skill and strength—
He fell not quickly, but he fell at length.
They quoted books, to him both bold and new,
And scorn'd as fables all he held as true—
" Such monkish stories and such nursery lies,"
That he was struck with terror and surprise.
   " What ! all his life had he the laws obey'd,
" Which they broke through and were not once afraid ?   20
" Had he so long his evil passions check'd,
" And yet at last had nothing to expect ?
" While they their lives in joy and pleasure led,
" And then had nothing, at the end, to dread ?
" Was all his priest with so much zeal convey'd,
" A part ! a speech ! for which the man was paid ?
" And were his pious books, his solemn prayers,

Crabbe   HH

" Not worth one tale of the admired Voltaire's?
" Then was it time, while yet some years remain'd,
" To drink untroubled and to think unchain'd,   30
" And on all pleasures, which his purse could give,
" Freely to seize, and while he lived, to live."
Much time he passed in this important strife,
The bliss or bane of his remaining life;
For converts all are made with care and grief,
And pangs attend the birth of unbelief;
Nor pass they soon;—with awe and fear he took
The flow'ry way, and cast back many a look.
The youths applauded much his wise design,
With weighty reasoning o'er their evening wine;   40
And much in private 'twould their mirth improve,
To hear how Abel spake of life and love;
To hear him own what grievous pains it cost,
Ere the old saint was in the sinner lost;
Ere his poor mind with every deed alarm'd,
By wit was settled, and by vice was charm'd.
For Abel enter'd in his bold career,
Like boys on ice, with pleasure and with fear;
Lingering, yet longing for the joy, he went,
Repenting now, now dreading to repent;   50
With awkward pace, and with himself at war,
Far gone, yet frighten'd that he went so far;
Oft for his efforts he'd solicit praise,
And then proceed with blunders and delays.
The young more aptly passion's calls pursue,
But age and weakness start at scenes so new,
And tremble when they've done, for all they dared to do. [ ]]
At length example Abel's dread removed;
With small concern he sought the joys he loved;
Not resting here, he claim'd his share of fame,   60
And first their votary, then their wit became;
His jest was bitter and his satire bold,
When he his tales of formal brethren told,
What time with pious neighbours he discuss'd,
Their boasted treasure and their boundless trust:
"Such were our dreams," the jovial elder cried;
"Awake and live," his youthful friends replied,

THE BOROUGH

Now the gay clerk a modest drab despised,
And clad him smartly as his friends advised;
So fine a coat upon his back he threw,   70
That not an alley-boy old Abel knew;
Broad polish'd buttons blazed that coat upon,
And just beneath the watch's trinkets shone—
A splendid watch, that pointed out the time,
To fly from business and make free with crime.
The crimson waistcoat and the silken hose
Rank'd the lean man among the Borough beaux;
His raven hair he cropp'd with fierce disdain,
And light elastic locks encased his brain:
More pliant pupil who could hope to find,   80
So deck'd in person and so changed in mind?
  When Abel walk'd the streets, with pleasant mien
He met his friends, delighted to be seen;
And, when he rode along the public way,
No beau so gaudy and no youth so gay.
  His pious sister, now an ancient maid,
For Abel fearing, first in secret pray'd;
Then thus in love and scorn her notions she convey'd: [ ]]
  "Alas! my brother! can I see thee pace
"Hoodwink'd to hell, and not lament thy case,   90
"Nor stretch my feeble hand to stop thy headlong race? [ ]]
"Lo! thou art bound; a slave in Satan's chain,
"The righteous Abel turn'd the wretched Cain;
"His brother's blood against the murderer cried;
"Against thee thine, unhappy suicide!
"Are all our pious nights and peaceful days,
"Our evening readings and our morning praise,
"Our spirits' comfort in the trials sent,
"Our hearts' rejoicings in the blessings lent,
"All that o'er grief a cheering influence shed—   100
"Are these for ever and for ever fled?
  "When in the years gone by, the trying years,
"When faith and hope had strife with wants and fears,
"Thy nerves have trembled till thou couldst not eat
"(Dress'd by this hand) thy mess of simple meat;
"When, grieved by fastings, gall'd by fates severe,
"Slow pass'd the days of the successless year;

GEORGE CRABBE

"Still in these gloomy hours, my brother then
"Had glorious views, unseen by prosperous men :
"And when thy heart has felt its wish denied,   110
"What gracious texts hast thou to grief applied ;
"Till thou hast enter'd in thine humble bed,
"By lofty hopes and heavenly musings fed ;
"Then I have seen thy lively looks express
"The spirit's comforts in the man's distress.
  "Then didst thou cry, exulting, ' Yes, 'tis fit,
"' 'Tis meet and right, my heart ! that we submit ; '
"And wilt thou, Abel, thy new pleasures weigh
"Against such triumphs ?—Oh ! repent and pray.
  "What are thy pleasures ?—with the gay to sit,   120
"And thy poor brain torment for awkward wit ;
"All thy good thoughts (thou hat'st them) to restrain,
"And give a wicked pleasure to the vain ;
"Thy long lean frame by fashion to attire,
"That lads may laugh and wantons may admire ;
"To raise the mirth of boys, and not to see,
"Unhappy maniac ! that they laugh at thee.
  "These boyish follies, which alone the boy
"Can idly act or gracefully enjoy,
"Add new reproaches to thy fallen state,   130
"And make men scorn what they would only hate.
  "What pains, my brother, dost thou take to prove
"A taste for follies which thou canst not love !
"Why do thy stiffening limbs the steed bestride—
"That lads may laugh to see thou canst not ride ?
"And why (I feel the crimson tinge my cheek)
"Dost thou by night in Diamond-Alley sneak ?
  "Farewell ! the parish will thy sister keep,
"Where she in peace shall pray and sing and sleep,
"Save when for thee she mourns, thou wicked, wandering
    sheep !   140[ ]]
"When youth is fall'n, there's hope the young may rise,
"But fallen age for ever hopeless lies :
"Torn up by storms and placed in earth once more,
"The younger tree may sun and soil restore ;
"But when the old and sapless trunk lies low,
"No care or soil can former life bestow ;

484

THE BOROUGH

"Reserved for burning is the worthless tree;
"And what, O—Abel! is reserved for thee?"
These angry words our hero deeply felt,
Though hard his heart, and indisposed to melt!   150
To gain relief he took a glass the more,
And, then went on as careless as before;
Thenceforth, uncheck'd, amusements he partook,
And (save his ledger) saw no decent book;
Him found the merchant punctual at his task,
And, that perform'd, he'd nothing more to ask;
He cared not how old Abel play'd the fool,
No master he, beyond the hours of school:
Thus they, proceeding, had their wine and joke,
Till merchant Dixon felt a warning stroke,   160
And, after struggling half a gloomy week,
Left his poor clerk another friend to seek.
Alas! the son, who led the saint astray,
Forgot the man whose follies made him gay;
He cared no more for Abel in his need,
[Than] Abel cared about his hackney steed;
He now, alas! had all his earnings spent,
And thus was left to languish and repent;
No school nor clerkship found he in the place,
Now lost to fortune, as before to grace.   170
For town-relief the grieving man applied,
And begg'd with tears what some with scorn denied;
Others look'd down upon the glowing vest,
And, frowning, ask'd him at what price he dress'd?
Happy for him his country's laws are mild,
They must support him, though they still reviled;
Grieved, abject, scorn'd, insulted, and betray'd,
Of God unmindful, and of man afraid—
No more he talk'd; 'twas pain, 'twas shame to speak,
His heart was sinking and his frame was weak.   180
His sister died with such serene delight,
He once again began to think her right;
Poor like himself, the happy spinster lay,
And sweet assurance bless'd her dying-day;
Poor like the spinster, he, when death was nigh,
Assured of nothing, felt afraid to die.

485

GEORGE CRABBE

The cheerful clerks who sometimes pass'd the door,
Just mention'd "Abel!" and then thought no more.
So Abel, pondering on his state forlorn,
Look'd round for comfort, and was chased by scorn.   190
And now we saw him on the beach reclined,
Or causeless walking in the wint'ry wind;
And, when it raised a loud and angry sea,
He stood and gazed, in wretched reverie;
He heeded not the frost, the rain, the snow;
Close by the sea he walk'd alone and slow.
Sometimes his frame through many an hour he spread
Upon a tombstone, moveless as the dead;
And, was there found a sad and silent place,
There would he creep with slow and measured pace.   200
Then would he wander by the river's side,
And fix his eyes upon the falling tide;
The deep dry ditch, the rushes in the fen,
And mossy crag-pits were his lodgings then:
There, to his discontented thoughts a prey,
The melancholy mortal pined away.
The neighb'ring poor at length began to speak
Of Abel's ramblings—he'd been gone a week,
They knew not where; and little care they took
For one so friendless and so poor to look;   210
At last a stranger, in a pedler's shed,
Beheld him hanging—he had long been dead.
He left a paper, penn'd at sundry times,
Intitled thus—"My Groanings and my Crimes!"
"I was a christian man, and none could lay
"Aught to my charge; I walk'd the narrow way:
"All then was simple faith, serene and pure,
"My hope was steadfast and my prospects sure;
"Then was I tried by want and sickness sore,
"But these I clapp'd my shield of faith before,   220
"And cares and wants and man's rebukes I bore.   []]
"Alas! new foes assail'd me; I was vain,
"They stung my pride and they confused my brain:
"Oh! these deluders! with what glee they saw
"Their simple dupe transgress the righteous law;
"'Twas joy to them to view that dreadful strife,

486

"When faith and frailty warr'd for more than life;
"So with their pleasures they beguiled the heart,
"Then with their logic they allay'd the smart;
"They proved (so thought I then) with reasons strong,   230
"That no man's feelings ever led him wrong;
"And thus I went, as on the varnish'd ice,
"The smooth career of unbelief and vice.
"Oft would the youths, with sprightly speech and bold,
"Their witty tales of naughty priests unfold;
"''Twas all a craft,' they said, 'a cunning trade,
"'Not she the priests, but priests religion made:'
"So I believed;"—No, Abel! to thy grief,
So thou relinquish'dst all that was belief;—
"I grew as very flint, and when the rest   240
"Laugh'd at devotion, I enjoy'd the jest;
"But this all vanish'd like the morning-dew,
"When unemploy'd, and poor again I grew;
"Yea! I was doubly poor, for I was wicked too.   [ ]]

"The mouse that trespass'd and the treasure stole,
"Found his lean body fitted to the hole;
"Till, having fatted, he was forced to stay,
"And, fasting, starve his stolen bulk away.
"Ah! worse for me—grown poor, I yet remain
"In sinful bonds, and pray and fast in vain.   250

"At length I thought: although these friends of sin
"Have spread their net and caught their prey therein;
"Though my hard heart could not for mercy call,
"Because, though great my grief, my faith was small;
"Yet, as the sick on skilful men rely,
"The soul diseased may to a doctor fly.

"A famous one there was, whose skill had wrought
"Cures past relief, and him the sinners sought;
"Numbers there were defiled by mire and filth,
"Whom he recover'd by his goodly tilth:—   260
"''Come then,' I said, 'let me the man behold,
"'And tell my case;'—I saw him and I told.

"With trembling voice, 'Oh! reverend sir,' I said,
"'I once believed, and I was then misled;
"'And now such doubts my sinful soul beset,
"'I dare not say that I'm a Christian yet;

GEORGE CRABBE

"'Canst thou, good sir, by thy superior skill,
"'Inform my judgment and direct my will?
"'Ah! give thy cordial; let my soul have rest,
"'And be the outward man alone distress'd;   270
"'For at my state I tremble.'—'Tremble more,'
"Said the good man, 'and then rejoice therefore;
"''Tis good to tremble; prospects then are fair,
"'When the lost soul is plunged in deep despair.
"'Once thou wert simply honest, just and pure,
"'Whole, as thou thought'st, and never wish'd a cure;
"'Now thou hast plunged in folly, shame, disgrace;
"'Now thou'rt an object meet for healing grace;
"'No merit thine, no virtue, hope, belief;
"'Nothing hast thou, but misery, sin, and grief,   280
"'The best, the only titles to relief.'   [ ]]
"'What must I do,' I said, 'my soul to free?'
"'—Do nothing, man; it will be done for thee.'
"'But must I not, my reverend guide, believe?'
"'—If thou art call'd, thou wilt the faith receive;'—
"'But I repent not.'—Angry he replied,
"'If thou art call'd, thou needest nought beside;
"'Attend on us, and if 'tis Heaven's decree,
"'The call will come—if not, ah! wo for thee.'
"There then I waited, ever on the watch,   290
"A spark of hope, a ray of light to catch;
"His words fell softly like the flakes of snow,
"But I could never find my heart o'erflow.
"He cried aloud, till in the flock began
"The sigh, the tear, as caught from man to man;
"They wept and they rejoiced, and there was I,
"Hard as a flint, and as the desert dry.
"To me no tokens of the call would come,
"I felt my sentence and received my doom;
"But I complain'd;—'Let thy repinings cease,   300
"'Oh! man of sin, for they thy guilt increase;
"'It bloweth where it listeth;—die in peace.'   [ ]]
"—'In peace, and perish?' I replied; 'impart
"'Some better comfort to a burthen'd heart.'—
"'Alas!' the priest return'd, 'can I direct
"'The heavenly call?—Do I proclaim th' elect?

488

"'Raise not thy voice against th' Eternal will,
"'But take thy part with sinners and be still [1].'
"Alas! for me, no more the times of peace
"Are mine on earth—in death my pains may cease.   310
"Foes to my soul! ye young seducers, know,
"What serious ills from your amusements flow;
"Opinions you with so much ease profess
"O'erwhelm the simple and their minds oppress:
"Let such be happy, nor with reasons strong,
"That make them wretched, prove their notions wrong;
"Let them proceed in that they deem the way,
"Fast when they will, and at their pleasure pray.
"Yes, I have pity for my brethren's lot;
"And so had Dives, but it help'd him not.   320
"And is it thus?—I'm full of doubts:—Adieu!
"Perhaps his reverence is mistaken too."

GEORGE CRABBE

NOTE TO LETTER XXI.

Note 1, page 489, line 308.

But take thy part with sinners and be still.

In a periodical work for the month of June last, the preceding dialogue
is pronounced to be a most abominable caricature, if meant to be applied
to Calvinists in general, and greatly distorted, if designed for an individual.
Now, the author in his preface has declared, that he takes not upon him the
censure of any sect or society for their opinions; and the lines themselves
evidently point to an individual, whose sentiments they very fairly represent,
without any distortion whatsoever. In a pamphlet intitled " A Cordial
for a Sin-despairing Soul," originally written by a teacher of religion, and
lately re-published by another teacher of greater notoriety, the reader is
informed that after he had full assurance of his salvation, the Spirit entered
particularly into the subject with him ; and, among many other matters of
like nature, assured him that " his sins were fully and freely forgiven, as if
" they had never been committed : not for any act done by him, whether
" believing in Christ, or repenting of sin; nor yet for the sorrows and
" miseries he endured, nor for any service he should be called upon in his
" militant state, but for his own name and for his glory's sake[1]," &c. And
the whole drift and tenour of the book is to the same purpose, viz. the
uselessness of all religious duties, such as prayer, contrition, fasting, and
good works : he shows the evil done by reading such books as the Whole
Duty of Man, and the Practice of Piety ; and complains heavily of his
relation, an Irish bishop, who wanted him to join with the household in
family prayer : in fact, the whole work inculcates that sort of quietism
which this dialogue alludes to, and that without any recommendation of
attendance on the teachers of the Gospel, but rather holding forth encouragement to the supineness of man's nature ; by the information that
he in vain looks for acceptance by the employment of his talents, and that
his hopes of glory are rather extinguished than raised by any application to
the means of grace.

[1] Cordial, &c. page 87.

THE BOROUGH.

LETTER XXII.

THE POOR OF THE BOROUGH.

PETER GRIMES.

———————Was a sordid soul,
Such as does murder for a meed;
Who but for fear knows no control,
Because his conscience, sear'd and foul,
Feels not the import of the deed;
One whose brute feeling ne'er aspires
Beyond his own more brute desires.
Scott, Marmion [Canto II.].

Methought the souls of all that I had murder'd
Came to my tent, and every one did threat———
Shakspeare. Richard III. [Aft v. Sc. 3, vv. 204-5].

The times have been,
That, when the brains were out, the man would die,
And there an end; but now they rise again,
With twenty mortal murders on their crowns,
And push us from our stools.
Macbeth [Aft III. Sc. 4. vv. 78-82].

THE BOROUGH.

LETTER XXII.

PETER GRIMES.

OLD Peter Grimes made fishing his employ ;
   His wife he cabin'd with him and his boy,
And seem'd that life laborious to enjoy.   [ ]]
To town came quiet Peter with his fish,
And had of all a civil word and wish.
He left his trade upon the sabbath-day,
And took young Peter in his hand to pray ;
But soon the stubborn boy from care broke loose,
At first refused, then added his abuse ;
His father's love he scorn'd, his power defied,   10
But, being drunk, wept sorely when he died.
   Yes ! then he wept, and to his mind there came
Much of his conduct, and he felt the shame :—
How he had oft the good old man reviled,
And never paid the duty of a child ;
How, when the father in his Bible read,
He in contempt and anger left the shed ;
"It is the word of life," the parent cried ;
—"This is the life itself," the boy replied ;
And while old Peter in amazement stood,   20
Gave the hot spirit to his boiling blood ;—
How he, with oath and furious speech, began
To prove his freedom and assert the man ;
And when the parent check'd his impious rage,
How he had cursed the tyranny of age ;—
Nay, once had dealt the sacrilegious blow
On his bare head, and laid his parent low ;

THE BOROUGH

The father groan'd—"If thou art old," said he,
"And hast a son—thou wilt remember me;
"Thy mother left me in a happy time,   30
"Thou kill'dst not her—Heav'n spares the double crime."
  On an inn-settle, in his maudlin grief,
This he revolved, and drank for his relief.
  Now lived the youth in freedom, but debarr'd
From constant pleasure, and he thought it hard;
Hard that he could not every wish obey,
But must awhile relinquish ale and play;
Hard! that he could not to his cards attend,
But must acquire the money he would spend.
  With greedy eye he look'd on all he saw;   40
He knew not justice, and he laugh'd at law;
On all he mark'd he stretch'd his ready hand;
He fish'd by water, and he filch'd by land.
Oft in the night has Peter dropp'd his oar,
Fled from his boat and sought for prey on shore;
Oft up the hedge-row glided, on his back
Bearing the orchard's produce in a sack,
Or farm-yard load, tugg'd fiercely from the stack; [ ]]
And as these wrongs to greater numbers rose,
The more he look'd on all men as his foes.   50
  He built a mud-wall'd hovel, where he kept
His various wealth, and there he oft-times slept;
But no success could please his cruel soul,
He wish'd for one to trouble and control;
He wanted some obedient boy to stand
And bear the blow of his outrageous hand;
And hoped to find in some propitious hour
A feeling creature subject to his power.
  Peter had heard there were in London then—
Still have they being!—workhouse-clearing men,   60
Who, undisturb'd by feelings just or kind,
Would parish-boys to needy tradesmen bind;
They in their want a trifling sum would take,
And toiling slaves of piteous orphans make.
  Such Peter sought, and, when a lad was found,
The sum was dealt him, and the slave was bound.
Some few in town observed in Peter's trap

GEORGE CRABBE

A boy, with jacket blue and woollen cap;
But none inquired how Peter used the rope,
Or what the bruise, that made the stripling stoop;   70
None could the ridges on his back behold,
None sought him shiv'ring in the winter's cold;
None put the question—"Peter, dost thou give
"The boy his food?—What, man! the lad must live:
"Consider, Peter, let the child have bread,
"He'll serve thee better if he's stroked and fed."
None reason'd thus—and some, on hearing cries,
Said calmly, "Grimes is at his exercise."
    Pinn'd, beaten, cold, pinch'd, threaten'd, and abused—
His efforts punish'd and his food refused—   80
Awake tormented—soon aroused from sleep—
Struck if he wept, and yet compell'd to weep:
The trembling boy dropp'd down and strove to pray,
Received a blow, and trembling turn'd away,
Or sobb'd and hid his piteous face;—while he,
The savage master, grinn'd in horrid glee:
He'd now the power he ever loved to show,
A feeling being subject to his blow.
    Thus lived the lad, in hunger, peril, pain,
His tears despised, his supplications vain.   90
Compell'd by fear to lie, by need to steal,
His bed uneasy and unbless'd his meal,
For three sad years the boy his tortures bore;
And then his pains and trials were no more.
    "How died he, Peter?" when the people said,
He growl'd—"I found him lifeless in his bed;"
Then tried for softer tone, and sigh'd, "Poor Sam is dead." [ ]
Yet murmurs were there, and some questions ask'd—
How he was fed, how punish'd, and how task'd?
Much they suspected, but they little proved,   100
And Peter pass'd untroubled and unmoved.
    Another boy with equal ease was found,
The money granted, and the victim bound;
And what his fate?—One night, it chanced he fell
From the boat's mast and perish'd in her well,
Where fish were living kept, and where the boy
(So reason'd men) could not himself destroy.—

THE BOROUGH

"Yes! so it was," said Peter; "in his play,
"(For he was idle both by night and day,)
"He climb'd the main-mast and then fell below;"— 110
Then show'd his corpse and pointed to the blow;—
"What said the jury?"—They were long in doubt;
But sturdy Peter faced the matter out:
So they dismiss'd him, saying at the time,
"Keep fast your hatchway, when you've boys who climb."
This hit the conscience, and he colour'd more
Than for the closest questions put before.
    Thus all his fears the verdict set aside,
And at the slave-shop Peter still applied.
    Then came a boy, of manners soft and mild— 120
Our seamen's wives with grief beheld the child;
All thought (the poor themselves) that he was one
Of gentle blood, some noble sinner's son,
Who had, belike, deceived some humble maid,
Whom he had first seduced and then betray'd.—
However this, he seem'd a gracious lad,
In grief submissive and with patience sad.
    Passive he labour'd, till his slender frame
Bent with his loads, and he at length was lame;—
Strange that a frame so weak could bear so long 130
The grossest insult and the foulest wrong;
But there were causes—in the town they gave
Fire, food, and comfort, to the gentle slave;
And though stern Peter, with a cruel hand,
And knotted rope, enforced the rude command,
Yet he consider'd what he'd lately felt,
And his vile blows with selfish pity dealt.
    One day such draughts the cruel fisher made
He could not vend them in his borough-trade,
But sail'd for London-mart; the boy was ill, 140
But ever humbled to his master's will;
And on the river, where they smoothly sail'd,
He strove with terror and awhile prevail'd;
But, new to danger on the angry sea,
He clung affrighten'd to his master's knee.
The boat grew leaky and the wind was strong,
Rough was the passage and the time was long;

His liquor fail'd, and Peter's wrath arose—
No more is known—the rest we must suppose,
Or learn of Peter ;—Peter says, he " spied   150
" The stripling's danger and for harbour tried ;
" Meantime the fish, and then th' apprentice died."   [ ]]
  The pitying women raised a clamour round,
And weeping said, " Thou hast thy 'prentice drown'd."
  Now the stern man was summon'd to the hall,
To tell his tale before the burghers all.
He gave th' account ; profess'd the lad he loved,
And kept his brazen features all unmoved.
  The mayor himself with tone severe replied,—
" Henceforth with thee shall never boy abide ;   160
" Hire thee a freeman, whom thou durst not beat,
" But who, in thy despite, will sleep and eat.
" Free thou art now !—again shouldst thou appear,
" Thou'lt find thy sentence, like thy soul, severe."
  Alas ! for Peter not a helping hand,
So was he hated, could he now command ;
Alone he row'd his boat ; alone he cast
His nets beside, or made his anchor fast ;
To hold a rope or hear a curse was none—
He toil'd and rail'd ; he groan'd and swore alone.   170
  Thus by himself compell'd to live each day,
To wait for certain hours the tide's delay ;
At the same times the same dull views to see,
The bounding marsh-bank and the blighted tree ;
The water only when the tides were high ;
When low, the mud half-cover'd and half-dry ;
The sun-burnt tar that blisters on the planks,
And bank-side stakes in their uneven ranks ;
Heaps of entangled weeds that slowly float,
As the tide rolls by the impeded boat.   180
  When tides were neap, and, in the sultry day,
Through the tall bounding mud-banks made their way,
Which on each side rose swelling, and below
The dark warm flood ran silently and slow :
There anchoring, Peter chose from man to hide,
There hang his head, and view the lazy tide
In its hot slimy channel slowly glide ;   [ ]]

THE BOROUGH

Where the small eels that left the deeper way
For the warm shore, within the shallows play;
Where gaping muscles, left upon the mud,   190
Slope their slow passage to the fallen flood :—
Here dull and hopeless he'd lie down and trace
How sidelong crabs had scrawl'd their crooked race;
Or sadly listen to the tuneless cry
Of fishing gull or clanging golden-eye;
What time the sea-birds to the marsh would come,   ⎫
And the loud bittern, from the bull-rush home,   ⎬
Gave from the salt-ditch side the bellowing boom.   [⎭]
He nursed the feelings these dull scenes produce,
And loved to stop beside the opening sluice;   200
Where the small stream, confined in narrow bound,
Ran with a dull, unvaried, sadd'ning sound;
Where all presented to the eye or ear
Oppress'd the soul with misery, grief, and fear.
  Besides these objects, there were places three,
Which Peter seem'd with certain dread to see;
When he drew near them he would turn from each,
And loudly whistle till he pass'd the reach[1].
  A change of scene to him brought no relief;
In town, 'twas plain, men took him for a thief: 210
The sailors' wives would stop him in the street,
And say, "Now, Peter, thou'st no boy to beat;"
Infants at play, when they perceived him, ran,
Warning each other—"That's the wicked man;"
He growl'd an oath, and in an angry tone
Cursed the whole place and wish'd to be alone.
  Alone he was, the same dull scenes in view,
And still more gloomy in his sight they grew.
Though man he hated, yet employ'd alone
At bootless labour, he would swear and groan,   220
Cursing the shoals that glided by the spot,
And gulls that caught them when his arts could not.

[1] The reaches in a river are those parts which extend from point to
point. Johnson has not the word precisely in this sense; but it is very
common, and I believe used wheresoever a navigable river can be found
in this country.

GEORGE CRABBE

Cold nervous tremblings shook his sturdy frame,
And strange disease—he couldn't say the name;
Wild were his dreams, and oft he rose in fright,
Waked by his view of horrors in the night—
Horrors that would the sternest minds amaze,
Horrors that demons might be proud to raise;
And, though he felt forsaken, grieved at heart,
To think he lived from all mankind apart;   230
Yet, if a man approach'd, in terrors he would start.   [ ]]
   A winter pass'd since Peter saw the town,
And summer-lodgers were again come down;
These, idly curious, with their glasses spied
The ships in bay as anchor'd for the tide—
The river's craft—the bustle of the quay—
And sea-port views, which landmen love to see.
   One, up the river, had a man and boat
Seen day by day, now anchor'd, now afloat;
Fisher he seem'd, yet used no net nor hook;   240
Of sea-fowl swimming by no heed he took,
But on the gliding waves still fix'd his lazy look;   [ ]]
At certain stations he would view the stream,
As if he stood bewilder'd in a dream,
Or that some power had chain'd him for a time,
To feel a curse or meditate on crime.
   This known, some curious, some in pity went,
And others question'd—"Wretch, dost thou repent?"
He heard, he trembled, and in fear resign'd
His boat; new terror fill'd his restless mind;   250
Furious he grew, and up the country ran,
And there they seized him—a distemper'd man.—
Him we received; and to a parish-bed,
Follow'd and cursed, the groaning man was led.
   Here when they saw him, whom they used to shun,
A lost, lone man, so harass'd and undone,
Our gentle females, ever prompt to feel,
Perceived compassion on their anger steal;
His crimes they could not from their memories blot;
But they were grieved, and trembled at his lot.   260
   A priest too came, to whom his words are told;
And all the signs they shudder'd to behold.

"Look! look!" they cried; "his limbs with horror
  shake,
"And as he grinds his teeth, what noise they make!
"How glare his angry eyes, and yet he's not awake.   [ ]
"See! what cold drops upon his forehead stand,
"And how he clenches that broad bony hand."
  The priest, attending, found he spoke at times
As one alluding to his fears and crimes:
"It was the fall," he mutter'd, "I can show   270
"The manner how—I never struck a blow;"—
And then aloud—"Unhand me, free my chain;
"On oath, he fell—it struck him to the brain;—
"Why ask my father?—that old man will swear
"Against my life; besides, he was'nt there;—
"What, all agreed?—Am I to die to-day?—
"My Lord, in mercy, give me time to pray."
  Then, as they watch'd him, calmer he became,
And grew so weak he couldn't move his frame,
But murmuring spake—while they could see and hear   280
The start of terror and the groan of fear;
See the large dew-beads on his forehead rise,
And the cold death-drop glaze his sunken eyes;
Nor yet he died, but with unwonted force
Seem'd with some fancied being to discourse.
He knew not us, or with accustom'd art
He hid the knowledge, yet exposed his heart;
'Twas part confession and the rest defence,
A madman's tale, with gleams of waking sense.
  "I'll tell you all," he said; "the very day   290
"When the old man first placed them in my way:
"My father's spirit—he who always tried
"To give me trouble, when he lived and died—
"When he was gone, he could not be content
"To see my days in painful labour spent,
"But would appoint his meetings, and he made
"Me watch at these, and so neglect my trade.
  "'Twas one hot noon, all silent, still, serene;
"No living being had I lately seen;
"I paddled up and down and dipp'd my net,   300
"But (such his pleasure) I could nothing get—

"A father's pleasure, when his toil was done,
"To plague and torture thus an only son!
"And so I sat and look'd upon the stream,
"How it ran on, and felt as in a dream—
"But dream it was not; no!—I fix'd my eyes
"On the mid stream and saw the spirits rise;
"I saw my father on the water stand,
"And hold a thin pale boy in either hand;
"And there they glided ghastly on the top   310
"Of the salt flood, and never touch'd a drop.
"I would have struck them, but they knew th' intent,
"And smiled upon the oar, and down they went.
  "Now, from that day, whenever I began
"To dip my net, there stood the hard old man—
"He and those boys; I humbled me and pray'd
"They would be gone;—they heeded not, but stay'd.
"Nor could I turn, nor would the boat go by,
"But gazing on the spirits, there was I;
"They bade me leap to death, but I was loth to die.   320[}]
"And every day, as sure as day arose,
"Would these three spirits meet me ere the close;
"To hear and mark them daily was my doom,
"And 'Come,' they said, with weak, sad voices, 'come.'
"To row away with all my strength I try'd;
"But there were they, hard by me in the tide,
"The three unbodied forms—and 'Come,' still 'come,'
    they cried.   [}]
  "Fathers should pity—but this old man shook
"His hoary locks, and froze me by a look.
"Thrice, when I struck them, through the water came   330
"A hollow groan that weaken'd all my frame;
"'Father!' said I, 'have mercy!'—He replied,
"I know not what—the angry spirit lied,—
"'Didst thou not draw thy knife?' said he;—'Twas true,
"But I had pity and my arm withdrew;
"He cried for mercy which I kindly gave,
"But he has no compassion in his grave.
  "There were three places, where they ever rose;—
"The whole long river has not such as those—
"Places accursed, where, if a man remain,   340

THE BOROUGH

"He'll see the things which strike him to the brain;
"And there they made me on my paddle lean,
"And look at them for hours—accursed scene!
"When they would glide to that smooth eddy-space,
"Then bid me leap and join them in the place;
"And at my groans each little villain sprite
"Enjoy'd my pains and vanish'd in delight.
  "In one fierce summer-day, when my poor brain
"Was burning hot and cruel was my pain,
"Then came this father-foe; and there he stood   350
"With his two boys again upon the flood;
"There was more mischief in their eyes, more glee
"In their pale faces when they glared at me.
"Still did they force me on the oar to rest,
"And when they saw me fainting and oppress'd,
"He, with his hand, the old man, scoop'd the flood,
"And there came flame about him, mix'd with blood;
"He bade me stoop and look upon the place,
"Then flung the hot-red liquor in my face;
"Burning it blazed, and then I roar'd for pain,   360
"I thought the demons would have turn'd my brain.
  "Still there they stood, and forced me to behold
"A place of horrors—they cannot be told—
"Where the flood open'd, there I heard the shriek
"Of tortured guilt no earthly tongue can speak:
"'All days alike! for ever!' did they say,
"'And unremitted torments every day!'—
"Yes, so they said;"—but here he ceased and gazed
On all around, affrighten'd and amazed;
And still he tried to speak, and look'd in dread   370
Of frighten'd females gathering round his bed;
Then dropp'd exhausted and appear'd at rest,
Till the strong foe the vital powers possess'd;
Then with an inward, broken voice he cried,
"Again they come," and mutter'd as he died.

THE BOROUGH.

LETTER XXIII.

PRISONS.

Pœna autem vehemens ac multò sævior illis,
Quas et Cæditius gravis invenit aut Rhadamanthus,
Noĉte dieque suum gestare in peĉtore testem.
Juvenal. Sat. 13. ll. 197–9.

Think [our] former state a happy dream,
From which awaked, the truth of what we are
Shows us but this,—I am sworn brother now
To grim Necessity, and he and I
Will keep a league till death.
Richard II. [Aĉt v. Sc. 1, ll. 18–22].

The Mind of Man accommodates itself to all Situations; Prisons otherwise would be intolerable—Debtors; their different Kinds: three particularly described; others more briefly—An arrested Prisoner: his Account of his Feelings and his Situation—The Alleviations of a Prison—Prisoners for Crimes—Two condemned: a vindiĉtive Female: a Highwayman—The Interval between Condemnation and Execution —His Feelings as the Time approaches—His Dream.

THE BOROUGH.

LETTER XXIII.

PRISONS.

'TIS well that man to all the varying states
    Of good and ill his mind accommodates;
He not alone progressive grief sustains,
But soon submits to unexperienced pains.
Change after change, all climes his body bears,
His mind repeated shocks of changing cares;
Faith and fair virtue arm the nobler breast;
Hope and mere want of feeling aid the rest.
  Or who could bear to lose the balmy air
Of summer's breath, from all things fresh and fair,   10
With all that man admires or loves below;   ⎫
All earth and water, wood and vale bestow,   ⎬
Where rosy pleasures smile, whence real blessings flow; [ ]]⎭
With sight and sound of every kind that lives,
And crowning all with joy that freedom gives?
  Who could from these, in some unhappy day,
Bear to be drawn by ruthless arms away
To the vile nuisance of a noisome room,
Where only insolence and misery come?
(Save that the curious will by chance appear,   20
Or some in pity drop a fruitless tear,)
To a damp prison, where the very sight
Of the warm sun is favour and not right;
Where all we hear or see the feelings shock,
The oath and groan, the fetter and the lock?

GEORGE CRABBE

Who could bear this and live?—Oh! many a year
All this is borne, and miseries more severe;
And some there are, familiar with the scene,
Who live in mirth, though few become serene.
Far as I might the inward man perceive,   30
There was a constant effort—not to grieve;
Not to despair, for better days would come,
And the freed debtor smile again at home;
Subdued his habits, he may peace regain,
And bless the woes that were not sent in vain.
Thus might we class the debtors here confined,
The more deceived, the more deceitful kind;
Here are the guilty race, who mean to live
On credit, that credulity will give;
Who purchase, conscious they can never pay;   40
Who know their fate, and traffic to betray;
On whom no pity, fear, remorse, prevail,
Their aim a statute, their resource a jail;—
These as the public spoilers we regard;
No dun so harsh, no creditor so hard.
A second kind are they, who truly strive
To keep their sinking credit long alive;
Success, nay prudence, they may want, but yet
They would be solvent, and deplore a debt;
All means they use, to all expedients run,   50
And are by slow, sad steps, at last undone.
Justly, perhaps, you blame their want of skill,
But mourn their feelings and absolve their will.
There is a debtor, who his trifling *all*
Spreads in a shop; it would not fill a stall:
There at one window his temptation lays,
And in new modes disposes and displays.
Above the door you shall his name behold,
And what he vends in ample letters told,
The words *repository*, *warehouse*, all   60
He uses to enlarge concerns so small.
He to his goods assigns some beauty's name,
Then in her reign, and hopes they'll share her fame;
And talks of credit, commerce, traffic, trade,
As one important by their profit made;

THE BOROUGH

But who can paint the vacancy, the gloom,
And spare dimensions of one backward room?
Wherein he dines, if so 'tis fit to speak,
Of one day's herring and the morrow's steak;
An anchorite in diet, all his care   70
Is to display his stock and vend his ware.
  Long waiting hopeless, then he tries to meet
A kinder fortune in a distant street;
There he again displays, increasing yet
Corroding sorrow and consuming debt:
Alas! he wants the requisites to rise—
The true connexions, the availing ties;
They who proceed on certainties advance;
These are not times when men prevail by chance.
But still he tries, till, after years of pain,   80
He finds, with anguish, he has tried in vain.
Debtors are these on whom 'tis hard to press,
'Tis base, impolitic, and merciless.
  To these we add a miscellaneous kind,
By pleasure, pride, and indolence confined;
Those whom no calls, no warnings could divert,
The unexperienced and the inexpert;
The builder, idler, schemer, gamester, sot—
The follies different, but the same their lot;
Victims of horses, lasses, drinking, dice,   90
Of every passion, humour, whim, and vice.
  See that sad merchant, who but yesterday
Had a vast household in command and pay;
He now entreats permission to employ
A boy he needs, and then entreats the boy.
  And there sits one, improvident but kind,
Bound for a friend, whom honour· could not bind;
Sighing, he speaks to any who appear,
" A treach'rous friend—'twas that which sent me here:
" I was too kind—I thought I could depend   100
" On his bare word—he was a treach'rous friend."
  A female too!—it is to her a home;
She came before—and she again will come.
Her friends have pity; when their anger drops,
They take her home;—she's tried her schools and shops—

GEORGE CRABBE

Plan after plan ;—but fortune would not mend,
She to herself was still the treach'rous friend ;
And wheresoe'er began, all here was sure to end.   [ ]]
And there she sits as thoughtless and as gay,
As if she'd means, or not a debt to pay—   110
Or knew to-morrow she'd be call'd away—
Or felt a shilling and could dine to-day.   [ ]]
While thus observing, I began to trace
The sober'd features of a well-known face—
Looks once familiar, manners form'd to please,
And all illumined by a heart at ease.
But fraud and flattery ever claim'd a part
(Still unresisted) of that easy heart ;
But he at length beholds me—" Ah ! my friend !
" And have thy pleasures this unlucky end ? "   120
" Too sure," he said, and, smiling as he sigh'd :
" I went astray, though prudence seem'd my guide ;
" All she proposed I in my heart approved,
" And she was honour'd, but my pleasure loved—
" Pleasure, the mistress to whose arms I fled,
" From wife-like lectures angry prudence read.
" Why speak the madness of a life like mine,
" The powers of beauty, novelty, and wine ?
" Why paint the wanton smile, the venal vow,
" Or friends whose worth I can appreciate now ?   130
" Oft I perceived my fate, and then would say,
" ' I'll think to-morrow, I must live to-day : '
" So am I here—I own the laws are just—
" And here, where thought is painful, think I must.
" But speech is pleasant ; this discourse with thee
" Brings to my mind the sweets of liberty ;
" Breaks on the sameness of the place, and gives
" The doubtful heart conviction that it lives.
" Let me describe my anguish in the hour
" When law detain'd me and I felt its power.   140
" When in that shipwreck, this I found my shore,
" And join'd the wretched, who were wreck'd before ;
" When I perceived each feature in the face
" Pinch'd through neglect or turbid by disgrace ;
" When in these wasting forms affliction stood

506

"In my afflicted view, it chill'd my blood ;—
"And forth I rush'd, a quick retreat to make,
"Till a loud laugh proclaim'd the dire mistake.
"But when the groan had settled to a sigh ;
"When gloom became familiar to the eye ;   150
"When I perceive how others seem to rest,
"With every evil rankling in my breast—
"Led by example, I put on the man,
"Sing off my sighs, and trifle as I can.
 "Homer ! nay, Pope ! (for never will I seek
"Applause for learning—nought have I with Greek—)
"Gives us the secrets of his pagan hell,
"Where ghost with ghost in sad communion dwell ;
"Where shade meets shade, and round the gloomy meads
"They glide and speak of old heroic deeds— 160
"What fields they conquer'd, and what foes they slew
"And sent to join the melancholy crew.
 "When a new spirit in that world was found,
"A thousand shadowy forms came flitting round ;
"Those who had known him, fond inquiries made :—
"'Of all we left, inform us, gentle shade,
"'Now as we lead thee in our realms to dwell,
"'Our twilight groves, and meads of asphodel.'
 "What paints the poet, is our station here,
"Where we like ghosts and flitting shades appear : 170
"This is the hell he sings, and here we meet,
"And former deeds to new-made friends repeat ;
"Heroic deeds, which here obtain us fame,
"And are in fact the causes why we came.
"Yes ! this dim region is old Homer's hell,
"Abate but groves and meads of asphodel.
 "Here, when a stranger from your world we spy,
"We gather round him and for news apply ;
"He hears unheeding, nor can speech endure,
"But shivering gazes on the vast obscure. 180
"We, smiling, pity, and by kindness show
"We felt his feelings and his terrors know ;
"Then speak of comfort—time will give him sight,
"Where now 'tis dark ; where now 'tis wo, delight.
 "'Have hope,' we say, 'and soon the place to thee

"'Shall not a prison but a castle be;
"'When to the wretch whom care and guilt confound,
"'The world's a prison, with a wider bound;
"'Go where he may, he feels himself confined,
"'And wears the fetters of an abject mind.'   190
"But now adieu! those giant keys appear,
"Thou art not worthy to be inmate here;
"Go to thy world, and to the young declare
"What we, our spirits and employments, are;
"Tell them how we the ills of life endure,
"Our empire stable, and our state secure;
"Our dress, our diet, for their use describe,
"And bid them haste to join the gen'rous tribe:
"Go to thy world, and leave us here to dwell,
"Who to its joys and comforts bid farewell."   200
Farewell to these; but other scenes I view,
And other griefs, and guilt of deeper hue;
Where conscience gives to outward ills her pain,
Gloom to the night, and pressure to the chain.
Here separate cells awhile in misery keep
Two doom'd to suffer; there they strive for sleep;
By day indulged, in larger space they range,
Their bondage certain, but their bounds have change.
One was a female, who had grievous ill
Wrought in revenge, and she enjoy'd it still.   210
With death before her, and her fate in view,
Unsated vengeance in her bosom grew;
Sullen she was and threat'ning; in her eye
Glared the stern triumph that she dared to die;
But first a being in the world must leave—
'Twas once reproach; 'twas now a short reprieve.
She was a pauper bound, who early gave
Her mind to vice, and doubly was a slave;
Upbraided, beaten, held by rough control,
Revenge sustain'd, inspired, and fill'd her soul.   220
She fired a full-stored barn, confess'd the fact,
And laugh'd at law and justified the act.
Our gentle vicar tried his powers in vain,
She answer'd not, or answer'd with disdain;
Th' approaching fate she heard without a sigh,

And neither cared to live nor fear'd to die.
  Not so he felt, who with her was to pay
The forfeit, life—with dread he view'd the day,
And that short space which yet for him remain'd,
Till with his limbs his faculties were chain'd.   230
He paced his narrow bounds some ease to find,
But found it not,—no comfort reach'd his mind.
Each sense was palsied; when he tasted food,
He sigh'd and said, "Enough—'tis very good."
Since his dread sentence, nothing seem'd to be
As once it was—he seeing could not see,
Nor hearing, hear aright;—when first I came
Within his view, I fancied there was shame,
I judged, resentment; I mistook the air—
These fainter passions live not with despair,   240
Or but exist and die:—Hope, fear, and love,
Joy, doubt, and hate, may other spirits move,
But touch not his, who every waking hour
Has one fix'd dread, and always feels its power.
  "But will not mercy?"—No! she cannot plead
For such an outrage;—'twas a cruel deed:
He stopp'd a timid traveller;—to his breast,
With oaths and curses, was the danger press'd:—
No! he must suffer; pity we may find
For one man's pangs, but must not wrong mankind.   250
  Still I behold him, every thought employ'd
On one dire view!—all others are destroy'd;
This makes his features ghastly, gives the tone
Of his few words resemblance to a groan.
He takes his tasteless food, and, when 'tis done,
Counts up his meals, now lessen'd by that one;
For expectation is on time intent,
Whether he brings us joy or punishment.
  Yes! e'en in sleep the impressions all remain;
He hears the sentence and he feels the chain;   260
He sees the judge and jury, when he shakes,
And loudly cries, "Not guilty," and awakes.
Then chilling tremblings o'er his body creep,
Till worn-out nature is compell'd to sleep.
  Now comes the dream again; it shows each scene,

GEORGE CRABBE

With each small circumstance that comes between—
The call to suffering and the very deed—
There crowds go with him, follow, and precede;
Some heartless shout, some pity, all condemn,
While he in fancied envy looks at them. 270
He seems the place for that sad act to see,
And dreams the very thirst which then will be;
A priest attends—it seems, the one he knew
In his best days, beneath whose care he grew.
    At this his terrors take a sudden flight,
He sees his native village with delight;
The house, the chamber, where he once array'd
His youthful person; where he knelt and pray'd.
Then too the comforts he enjoy'd at home,
The days of joy; the joys themselves are come— 280
The hours of innocence—the timid look
Of his loved maid, when first her hand he took
And told his hope; her trembling joy appears,
Her forced reserve and his retreating fears.
    All now is present;—'tis a moment's gleam
Of former sunshine—stay, delightful dream!
Let him within his pleasant garden walk,
Give him her arm, of blessings let them talk.
    Yes! all are with him now, and all the while
Life's early prospects and his Fanny's smile: 290
Then come his sister and his village-friend,
And he will now the sweetest moments spend
Life has to yield;—no! never will he find
Again on earth such pleasure in his mind:
He goes through shrubby walks these friends among,
Love in their looks and honour on the tongue;
Nay, there's a charm beyond what nature shows,
The bloom is softer and more sweetly grows;—
Pierced by no crime, and urged by no desire
For more than true and honest hearts require, 300
They feel the calm delight, and thus proceed
Through the green lane—then linger in the mead—
Stray o'er the heath in all its purple bloom—
And pluck the blossom where the wild bees hum;
Then through the broomy bound with ease they pass,

510

THE BOROUGH

And press the sandy sheep-walk's slender grass,
Where dwarfish flowers among the gorse are spread,
And the lamb browses by the linnet's bed;
Then 'cross the bounding brook they make their way
O'er its rough bridge—and there behold the bay!—
The ocean smiling to the fervid sun—
The waves that faintly fall and slowly run—
The ships at distance and the boats at hand;
And now they walk upon the sea-side sand,
Counting the number and what kind they be,
Ships softly sinking in the sleepy sea;
Now arm in arm, now parted, they behold
The glitt'ring waters on the shingles roll'd;
The timid girls, half dreading their design,
Dip the small foot in the retarded brine,
And search for crimson weeds, which spreading flow,
Or lie like pictures on the sand below;
With all those bright red pebbles that the sun
Through the small waves so softly shines upon;
And those live lucid jellies which the eye
Delights to trace as they swim glitt'ring by:
Pearl-shells and rubied star-fish they admire,
And will arrange above the parlour-fire,—
Tokens of bliss!—"Oh! horrible! a wave
"Roars as it rises—save me, Edward! save!"
She cries—Alas! the watchman on his way
Calls and lets in—truth, terror, and the day!

310

320

330

THE BOROUGH.

LETTER XXIV.

SCHOOLS.

Tu quoque ne metuas, quamvis schola verbere multo
Increpet et truculenta senex geret ora magister;
Degeneres animos timor arguit; at tibi consta
Intrepidus, nec te clamor, plagæque sonantes,
Nec matutinis agitet formido sub horis,
Quod sceptrum vibrat ferulæ, quod multa supellex
Virgea, quod molis scuticam prætexit aluta,
Quod fervent trepido subsellia vestra tumultu;
Pompa loci, et vani fugiatur scena timoris.
Ausonius in Protreptico ad Nepotem [vv. 24-33].

Be it a weakness, it deserves some praise,—
We love the play-place of our early days;
The scene is touching, and the heart is stone
That feels not at that sight—and feels at none.
The wall on which we tried our graving skill;
The very name we carved subsisting still;
The bench on which we sat while deep employ'd,
Though mangled, hack'd, and hew'd, yet not destroy'd.
The little ones unbutton'd, glowing hot,
Playing our games, and on the very spot;
As happy as we once to kneel and draw
The chalky ring and knuckle down at taw.
. . . .
This fond attachment to the well-known place,
When first we started into life's long race,
Maintains its hold with such unfailing sway,
We feel it e'en in age, and at our latest day.
Cowper [Tirocinium, ll. 296-317].

Schools of every Kind to be found in the Borough—The School for
Infants—The School Preparatory: the Sagacity of the Mistress in
foreseeing Character—Day-Schools of the lower Kind—A Master
with Talents adapted to such Pupils; one of superior Qualifications—
Boarding-Schools: that for young Ladies: one going first to the
Governess, one finally returning Home—School for Youth; Master
and Teacher; various Dispositions and Capacities—The Miser-Boy—
The Boy-Bully—Sons of Farmers: how amused—What Study will
effect, examined—A College Life: one sent from his College to a
Benefice; one retained there in Dignity—The Advantages in either
Case not considerable—Where then the Good of a literary Life?—
Answered—Conclusion.

THE BOROUGH.

LETTER XXIV.

SCHOOLS.

TO every class we have a school assign'd,
Rules for all ranks and food for every mind;
Yet one there is, that small regard to rule
Or study pays, and still is deem'd a school:
That, where a deaf, poor, patient widow sits,
And awes some thirty infants as she knits;
Infants of humble, busy wives, who pay
Some trifling price for freedom through the day.
At this good matron's hut the children meet,
Who thus becomes the mother of the street.   10
Her room is small, they cannot widely stray—
Her threshold high, they cannot run away;
Though deaf, she sees the rebel-heroes shout;—
Though lame, her white rod nimbly walks about;
With band of yarn she keeps offenders in,
And to her gown the sturdiest rogue can pin.
Aided by these, and spells, and tell-tale birds,
Her power they dread and reverence her words.
To learning's second seats we now proceed,
Where humming students gilded primers read;   20
Or books with letters large and pictures gay,
To make their reading but a kind of play—
"Reading made Easy," so the titles tell;
But they who read must first begin to spell.
There may be profit in these arts, but still
Learning is labour, call it what you will—

Upon the youthful mind a heavy load;
Nor must we hope to find the royal road.
Some will their easy steps to science show,
And some to heav'n itself their by-way know;   30
Ah! trust them not;—who fame or bliss would share,
Must learn by labour, and must live by care.
    Another matron of superior kind
For higher schools prepares the rising mind;
Preparatory she her learning calls,
The step first made to colleges and halls.
    She early sees to what the mind will grow,
Nor abler judge of infant-powers I know;
She sees what soon the lively will impede,
And how the steadier will in turn succeed;   40
Observes the dawn of wisdom, fancy, taste,
And knows what parts will wear and what will waste:
She marks the mind too lively, and at once
Sees the gay coxcomb and the rattling dunce.
    Long has she lived, and much she loves to trace
Her former pupils, now a lordly race;
Whom when she sees rich robes and furs bedeck,
She marks the pride which once she strove to check.
A burgess comes, and she remembers well
How hard her task to make his worship spell;   50
Cold, selfish, dull, inanimate, unkind,
'Twas but by anger he display'd a mind;
Now civil, smiling, complaisant, and gay,
The world has worn th' unsocial crust away;
That sullen spirit now a softness wears,
And, save by fits, e'en dulness disappears:
But still the matron can the man behold,
Dull, selfish, hard, inanimate, and cold.
A merchant passes;—"probity and truth,
"Prudence and patience, mark'd thee from thy youth."   60
Thus she observes, but oft retains her fears
For him, who now with name unstain'd appears;
Nor hope relinquishes for one who yet
Is lost in error and involved in debt;
For latent evil in that heart she found,
More open here, but here the core was sound.

THE BOROUGH

Various our day-schools : here behold we one
Empty and still ;—the morning duties done,
Soil'd, tatter'd, worn, and thrown in various heaps,
Appear their books, and there confusion sleeps ;   70
The workmen all are from the Babel fled,
And lost their tools, till the return they dread.
Meantime the master, with his wig awry,
Prepares his books for business by-and-by.
Now all th' insignia of the monarch laid
Beside him rest, and none stand by afraid ;
He, while his troop light-hearted leap and play,
Is all intent on duties of the day ;
No more the tyrant stern or judge severe,
He feels the father's and the husband's fear.   80
    Ah ! little think the timid trembling crowd,
That one so wise, so powerful, and so proud,
Should feel himself, and dread the humble ills
Of rent-day charges and of coalman's bills ;
That, while they mercy from their judge implore,
He fears himself—a knocking at the door ;
And feels the burthen as his neighbour states
His humble portion to the parish-rates.
    They sit th' allotted hours, then eager run,
Rushing to pleasure when the duty's done ;   90
His hour of leisure is of different kind,
Then cares domestic rush upon his mind ;
And half the ease and comfort he enjoys,
Is when surrounded by slates, books, and boys.
    Poor Reuben Dixon has the noisiest school
Of ragged lads, who ever bow'd to rule ;
Low in his price—the men who heave our coals,
And clean our causeways, send him boys in shoals.
To see poor Reuben, with his fry beside—
Their half-check'd rudeness and his half-scorn'd pride—   100
Their room, the sty in which th' assembly meet,
In the close lane behind the Northgate-street ;
T' observe his vain attempts to keep the peace,
Till tolls the bell, and strife and troubles cease,
Calls for our praise ; his labour praise deserves,
But not our pity ; Reuben has no nerves.

GEORGE CRABBE

'Mid noise and dirt, and stench, and play, and prate,
He calmly cuts the pen or views the slate.
But Leonard !—yes, for Leonard's fate I grieve,
Who loathes the station which he dares not leave ;   110
He cannot dig, he will not beg his bread ;
All his dependence rests upon his head ;
And, deeply skill'd in sciences and arts,
On vulgar lads he wastes superior parts.
Alas ! what grief that feeling mind sustains,
In guiding hands and stirring torpid brains ;
He whose proud mind from pole to pole will move,
And view the wonders of the worlds above ;
Who thinks and reasons strongly—hard his fate,
Confined for ever to the pen and slate.   120
True, he submits, and when the long dull day
Has slowly pass'd, in weary tasks, away,
To other worlds with cheerful view he looks,
And parts the night between repose and books.
Amid his labours, he has sometimes tried
To turn a little from his cares aside ;
Pope, Milton, Dryden, with delight has seized,
His soul engaged and of his trouble eased.
When, with a heavy eye and ill-done sum,
No part conceived, a stupid boy will come ;   130
Then Leonard first subdues the rising frown,
And bids the blockhead lay his blunders down ;
O'er which disgusted he will turn his eye,
To his sad duty his sound mind apply,
And, vex'd in spirit, throw his pleasures by.   [ ]]
Turn we to schools which more than these afford—
The sound instruction and the wholesome board ;
And first our school for ladies :—pity calls
For one soft sigh, when we behold these walls,
Placed near the town, and where, from window high,   140
The fair, confined, may our free crowds espy,
With many a stranger gazing up and down,
And all the envied tumult of the town ;
May, in the smiling summer-eve, when they
Are sent to sleep the pleasant hours away,
Behold the poor (whom they conceive the bless'd)

THE BOROUGH

Employ'd for hours, and grieved they cannot rest.
Here the fond girl, whose days are sad and few
Since dear mamma pronounced the last adieu,
Looks to the road, and fondly thinks she hears   150
The carriage-wheels, and struggles with her tears.
All yet is new, the misses great and small,
Madam herself, and teachers, odious all;
From laughter, pity, nay command, she turns,
But melts in softness, or with anger burns;
Nauseates her food, and wonders who can sleep
On such mean beds, where she can only weep.
She scorns condolence—but to all she hates
Slowly at length her mind accommodates;
Then looks on bondage with the same concern   160
As others felt, and finds that she must learn
As others learn'd—the common lot to share,
To search for comfort and submit to care.
There are, 'tis said, who on these seats attend,
And to these ductile minds destruction vend;
Wretches (to virtue, peace, and nature, foes)
To these soft minds, their wicked trash expose;
Seize on the soul, ere passions take the sway,
And lead the heart, ere yet it feels, astray:
Smugglers obscene!—and can there be who take   170
Infernal pains, the sleeping vice to wake?
Can there be those, by whom the thought defiled
Enters the spotless bosom of a child?
By whom the ill is to the heart convey'd,
Who lend the foe, not yet in arms, their aid,
And sap the city-walls before the siege be laid?   [ ]
Oh! rather skulking in the by-ways steal,
And rob the poorest traveller of his meal;
Burst through the humblest trader's bolted door;
Bear from the widow's hut her winter-store;   180
With stolen steed on highways take your stand,
Your lips with curses arm'd, with death your hand;—
Take all but life—the virtuous more would say,
Take life itself, dear as it is, away,
Rather than guilty thus the guileless soul betray.   [ ]
Years pass away—let us suppose them past,

GEORGE CRABBE

Th' accomplish'd nymph for freedom looks at last;
All hardships over, which a school contains,
The spirit's bondage and the body's pains;
Where teachers make the heartless, trembling set   190
Of pupils suffer for their own regret;
Where winter's cold, attack'd by one poor fire,
Chills the fair child, commanded to retire;
She felt it keenly in the morning air,
Keenly she felt it at the evening prayer.
More pleasant summer; but then walks were made
Not a sweet ramble, but a slow parade;
They moved by pairs beside the hawthorn-hedge,
Only to set their feelings on an edge;
And now at eve, when all their spirits rise,   200
Are sent to rest, and all their pleasure dies;
Where yet they all the town alert can see,
And distant plough-boys pacing o'er the lea.
   These and the tasks successive masters brought—
The French they conn'd, the curious works they wrought,
The hours they made their taper fingers strike,
Note after note, all dull to them alike;
Their drawings, dancings on appointed days,
Playing with globes, and getting parts of plays;
The tender friendships made 'twixt heart and heart,   210
When the dear friends had nothing to impart:—
   All! all! are over;—now th' accomplish'd maid
Longs for the world, of nothing there afraid.
Dreams of delight invade her gentle breast,
And fancied lovers rob the heart of rest;
At the paternal door a carriage stands,
Love knits their hearts, and Hymen joins their hands.
   Ah!—world unknown! how charming is thy view,
Thy pleasures many, and each pleasure new!
Ah!—world experienced! what of thee is told?   220
How few thy pleasures, and those few how old!
   Within a silent street, and far apart
From noise of business, from a quay or mart,
Stands an old spacious building, and the din
You hear without, explains the work within;
Unlike the whispering of the nymphs, this noise
518

THE BOROUGH

Loudly proclaims a "boarding-school for boys."
The master heeds it not, for thirty years
Have render'd all familiar to his ears ;
He sits in comfort, 'mid the various sound
Of mingled tones for ever flowing round ;
Day after day he to his task attends—
Unvaried toil, and care that never ends.
Boys in their works proceed ; while his employ
Admits no change, or changes but the boy ;
Yet time has made it easy ;—he beside
Has power supreme, and power is sweet to pride.
But grant him pleasure ;—what can teachers feel,
Dependent helpers always at the wheel ?
Their power despised, their compensation small,
Their labour dull, their life laborious all ;
Set after set, the lower lads to make
Fit for the class which their superiors take ;
The road of learning for a time to track
In roughest state, and then again go back ;
Just the same way on other troops to wait—
Attendants fix'd at learning's lower gate.
   The day-tasks now are over ;—to their ground
Rush the gay crowd with joy-compelling sound ;
Glad to [elude] the burthens of the day,
The eager parties hurry to their play.
Then in these hours of liberty we find
The native bias of the opening mind ;
They yet possess not skill the mask to place,
And hide the passions glowing in the face ;
Yet some are found—the close, the sly, the mean,
Who know already all must not be seen.
   Lo ! one who walks apart, although so young,
He lays restraint upon his eye and tongue ;
Nor will he into scrapes or dangers get,
And half the school are in the stripling's debt.
Suspicious, timid, he is much afraid
Of trick and plot—he dreads to be betray'd ;
He shuns all friendship, for he finds they lend,
When lads begin to call each other friend.
Yet self with self has war ; the tempting sight

GEORGE CRABBE

Of fruit on sale provokes his appetite;—
See! how he walks the sweet seduction by;
That he is tempted, costs him first a sigh—
'Tis dangerous to indulge, 'tis grievous to deny!   270 [∫]
This he will choose, and whispering asks the price,
The purchase dreadful, but the portion nice;
Within the pocket he explores the pence;
Without, temptation strikes on either sense,
The sight, the smell;—but then he thinks again
Of money gone! while fruit nor taste remain.
Meantime there comes an eager thoughtless boy,
Who gives the price and only feels the joy:
Example dire! the youthful miser stops,
And slowly back the treasured coinage drops.   280
Heroic deed! for should he now comply,
Can he to-morrow's appetite deny?
Beside, these spendthrifts who so friendly live,
Cloy'd with their purchase, will a portion give.—
Here ends debate, he buttons up his store,
And feels the comfort that it burns no more.
   Unlike to him the tyrant-boy, whose sway
All hearts acknowledge; him the crowds obey:
At his command they break through every rule;
Whoever governs, he controls the school;   290
'Tis not the distant emperor moves their fear,
But the proud viceroy who is ever near.
Verres could do that mischief in a day,
For which not Rome, in all its power, could pay;
And these boy-tyrants will their slaves distress,
And do the wrongs no master can redress.
The mind they load with fear; it feels disdain
For its own baseness; yet it tries in vain
To shake th' admitted power;—the coward comes again. [∫]
'Tis more than present pain these tyrants give,   300
Long as we've life some strong impressions live;
And these young ruffians in the soul will sow
Seeds of all vices that on weakness grow.
   Hark! at his word the trembling younglings flee;
Where he is walking none must walk but he;
See! from the winter-fire the weak retreat;

THE BOROUGH

His the warm corner, his the favourite seat,
Save when he yields it to some slave to keep
Awhile, then back, at his return, to creep.
At his command his poor dependents fly,   310
And humbly bribe him as a proud ally ;
Flatter'd by all, the notice he bestows
Is gross abuse, and bantering and blows ;
Yet he's a dunce, and, spite of all his fame
Without the desk, within he feels his shame :
For there the weaker boy, who felt his scorn,
For him corrects the blunders of the morn ;
And he is taught, unpleasant truth ! to find
The trembling body has the prouder mind.
   Hark to that shout, that burst of empty noise, 320
From a rude set of bluff, obstreperous boys ;
They who, like colts let loose, with vigour bound,
And thoughtless spirit, o'er the beaten ground ;
Fearless they leap, and every youngster feels
His Alma active in his hands and heels.
   These are the sons of farmers, and they come
With partial fondness for the joys of home ;
Their minds are coursing in their fathers' fields,
And e'en the dream a lively pleasure yields ;
They, much enduring, sit th' allotted hours,   330
And o'er a grammar waste their sprightly powers ;
They dance ; but them can measured steps delight,
Whom horse and hounds to daring deeds excite ?
Nor could they bare to wait from meal to meal,
Did they not slyly to the chamber steal,
And there the produce of the basket seize,
The mother's gift ! still studious of their ease.
Poor Alma, thus oppress'd, forbears to rise,
But rests or revels in the arms and thighs[1].
   " But is it sure that study will repay   340
" The more attentive and forbearing ? "—Nay !
The farm, the ship, the humble shop have each
Gains which severest studies seldom reach.
   At college place a youth, who means to raise

---

[1] Should any of my readers find themselves at a loss in this place, I beg leave to refer them to a poem of Prior, called Alma, or the Progress of the Mind.

His state by merit and his name by praise;
Still much he hazards; there is serious strife
In the contentions of a scholar's life.
Not all the mind's attention, care, distress,
Nor diligence itself, ensure success;
His jealous heart a rival's power may dread,   350
Till its strong feelings have confused his head,
And, after days and months, nay, years of pain,
He finds just lost the object he would gain.
　But, grant him this and all such life can give,
For other prospects he begins to live;
Begins to feel that man was form'd to look
And long for other objects than a book.
In his mind's eye his house and glebe he sees,
And farms and talks with farmers at his ease;
And time is lost, till fortune sends him forth   360
To a rude world unconscious of his worth;
There in some petty parish to reside,
The college-boast, then turn'd the village-guide;
And, though awhile his flock and dairy please,
He soon reverts to former joys and ease:
Glad when a friend shall come to break his rest,
And speak of all the pleasures they possess'd—
Of masters, fellows, tutors, all with whom
They shared those pleasures, never more to come;
Till both conceive the times by bliss endear'd,   370
Which once so dismal and so dull appear'd.
　But fix our scholar, and suppose him crown'd
With all the glory gain'd on classic ground;
Suppose the world without a sigh resign'd,
And to his college all his care confined;
Give him all honours that such states allow,
The freshman's terror and the tradesman's bow;
Let his apartments with his taste agree,
And all his views be those he loves to see;
Let him each day behold the savoury treat,   380
For which he pays not, but is paid to eat;
These joys and glories soon delight no more,
Although, withheld, the mind is vex'd and sore;
The honour too is to the place confined;
Abroad they know not each superior mind:

THE BOROUGH

Strangers no *wranglers* in these figures see,
Nor give they worship to a high degree.
Unlike the prophet's is the scholar's case,
His honour all is in his dwelling-place;
And there such honours are familiar things; 390
What is a monarch in a crowd of kings?
Like other sovereigns he's by forms address'd,
By statutes govern'd and with rules oppress'd.
  When all these forms and duties die away,
And the day passes like the former day,
Then, of exterior things at once bereft,
He's to himself and one attendant left;
Nay, John too goes; nor aught of service more
Remains for him; he gladly quits the door,
And, as he whistles to the college-gate, 400
He kindly pities his poor master's fate.
  Books cannot always please, however good;
Minds are not ever craving for their food;
But sleep will soon the weary soul prepare
For cares to-morrow that were this day's care;
For forms, for feasts, that sundry times have past,
And formal feasts that will for ever last.
  "But then from study will no comforts rise?"
Yes! such as studious minds alone can prize;
Comforts, yea! joys ineffable they find, 410
Who seek the prouder pleasures of the mind:
The soul, collected in those happy hours,
Then makes her efforts, then enjoys her powers;
And in those seasons feels herself repaid,
For labours past and honours long delay'd.
  No! 'tis not worldly gain, although by chance
The sons of learning may to wealth advance;
Nor station high, though in some favouring hour
The sons of learning may arrive at power;
Nor is it glory, though the public voice 420
Of honest praise will make the heart rejoice;
But 'tis the mind's own feelings give the joy,
Pleasures she gathers in her own employ—
Pleasures that gain or praise cannot bestow,
Yet can dilate and raise them when they flow.
  For this the poet looks the world around,

GEORGE CRABBE

Where form and life and reasoning man are found.
He loves the mind in all its modes to trace,
And all the manners of the changing race;
Silent he walks the road of life along, 430
And views the aims of its tumultuous throng;
He finds what shapes the Proteus-passions take,
And what strange waste of life and joy they make,
And loves to show them in their varied ways,
With honest blame or with unflattering praise.
'Tis good to know, 'tis pleasant to impart,
These turns and movements of the human heart;
The stronger features of the soul to paint,
And make distinct the latent and the faint;
Man as he is, to place in all men's view, 440
Yet none with rancour, none with scorn pursue;
Nor be it ever of my portraits told,—
"Here the strong lines of malice we behold."—

 THIS let me hope, that when in public view
I bring my pictures, men may feel them true;
"This is a likeness," may they all declare,
"And I have seen him, but I know not where;"
For I should mourn the mischief I had done,
If as the likeness all would fix on one.
Man's vice and crime I combat as I can, 450
But to his GOD and conscience leave the man;
I search (a [Quixote!]) all the land about,
To find its giants and enchanters out,
(The giant-folly, the enchanter-vice,
Whom doubtless I shall vanquish in a trice;)
But is there man whom I would injure?—no!
I am to him a fellow, not a foe—
A fellow-sinner, who must rather dread
The bolt, than hurl it at another's head.
 No! let the guiltless, if there such be found, 460
Launch forth the spear, and deal the deadly wound;
How can I so the cause of virtue aid,
Who am myself attainted and afraid?
Yet, as I can, I point the powers of rhyme,
And, sparing criminals, attack the crime.

ERRATA

[Except in the case of short poems with unnumbered lines, or in that of prefaces, mottos, notes &c. the line of the poem, not the line of the page, is cited.]

PAGE 1 l. 11 for *chests* read *chiefs.*   p. 3 l. 5 for *she's a* read *she,* " '*s a.*
p. 4 l. 2 for *beaut'y* read *beauty's.*   p. 5 l. 18 for *moans* read *mourn.*   p. 7
l. 9 for *stand* read *stands.*   p. 9 l. 1 for *Shenstone's* read *Byrom's.*   p. 14
l. 31 for *nature* read *Nature's.*   p. 20 l. 75 for *devine* read *divine.*   *ib.* l. 90
for *unwraught* read *unwrought.*   *ib.* l. 102 for *pleasures* read *pleasure's.*
p. 21 l. 116 for *distant* read *distance.*   p. 23 l. 186 for *desturb* read *disturb.*
ib. l. 196 for *titt'ring* read *titt'rings.*   *ib.* note for *puris* read *purus.*
p. 24 l. 214 for *sits* read *sets.*   *ib.* l. 226 for *fall* read *pall.*   *ib.* for *refind*
read *refin'd.*   p. 27 l. 82 for *to humble or to brave* read *too humble or too
brave.*   p. 28 l. 101 for *Errors* read *Error's.*   p. 30 l. 153 for *be* read *by.*
p. 48 l. 41 for *Meonides* read *Mæonides.*   *ib.* l. 54 for *triump'd* read *triumph'd.*
ib. l. 61 for *Wonders* read *wanders.*   p. 49 l. 67 for *Titerus* read *Tityrus.*
ib. l. 69 for *Neareds* read *Nereids.*   *ib.* l. 83 for *glomiest* read *gloomiest.*
ib. l. 87 for *Thompson* read *Thomson.*   *ib.* l. 89 for *years Verdent* read *year's
Verdant.*   *ib.* l. 91 for *Aspin* read *Aspen.*   p. 50 l. 104 for *Vally* read *Vally.*
Valley.   *ib.* l. 111 for *glomier* read *gloomier.*   *ib.* l. 118 for *Challange*
read *Challenge.*   p. 51 l. 142 for *Disapointment* read *Disappointment.*   *ib.*
l. 149 for *Currant* read *Current.*   *ib.* l. 160 for *Eccho's* read *Echo's.*   p. 52
l. 185 for *ignious* read *igneous.*   *ib.* l. 201 for *not* read *out.*   *ib.* l. 212 for
ages read *age's.*   *ib.* l. 215 for *ratling* read *rattling.*   p. 53 l. 235 for
Simphony read *Symphony.*   *ib.* l. 237 for *Scence* read *Scene.*   p. 55 l. 295
for *Fiend, fang'd* read *Fiend and fang'd.*   *ib.* l. 297 for *thretned* read
threaten'd.   *ib.* l. 313 for *Rotteness* read *Rottenness.*   p. 56 l. 343 for
distinguis'd read *distinguish'd.*   *ib.* l. 351 for *Worldwind's* read *Whirlwind's.*
p. 57 l. 379 for *dispis'd* read *despis'd.*   p. 59 l. 439 for *beseige* read *besiege.*
ib. l. 441 for *tenaceous* read *tenacious.*   *ib.* l. 446 for *Death Thoughts* read
Death, Thought's.   *ib.* l. 466 for *Emminence* read *Eminence.*   p. 82 note
for *Od.* 8 read *Od.* 6.   p. 87 l. 8 for *Paneg. ad Pisones, Lucan* read *Paneg.
ad Pisones.*   p. 115 l. 543 for *reverend* read *reverent.*   p. 123 l. 118 for
Theirs read *Their.*   p. 146 l. 157 for *Indited* read *Indicted.*   p. 152 l. 393
for *silly* read *slily.*   p. 155 l. 8 for *teneres* read *teneras.*   *ib.* l. 15. The reading
in Shakspere is not *furnish up,* but *finish up.*   p. 158 l. 8 for *restat* read
restet.   p. 161 l. 139 for *cives* read *chives.*   p. 182 l. 63 not in inverted
commas.   p. 187 ll. 235-6 not in inverted commas.   p. 205 l. 270
for *passion* read *passions.*   p. 211 l. 507 for *Snowden's* read *Snowdon's.*
p. 212 ll. 551-2 not in inverted commas.   p. 230 l. 214 for *One* read *one.*
p. 232 l. 319 for *Reubens* read *Rubens.*   *ib.* l. 320 for *shall* read *shalt.*

ERRATA

p. 237 l. 96 for *If* read *In.*   p. 238 l. 11. *I'll know no more,* not printed as beginning of new stanza.   p. 239 l. 36 not printed as beginning of new stanza.   *ib.* not in inverted commas.   p. 251 l. 4 for 22 read 22 *and* 23.   p. 252 l. 5 for *dolor* read *labor.*   p. 256 l. 4 for *deplorant* read *deplangunt.* p. 257 l. 22 for *elmin* read *elmen.*   p. 284 l. 7 for *scenes* read *place hath. ib.* l. 15 for *discutient* read *discutiunt.*   *ib.* l. 17 for *ver.* 520 read vv. 519–523. p. 289 l. 154 (Lonely yet public stands) not enclosed *sic* in brackets.   p. 292 l. 299 for *suceeds* read *succeeds.*   p. 301 l. 266 for *thoughts* and *spirits* read *thoughts'* and *spirit's.*   p. 303 l. 13 for *of* read *o'er.*   *ib.* l. 14 for *while* read *whilst.*   p. 307 l. 132 for *Comes* read *Come.*   p. 313 l. 6 for *Churches* read *Church's.*   *ib.* l. 12 for *knew* read *know.*   *ib.* l. 14 for *Oh!* read *Ah!*   p. 327 l. 528 for *staid* read *stay'd.*   p. 328 l. 12 for xxvii. read xxviii.   p. 329 l. 6 for *leader* read *captain.*   *ib.* l. 8 for *beer: all* read *beer......all. ib. ib.* for *I* read *and I.*   *ib.* ll. 10, 11 for *and they shall all worship me as* read *and worship me.*   p. 336 l. 7 for *Manilius* read *Plaut. Trucul.*   p. 340 l. 114 for *professions* read *professions'.*   p. 347 instead of ll. 4, 5 read as in text :

> *Finirent multi letho mala ; credula vitam*
> *Spes alit, et melius cras fore semper ait.*

p. 364 l. 6 for *Catull,* lib. 3 read (*Dionys.*) *Cato De Moribus* III. 7.   *ib.* l. 7 for *fatiscat* read *fatiscit.*   p. 374 l. 14 for *Et* read *Sed.*   *ib.* for *juncta* read *multa.*   p. 407 l. 7 for *pool* read *pond.*   *ib.* l. 9 is followed in Shakspere by the line :

> ' *Of wisdom, gravity, profound conceit.*'

p. 417 l. 5 for *quia* read *quam.*   *ib.* l. 12 for *tibi* read *cui.*   *ib.* l. 15 for *blessing* read *blessings.*   p. 422 l. 147 for *reverend* read *reverent.*   p. 428 l. 114 for *blissing* read *blessing.*   p. 431 l. 5 six lines follow after 'Burning Lamp.'   *ib.* for *wast* read *wert.*   *ib.* l. 7 five lines follow after *this fire. ib.* 'An everlasting bonfire light !' follows after 'perpetual triumph.'   *ib.* l. 8 for *in a* read *with thee in the.*   p. 439 l. 4 for *who* read *that.*   *ib* l. 5 for *in time* read *in the time.*   p. 451 l. 71 for *birth* read *berth.*   p. 480 l. 4 for *Coepis* read *Coepisti.*   *ib.* for *desines* read *desinis.*   p. 485 l. 166 for *then* read *than.*   p. 502 l. 7 for *my* read *our.*   p. 512 l. 24 six lines follow after *at taw.*   p. 519 l. 250 for *illude* read *elude.*   p. 524 l. 452 for *Quixotte !* read *Quixote !*

The (mis)quotation from Ovid in p. 5 cannot be identified ; the lines quoted on p. 284 as 'Pope's Homer's Iliad, bk. vi. line 45' are not to be found in that work ; and the stanza attributed on p. 294 to Percy is not traceable to the *Reliques.*

VARIANTS.

POEMS. Dedication and Preface. Variants in edition of 1807 (first edition).

Dedication: p. 88, l. 2. Henry-Richard.

p. 89, l. 5. judgement. l. 10. have taught.

Preface : p. 90, l. 11. enquiry. l. 27. judgement.

p. 91, l. 23. among. l. 32. as Mr Boswell (since Lord Auchinleck) has told.

p. 92, l. 7. suspence.

p. 93, l. 2. my friends. l. 5. judgement. l. 9. blameable.

p. 94, l. 13. such opinion. l. 18. Charles-James. l. 28. criticizing. l. 36. judgement.

p. 95, l. 12. judgement. l. 15. Lope de Vega. l. 22. an high degree. l. 26. Lope de Vega.

p. 96, l. 20. judgement. l. 26. in a beneficed clergyman.

p. 97, l. 23. Baptisms. l. 31. enquiry.

p. 98, l. 25. judgement. l. 26. intitled.

p. 99, l. 8. judgement. l. 14. or the exultation.

THE LIBRARY. Variants in edition of 1781 (first edition).

l. 16. *for* wo: woe. l. 22. prevail. l. 28. her old. *instead of* ll. 51—54 : Come then, and entering view this spacious scene,
   This sacred dome, this noble magazine;

l. 57. asswage. *instead of* ll. 63—178 :

  In this selection, which the human mind
  With care has made, for Glory has design'd,
  All should be perfect; or at least appear
  From falshood, vanity, and passion clear:
  But man's best efforts taste of man, and show
  The poor and troubled source from whence they flow;
  His very triumphs his defeats must speak,
  And ev'n his wisdom serves to prove him weak.
  Fashion, though Folly's child, and guide of fools,

VARIANTS

Rules e'en the wisest, and in Learning rules;
From courts and crowds to Wisdom's seat she goes,
And reigns triumphant o'er her mother's foes:
Yon Folio's, once the darlings of the mode,
Now lie neglected like the birth-day ode;
There Learning, stuff'd with maxims trite though sage,
Makes Indigestion yawn at every page;
Chain'd like Prometheus, lo! the mighty train
Brave Time's fell tooth, and live and die again;
And now the scorn of men and now the pride,
The sires respect them, and the sons deride.

l. 183. every note and every comment. l. 197. is. l. 200. your
judges are your rivals. *instead of* ll. 201—322:

But ne'er, discourag'd, fair attempts lay by,
For Reason views them with approving eye,
And Candour yields what cavillers deny.
She sees the struggles of the soul to steer
Through clouds and darkness, which surround us here,
And, though the long research has ne'er prevail'd,
Applauds the trial and forgets it fail'd.

followed by ll. 105—140 *of the text; then continuing*:

Wits, Bards and Idlers fill a tatter'd row;
And the vile Vulgar lie disdain'd below.

Amid these works, on which the eager eye
Delights to fix, or glides reluctant by
Where all combin'd their decent pomp display,
Where shall we first our early offering pay?

To thee PHILOSOPHY! to thee, the light,
The guide of mortals through their mental night,
By whom the world in all its views is shown,
Our guide through Nature's works, and in our own;
Who place in order Being's wondrous chain,
Save where those puzzling, stubborn links remain,
By art divine involv'd, which man can ne'er explain.
These are thy volumes; and in these we look,
As abstracts drawn from Nature's larger book;
Here first describ'd the humble glebe appears,
Unconscious of the gaudy robe it wears;
All that the earth's profound recesses hide,
And all that roll beneath the raging tide;
The sullen gem that yet disdains to shine,
And all the ductile matter of the mine.
Next to the vegetable tribes they lead,
Whose fruitful beds o'er every balmy meed
Teem with new life, and hills, and vales, and groves,
Feed the still flame, and nurse the silent loves;
Which, when the Spring calls forth their genial power
Swell with the seed, and flourish in the flower:
There, with the husband-slaves, in royal pride,

Queens, like the Amazons of old, reside;
There, like the Turk, the lordly husband lives,
And joy to all the gay seraglio gives;
There, in the secret chambers, veil'd from sight,
A bashful tribe in hidden flames delight ;
There, in the open day, and gaily deck'd,
The bolder brides their distant lords expect ;
Who with the wings of love instinctive rise,
And on prolific winds each ardent bridegroom flies.
   Next are that tribe whom life and sense inform,
The torpid beetle, and the shrinking worm ;
And insects, proud to spread their brilliant wing,
To catch the fostering sunbeams of the spring ;
That feather'd race, which late from winter fled,
To dream an half-existence with the dead ;
Who now, returning from their six months' sleep,
Dip their black pinions in the slumbering deep;
Where, feeling life from stronger beams of day,
The scaly myriads of the ocean play.
   Then led by Art through Nature's maze, we trace
The sullen people of the savage race ;
And see a favourite tribe mankind attend,
And in the fawning follower find the friend.

l. 346.   virtues seek.   l. 390.   subtle.   l.   408.   a   song.
l. 410.   did ne'er   l. 422.   Abridgements.   l. 431.   cries.   *instead of*
l. 432 :   Ere laws arose, ere tyrants bade them rise ;   l. 435.   no tumults.
instead of ll. 441—2 :

> Bound by no tyes but those by nature made,
> Virtue was law, and gifts prevented trade.

l. 444.   chearless.   *instead of* l. 454 :   Taught by some conquering friends
who came as foes.   l. 477.   Primæval.   *After* l. 478 :

> Now turn from these, to view yon ampler space,
> There rests a sacred, grave and solemn race ;
> There the devout an awful station keep,
> Vigils advise and yet dispose to sleep;
> There might they long in lasting peace abide   ⎫
> But controversial authors lie beside,   ⎬
> Who friend from friend and sire from son divide: ⎭
> Endless disputes around the world they cause
> Creating now, and now controuling laws.

followed by ll. 223—266 *of the text, with the ensuing variations* :

ll. 237—244 :   Calvin grows gentle in this silent coast,
                     Nor finds a single heretic to roast:
                     Here, their fierce rage subdu'd, and lost their p ide
                     The Pope and Luther slumber side by side:

l. 245.   whom the Church's.   l. 248.   Crumbs.   ll. 249—256 *omitted*.
instead of l. 257 :   And let them lie—for lo! yon gaudy frames.   l. 259.
dread.   l. 260.   sparks of Grace.   l. 265.   prophane, or impiously.
l. 537.   What tho' neglect has shed.   l. 550.   dæmons.   l. 555.   strait.
l. 578.   tipling.   l. 595.   fancy'd.

VARIANTS

THE VILLAGE. Variants in edition of 1783 (first edition).

Book I.

Synopsis of contents omitted.

l. 5. forms. *instead of* ll. 7—8 :

> Fled are those times, if e'er such times were seen,
> When rustic poets prais'd their native green ;

l. 18. echo's. l. 31. one chief cause. *instead of* ll. 33—35 :

> They ask no thought, require no deep design,
> But swell the song and liquefy the line ;
> The gentle lover takes the rural strain.

l. 40. gazes. l. 59. sooth. l. 76. And the wild tare clings round. *instead of* ll. 99—100 :

> And foil'd beneath the young Ulysses fell ;
> When peals of praise the merry mischief tell ?

l. 107. Or, yielding part (when equal knaves contest). l. 108. for the rest. l. 118. their's. *after* l. 143 :

> Like him to make the plenteous harvest grow,
> And yet not share the plenty they bestow ;

l. 153. as luxury. *instead of* ll. 166—7 :

> Or will you urge their homely, plenteous fare,
> Healthy and plain and still the poor man's share ?

instead of l. 171 :

> As you who envy would disdain to touch.

l. 183. its own. l. 189. straitest. l. 197. And urge the efforts. l. 204. rouz'd. l. 219. Slow in their gifts, but. l. 223. woe. l. 265. is all. l. 271. Nor wipes. l. 273. Nor promise. l. 295. mutely hastens to the grave. *instead of* ll. 312—13 :

> Sure in his shot his game he seldom mist,
> And seldom fail'd to win his game at whist ;

l. 325. oh! Death. l. 327. farmer gets.

THE VILLAGE.

Book II.

Synopsis of contents omitted.

l. 30. began. l. 52. the Lord's. l. 55. Hear too. *instead of* ll. 59—62 :

> How their maids languish, while their men run loose,
> And leave them scarce a damsel to seduce.

instead of l. 68 :

> One cup, and that just serves to make them foes ;

VARIANTS

l. 70. And batter'd faces end.   l. 85.   faultering.   l. 102.   you reckon great.   *instead of* ll. 111—112:

> Who gave up pleasures you could never share,
> For pain which you are seldom doom'd to bear,

instead of ll. 161—2:

> But Rutland's virtues shall his griefs restrain,
> And join to heal the bosom where they reign.

l. 165.   Hush the loud grief.   l. 168.   can please.   l. 172.   not valu'd.
l. 176.   terror.   *instead of* l. 177:

> But 'tis the spirit that is mounting high.

l. 178.   a native.   l. 193.   nearer woes.   *after* l. 197:

> Victims victorious, who with him shall stand
> In Fame's fair book the guardians of the land;

l. 201.   streams go murmuring by.   l. 204.   strong stream.

THE NEWSPAPER.   Variants in edition of 1785 (first edition).

l. 37.   Yet you in pity check.   l. 38.   and still vouchsafe to write.
instead of ll. 39—40:

> (While your choice works on quiet shelves remain,
> Or grace the windows of the trade in vain;
> Where ev'n their fair and comely sculptures fail,
> Engrav'd by Grignion, and design'd by Wale)—

instead of ll. 47—48:

> But lend your aid to make my prowess known,
> And puff my labours as ye puff your own.

l. 51.   or what the time they fly.   *instead of* ll. 57—60:

> Gray evening comes, and comes not evening gray
> With all the trifling tidings of the day?

instead of ll. 71—72:

> Yet soon each reptile tribe is lost but these,
> In the first brushing of the wintry breeze;

l. 73.   These still remain.   *after* l. 78:

> (The Oglio now appears, a rival name,
> Of bolder manners, tho' of younger fame);

l. 83.   lye.   l. 85.   holy day.   *instead of* l. 92:   Tomorrow Woodfall, and the world below.   l. 104.   the weak man's brain.   *after* l. 126:

> Soon as the chiefs, whom once they choose, lie low,
> Their praise too slackens, and their aid moves slow;
> Not so, when leagu'd with rising powers, their rage
> Then wounds th' unwary foe, and burns along the page.

l. 132.   nor leaves the winter one.   l. 134.   Fly in successive troops this fluttering race.   *after* l. 136:

> Or are there those, who ne'er their friends forsook,
> Lur'd by no promise, by no danger shook?

VARIANTS

Then bolder bribes the venal aid procure,
And golden letters make the faithless sure:
For those who deal in flattery or abuse,
Will sell them when they can the most produce.

l. 155. Justice, Rector and Attorney.   l. 160. tythe.   *instead of* ll. 163—4 :

Here comes the neighbouring Squire, with gracious air,
To stamp opinions, and to take the chair;

l. 172. plagues.   l. 175. Brook's and St Albin's.   l. 178. owes. *instead of* ll. 190—192 :

"Strive but for power, and parley but for place;"
Yet hopes, good man! "that all may still be well,"
And thanks the stars that he's a vote to sell.

after l. 192 :

While thus he reads or raves, around him wait
A rustic band and join in each debate ;
Partake his manly spirit, and delight
To praise or blame, to judge of wrong or right ;
Measures to mend, and ministers to make,
Till all go madding for their country's sake.

l. 193. th' all-teeming Press.   l. 194. These pois'nous.   *instead of* ll. 211—12 :

Studious we toil, correct, amend, retouch,
Take much away, yet mostly leave too much;

l. 230. deny'd.   l. 253. chearful.   l. 260. And slighting theirs, make comments of their own.   l. 266. monies.   *instead of* ll. 267—8 :

While the sly widow, and the coxcomb sleek,
Dive deep for scandal through a hint oblique.

instead of ll. 273—4 :

Hence on that morn no welcome post appears,
That luckless mind a sullen aspect wears;

l. 279. Such restless passion.   l. 280. Worse than an itch for Music or the Muse.   l. 284. Has neither chance for cure, nor intervals of rest.   *after* l. 284 :

Such powers have things so vile, and they can boast
That those peruse them who despise them most.

l. 285. Thus sung—say Muse.   l. 294. Or coin fresh tales.   l. 300. No British widow turns Italian bride.   l. 304. peers give place, and own her fair.   *instead of* ll. 309—312 :

Such tales as these with joy the many read,
And paragraphs on paragraphs succeed;
Then add the common themes that never cease
The tide-like Stocks, their ebb and their increase;

instead of l. 336 : And nameless murder'd in the face of day.   l. 337. Here, first in rank, the Stage.   l. 344. From self, and.   l. 346. try'd.   l. 373. gray.   *instead of* ll. 379—80 :

Such are their puffs, and would they all were such,
Then should the verse no poet's laurel touch;

VARIANTS

l. 386. frizeurs. l. 416. sacred labours. l. 428. On the scroll'd bar-
board, view'd too long before. l. 429. tipling. l. 438. For these no
more shall live, than they shall die. *instead of* ll. 449—50 :

> Nameless you this way print your idle rhymes,
> A thousand view them, you a thousand times:

l. 462. Leave wealth, indulge not these but nobler fires. Note 1. SPLEEN,
a poem.

The following footnotes appear in the first edition of The Newspaper, *but
were not reprinted:*

l. 1. The greatest part of this Poem was written immediately after the
dissolution of the late parliament

l. 68. The Ephemera, or May-fly, is an insect remarked by naturalists for
the very short time it lives, after assuming its last and more perfect form.

l. 78. [See Variant.] The OGLIO, a Sunday paper, advertised about October
last.

THE PARISH REGISTER. Variants in edition of 1807 (first edition).

Part I.

Instead of ll. 43—50 :

> Above the mantel bound with ribband blue,
> The Swain's emblazon'd Arms demand our view.
> In meadow *Vert*, there feeds in *Gules* a cow,
> Beneath an *Argent* share and *Sable* plough ;
> While for a crest, an *Azure* arm sustains
> In *Or* a wheatsheaf, rich with bristling grains.

l. 53. when tried. l. 54. who prov'd misfortunes. l. 61. that England
fed. l. 66. That nations dreaded and that Nelson beat. *instead of*
ll. 67—8 :

> And here will soon that other fleet be shown,
> That Nelson made the ocean's and our own.

l. 85. by famous Heads made out. l. 86. That teach the simple reader
where to doubt. l. 87. That made him stop. l. 88 And where he
wonder'd then. l. 112. Laid. *instead of* ll. 127—8 :

> These hear the parent Swain, reclin'd at ease
> With half his listening offspring on his knees.

l. 140. The tall *Leek*, tapering with his rushy stem ; l. 177. who knew
not sex. l. 193. gutters flow. l. 197. woe. l. 248. drink and
play. l. 270. Glories unsought, the Fathers. l. 309. an haughty soul.
l. 310. controul. l. 314. seldom shed. l. 339. What then was left,
these Lovers to require? l. 368. Higler's. l. 369. antient. *instead
of* ll. 371—2 :

> Day after day were past in grief and pain,
> Week after week, nor came the Youth again ;

instead of ll. 417—18 :

> Few were their Acres,—but they, well content,
> Were on each pay-day, ready with their rent ;

533

VARIANTS

instead of ll. 453—60 :

> 'Far other thoughts, your Reverence, caus'd the ill,
> '"Twas pure good-nature, not a wanton will;
> 'They urg'd me, paid me, beg'd me to comply, }
> 'Not hard of heart, or slow to yield am I, }
> 'But prone to grant as melting charity. }
> 'For wanton wishes, let the frail-ones smart,
> 'But all my failing is a tender heart.'

l. 470.   Gerrard.   *instead of* ll. 471—2 :

> Seven have I nam'd, and but six years have past
> By him and Judith since I bound them fast.

l. 477.   he would no more increase.   l. 481.   humbled.   l. 521.   pedlar's.
l. 539.   woe with woe.   l. 540.   "Ah! Humphrey! Humphrey!   l. 558.
said Humphrey.   l. 559.   an husband's.   l. 569.   antient.   *instead of*
ll. 582—3 :

> To prove these arrows of the giants' hand,
> Are not for man to stay or to command.

instead of l. 604 :

> Of news or nothing, she by looks compel.

l. 628.   *Artimisia.*   l. 631.   *Senecio.*   l. 649.   turged *Anthers.*   *instead of* l. 650 :

> "But haste and bear them to their spouse away;
> "In a like bed you'll see that spouse reclin'd,
> ("Oh! haste and bear them, they like love are blind,)

l. 652.   make the marriage sure.   l. 663.   to life's great duty, Love.
l. 676.   some notice they will claim.   *instead of* ll. 678—9 :

> The straitest furrow lifts the ploughman's heart,
> Or skill allow'd firm in the bruiser's art.

l. 700.   For he who lent a name to babe unknown.   l. 702.   they ask'd
the name of all.   l. 713.   controul.   l. 743.   that seem'd.   l. 744.
that nothing meant.   l. 748.   steelly.   l. 751.   still more sure about the
world.   l. 784.   Keeps looking on the ground.   l. 785.   These looks and
sighs.   l. 803.   transcendant.   l. 811.   Bishoprick.   l. 826.   Passions.
l. 833.   Spencer; Spencer's.

The note to l. 833 *is omitted in the first edition.*

Part II.

Instead of ll. 5—6 :

> If Poor, Delay shall for that Want prepare,
> That, on the hasty, brings a World of Care;

instead of l. 17 :

> Yet thee too long, let not thy Fears detain

l. 19.   tied.   l. 26.   Banns.   instead of ll. 34—60.

> Fie, Nathan! fie! to let a sprightly Jade
> Leer on thy Bed, then ask thee how 'twas made
> And lingering walk around at Head and Feet,
> To see thy nightly Comforts all complete;

534

VARIANTS

Then waiting seek—not what she said she sought,
And bid a Penny for her Master's Thought;—
(A Thought she knew, and thou could'st not send hence,
Well as thou lov'dst them, for ten thousand Pence!)
And thus with some bold Hint she would retire,
That wak'd the idle Wish and stirr'd the slumbering Fire;
Didst thou believe thy Passion all so laid
That thou might'st trifle with thy wanton Maid,
And feel amus'd, and yet not feel afraid?
The dryest Faggot, Nathan, once was green,
And laid on Embers, still some Sap is seen;
Oaks, bald like thee above, that cease to grow,
Feel yet the Warmth of Spring and Bud below;
More senseless thou than Faggot on the Fire
For thou could'st feel and yet would'st not retire;
Less provident than dying Trees,—for they
Some vital Strength, some living Fire display,
But none that tend to wear the Life itself away.
Ev'n now I see thee to the Altar come;
Downcast thou wert and conscious of thy Doom:
I see thee glancing on that Shape aside,
With blended Looks of Jealousy and Pride;
But growing Fear has long the Pride supprest,
And but one Tyrant rankles in thy Breast;
Now of her Love, a second Pledge appears,
And Doubts on Doubts arise, and Fears on Fears;
Yet Fear defy, and be of Courage stout,
Another Pledge will banish every Doubt;
Thine Age advancing as thy Powers retire,
Will make thee sure—What more would'st thou require?

l. 68. antient.   l. 96. Drew Oil, drew Essence.   l. 100. Mrs.   l. 269.
And hid the Snare, prepar'd to catch the Maid.   l. 290. Scrolls.   *instead*
of ll. 301—308 :

> Is it that strong and sturdy in the Field
> They scorn the Arms of idle Men to wield
> Or give that Hand to guide the Goosequill Tip,
> That rules a Team, and brandishes a Whip?
> The Lions they, whom conscious Power forbid,—
> To play the Ape and "dandle with the Kid."

l. 313. For Bridget Dawdle.   l. 317. To Roger Pluck.   l. 321. In all
his Dealings, Hodge was just and true.   l. 340. Bridget's.   l. 341.
Roger.   l. 351. Bridget.   l. 353. Roger's.   l. 355. Roger's *bis.*
instead of ll. 372—375 :

> So two dried Sticks, all fled the vital juice,
> When rubb'd and chaf'd, their latent Heat produce;
> All in one part unite the cheering Rays,
> And kindling burn with momentary Blaze.

l. 380. when touch'd with Galvin's Wire.   *instead of* ll. 400—1 :

> No more she plays, no more attempts to fit
> Her Steps responsive to the squeaking Kit,

535

VARIANTS

l. 419. in room apart.　l. 424. And Wives like these assert and prove their own;　l. 430 (*note*). Spencer.　l. 437. Nor sought their Bliss, at *Cupid's* wild Commands,　l. 444. was her Reuben's Care;　*instead of* ll. 461—66:

> Nor these alone, (though favour'd more) are blest;
> In time, the Rash, in time, the Wretched rest;
> They first-sad years of Want and Anguish know,
> Their Joys come seldom, and their Pains pass slow;

instead of ll. 473—4:

> When Life's Afflictions long with dread endur'd,
> By Time are lessen'd, or by Caution cur'd;

l. 477. And calm in Cares, with Patience, Man and Wife,　l. 490. Coite. *instead of* ll. 491—2:

> For me, (he thinks,) shall soon this Deed be done,
> A few steps forward, and my Race is run;

l. 499. He gives his Friend a tear, and heaves himself a sigh.　l. 516. Plowman's.　l. 521. spare, for Rapture to enjoy?　*instead of* ll. 565—7:

> Who caus'd the Anguish they disdain'd to heal,
> Have at some time, the Power of Virtue known,
> And felt another's good promote their own:

l. 568. the youth.　l. 569. Who took the Maid, with innocence and truth; l. 572. its vigour keep.　l. 583. When Beauty all decays.

Part III.

l. 33. that sad submission.　l. 48. as a Sinner's Right.　l. 49. God is good.　l. 50. And, none have liv'd, as Wisdom wills they should. l. 54. To think about beginning to repent.　l. 65. That feels the useful Pain, Repentance brings.　l. 66. Dejection's Sorrows.　l. 67. And then, the Hope, that Heaven these Griefs approve.　l. 68. And lastly Joy that springs.　l. 75. Collet.　*instead of* ll. 151—2:

> Like that industrious Kind, no thoughts of Sex
> No cares of Love, could her chaste Soul perplex.

l. 159. welcome at her Board to share.　*After* l. 172: As Bridget churn'd the Butter, for her Hand.　l. 173. (Geese, Hens, and Turkeys following where she went.)　l. 185. as the more.　l. 186. She grasp'd with greater force.　l. 212. To bear a Grandchild.　l. 219. check the passions.　l. 220. Youth's Disappointments, the Regrets of Age. *instead of* ll. 225—31:

> Blest is the Nurseling never taught to sing,
> But thrust untimely from its Mother's Wing;
> Or the grown Warbler, who, with grateful Voice,
> Sings its own Joy and makes the Grove rejoice;
> Because, ere yet he charm'd th' attentive Ear.

l. 278. aweful.　l. 283. woe's.　l. 297. Studds.　l. 329. Catharine's. l. 345. And held the Golden Watch, the Ruby-Rings.　l. 357. the Lady's. l. 381. On Pride that governs, Pleasure that will grow.　l. 394. Bawbles.

VARIANTS

l. 412. Catharine. l. 428. the Joy. l. 431. that wounds. l. 432. Who miss one Comfort that. l. 434. He felt with many. l. 436. an old Neighbour. l. 443. he knew. l. 444. More skilful none, and skill'd like him, but few. *instead of* 458—60:

> By the new Light, to the new Way direct;—
> "Mine now are Faith and Hope," he said; "Adieu!
> "I fear to lose them, in a way so new."

instead of ll. 467—8:

> His honest Fame he yet retain'd; no more,
> His wife was buried, and his Children poor;

l. 473. And just, as kind. l. 474. And then for Comforts. l. 477. with him to live. l. 478. Who, while he feeds me, is as loath to give l. 480. guages. l. 485. to mourn my Lot is vain. l. 486. Mine it is not to choose but to sustain. l. 495. aweful. l. 499. that suppliant Look. l. 500. Nor that pure Faith, that gave it Force are there. l. 510. Intic'd. l. 565. An House. l. 573. And thus he rose, but tried. *instead of* ll. 594—6:

> And all was Terror, till all Hope was gone;
> Was silent Terror, where that Hope grew weak,
> Look'd on the Sick, and was asham'd to speak.

l. 601. So sure. l. 654. Glib. l. 664. Glib. l. 670. With Luck and Leah. l. 675. "Nay, but," he said "and dare you. l. 700. Judgement. l. 715. Woe. l. 825. Ailes. l. 848. sly Dissenters. l. 863. An whoreson Cough. l. 882. Gypsies. l. 891. Aile. l. 921. antient. l. 966. while Parents them and us forsake.

THE BIRTH OF FLATTERY. Variants in edition of 1807 (first edition).

l. 1. Spencer. l. 15. Siren. l. 21. An hireling. l. 50. Dissentions. l. 52. Say what Success has one Projection crown'd? l. 60. Ingulph'st. l. 65. worthless Arts. l. 111. nuptual. l. 125 repay'd. l. 191. antient. l. 213. controul. l. 304. *Gorze.* l. 317. Tenniers. l. 333. Mein. l. 344. that well their Worth she knew. l. 347. While all Disgrace attend.

SIR EUSTACE GREY. Variants in edition of 1807 (first edition).

l. 23. Will sometimes point. l. 24. And will with. l. 26. Will veil. l. 37. Well! I am calm. l. 38. woe. l. 58. an. l. 171. Dæmons. l. 234. Travellers.

Note 3, l. 5. Intended to cast ridicule on any religious persuasion. l. 8. enthusiastical.

The notes appear as footnotes in the first edition.

THE HALL OF JUSTICE. Variants in edition of 1807 (first edition).

Part I.

l. 11. forbad. l. 36. woe. l. 41. on Want and Error.

VARIANTS

WOMAN! Variants in edition of 1807 (first edition).
l. 1. Africk's. l. 4. Dæmons.

THE BOROUGH. Variants in the edition of 1810 (first edition).
Preface. p. 266, l. 9. may fairly be. l. 24. values. p. 268, l. 16. connections. p. 269, l. 12. an hope. p. 271, l. 5. enquiries. p. 273, l. 13. enquiry. *ib.* l. 28. controul. p. 274, l. 35. attornies. p. 275, l. 2. license. *ib.* l. 39. set down. p. 276, l. 7. give us more favourable view. p. 277, l. 33. an hundred. p. 278, l. 2. an happier. *ib.* l. 31. immoveable. p. 279, l. 14. *after* insane, : and why the visions of his distempered brain should be of so horrible a nature. p. 282, l. 7. mottos.

Letter 1. l. 85. wreathes. l. 153. an House. l. 156. tipling. l. 175. stoney Beech. l. 195. o'ershrowd. l. 290. rimpling.

Letter 2. Synopsis, l. 2. Columns and Aysles; l. 8. Grief in the surviver.
l. 29. Yet Gothic all, l. 34. aisle. l. 40. grey. l. 57. greys. l. 62. grey. l. 76. The stoney Tower as grey. l. 114. Woe. l. 127. teiz'd.

Letter 3. l. 46. inlists. l. 62. antient. l. 105. charardes. l. 127. antient. l. 132. aisle...aisle. l. 137. woe. *instead of* ll. 158—159 :
> Mamma approv'd a safe contented guest
> And Miss a Friend to back a small request;

instead of ll. 202—205 :
> Oh! had he learn'd to make the Wig he wears,
> To throw the Shuttle or command the Sheers,
> Or the strong Boar-skin for the Saddle shap'd,
> What pangs, what terrors had the Man escap'd.

l. 214. woeful.

Letter 4. Synopsis, l. 3. Swedenburgeans. ll. 5, 9. Armenian l. 12. extatic. l. 21. doat, extacies. l. 70. tye. l. 75. Dioclecian. l. 120. antient. l. 129. antient. l. 168. Swedenbourgeans. l. 184. Phaætons. l. 191. chastizing. l. 205. rev'rendly. l. 230. byeword. l. 255. antient. *instead of* ll. 258—259 :
> True *Independants* : while they *Calvin* hate,
> They heed as little what *Socinians* state;
> They judge *Arminians Antinomians* stray
> Nor *England's Church*, nor Church on Earth obey ;

l. 260. But for themselves. l. 264. inlists. l. 267. Westley. l. 299. an helping hand. l. 338. ingulph'd. l. 389. antient, Westley. l. 419. naught. l. 477. stoney. l. 487. stoney-cold. l. 500. aweful. l. 503. woe.

Letter 5. l. 92. for then he's most. l. 113. burrs. *instead of* ll. 167—170 :
> In fact the Fisher was amaz'd ; as soon
> Could he have judg'd Gold issued from the Moon ;
> But being taught, he griev'd with all his heart,
> For lack of knowledge in this precious art;

VARIANTS

Letter 6. l. 52. Socilitor.   l. 64. the far-resounding.   l. 75. buz.
l. 108. controul.   l. 114. Whose Sons aspiring, for Professions call.
l. 292. dosing.   l. 295. if he try.   l. 298. strait.   l. 306. doat.
l. 335. He'd balked.

Letter 7. Synopsis, l. 6. Empiricks.   l. 8.   Empirick.   *instead of* ll. 1—4 :

> From Law to Physic stepping at our ease,
> We find a way to finish—by degrees;
> Forgive the quibble, and in graver style,
> We'll sing of those with whom we seldom smile.

l. 15. an hope.   l. 19. Physician.   *instead of* l. 59 :

> So Merit suffers, while a Fortune's made.

l. 64. the licenc'd Tribe.   l. 79. Coblers.   l. 80. Lyars.   l. 96.
their Patents.   l. 111. Schirrus.   l. 124. Empirick's.   l. 147. fewel.
l. 156. intreats.   l. 257. controul.   l. 262. bar'd   l. 268. Ev'n.
some who'd known him.   l. 271. neither reason.

Letter 8. Synopsis, l. 5. *After* 'The Weaver an Entomologist, etc.
insert 'Hunting Butterflies,' etc.
l. 18. an high.   l. 27. expence.   l. 30. Th' estimate that's made.
l. 216. controul

Letter 9. l. 17. an Hall.   l. 27. Sheers.   l. 64. Where.
l. 152. Expence.   l. 154. favouring Gale.   l. 176. this Envy.   l. 197.
on the Waters float.   l. 198. Note.   l. 216. Shores to Shores.

Letter 10. Synopsis, l. 5. Petulences.
l. 121. an happier few.   l. 123. not fretful.   l. 129. antient.
instead of ll. 165—6 :

> Against their Nature they might show their Skill
> With small Success, who're Maids against their will.

l. 167. bashful muse.   l. 253, 258. Aye.   l. 293. Gulph.   l. 353.
gregareous.   l. 382. tye.   l. 385. Himself to strengthen, or himself to shun ;

Letter 11. l. 55. Ribbands.   l. 78. the work of Treason done.
instead of ll. 79—80 :

> Have, like the *Guillotine*, the royal Neck
> Parted in twain—the Figure is a Wreck ;

l. 102. antient.   l. 136. Styes.   l. 143. Basons.   l. 185. antient.
l. 286. Controul.   l. 287. an Home.

Letter 12. Synopsis, l. 6. An Heroine;   l. 8. Frederic.
l. 21. an House.   l. 54. an Hero's.   l. 65. Havock.   l. 75. Woe.
l. 87. Wane.   l. 94. in the appointed Course.   l. 105. pityful.   l. 136.
Woe.   l. 148. Woe.   l. 185. teiz'd.   l. 195. Taylor's.   l. 202.
Frederic.   *instead of* ll. 205—6 :

> It was not quite within the Merchant's line.
> To think of College, but the Boy would shine.

VARIANTS

l. 207. he'd prosper, none could doubt.   l. 214.   Frederic.   l. 222.
Frederic.   l. 236.   authoriz'd.   *between* ll. 266—7 :

> Vice, dreadful habit ! when assum'd so long,
> Becomes at length inveterately strong ;
> As more indulg'd it gains the Strength we lose,
> Maintains its Conquests and extends it Views ;
> Till the whole Soul submitting to its Chains,
> It takes possession, and for ever reigns.

l. 282. an Home.   l. 298.   an Home.   l. 330.   an Hoy.   l. 332.
Frederic.   l. 339.   Enquiries.   l. 341.   Frederic.   l. 347.   Enquiry.
l. 356. an happier.   l. 369.   Woe.

Letter 13. *Instead of* ll. 5—6 :

> He wore his Coat till every Thread was bare,
> And fed his Body with the meanest Fare ;

l. 13. Crumbs.   l. 25. favorite.   *instead of* ll. 27—28 :

> Haunts have been trac'd to which he nightly went,
> And serious Sums in private Pleasures spent ;

l. 78. Controul.   l. 107.   controul.   l. 121.   Detracter.   l. 135.
Enquiry.   *instead of* l. 173 : Small is his private Room : you'd find
him there.   l. 188.   an herd.   *instead of* ll. 191—2 :

> You'd meet Sir Denys in a morning Ride,
> And be convinc'd he'd not a spark of Pride ;

l. 202. Equipt.   l. 203.   an Horse.   l. 207.   An handsome Youth *Sir
Denys* ; and an Horse.   l. 214.   Aye.   l. 226.   cloath'd.   l. 244.   controul'd.   l. 275.   try'd.   l. 296.   t' asswage.

Letter 14. Synopsis, l. 6.   Connections.

l. 17. Enquiry.   l. 31.   Expences.   l. 49.   try'd.   l. 58.   antient.
l. 120. this final Hoard.   *instead of* l. 138 : Those whom he'd daily shaken
by the hand.   l. 145.   Billedeux.   l. 148.   an useful.   *instead of*
l. 165 : He'll even read to learn the Ill they've done.   l. 169.   he'll dispose
the Mind.   l. 212.   antient.

Letter 15. l. 19.   and Poems.   l. 93.   an Heart so fond, an Hand so
priz'd ;   l. 108.   straiter.   l. 152.   try'd.   l. 216.   antient.

Letter 16. Synopsis, l. 11.   Dolly.

l. 86. Vallies.   l. 90.   forebore.   l. 127.   'twould not believe its
Eyes.   l. 128.   'Twould sadly glide.   l. 132.   an huge.   l. 133.
an huge.   l. 156.   Breakfasts.   l. 159.   teiz'd.   l. 183.   ratling.
l. 209. She held him babish and his Captives blind.   *instead of*
ll. 211—213 :

> Her Sexe's Pattern, without Thoughts of Sex ;
> Our timid Girls and Lovers half afraid,
> All shunn'd the Speeches of the frank old maid.

l. 230. antient.

540

VARIANTS

Letter 17. l. 7. Woe. l. 17. all have. l. 41. inclose. l. 48. has never heard. l. 78. Woe. l. 113. bruize. l. 138. an House. l. 208. Tyes. l. 248. place in view. l. 261. well-dry'd. l. 277. do the work.

Letter 18. Synopsis, l. 8. Bye-Ways.
l. 12. antient. l. 24. antient. l. 94. antient. l. 130. Woe. l. 199. try'd. l. 218. 'till he's run his Race. l. 222. antient. *instead of* l. 264:
> Which that low Paling, form'd of Wreck, surround;

l. 270. relicks. l. 318. an Handmaid. l. 327. Virtue's. l. 332. an Humourist. l. 336. an Home. l. 365. antient. l. 369. contain. l. 389. fry'd.

Notes. *These appear in the first edition as footnotes.*

Letter 19. *Instead of* ll. 18—19:
> This book-taught Man, with ready mind receiv'd
> More than Church commanded or believ'd;

l. 64. their very Look's a charm. l. 94. try'd. l. 110. Abash'd. l. 131. an hearing. l. 196. Aisle. l. 259. cry'd. l. 269. *not in inverted commas.* l. 299. enquir'd.

Letter 20. Synopsis, l. 6. An Husband. l. 7. The Men's.
l. 34. *Darnly-Cottages.* l. 59. Chateux. l. 97. an Hound. l. 101. Woe. l. 112. Woe. l. 135. teiz'd. l. 182. an Hovel's. l. 196. affrighten'd. *instead of* ll. 262—3:
> I would all Memory of his Fate were fled
> He was our second Child, our darling *Ned*;

l. 269. Slight. l. 283. Tyger. l. 299. might be proud.

Notes. *These appear in the first edition as footnotes.* Note 1. l. 1. Southerwood. l. 2. *Artimisia.* Note 2. l. 2. tenor. l. 6. teazing. l. 10. teazed.

Letter 21. l. 51. aukward. l. 86. antient. l. 110. thine Heart. l. 122. (thou had'st them). l. 183. laid. l. 184. blest the dying Maid. l. 211. Pedlar's. l. 214. Entitled. l. 218. stedfast. l. 231. lead. *instead of* l. 263:
> Oh! please your Rev'rence, rev'rendly I said.

l. 289. woe.

Note. *This does not appear in the first edition.*

Letter 22. Synopsis, l. 6. insipient.
l. 30. an happy Time. l. 54. controul. l. 69. enquir'd. l. 165. an helping Hand. l. 228. Dæmons. l. 259. could'nt. l. 361. Dæmons.

VARIANTS

Letter 23. Synopsis, l. 6. an Highwayman.
l. 78. succeed. l. 89. The Folly diverse. l. 102. an Home.
l. 105. try'd. l. 165. enquiries. l. 184. Woe. l. 219. Controul.
l. 308. brouzes.

Letter 24. l. 27. an heavy Load. l. 104. Strife on both sides.
l. 129. an heavy Eye. l. 188. All Hardship. l. 250. illude the Burdens.
instead of l. 276:

Of Money wasted! when no taste remain.

l. 290. controuls. l. 310. Dependants. l. 334. bear. l. 335.
slily. l. 339, footnote, *not in first edition.* l. 380. savory. l. 387.
an high degree.

END OF VOL. I.

For EU product safety concerns, contact us at Calle de José Abascal, 56–1°, 28003 Madrid, Spain or eugpsr@cambridge.org.

www.ingramcontent.com/pod-product-compliance
Ingram Content Group UK Ltd.
Pitfield, Milton Keynes, MK11 3LW, UK
UKHW012335130625
459647UK00009B/304